It's a play, it's a music blog, it's a socio-political commentary of July 2020 through March 2021, it's...

Bottle of Beef Book 2: The Media Empire of Doom
by
Paul Tompkins

Welcome to book 2, the book about the making of the books that weaves back around and devours its own tail. You can call me Bottle. Personally, I don't think there's any preamble that could prepare you for the insanity ahead, but maybe wear a helmet? I'm perfectly happy to reside wherever you place me in the pantheon of acutely obtuse writers, but it might be helpful to keep in mind that just because I wrote it in chronological order, doesn't mean it actually works that way. If you survived the first book, then congratulations, I'll try harder this time.

Technical note, this book contains characters. They are not based on actual people. Except for the ones about actual people, but what you know about those actual people is probably not what those people were actually like. Anywho, good luck, I'm as surprised as anyone at how it turned out.

Sincerely,
Bottle

© Paul Tompkins 2021, All rights reserved

Contents:

I: Who Died and Made Skip the Editor? 5

II: Scenes from the Blog I 45

III: Bottle vs. The Compiler 71

IV: Scenes from the Blog II 95

V: Skip the Editor and The Compiler proudly
    bring you this appendix of references from
    The Explanatory Pamphlet of Doom,
    with annotations as necessary 99

  IV (Again): Scenes from the Blog II 105

VI: Capital with Bottle (an adventure in
    its own right) 185

VII: Scenes from the Blog III 209

VIII: Have Fun Storming the Castle 299

IX: The Great Unbottling 359

X: Final Sequence: The End is Somewhere in the
    Beginning of the Middle 437

[This field intentionally left fallow]

I. Who died and made Skip the Editor?

The Explanatory Pamphlet of Doom[1]

521 Anywhere Ave. I keep waiting for the sun, but as they say, no one here gets out alive. It doesn't look particularly impressive from the outside. Some people might do a double take at an anachronistic farmhouse nestled back in the shadows between two Brownstones, but such a thing isn't completely uncommon. Strange place for a supposedly productive record label, but lawyers and dentists like these architectural anomalies, why can't we? Surely some interesting story will soon ensue.

"Heads up, Bottle. You might make a new friend today."

You wouldn't know from looking at her grandmotherly smile, but Gladys is a right mean old bird. 80-year-old receptionist at the sausage factory, I mean the worst imaginary record label in town is a career that rewards sharp wit. Plus, she's had about 30 years of practice stabbing thieves

---

[1] Hi. Marvin, sorry, Skip here. First, I have to tell you that this is weird. I really am "the Editor" around here now; a name plaque just appeared on my makeshift desk, but no one seems to know where it came from. Second, it's kind of creepy how accurate Bottle is in telling this little story. I read it and think "yeah, that *is* what we said." I'll try not to barge in on the story too much, but know that the footnotes are from me. Third, Bottle really talks like that. It's confusing as hell, but I'm starting to catch on to some of the metaphors and idioms he frequently uses. He has a tendency to formulate ideas from whatever he's been listening to recently. Maybe you'll spot the references to the Doors in the opening paragraph, or maybe you won't (of course you will, I just told you). That's another thing he does, whenever he catches himself making an assumption about what someone else is thinking, he immediately counteracts it. It's kind of endearing, actually. He might be the most honest person I've ever met, and believe it or not that is incredible confusing. Regardless, I'll reserve my editorial contributions for some of his more esoteric moments, places where it might be helpful for you. The story is quite readable if you ignore them, so don't imagine that it's mandatory.

and liars with her knitting needles. I think her late husband was a clergyman, or something.²

"Yay?" The one nice thing about old houses is you don't need an intercom. You can hear each other just fine as though the floors and ceilings aren't even there. "Don't do too much damage. I think you're inadvertently accelerating the exploding part of this whole cursed operation."

"Ok, I'll be subtle."

Subtle. Indeed. Poor kid won't know what hit him, or poked him (not to be confused with "fatally stabbed him") in the ribs. I just wish I knew why they always spontaneously combust, or inexplicably electrocute themselves after a while. Se la mort, I guess... Op! There's the confuddling sound of somebody losing their footing on the old eternal escalator of doom. 3, 2, 1, *THUD*.

"Oof."

This should be fun, or at least temporarily amusing.

---

[2] That's a reference to the band Ministry. I'll stop pointing them out now, seeing as I just received the memo that figuring them out is supposed to be part of the fun. I'm not sure the word "fun" means what Bottle thinks it means, but it's not inconceivable that you'll find some humor in it.

Chapter 1[3]

B: Welcome to the bunker.[4] What's your name, Skip?

E: Um, Marvin, sir.

B: Nice to meet you, Skip. No need for formalities around here, call me Bottle.

E: Um, sorry sir. My name is Marvin, sir.

B: Look Skip, Sir works in accounting, and since we don't make any money here, there's no Sir. Get it? Got it? Good. My name is not Bottle. You can call me Bottle, and Bottle calls you Skip. I don't make the rules.

E: But aren't you the boss, Mr. Bottle?

B: Mister waters the plants mid-morning, just Bottle. You're not making this easy on yourself, Skip. I'm positively certain Gladys explained this to you up front, because you came down the one-way escalator, and you're here now.

E: I thought I was interviewing for an internship...um...Bottle.

B: No boats around here that I know about. Intern. Our ad specifically asks "wanna be an intern?" Deal's done, you're interned. Either you make the best of it, or you explode. Let me show you around, introduce you to the lunatics you'll run into if you aren't paying attention to which hallway you traverse.

E: Wait, you mean I can't leave?

---

[3] The next bit of the story is written in dialogue. I thought about making him add some actual narrational text, but it's totally readable, so we compromised and added cues; B: for Bottle, E: for Editor, and so on. New characters will get similar treatment.

[4] Here's a good example of the song lyrics thing I mentioned. I've heard him do it enough to know that's Guns 'N Roses, he's just substituting a word with the right syllables and vowel sounds: jungle/bunker, get it? Once you learn to recognize it, you realize he does it *all the time*.

B: I'm certain I didn't say that, Skip. I have no idea if you can or not. What I do know is that p(nmi)t seems to come and go as he pleases, but when I try to run up the escalator it just brings me back down faster. Trap door, maybe? Some days I wake up to the smell of spontaneous combustion, and find that all the interns have exploded again. It stopped making sense a long time ago, so why worry? It's good exercise, though. Like an ambition treadmill, or something.

E: Ooooh, intern. Like, you mean "prisoner?"

B: Of war maybe, but good job, Skip. That only took what, 10 minutes? That's a new record. I'm gonna miss you if you explode tomorrow.

E: I'm not sure how to take that, Sir, I mean Bottle.

B: Sorry, I have a tendency to sound sarcastic even when I'm not. You'll probably get used to it. Or, you won't. That's your own problem, I'm afraid. For what it's worth, some people say it's easiest to just take my words at face value.

E: Um, ok.

B: Please stop saying "um," it's distracting.

E: Sorry.

B: That's the spirit. Now where was I? Oh, yeah. There's like millions of peaches down here, but you're really only ever gonna see Gregory, Sandra, and Carl.

E: Didn't you say something about a Petey?

B: No, I said p(nmi)t. You have to listen real close for the parenthetical insertion. I doubt you'll ever see him. You'll know he was here 'cause Carl will be cleaning up whatever horribly absurd mess he made, and we'll have like 5 new EPs to publish (which I don't necessarily recommend listening to on an empty stomach), but all I ever see of him is beard trimmings around the sink. He's been on vacation for a while. It's been great, I can listen to my record collection, there aren't any memos, everything stays in the same place.

E: Wait, what?

B: Oh, sorry. He moves things. Your eyes flip on and everything's in a different place, assuming it didn't get broken and end up in multiple places. You get used to it. Now, in reverse order: my personal theory is that Carl's in charge, but for lack of a better term, he's the janitor.[5] Sandra is our HR department. That's an inside joke, there are no humans here.

E: What!? I'm human.

B: No, no, no. You used to be human, but now you're just a function. You didn't notice it happen, I mean you've been here what, 45 minutes now? Rage all you want, you're a part of the machine. Bottle of Beef: we're all dead on the inside, tee hee. It's not a motto, it's a lifestyle. Skip, you're giving me that look that sheepishly admits you never actually thought about demeaning of "human resources" before. And, you didn't even notice that pun. I take it back, 'splode away.

E: Ah! What? Dude! I mean, Bottle. You're just going so fast, and I'm really confused, and...

B: Great news! Skip's here, everybody! Questions for the end, you didn't let me warn you about GREGORY. Nice guy, but stay out of his way. If you're going into a room, make sure there's no sign hanging on it that says "CLOSET." One way ticket to splodey town if you catch him by surprise. I got him to use the sign, and wear a top hat, and I call that a win.

E: Wait. Why "closet"?

B: Because he's a skeleton. Duh, duh, dumbass, Bottle. Of course you didn't get the memo, you just got here. Puns are

---

[5] Sorry to intrude again, but I'm actually super proud of figuring this one out. Bottle has this running gag about the movie Billy Madison. You remember, at the end Carl inherits the company because Billy decides he wants to be a teacher. One of Bottle's favorite non-sequiturs is "the H is silent." When you put them together it's "Charles in Charge (the "h" is silent)." I didn't say it was actually funny, I just said I was proud of figuring it out. Apologies, Bottle's overwhelming sense of honesty is a little bit contagious.

real, puns are important, as Gladys likes to say, "guns for nuns, watch out for the puns, and if you don't be prepared for the runs."[6] As in, run away and/or crap your pants. She has a wicked sense of humor. Any questions?

    E: Several dozen.

    B: Great! Hold it for a minute, 'cause I can't. Reverse coffee break.

    E: Huh?

    B: Bathroom, Skip. Bathroom.

---

[6] I can confirm, she does indeed say that phrase.

Chapter 3

B: Much better. Oh, hello Skip. You're still here? Great! You were about to try to figure things out, I believe.

E: So, what am I supposed to do, Bottle?

B: I don't know. We're an imaginary record label. Find an empty office, there's loads of 'em now that nobody buys physical media anymore. Imagine up a band or 12 and then fire them. I mean, I guess if you're really looking to suffer you can edit my album review blog into book form. Ceiling's the limit.

E: What kind of book?

B: An unguided tour of completely random albums. Every night for a whole year I listen to an album and write an essay while the pages of a calendar blow away like in an old movie transition. A Year in the Life of Bottle the Curmudgeon. I squeezed in about 400 albums and it only took me 10 months.

E: That sounds terrible.

B: Compared to what? Inventing imaginary employees for Sandra to scold? Well then, what are you waiting for? Have fun. Try to make it not suck, if possible. Or, maybe make it really suck. I don't care. Skip, the Editor. Good job title, even if I do say so myself.[7]

---

[7] Yep, that's exactly how that conversation ended. He just walked away after "I don't care," mumbling the rest to himself.

Chapter 4

Not many people understand the idea of an imaginary record label. They think there's like a rule book, or something. Like a bunch of rich guys are just sitting around discussing the best way to disseminate the real art form of popular music to the discerning consumer. Have you ever met anyone like that?

Think about it. You've just got your hands on a couple million dollars through (let's be generous) only slightly mean spirited, but completely legal, activities. No way in hell you're going to pay taxes on that hard earned money, so the plan is to invest it in some useless crap actual working people will buy for fun, and only pay taxes on a portion of the profits from that investment. Sure, you could just open a few savings accounts and live comfortably off the federally insured interest they generate while using that money to actually make the world around you slightly nicer, but that's boring as hell. Now, we don't want to do any actual work, so we'll look for bands that are starting to make some money and generate a fan base all on their own, work up some truly confusing contract that gets them to pay for the whole thing themselves like they were already doing, and pay them whatever trivial amount they think is worth it. If we have to. If someone makes us.

Now, obviously things are going to randomly happen to mess that up, so we need some contingency plans. Little stuff. A few dollars to DJs to play our songs more often, a few dollars to certain clubs and whatnot. Maybe it's a bad year, why not invent an act that will definitely sell and worry about the trivial problem of finding actual musicians later?

Oh crap, oh crap, oh crap, this all got way out of hand real quick, and now we have to buy any band that shows even a hint of possible success before those other guys snag them and we have to start using our own money. UMG wants to buy us? Why didn't you sell us to them yesterday? Thank goodness for our corporate overlords, or I'd have to sell my 15th mansion just to pay the electric bill for the other 14. Dodged a bullet on that one.

    Can somebody tell me where in the hell all these speed freaks and heroin addicts came from? Oh, these are our bands? Sane people figured out they really could just do it themselves for more profit? Crap. What if we just lean into it? I mean, really go after the most unstable people we can find. Who says they have to actually play on their own albums? Yeah, sure, let the good ones play or hire them as staff and use their overdubs. Just find out what the last thing people bought was, and make 20 more of it. The hits will pay for the rest, nothing to worry about. Easy, Breezy, Beautiful. That reminds me, find pretty guys who don't mind wearing makeup. No, I'm not a pervert, hire ugly guys too, I just have a hunch that people really are that shallow and I want to see if it's true. Call it "market research" or whatever nonsense let's you write it off next quarter.[8]

    Personally, I think all that unplanned business buffoonery sounds like a lot of needless emotion, and stupidity, and work. I say, cut out the middle man and just pretend you're doing it. Little men try, don't get a lot done, all I really need is just somewhere to hide away. Know what I mean, Verne? Ernesty is the best policy, in my opinion.[9]

---

[8] Be patient, he'll get back to the actual story pretty soon.

[9] Don't tell Bottle I said this, but my lord that's bad. No one should have to walk around with all of the Ernest movies lodged in their head.

Chapter 5

S: How's the new guy?[10]

B: Nougat? Noogie? New guy? Oh, Skip! Is he still here? I guess so. I haven't heard any screaming, or loud booms. I haven't said any swear words recently, so give that guy a raise. Hi, Sandra!

S: Shut up, Bottle. What are you working on?

B: I had this idea for a band called Pregnant Paws. They'd wear cat costumes, but I don't think I could find an entire band of expecting ladies for more than 3 weeks' worth of shows, and I'm worried someone might sue us for child labor. Still a good idea, though.

S: Har, har, you'll find a better idea soon. As you often say, you can unscrew a light bulb.

B: My Blue Heaven. Steve Martin explains why it's important to take off your pants as soon as you get home.

S: Shut up, Bottle. Carl's worried.

B: About what?

S: About you know who.

B: I don't want to marry you.[11]

S: Shut. Up. Bottle. When Carl gets worried I get worried, and when I get worried I tell Gladys to make you wish I wasn't worried.

B: What do you expect? 4 manic years of sound vomit. Have you listened to the last few EPs? He lost any sense of direction or focus. Then GREGORY showed up, and do you have any idea how hard it was to imagine up an actual top hat

---

[10] S: is for Sandra.

[11] Bottle has this weird lateral thought process where he knows what he's about to say and skips right over it to a humorous tangential thought. Most people seem to ignore it, and he doesn't seem to care either way. The logical response in this case was "I do?"

for an anthropomorphic skeleton. The bitey, Army of Darkness kind, not the kooky xylophone playing cartoon kind. He'll terrorize us all again when he's ready. Who knows? It might even be good next time around.[12]

S: Yeah, I kind of zoned out after the bird and the tape recorder thing. Your guitarchestra club had all just exploded, and Carl couldn't find his favorite mop, and I just...

B: Trust me, you aren't missing the red and yellow.

S: Ok, you stumped me on that one.

B: They blew.

S: Gotcha. Go see how the new recruit is getting along. I hope you didn't give him anything too stressful to worry about.

B: No comment. Don't eyebrow me. Yes, Ma'am.

---

[12] I've heard a lot of stories about p(nmi)t in my short time here. No, I haven't met him, but I have a hunch that everyone is blowing it a little out of proportion. Regardless, I'm just the Editor. I honestly can't imagine it will be any different than the boring stuff I'm already doing.

Chapter 6

B: Hi, Skip. How goes it?

E: Fine. I'm not quite halfway through copying all the posts.

B: You're actually doing it?

E: What else is there for me to do? I do wonder, though, if you don't mind my asking, why you didn't keep offline copies. You know, a more accessible format?

B: I'm gonna let you in on a little secret, Skip. I don't worry about stuff like that. I have an idea, the idea gets made, I shove it in the tube, and start over again. Bridbrad did all the fiddly bits.

E: Who's Bridbrad?

B: Bridbrad McStabbinstuff. He was our PR guy on the outside. Good at talking to people, so I didn't have to.

E: Did he explode?

B: No, no, nothing like that. We haven't been doing much lately, so he probably just found something more entertaining than waiting for the mail. He'll wander back eventually, like he always does when p(nmi)t's doing whatever he does. Nice guy.

E: I've been meaning to ask, is PT our only actual musician?

B: You're pronouncing it wrong, it's "p(nmi)t." It helps if you pretend to cup your hand around your mouth in the middle, like you're sharing a secret.

E: p.t.?

B: Closer. Maybe try shifting your eyes to the left as you say it.

E: P(nmi)t.

B: I got a whiff of cigar smoke there. A little less emphasis, like you don't actually want to say it.

E: p(nmi)t.

B: There you go. Class adjourned. Shhhh. I won't forget to answer your next question tomorrow, but that jab is gonna connect.[13]

---

[13] That's Bottle-speak for "lights out." He wasn't joking, it was like a total black out. I don't remember anything in between. One moment he was here, the next he was gone, and I was wearing different clothes. I wouldn't say I'm used to it now, but I still don't have any reasonable explanation.

Chapter 7

Sometimes people say things like "how do you remember all this stuff?," and sometimes I forget that I remember all that stuff and worry that I'm psychic. I'm not psychic. Patterns, and such. I don't know. If it ends up being important, it usually turns out I remember it. Like Sandra talking to Skip. It's not that I'm clairvoyant, sound travels freely down here. Now that I'm writing this story, it turns out I remember hearing their conversation. See, not weird or spooky at all. Just one of those boring, mundane, real life things that no one else seems to notice.

S: Knock, knock.[14]

E: Oh, hello. We haven't met yet, I'm Marvin, Marvin...

S: No, no, no, don't tell me your last name. I have a feeling I already know what it is.

E: Okay? Bottle calls me Skip for some unknown reason.

B: New Editor, new addition. How droll.[15] You can call me Sandra. How are you feeling?

E: If I'm being honest, I have no idea. I don't seem to notice that I'm doing much of anything until someone interrupts me. Not that you're interrupting, I mean, um....

S: The good news is that's completely normal around here. The bad news is you'll never get used to it. If you ever need to talk, my office is three lefts and a right away. It's hard coded, so even if everything else is in a different place you can find me. Once you get the hang of it, you won't even have walk anywhere.

---

[14] Sandra does in fact say "knock, knock," without actually knocking. I get the feeling she secretly wants you to ask "who's there?," because more than once I've overheard Bottle respond with the word "punch bowl" in his strangely expressive, but monotone voice.

[15] Ooooh. Now I get it. Droll indeed.

E: Um, what does that mean?

S: Easy on the "ums," Skip. They remind Bottle of a bad idea.

E: What?

S: Something about a Pink Floyd album. It's not really important. Cooperation is the key. It doesn't do any good to win if you still have to sit in the same room with all the losers, now does it?

E: That thought has never occurred to me in that form, but now that you say it, it makes total sense.

S: I can't take credit, that's one of Bottle's more lucid epiphanies. Nice chatting with you, Skip. Toodles….

Sandra's really nice. I don't know if I imagined her up, or if she was always here and I just stumbled down her hallway by accident. Not really important, I suppose. I'm not sure what her actual function is, but she seems to turn up exactly when you least expect it to tell you things she thought you should know, or do. It's true about her office. No matter how many new weird hallways appear when the lights flick on, if you turn left three times then turn right you'll be standing in front of her office. I don't understand her computer type lingo thing, but it works in both digital and analog formats. Like, you can tap three times with your left finger and once with your right, and presto dinero there's her door. Or, like if you're looking for something and you accidentally turn around 270 degrees and back to 180, she'll be standing there with your keys dangling from her finger, or holding your coffee cup, or whatever. I don't go to parties, but that's a top shelf trick.[16]

---

[16] I know I'm not supposed to keep pointing them out, but I actually like this one. Top shelf, expensive as opposed to cheap, Cheap Trick. I suppose it is a fun little game to play. A side quest, to borrow Sandra's terminology.

Now, you're probably wondering why I'm telling you all this (or at least you should be), and the answer is I'm just not feeling it, you know. The ideas aren't popping like they used to. Not that that's a problem, it's just uncomfortable. Enough of that mopey junk, these bands aren't going to imagine themselves. Think Lizards? Nah, too frat-rock for my taste....[17]

---

[17] Note to self: explain to Bottle that trailing off as you walk away doesn't work well in a written context.

Chapter 8

E: Excuse me, Bottle. Sorry to interrupt, but I have some questions if you have some time.

B: Skip! How's Eternity treating you?

E: Oh, the album reviews? Fine. The "c" and "v" are wearing off my keyboard, and the control key has a noticeable dent, but it's going good. It's the other book I wanted to ask about. I'm not sure what I'm actually supposed to be doing.

B: How would I know? You're the Editor. The music world is sort of at a standstill at the moment, so I thought I might try writing a book. Is it terrible?

E: No, no, but you only gave me two chapters the first day, and every so often a new one appears on my desk. How am I supposed to edit a book you're still writing? I don't have any idea where it's supposed to be going.

B: Oh. Okay. Well, see I was thinking it would be like a biography of this place. How it works, the silly things that happen down here. Then I thought, Skip's new here, it might be interesting to get his take on the story as it's happening. Brilliant idea! Shoe songs. There's a face on your face, Skip. Where did I lose you? Oh, I know. Sorry, footnotes. A guy I like did that a lot. Molly Prattfall, or something.[18] Doesn't matter. Whenever I do something worth talking about, put it in the shoe store [snap, snap] meat locker [snap, snap, snap] footnote. I'll show you mine if you show me yours.

E: That's a little weird.

B: Weird is good. Weird like science. Makes things interesting.

E: Ok. Yeah, I guess that could work. If that doesn't bother you. I mean, I feel like I might accidentally hurt your feelings.

---

[18] I must admit, I'm still stumped on this one. I think it's maybe an author and a band smashed together, but I don't know for sure.

B: I don't have feelings. That's not true. I have feelings, they just tend to be really big feelings. I know there are in between-y bits, I just think them as opposed to feeling them. Clear as mud?

E: Sure, I guess. I'll give it a try, but I still don't know how it's supposed to unfold.

B: Oh, there are no morals to these stories at all. I work exclusively from start to finish, changing earlier things to match what I just did. I read writers saying second/third draft nonsense, and I think "are you lazy?" Just do all the thinking as you're thinking it. Every sentence I write has already gone through 14 or 15 revisions. I'm done after I puke it out. I'm not bobbing for Snapple here. No prize for being the best, just more pointlessly boring work and 3 times as many welfare wombats up on Mt. Interest. Who told you you're not allowed to suck, and why am I not allowed to enjoy it? Those are my questions.

E: That's certainly an interesting way to put it.

B: I was going for refreshing. Thanks Skip, I'm feeling better already.[19]

---

[19] This is just my personal opinion, but I think Bottle forgets that you don't know what he's thinking. He watches your face for signs of confusion and reformulates what he's saying as he goes. I don't know if snapping helps or not. I asked Sandra about it, but all she said was "reticulating splines," whatever that means. It seems like he's physically trying to stop his train of thought.

Chapter 9

I think of myself as an idea guy. Every band needs a story, a gimmick, a raisin to eat.[20] Long gone are the days when you can just be a t-shirt and jeans kind of band. You can't just laser-point a blinking eyeball on your forehead and phone it in, you gotta be the most original wackos on the planet these days. Costumes, live barnyard animals, concerts inside an active volcano[21], it's ridiculous out there.

I've had a few big breaks. Arséne Face, Suburban Insider, Cattlemast. My latest group was The Moontown Brats: all their songs are about how boring and pointless life is at the lunar way station ever since the Office of Interplanetary Negotiation Knights signed a deal with the Omicronian War Gods making it completely legal to harvest the stomach acid of lunar citizens. Big in Portugal, for some reason.[22]

Is it ridiculous? Yes, of course it is. You see, back when there wasn't much to do for fun, people liked to get drunk and watch another bunch of drunk people try to make music. The point was to laugh and have a good time because you had to go back to shoveling babies into a furnace on a locomotive, or dynamiting a mountain to look like racist presidents, or whatever people did before TV. Then, out of nowhere, the Orangutans thought "this is all Lady Elaine in the land of Make It Bleed, right? Why not just go full cartoon and put an actual curtain between us and the Bozos four feet below us?"

---

[20] I think he means raison d'être.

[21] Metalocalypse?

[22] I'm obviously new here, but I don't have the foggiest idea what he's talking about. I did once stumble down the wrong hallway and see a bunch of photos hanging on the wall, but they all looked suspiciously like those stock photos of families that come in pre-made picture frames. I'm still not comfortable enough to actually ask about it.

That was it. We found out that circuses and zoos treated their wild animals like crap, so we needed something to keep us entertained. Some guys went mild and just dressed up like imaginary superheroes. Some people went guano and drove ten-penny nails into their septums. Matching Cosby sweaters, inflatable architecture, you name it. Pretty soon, you had to have a college degree in Astrophysics and pass a NASA administered polygraph test to play the Maracas, because who's gonna listen to 90 minutes of chopped and screwed take out menu options if you aren't broadcasting it from the Gamma Quadrant?

Every once in a while, somebody slips a normal, boring old band by the Auditors, but three weeks later it's like they aren't even speaking our language anymore. We don't have rocket ship money, and the Corncob Conglomeration owns 93% of the audible frequency spectrum anyway, so I just said buggerit.[23]

---

[23] Maybe the fumes are getting to me, but some of this is starting to make sense. Still, that's a lot of hyperbole to digest in one sitting.

Chapter 10

Like I said, we're an imaginary record label. No overhead, no insurance premiums, no phony phone calls or publicity scams, no accountants to pay for it all. It's fantastic. We do however have one actual, real life artist (and I use those three terms as loosely as possible). We are the publishing house of p(nmi)t. How to describe his music? I can't. Looped improvisation? Texture music? Antithetical constructionism? None of those words seem to do it justice. I've tried, but I'll be damned if I can find the right description.

He runs his own Bandcamp page, but we've put out a few compilations of his music. Believe me, filtering through his cornucopia of noise takes a certain, shall we say, flammable mindset. What does he do? He makes EPs.

Now, Bottle's Taxonomy of Recorded Music (I took the liberty of naming it after myself) is really simple. Singles: that's two tracks, a thing you want to hear, and another thing you might also be interested in; EPs: that's a self-contained work that fits on one side of a record or cassette; and LPs: these are two sides of a record or cassette, or like a 30-45 minute CD. Anything longer than that is nonsense. You could get more fiddly than that, but why?

Why keep him around? Well, he's interesting. You get to a point where you think there's nothing new under the sun, like you're stuck. We've chewed up and extracted all the nutrients from history, we've got some really great ideas about what to do in the future, but all that stuff costs money and no one wants to let us use that money to do it. It's childish, but who wants to spend all their time fighting about whether or not it's your turn on the tire swing? The guy who doesn't want to share the tire swing, of course.

If you like painting portraits of people and their pets, just go ahead and do it. If you like playing the same 3 chords and screaming restaurant reviews into a megaphone while your little brother plays the harmonica, go right ahead. If that means you make $27 every 3 months, then that's what it means. You can be in charge and boss people around for money, or you can do what you like and get bossed around for money. Neither side actually wins a prize, everybody is secretly miserable, but the only thing they both agree on is that changing that system is the worst idea in the history of the universe.[24]

My philosophy of the world is pretty simple: if you can understand the me, then I can understand the you. On the other hand, if you're gonna put on your aluminum foil cowboy hat and tell me that some guy 5,000 miles away has a personal interest in wanting me to be homeless while proclaiming that turkey bacon is morally preferable to pig bacon, then I'm going to point out that we've been making important socio-political decisions based on the supposed psychology attached to the shape of peoples' genitalia for centuries. The fact that you forgot that you're just some psychotically malfunctioning primate is exactly why we can't be friends. Ok, maybe that's too harsh. My point is, wouldn't it be more useful to combine our ideas into something fun, rather than argue about which shampoo makes your hair more shiny? After all, I have to assume that you actually believe the ideas you use to punish me in ways I haven't even bothered to imagine. I think you want me to be mad because you're intellectually lazy, so I try to make that whole situation as pointless as possible.

---

[24] Stuck, childish, do what you enjoy doing, this all sounds a lot like an English art movement.

Chapter 11

Bankruptcy is an insane concept invented from the fear of going bankrupt. Hello, tautology. [25]

---

[25] I feel like we've reached the middle of the book, and Bottle is just flailing for ideas to write about. I'm sorry, Bottle, I'm going to ask Sandra if we can have an intervention.

Chapter 12

S: Before we all explode, shut up, Bottle. Skip is very confused, and I don't blame him. You gave him a project to work on, but then threw an even more confusing curveball at him. How was he supposed to react to the clash of opposing timelines without any way to talk to you about them?

B: I wasn't trying to be a jerk, and I told him I don't think about that stuff.

S: Yes, but Skip has only been here a week or so, and he doesn't feel comfortable with your nonsense. Is that accurate, Skip?

E: I, I wouldn't call it nonsense, but yeah. I don't know what I'm doing.

S: Ok, then let's establish some rules going forward. First, Skip's project should be the book of the blog of the album anecdotes. Bottle, you need to find out where p(nmi)t is hiding, and get him back to work. You forgot that he was just working from some of your more coherent ideas anyway, and you're subconsciously grumpy that GREGORY ate your minions. Second, speaking of GREGORY, give him something to do as well because Carl is tired of searching for his mop every time GREGORY moves to a different closet. Third, Skip, you're in need of some reassurance. Bottle has no secret agenda or hidden animosity toward anyone, and he will be the first to tell you that you should point out his mistakes. Is that accurate?

B: Exactly. I'm like the Scarecrow, eyes without a face, I mean mouth without a brain.

S: But, you are also hyperbolically self-critical, and that can be even more confusing.

B: Fair enough. Skip, just say what you're thinking and I'll do whatever I think Sandra would tell me to do, and try to convince Bridbrad to find us a smallish amount of money to buy GREGORY an electric piano.

S: Excellent, now if you'll excuse me, I'll be in my office drawing pictures of imaginary flowers until old whatshisname gives me some albums in need of cover art.

B: At the risk of sounding sarcastic when I'm not, thanks for being so nice, Sandra.[26]

S: Shut up, Bottle.

---

[26] I have to agree, Sandra is really nice. I still don't know what book we're actually writing, but it sounds like we're at least on the same blank page now.

Chapter 13

That was a productive meeting. For starters, I learned that Sandra is responsible for the cover art on p(nmi)t's albums. Honestly, I thought he did them himself. Skip has done some really great work on the album reviews, now that I'm reading his fresh prints DJ Jazzy Jeff style. I should just write while I wait for our benevolent underlord to noodle up some musical macaroni. Back to square one (that's the loneliest number, no matter how many times you multiply). Which brings us to the G Thang.

Skeletonus Anthropomorphii is a fairly diverse family of former vertebrates, generally divided into two behavioral subgroups: Buffo and Profundo. Not surprisingly, they are overwhelmingly drawn to the world of music. Skeletonus Buffos are the happy-go-lucky goofballs of the bunch. As you might suspect, they gravitate toward percussion instruments, and you'll often find them playing bass drums and xylophones with their own leg bones. Skeletonus Profundo, however, prefer organs. Give them a keyboard and they are as happy, productive, and docile as can be. Don't give them a keyboard, and they'll happily take advantage of our haphazard human homonyms. When left to congregate freely, they tend to form warrior-based hierarchies and attack unsuspecting travelers. They've even been known to dig vast networks of tunnels in areas with good soil aeration, and snatch passing prey by simply punching up through the ground. GREGORY, I'm afraid, is profoundly Profundo.

Now, being the Jack Skellington of all trades that I am, I've learned a trick or two. Everyone has a skeleton in their closet. Why? Because that's where the skeleton wants to be. He doesn't want to spend the whole rest of his day sword fighting because he unthinkingly disemboweled your Chihuahua out of boredom; he doesn't have a brain to tell his fingers to stop wiggling like that. It's not his fault that a hole opened up into fifth dimensional fear-space. Oh, you probably didn't know that. Humans are 3-dimensional creatures, but they are really good at imagining the higher dimensions. So good in fact, that they found "the monster." Does that affect you? No. Does it affect me? Yes. We Imagineers are pretty impartial, but figuring out *why* the largest group of all symmetries exists is a frightening prospect. The random edge of existence is just loitering at the corner of 196,883 dimensions like the gatekeeper of nothingness? Count me out. Just like you humans can't see the fourth dimension of time but you can see its effects, we can see time like a film reel of experience, but we can't see the dimension in which time itself exists. We can see the funky shadows it produces, and those shadows are fear.

Obviously, I sound like a lunatic saying that stuff, so I'll say it a different way. Skeletons don't just walk around without their flesh armor, of course they don't, but they do walk around inside your head. The only thing keeping you from living in constant fear of imaginary Skullboy McBitesyourface is the differentiation between real and imaginary. Poke a hole in that boundary between the imaginable and the unimaginable, and imagine how unimaginably imaginable all that terrifying nonsense might become. Time literally stopping because you wanted to watch that photon party trick, all the gravity actually being localized in one corner of your bedroom, bumping into your personal DMT Elves at the grocery store. Width, Depth, Volume, Change, and Uncertainty, the 5 dimensions of the Imaginarium. Hi, I'm Alice, welcome to my nightmare.

So, to quote the Squirrel Nut Zippers (a stupendous name that I wish I had thought up), "put a lid on it." That is definitely not to be confused with "put a bird on it," which will not work given their inability to differentiate between the inner workings of animals and instruments. The top hat doesn't so much prevent your inevitable gory end, it just gives you the chance to close the door and run away while he's doffing it.

Chapter 14

E: Ok, Bottle. I think A Year in the Life is finished with the standard margin for typographical error.

B: Great, we'll shove it in the tube.

E: That's it? Don't we need to format it for publication?

B: No, no, no, no. We just publish it. Put it in a few different places, and tell the 14 people who care where to find it.

E: But don't we need to file the copyright, and have proofs made, and write up a press release and…

B: No. By all means, imagine that we did all that stuff. Nobody cares. We made it, it's done. There's that face on your face again. You read the things I have to say about the nonsensical real world. It's garbage, right? We're imaginary, we don't have to deal with that stuff. Ok, I've finished the main character introductions for this new book, the next chapter will answer a lot of those questions, I promise. Just take a break. Maybe see if Sandra has some interesting drawings to look at.

Chapter 15

Copyrights, and trademarks, and branding, and distribution, and all that nonsense are simply the rule book for litigation. As in, that guy made a bunch of money by stealing my property and selling it. He won't just give me some of that money, so I sue him and lawyers and judges comb through all the contracts, and deals, and legislation, and stuff, and decide who actually gets the part of the money left over after they take their own fees for representing us.

Who's going to steal my book? Furthermore, who's going to steal the Bottle of Beef brand? Even further than more, who's going to spend thousands and thousands of dollars trying to claim that I don't own my own web pages, or that I didn't type the words myself from my own brain?

Publish means make available for public consumption. Done. I made a thing and published it. No money involved at all. Anything beyond that, I have to pay someone else to do. I don't have any money to pay someone else, and no one else is paying me to do it in the first place, so all that stuff is complete nonsense.

The problem is that we've substituted money for cooperation, like you're somehow breaking the law for using your skills and talents to create interesting things for fun when you should be doing whatever I tell you to do. Somewhere along the way we got this bizarrely twisted idea that people are inherently evil, and that the best way to be happy is to hire the meanest guy we can find to fight all the other people who won't leave us alone for us. That's dumb. You can tell that's dumb because at a certain point the mean people with all of the money can't even figure out how to spend it anymore. All they know is that if they give it away someone else might be happier than they are, and clearly that's not fair. See, dumb. Now, if you turned it around the other way and offered me money to do the things I like to do, then we might get somewhere. For starters, I'd try to do a good job. I don't want you to be sad or grumpy. Sure, I might say "no," but you can always offer me more and see if that changes my mind.

The point is that there has to be some reason to make a deal in the first place. Who in their right mind would think I deserve two-thousand dollars for making jokes about the Christmas albums in my record collection? An occasional 5 bucks from people who already enjoy my macabre sense of humor? That's more reasonable. If you have 3 million dollars collecting interest in 7 different bank accounts, but I can't do anything worth a Jackson, a measly Jermaine, or even a Tito, for you,[27] then what use is even trying?

The problem is that the people who can pay us to do good work won't because they've made selling the product more valuable than making it. Everyone I know is just as broke as me. Offer to buy my creative output up front, and I'll gladly let you become a billionaire from the 3 good things I made on your own hustle.

M: But Bottle, the music you publish is terrible![28]

B: Clearly you didn't read my last book, Milton. There's no possible way anyone could predict what I do or don't like. For five bucks, I'll listen to anything you send me and write an honest 1,000 word essay about how it makes me feel. It might even be funny. I listened to the entire David Bowie discography in 4 days, even the terrible albums from the 80s.

---

[27] I know I shouldn't find that funny, but turning the portrait of Andrew Jackson on the $20 bill into a reference to the less famous brothers from the Jackson 5 is pretty creative. This place is getting to me.

[28] You haven't met Milton yet, but you will, so I'm just trying to be consistent.

What would I do with a million dollars? Pay people to help me make more music, of course. I don't need more stuff, I need more people with interesting ideas. Not even good ideas, just new ones. Artists value ideas no matter where they come from or how poorly they might be executed, but business just sinks to the most palatable mediocrity and rewards the guy who can churn it out fastest for cheap.

If all that sounds bitter or whiny, then you're reading it wrong. I assure you, it's actually quite the opposite.

Chapter 16

Funny thing, Skip just sent me a memo. Apparently, my last couple chapters come off a little too ranty. That's fair, I guess. I mean, I could certainly counter argue that I have no idea how to write a book, so you're going to get whatever spills out. What story could I possibly write? What plot is there to deftly unfold? Believe it or not, I'm not a particularly ambitious person. I'd much rather help someone else accomplish their own ideas and goals. That's probably why I secretly like p(nmi)t so much, he clearly doesn't care if it's good or bad, or if anyone understands it. Tracks show up, I maybe tweak the order or filter out a little noise, only occasionally chuck one or two in the trash can or save them for some better context, upload it and say a few wordy words. Simple as that. That's all anybody actually does. Some guys like to imagine that market research and staff meetings and paintball tournaments help, but you either have an audience or you don't. You're either paying for advertising or you're not. Thankfully, we don't have an audience, and we don't have to pay anyone.

Now, obviously that makes it hard to exist in the real world. Food, bathrooms, utility bills, and all that obvious stuff gets jettisoned immediately. That's not the end of it though. No home to go to, so you're stuck here, or you just eliminate the concept of home altogether. Then you have to say, where is here? Well, neverwhere. Just a pure imaginary space. Ok, not pure. I mean, it has to exist somewhere, right? Well, it's in a dream. Someone's dream. I don't know his name. I don't want to know his name.

Don't get all fussy and do the Bushwhacker arm flail on me, we aren't doing him any harm. He doesn't even notice…mostly. There might be some occasional crossover or feedback, but it's not like we're siphoning off his brainpower or anything. Technically this space is like a little psychic cyst, or a tiny little neural resistor. We let the stray currents pass through, just enough to keep the lights flickering. I push most of that energy right back out the other side, and when he wakes up we just go dark. A little bit of middle-aged slowing down is normal.

Now, before Skip gets all Toe Jam Football on me, I've considered the possibility that our host is p(nmi)t himself. It's a reasonable assumption, but given what I've just told you it's also reasonable to assume that p(nmi)t is just another psychic parasite. I mean, who's to say he doesn't have his own little bungalow over on Thalamus Lane, or somewhere, shoving his own garbled slag into the tube that eventually leads here. Hell, all these ideas could just be a whole infection of dream weevils sucking in the boring bits of some completely normal human experience and spitting them back out a different color. Maybe that's why the minions explode; I get carried away and try to siphon off too much energy. That's as good an explanation as any, I suppose. Then again, suppository statements tend to make your arguments all runny, and we do technically have a bathroom, or at least a place to get rid of all the coffee that only I seem to drink. Maybe I'm just imagining all the coffee. Maybe we're all just imagining that anything is real. Some things are just too big and silly to think about, so I don't.[29]

I think about little things; about how you can connect those little things into bigger things. A lot of those bigger things are silly, or scary, or just dumb, but you can just pull it all apart again and start over. That's really what an album is, right? You take some songs or music and stick them together to see what sculptures you can build. Most of them are terrible, but every once in a while, something really good shows up. Take 5 songs and smash them together, find an

---

[29] Existential conundrums aside, I've never actually seen him drink coffee, but he's always asking if you've seen his mug. Come to think of it, I don't eat or drink anything, and I didn't even notice that strange fact until now.

image that connects them in some way, have somebody look at it to find the parts that don't fit right, let Carl come back afterward and clean up the mess. All it takes is cooperation. Trying to do it the other way around makes everything a dull shade of grayish-brown, and you end up with 27 jingles for illicit weight loss supplements and a song about the virtues of oatmeal. I'd rather sift through Carl's box of slightly dented cookware and Gladys' yarn scraps.

Chapter 17

The humble escalator has long since lost any place of prestige on the tour of architectural wonders in our modern age. Moving staircase, how quaint. Yet, our escalator of doom is truly a marvel. But Bottle, you opine, surely you jest. No. Could it not be said that the fool is the wisest of men, albeit inside the universal irony? Let us begin at the mouth of madness.

You say to me, all escalators are "one-way," they move only in one direction. No, I reply with a sympathetic tilt and wiggle of the head. Your real escalator is a circle, bisected by the divide between the functional and the Newtonian consequence of that functionality. If you transported your funky wheel into my Imaginarium, I would need only stand my ground and refuse to disembark, thus riding back up and rendering your machinery useless for the purpose of doom. Real escalators are a two-way street.

One must instead imagine that there is no hidden underbelly, no secret trick, no illogical logic to exploit. The escalator of doom is an infinite wave with a source but no termination. It travels in exactly one direction, and the idea that running against it only accelerates your descent into nothingness adds that grey soupçon of terror that only high-quality mustard enthusiasts will appreciate.[30]

We have lots of other interesting architectural insanities here too, but they are a little harder to conceptualize. It's a lot like walking around in those MC Hammer drawings, but the birds have arms instead of wings, and the reflection in the mirror might accidentally pick your nose instead of her own. I don't want to drag you through the details, so we'll just

---

[30] A Grey Poupon joke? Really? Maybe I'm being too critical. At least Bottle seems surprisingly happy with the table of Alt-codes I asked Sandra to give him. Lowercase C-cedilla is Alt+0231, in case you were curious.

say that whatever you thought something was supposed to be, it turns out to be the opposite.[31]

---

[31] I mentioned the hallway of stock photos a while back, and I've now had the unfortunate experience of standing in front of that particular mirror. It's like the inaugural meeting of Fight Club, or a really unpleasant Three Stooges routine with razor blades and toothpaste.

Chapter 18

Speaking of skipping the details, I had an interesting conversation with Skip in the space between the last two pages, and we both agreed that I've reached the beginning of the end, as far as this unexplanatory pamphlet is concerned. I mean, you got your setting, your characters, that riveting climax of a board meeting where we all agreed to just do what we do while the time passes until something more interesting happens, I ranted about my particular brand of nonsense, Skip got frustrated a couple times, and all that's left is some cathartic conclusion where you get the sense that the other characters could have their own books all to themselves, and that's what an idea guy does, right? Good job, Bottle.

Unbeknownst to you, I've also got this handy little counter in the bottom left of my screen that tells me I've passed nine thousand substantive words. Not long enough to be a novel, but way longer than the purported pamphlet.

Structurally speaking, this house of cue cards is complete. If it were a movie, we'd be panning out at dusk for a clearer view of the stilts that comically hold the whole thing up so it doesn't slide off the cliff into the ocean below. Take it away artificial computer voice-over lady, whom we find out later is played by David Sedaris for the made for TV adaptation, or possibly Maryanne Faithful as GREGORY if it all turns out to be an M. Night Shaboopy cocktail:

As the sun sets in the sky, everybody waves bye-bye, and files back down the rabbit hole… only to suddenly reemerge in the lake and drag that poor lady from her canoe to her watery doom.[32]

---

[32] Damnit! That's the Teletubbies combined with Friday the 13th. As Sandra would say: "shut up, Bottle." Good night, and have some appropriate kind of tomorrow. Geez, now I'm doing it too. Why is the intercom crackling like

a plague of locusts? Who turned on the sprinkler!? Maybe p(nmi)t *is* exactly as terrible as everyone says he is. Why is my door rotating counterclockwise? Ctrl+P before flames start shooting out of my USB ports, or something even more bizarre!

II. Scenes from the blog

The First Day of the Rest of Our Lives

Holy guacamole, a can of frijoles, you will not believe what showed up at my house earlier today. This one time back in April, I thought it would be insane to order a record from Switzerland. Swiss label WRWTFWW records reissued an obscure 1978 album by French composer Dominique Guiot, L'Univers De La Mer. I gave up on it in June, but here it is.

As best I can tell, this thing involved 3 countries and at least two international importer/exporters. Swiss label, German exporter, and an importer in Washington who wrapped it in cardboard and mailed it to me in Iowa. That is insane, and I kind of feel like I should contact all these companies and make sure they didn't lose money on making it happen. I'm not going to, but how could 45 dollars really cover all that? Perhaps Further Records in Kirkland, WA deserves some future business (wink, wink). And, by the way, it's sold out now, so nah nah ne boo boo.

This is not cheesy electronic dance music, these are wonderfully serious compositions. Remember, it's 1978. Full on Disco, Cock Rock, and Punk are the mainstream over here. Bowie is touring Low and Heroes, MC5 are white panthering, this is like a breath of fresh, slightly salty air cutting through the British/American chaos. How could you not enjoy?

Roulette Winners of 1964

I've been relatively silent for a day or two. I hope you didn't miss me too much. I've been quite busy, actually. I really am cooking a book. Two books actually, but who's counting?

I'm feeling sassy, let's take a gamble on a compilation from Roulette Records. You're a winner! Wait a minute, what did these bands win? Great news guys, you're so popular, we're going to publish one of your songs on this compilation and give you no royalties a month for the next two years (then whack you)!

Thumbtack shoulder smack, I wish I could unhear My Boy Lollipop by Millie Smalls. How was that enjoyable, even in 1964? Maybe that's unfair, but there is absolutely no preparation for her nasally cheese grater of a voice. It just smacks you right in the temple, then disappears into more familiar 60s Soul.

Nevertheless, this is a surprisingly good comp. Cue the laughing out loud, it's a "mob label" formed in a desperate attempt to pay off gambling debts. I was just joking when I phrased it that way, but damned if it wasn't an actual, real-life Genovese front. Levy funded the Sugar Hill Gang and thus started rap before finally getting arrested? Nice. It's just a tombstone in the Warner cemetery now, but that's a fascinating origin story.

It really is good though, assuming you can still stand to listen to these incredibly big hits knowing that the musicians got seriously ripped off every waking moment of their careers. Then there's Leader of the Laundromat by The Detergents, a ridiculous spoof on Leader of the Pack. A true classic.

In the bizarre chance you actually run across this album somewhere, you really should grab it. You can feel the irony seep right into your bloodstream like it's soluble in DMSO as you hold it in your hand. Good times.

Linda Ronstadt – Prisoner In Disguise

Heart Like a Wheel was Linda Ronstadt's big breakthrough, so let's hear what she did after that. I know it's going to be country, maybe a little rock hiding in there, but the cover suggests I'm actually going to like it.

Here's the deal, that's a concept cover. It just screams showbiz vs. reality. She picked songs by her friends and got them to write the lyrics in their own handwriting for the fold. So, before we even start this is easy. It will either be awesome or absolute rubbish. There isn't any mediocre middle room to flounder in with a concept like that.

What are the criteria? Well, either she's a great singer, or she's not. Either the songs are carefully chosen to be about that conflict between outward appearance and inner turmoil, or they are pointless misogynistic drivel. Either she had a killer backup band, or she wanted to watch the can of thermite drop right through the engine block of her career. I think you can guess where this is going. Yeah, it's an amazing album. And the duet with Emmylou Harris is really fantastic.

But more importantly, the fiddle parts are just lovely. Now, who might be the fiddler? Does the name David Lindley ring a bell? It should. I've mentioned him. He does a mean Carol Channing impression. Yeah, the same David Lindley from Jackson Browne's "The Load Out/Stay," Mr. Muttonchops himself.

That's nothing. You might want to sit down for this next one. I don't expect David Campbell to mean anything to you. 450 gold/platinum records is impressive, but what casual listener really puts much thought into the arranger/conductor for these big albums? Hows'bout I say it a different way? You remember how I told you David Paich was born inside the matrix? Well, a couple pods away this other guy was born in there too and he became pretty famous. Every once in a while, he left the two turntables and a microphone at home and asked his dad to orchestrate some stuff for him. Yeah, don't let his mother's maiden name fool you, that's Beck's dad. Might I suggest drowning out that song from the ride at Disney World with a lovely album by Linda Ronstadt? Another actually good Country album in the Bibliography of Beef? Who'd a thunk it?

Smash Mouth – Fush Yu Mang

What do you get when you cross spaghetti and meatballs for dinner, looking at Jupiter and stuff through a telescope, and my wife reading a post about translating All-star into Aramaic and back?

You get the shocking revelation that I adore the first Smash Mouth album, Fush Yu Mang. Believe it or not, this is pop punk/ska and the songs are super catchy. They do other retro things too. It's easy to make fun of Smash Mouth, but it's the traditional running game, and it's effective. Possession time is much higher for a running offense, and all of a sudden that long pass takes the defense by surprise.

Lately, I've been thinking about the past. I love caffeino and a mean spaghetti sauce. I think I'm just paranoid. I moved away from all the whiny neighbors. Fuck it, let's rock.

If you only remember them from Shrek, or Lizzy McGuire, or something, then you're missing out. Their first album is snarky, fun, catchy, not embarrassing at all. Are they just the west coast's Mighty Mighty Bosstones? Maybe, but who says you can't like both. Why can't we be friends? I think I legitimately wore out my cassette as a teenager, and this still sounds as fun as it ever did.

Aw, man what's this "acoustic" version garbage? No bueno. Go listen to a playlist of the actual original, and pretend this was all they ever did, like I do.

The Grasshoppers

I've got a weird record for you tonight. It's Sing Along with the Grasshoppers.

But, but, but, that's just a rip off the Chipmunks!

To which I reply: among like a dozen other groups. And, Dave and Alvin and Simon and Theodore were really just a musical version of Chip and Dale, which evolved out of the mice from Cinderella, which used the relatively simple concept of recording slow audio and speeding it up. Which is to say, it's hard to copyright the idea that you can play back recorded audio at a faster speed. I mean it's the standard technique for the person on the other end of a phone conversation from at least the 40s.

Is Eddie Maynard and his Orchestra better than Ross Bagdasarian and his Orchestra? No? Can you even tell the difference? Nooo??? Does it matter? Noooooo?????

Everybody sounds pretty much the same if you record them in a low octave at 1/4 speed and play it back 2 times faster. Need I even mention Sir Mix-A-Lot's "Buttermilk Biscuits?"

Sadly, there aren't any funky beats on this Spinorama knock-off children's classic. Plus, I'm kinda freaked out by the story about stomping on them because they won't sing (I have an active imagination), and don't even get me started on feeding girls fruit or popcorn to get them to kiss you.

I guess I'm kind of stuck on one particular question, and that question is who in their right mind would hire lawyers and spend all their money trying to defend their copyright for something like this?

The answer is no one. Bagdasarian was the piano player in Rear Window, wrote an actual hit song for Dean Martin, and first uttered the phrase "oo ee oo aa aa, ting, tang, walla walla bing bang." Eddie Maynard doesn't even have a wikipedia page, and even I can't pretend it's the same Grasshoppers that Ben Orr played in before meeting Ric Ocasek. It'd be funny if it were, though.

Once upon a time, some musicians were so hard up for a gig that they just rerecorded songs from David Seville and the Chipmunks to sell to parents who wanted their kids to go be entertained in a different room for 35 minutes. And being the kindhearted soul that he was, Bagdasarian just shook his head and said have at it losers, you're not exactly cramping my style. Where's my hula hoop?

Mumford's Triple Trinities

Tonight's album is from the imagineer of Maximum Ames Records himself, Nate Logsdon. I heard about Nate and sent him an email when I moved to Iowa. The cool guy that he is invited me down to his favorite coffee shop/record store and then just invited me along to a board meeting for the local radio station they were building.

I have a copy of Mumford's Triple Trinities (that's a great portrait of Nate doing his Ray Liotta impression from whichever Shut Up Sheep movie that was), and I love it. This is one of those albums that is going to confuse, amuse, and abuse your brain. Nate is an interesting character in his own right, and he takes a very literary approach to songwriting. He does a lot of other stuff too, and I'd really like to get back in touch with him. In the meantime, enjoy this really interesting mish-mash of indie ska folk funk silliness.

Squirrel Nut Zippers – Hot

Let's talk retro throwback gimmick bands. The 90s were a kind of crisis decade, and revivals became a marketable enterprise. Obviously, we had the punk revival, but we also had real retro Rockabilly, Swing, and possibly weirdest of all, 30s Gypsy Jazz; the most notable band of that genre being Squirrel Nut Zippers.

Part of the reason we just let it slide is that we all kind of collectively nodded our heads and said "yeah this is an obvious manifestation of mainstream postmodern irony and we'll have a stroke in 2001 and move on." Go look up my review of the Strokes. Is Volbeat any different now? It's all Taco's Puttin' on the Ritz, right?

I bring it up because we stepped through the looking glass and we're fighting the Jabberwocky. We know these guys and gals take what they do seriously, even if everyone thinks it's silly. I don't think it's silly, I love Hot. The irony is that for a brief few minutes in the late 90s the Majors didn't know what to do, so they just paid for it while we laughed.

Believe it or not, SNZ goes right on the list of bands who built their careers directly with their fans, like NOFX, Modest Mouse, etc. They took that brief moment of mainstream attention as a blip in their self-made careers, and kept right on going. Fun stuff.

AWOLNATION

I have absolutely no idea why I thought of Sail and Kill Your Heroes earlier today, but who says I can't go listen to the entire AWOLNATION discography on youtube? Of course I can. I might have to stop in the middle and feed chickens, or have ice cream, or refresh my adult beverage a couple times, but I was going to do that anyway. Skip the first EP, on with the show.

Megalithic symphony: Hip-hop intro robot name check. Some lady singing "wake up." So, you should know what you're going to get. Like if Justin Timberlake joined Fallout Boy. No, seriously, this is going to be a mishmash of alternative rock and hip-hop from top to bottom, with a couple ballads here and there. Let go of the "pop" and "rock" labels, and think about what you're really going to get. 1) beatwork, 2) borderline rap and soul style verses, 3) catchy sing-along choruses. They are not a "rock band," so approaching it that way is a recipe for hating them. The chorus to Not Your Fault is awesome. Gospel ballad thing, sure I'm smiling, it's nice. Tell me "Canadian Tour" isn't a Backstreet Boys or N'Sync track. I like that Castles Nintendo beat feel. This is white guy hip-hop. It's not offensive, it's mildly goofy, it's fun. Short spoken word story. Soul Wars is straight up dance, like Fallout Boy's similar efforts. People is festival dance junk, but it's fun. The last few tracks are the same, Sail and Kill Your Heroes are the obvious singles from the album, that snark is like a delicious candy bar with nuts and nougat, and it's all capped off with some live snippets from the recording session. As albums go, it's structured really well, and it's not at all hard to listen to for anyone who likes great beats and catchy tunes.

What's Run have for us? Electronic beat work, and humans doing terrible things according to the title track. This is definitely darker than anything on the first album. Will that keep playing out? Wait, now you're awake? You just said you weren't awake and you were a bad guy on the last track. Now a love song? Yelling "fat face" is confusing. Is this like a fractured personality album? Bad wolf? Like you're Rose with the time vortex in her head? I get it though, it's you dealing with your own insecurities. Dark beats and singy screamy stuff. It's fine. Not like earth shattering, but enjoyable. You know what it reminds me of? Dark Side of the Moon. Remember when I said Roger Waters' statement was that all this feel bad dark stuff is what actually connects us as a collective humanity? But, it's too sentimental for my taste. This isn't a sit down and listen album, it's a headphones at the gym workout album, but it's also about 5 tracks too long.

Here Come the Runts. Or rather, here comes an unproduced AWOLNATION album. Cold start, you might not like it. It's growing on me thought. Is Aaron Bruno's falsetto great? No. How much did the Duff Mckagen and Rick Rubin cameos in Seven Sticks of Dynamite cost? This is the most eclectic album so far, but the recipe is pretty much the same. Look, this hour plus stuff is too much. Why don't I like it? Because once you pass 50 minutes I think that you think you're never going to get to make another album, so you just smash everything into it. A DIY album where the songs are literally your rescue dogs is a 30-minute album tops, and at least 6 of these tracks don't need to be here. I'm not gonna tell you which ones to cut, and I'm not gonna lie and say any of them are bad, but there's no reason to have interludes on this thing.

Which brings us to April 2020. This will either be prescient or pointless. Great news, the studio beatwork is back. Slam is pretty good, if comparatively down tempo. But, he's consistently painting half his face, going back and forth between dumb optimism and broody noirish conflict. Fiesta fever running through my veins? No it's not. And I can't do Lightening Riders. Please stop glowing in the dark. I can't sugar-coat it, the choruses suck now and he actually says "remember the 9th of November."

Now, I didn't mention it the few times it happened before, but AB quite often just vamps on the song title. Radical is the absolute worst. Blech. Don't listen to the second half, it's like Imagine Dragons, but like the cross-eyed knock-off brand dragons with uneven nostrils.

So, what happened over the last 9 years? Aaron Bruno lost all sense of humor about anything and now he's like "I know things are tough right now guys, but think positive and we can win third all around at the swim meet. Let's overcome our depression and go out for pizza." Barf.

I like AWOLNATION quite a lot, but they don't make albums. They don't. It's 14 songs from whatever ideas they worked on over the last couple years. They should be an EP band, pick the five best songs and really sell it. Don't make me pick out the 3 songs I really like from each album for my "I'll exercise tomorrow" playlist.

Well, that was something. I hope we all learned a little bit about one of the lesser-tier, quickly forgotten rock-hop bands of the last decade. I'll stick with that first album, thanks.

The Misfits – Static Age

What is Static Age? It's The Misfits' first album. G'night.

As origin stories go, though, it's pretty awesome. They released their first single on Glenn Danzig's properly paper-worked and trademarked Blank Records. Then Mercury wanted to use that name, and Danzig accepted a deal for 30 hours of studio time in exchange for the name, because you can just go fill out the paperwork again with a different name, Plan 9 in his case. There's always strings attached though, so those 30 hours happened late at night, and the engineers wasted most of that time getting levels, so they just bashed out 18 songs of highly varying quality. Musically it's fantastic, but lyrically it runs the gamut from truly shocking classic tracks like Last Caress and Bullet, to enjoyable mid-level songs on various topics, to simply listing the cast of the movie Return of the Fly. It's fantastic (if not exactly intelligent) late 70s punk. Supposedly Sid Vicious' mom was a random guest of the sessions. They were all hanging out with Sid, and she tagged along the night after he ODed. Who am I to assume Glenn and Jerry (their ice cream flavor would of course be Gravel Road, ba dum ching) were more interested in her wares than her celebrity? If you don't know that story, I'll give you the short version: Sid just got out of prison on bail, and most everyone thinks she gave him uncut dope (that would kill pretty much anybody) to spare him from his future return to said fine dining establishment where he would almost certainly be going in the near future. She was a professional mule, after all. Beverly was not a particularly nice human being.

Trouble is, sure they recorded it for free, but nobody wanted to pay to publish it. Two decades of randomly flicking the tracks out on other smaller projects, they finally released the whole thing in the 90s. It's awesome though. I mean, who doesn't want Glenn Danzig to kill their baby?

Dan Vapid and the Cheats

Remember that time two months ago when I ordered the first two Dan Vapid and the Cheats CDs? They made it here today!

There's no arguing about it, they sound like the best possible cross of Green Day and the Ramones. This is real pop punk, these are real 50s pop and rock songs with complex harmonies and catchy as hell melodies.

Please, as a personal favor to me, go buy their music so they can afford to put out their third album so I can buy it.

Then, drive around your town playing it loud enough that everyone can hear it and say "that's awesome, who is it?" Then you can reply "Dan Vapid and the Cheats!," and the world will be a little bit better.

Or don't, and the world will suck a little more than it has to, but to be honest that's pretty selfish, don't you think?

The Juliet Letters and The Gorey End

You know what I did? I accidentally crisscrossed (jump, jump, I missed the bus 'cause it's hard to run in backwards pants) the Kronos and Brodsky quartets in my review of Black Angels. I hid my blunder on the blog, but it's still sitting right there in A Year In The Life... for your eyes and brain to gawk at. Hop, Skip, and jump around while fixing it! Honest explanation for an honest mistake, because the 40 something albums of Kronos involve all kinds of collaborations and even I can't tackle that fondant covered football themed wedding cake. See what I did there? Tackle, football? Bottle's back everybody, put on your hip waders (again with the tackle jokes, did somebody spike my not particularly strong rum and punch?).

Whatsamawhosits aside, let's make it up to Declan and the Brods by comparing the two albums side by side.

I'm not about to do a head-to-head/which is better review, because both of these albums are fantastically amazing in their own special way. Apples vs. Beef Stroganoff. I'll simply say that they are very experimental in terms of string quartets accompanying things that no other string quartet would even dream of doing. Remember when Apocalyptica was just a couple Finnish cellists playing Metallica covers? That's the kind of crazy thing we're talking about.

First up, the maligned by me Brodsky Quartet and their collaboration with Elvis Costello, The Juliet Letters. That title comes from the weirdly Italian tradition of writing letters to the actual character from whatever play that guy wrote.

They all contributed to writing actual letters from various viewpoints, junk mail, bathroom graffiti, love letters, confessions, etc. I think Mr. MacManus sums it up best as not in any way being a "crossover" album. It is completely unique and one of my favorite albums of all time. Definitely go check it out.

The other album isn't really a "crossover" album either. I say that because both Tiger Lillies and Kronos built their careers doing, pardon my Portuguese, weird shit. Edward Gorey loved them so much that he literally sent them a cardboard box full of his unpublished writings and said "hey, weirdoes, make an album from this." They did. He even drew the artwork for it. Not gonna lie, there's a whole lot of vaudevillian falsetto on this album, and you might need to adjust your diet accordingly going into it (snails, and salmon mousse, and anything else that might give you an urge to lie down and die), but if you want to hear an album that Edward Gorey himself asked Martyn Jacques to make but died before he could hear, then pony up for the repub cause you can't have mine.

Die Krupps II (the final option)

Jürgen Engler is just an awesome dude. Write your own coffee grinder review...

... I'm kidding, of course I'll do it for you. For starters, the coffee grinder company doesn't have enough letter Ps. Then you gotta deal with that goddamned WWII thing where half the world wants to be fascist, and you have to say "oh, ok here's a guy who didn't like growing up in Germany at all, because actual real old-school Nazis would threaten children like him. England's a pretty Nazi friendly island as well, what with their national institutions of cultural segregation and hard right social politics. America is pretty freakin' sweet because at least you can see the security cameras, everybody knows they are being watched, and it takes an actual personal grievance to get you arrested." Granted, the Trump-dumpster is in need of being emptied at the moment, but we're closer to remembering how easy it is to start lighting your trash on fire again.

The politics of Engler and Die Krupps is elegantly simple: yes, complete freedom has its downsides and complications, but that's better than genocide. So what if we're "living in 1984?," that's a fantastically exciting environment for creativity, and in certain ways it does actually help reduce a little bit of crime.

Musically, Die Krupps is probably the most influential band of my beloved industrial metal genre. They evolved from straight industrial noise to experimenting with electronic dance and metal. Remember how you didn't realize that Vanilla Fudge and Spirit were the actual influences on all those famous 70s rock bands? Yeah, industrial metal sprang from a phase Die Krupps went through where Engels experimented with heavy metal guitar riffs. Plus, he thinks trying to colonize Mars is dumb, and since I wholeheartedly agree, it's pretty hard not to mention it.

Now, obviously you should get to know their entire discography, but since you're lazy (no, don't get mad at me, you are, you aren't going to spend your Thursday night listening to Die Krupps, and pretending that you will is what got us into this mess in the first place) we'll just focus on II - The Final Option. To the best of my knowledge, Marilyn Manson didn't steal any riffs from it like III, so it shouldn't confuse you too much. Plus, it's the one with "To the Hilt," and who doesn't want to watch two old men slow dance with each other in a dirty bathroom (go find the video, it's great)? That song is about how decidedly not-German he feels about being German.

If you need a more coherent frame of reference, it's the standard Mr. Mackey quote "fascism is bad, m'kay?" Real people experienced that garbage with their own eyes, and Die

Krupps is here to say "yes, that crap actually happened, please don't do it again."

Now more than ever you need to hear II, and realize that the final option is run away to a place where there aren't as many fascist imbeciles (sadly, America's form of that particular vermin is getting a whole lot of free advertising right now under the blatantly false blanket of "political conservatism." Conserving what? Racism, poverty, and disease as an economic weapon, of course. Are you new?)

AC/DC – Back in Black

I never originally planned to write about Back in Black. Partly, I had no idea what I would say, but also because I'm meh on AC/DC, I don't have the jacket, there's no room to argue that it isn't a classic album, it's not going to be particularly funny or clever or...

No, you know what? Screw it. Nobody even noticed that it's an ironic album. Bon Scott died, nobody cared that they auditioned like 47 sound-a-likes 'cause Bon Scott was already the second singer, and everybody said "hello, Brian Johnson. That'll do, pig. That'll do." I don't have any sentimental attachment to any of them, but I also can't argue that they sucked. Even their dumbest of dumb songs are great rock and roll. I accept full responsibility for not caring, so roll that beautiful bean footage.

They come from the land down under, where women blow and men chunder... no sorry "Thunder" isn't from this album... um... oh, I know, AC/DC is the Australian ZZ Top. They aren't singing these songs about your Christian Mingle, loving mother, PTA mom type of lady. They're singing about the type of empowered entrepreneur who will gladly kick you in the testicles for 40 dollars, and file the appropriate tax paperwork later. It's a gimmick, not real life. It was always a joke, and it never stopped being a joke all the way to the end.

We had congressional hearings about this stuff. Dee Snyder of all people testified before Congress. The problem isn't good people with macabre or even crass artistic personas and senses of humor, the problem is nasty people hiding under the facade of wholesomeness while committing heinous crimes in their personal free time and teaching that lying two-faced garbage to the heirs of their fortunes. Potato chip fights and toilet paper hoarding was a serious problem three months ago, and we won't even go near the concept of sexually fetishizing My Little Pony. Not my fault that you're psychotic. It's supposed to be offensive; metal is the appropriate place to give those horrible ideas a safe outlet as the horrible ideas they are.

I know that can be a difficult distinction, but pretending to be bad for entertainment is better than pretending to be good to get away with the bad stuff in real life. The appropriate response is "yay that was fun, I'd get dead if I acted that way in real life."

Even Christgau and the other guys who hated it admitted it was an excellent example of what it was supposed to be: crass, misogynistic, and juvenile. Cattle prod to the scrotum, indeed. Show me the guy who takes this serious as opposed to tongue in cheek and I guarantee the head banging didn't exacerbate his already established spiral into psychosis; he was long gone before AC/DC became a convenient scapegoat.

Feminist critics frequently sit on the fence because as I said about ZZ Top, the context is not taking advantage of women. The context is clearly defined as speaking to women who told them to speak that way. There's no confusion, they are simply filling their own role in this mutually agreed role-play, and naively misunderstanding that context is hard to defend from an analytical perspective. How dare the farcically juvenile macho bad guy says he's going to do naughty things to the poor innocent damsel! Are you mental? Again and again, the women are in charge of these situations because that's the emasculating fantasy at play here. "I like women who aren't afraid to put me in my place" is quite obviously different from "I like to drug women and take advantage of them like an actual psychotic pervert." It frightens me when an analyst can't tell the difference.

So, to sum up, the women on this album aren't Trisha Yearwood, or Tori Amos, or The GoGos, Brian's singing to Peaches, or L7, or Lita Ford, or Joan Jett. Notice he isn't calling them bimbos, hos, or bitches, he's having an imaginary conversation, and most of the time he's the one taking orders.

You're still allowed to not like it, and I'm still allowed to be "meh," but again those are the appropriate responses to the subject matter. It's fantasy kept as fantasy the way it should be. And, it sounds amazing.

Song in the Key of X

Noir is one of those confusing umbrella concepts for a feeling. Or rather, it is the combination of characteristics that produce a certain ambiguous unease.

Those characteristics are generally cynicism, moral ambiguity, fatalism, and often paranoia. You might be familiar with its manifestation as Crime Fiction. Black and white, the good guy isn't necessarily good and the bad guy isn't necessarily bad, everybody distrusts each other to the point that it doesn't even matter because it will play out exactly as bad as it should. Or, maybe you remember my pointing it out in the contexts of Thomas Dolby and Pink Floyd. I'd call it a doorway to doom.

I've got an album for that: Songs in the Key of X. It answers the important question "what would the soundtrack of The X-Files sound like if you guys and dolls wrote songs inspired by The X-Files?" A few of the tracks weren't made for the album, like the song that inspired the idea in the first place, Red Right Hand, or Frenzy from Screamin' Jay Hawkins, but the ethos is undeniable.

It's a smorgasbord of everything, and it's also probably the only place in the universe where Sheryl Crow, Danzig, and P.M. Dawn could appear courtesy of apprehensive spookiness for fun. How *do* you define normal, David Duchovny?

The Lazy Cowgirls

I'm in the mood for some mid-80s garage-punk. Nonononono, don't run for the egress, it's good. Geez, why do different people take things so differently?

It's just trashy rock and roll, like the Stooges or the Ramones. There was a real proto-punk Renaissance in California in the 80s, and you're gonna love the self-titled debut from The Lazy Cowgirls. It's not political, or offensive, or obnoxious (well, yes of course it's obnoxious, but that's the fun part).

They really were compared to those great Detroit rockers, or like a hybrid New York Dolls/Sex Pistols type band, but they are much more fun. Look, it's 1985, whether you liked New York Dolls or not, Johnny Thunders is dead (not literally), David Johansen is pretending to be Buster Poindexter, and all those kids who moved from Nowheresville, Indiana to LA just wanted to rock. This one'll hit you like a punch in the face, but in a good way. There're some killer bass lines, a whole lot of guitar chugging, songs about stuff and things that happen like Grandma Newman used to write. Plus, it has the coincidentally relevant "Read That Book" like I've been asking you to do. I'm sure I've mentioned I don't plan this stuff, it just happens.

So, please enjoy The Lazy Cowgirls, and note the very definite parody of MC5 on track 11. When only the finest trash rock will do, The Lazy Cowgirls deliver the goods.

Michael McDonald – Blue Obsession

I once said a mean thing about Michael McDonald. I called him the Nickelback of Adult-Contemporary R&B. I'm wearing big-boy pants, I said it and I accept the consequences. Now, being the smooth negotiator that I am, I plead no contest because I am perfectly willing to accept the punishment for my actual crime. Most people won't accept my differentiation that Nickelback is a great rock band who play terrible songs on purpose because they mistakenly think those songs are good, so while I'm willing to accept penalty for the insult, I think the judge will understand the simple motivation for my sensational claim: McDonald sounds like he's working through the pain of a particularly nasty hernia, and that is pure useless opinion on my part. In short, it's a false comparison, because McDonald is actually good, and I'll prove it.

Skip tells me I have a penchant for prolonging the perplexity, so I'll paraphrase. Your other brother Doobie is the real deal OG: Steely Dan, Bonnie Raitt, Queen Aretha, you name it, and his five-grammy palm exploding heart maneuver is killer. And let's not forget that "I Keep Forgetting" is the sample for Warren G's "Regulate."

I politely explained that to Sandra, and her verdict was quite reasonable. Given that I operate exclusively inside the context of full albums, my sentence can reasonably be commuted to listening to the first real solo album that pops up in a youtube search, with the condition that vocal delivery is off the table as far as criticism goes. So, finally, I give you Michael McDonald's 2007 album Finally. Coincidentally, I called Randy Newman my grandmother last night and this one has a track called "Grandmother." You might cry foul at not listening to one of his albums from the 70s, 80s, or 90s, but youtube's search algorithm is well outside my control, it's the first one that popped up after all...

... Sadly, Sandra is wise to all of my tricks, and she quickly punched me in the eye for trying to slip a random Finnish singer/songwriter with the same name past the Auditors, even though the playlist hilariously shows up on the actual Michael McDonald page. So, Blue Obsession it is.

It's from 2000, and it's Blue-eyed Soul according to wikipedia. Again, you could fault me for avoiding the real subject matter of the godfather of Yacht Rock, but UMG and I aren't friends, they don't want me to hear those albums. Again again, you takes what youtube gives you, and you row.

We can't compare him to Otis, or Eddie, or Sam. Like it or not, we have to compare him to Art, and Chriscross, and Dionne Warwick, and Rod McKuen. This is masculine men expressing real emotion in a strangely insulated world of sincerity and individualism, completely divorced from the political and social environment of the real world. In short, it's only corny if you're a jerk. In long, I've pointed out how the collective idealism of the 60s died in tragically hilarious ways like 300 times, and this is literally the psychological extension of that phenomenon. Just like metal is the outlet for all those bad naughty thoughts, Adult-Contemporary is the outlet for all those real feelings we're supposed to be suppressing like the lumbersexuals we really are. If your old friend Bottle is secretly a cross between Norm and Cliff, then McDonald is as good a doppelganger as I can think of. He's smooth and funky, and I can't pretend he's not appealing in the proper context. As you should have expected, Cheers.

Mastodon – Laviathan

Call me Bottle. Not quite a year ago, I began a voyage into the salty sea of album reviews. Not so much to purge the spleen, but to snap me out of the drizzly late October nights of my imagination. Better than punching people in the queequeg, am I right?

But look! Have I got a Matryoshka doll of an album for you: Mastodon's Leviathan. It's their first concept album, loosely based on Moby Dick. Sea monsters and stuff. Loosely in the same sense that Uriah Heep' The Magician's Birthday Party tells a story, or that p(nmi)t and Sandra are "artists." Loose lips sink ships, but not as impressively as albino Sperm Whales.

Melville's novel is equally loosely based on the story of the Essex, which if you're at all squeamish about ironic cannibalism, the part of American history that ran on Nantucket's whale fluid industry, the very real whale named Mocha Dick, and PR nightmares regarding race relations re said cannibalism, you should just avoid altogether. Mastodon's a boat load of wacky prog-metal graham cracker goodness by comparison.

Melville was actually a sailor on a whaler, and his gory details about harvesting barrels and barrels of spermaceti from their heads and ambergris from their intestines are quite accurate. Mastodon might have gotten drunk on a pontoon boat 3 or 30 times. Calm down, I adore Mastodon and they can handle my trash talk. Plus, it's a fantastic album. Granted, there's very little of what you might call "singing," but Troy is more gruff than growl. This isn't death metal, it's prog.

I only bring it up because we were talking about the historical return to individualism that happened with Yacht Rock yesterday. Literary criticism pretty strongly pits Melville against Thoreau in that regard. See, not as ridiculous a non-sequitur as you thought. That comes in the form of the closing instrumental track, Joseph Merrick. He was decidedly not a sea creature, but he was mistakenly called John a lot. It's still the right century, turnabout is fair play, so we're well within the standard marijuana margin for error.

That was a lot of unpacking. Please enjoy one of my favorite albums along with me.

The Most Happy Fella

Oh boy, oh boy. It's time for everybody's favorite game: What's this musical I've never heard of about, then? It's the best thing since sliced bread according to the back blurb. It's practically an opera! More musicians and chorus members than any Fire Marshall would allow if we told him about it. The music never stops (except when it has to for those stupid spoken lines a play has for some reason). Meet you on the other side.

But first, a word from our sponsor, Glick's Hardware in Cold Spring, NY. Do you need a 29-cent thing? Well, we've got it, just see if we don't! Skip says I should point out that my dad's side of the family lives in and around there. I have lots of vague childhood memories of the village, and if I ever travel again, I just might go there for a visit. Now, on with the show.

It's closing time, turn all of the lights off over every boy and every girl. Except this girl. It's tough being a waitress and her feet hurt. I hear ya, sister.

I want you to want me, I need you to need me. I mean yeah, sure, it's nice to know that somebody somewhere says swell stuff about you.

It's a me, Mario! The most happiest fellow. I shave a da face, I pulla da toot! (For my Sweeny Todd friends out there).

A song about bird watching. They are metaphorical cats, imagining catching and eating one of the girls walking by. Remember, you can't go to jail for what you're thinking....

The wind is like a perfumed woman, smelling like where she's been. That's certainly some kind of simile you got there, Joey. I agree, move it along. Go already.

So, they are pen pals, but he's worried that she doesn't know he's an "older gentleman"?

Abundance! But it's like bon voyage, or have fun, or break a leg, or like a send off.

Maiwage! Maiwage is watt bwings us here...

Now Joey's singing to sad barnyard animals for some reason.

Just like Lucy, Side B's got some a 'splainin' to do.

Ok, they are meeting for the first time. Yuck, that accent gets really bad. What accident?

Who knew "evening, ma'am," was such a smooth line? Oh, thank goodness it's about them both being from Dallas. "Big D" is a troublesome title, but I have actually heard this song before. I don't know why, but I have.

You make me...Glad all over, I mean warm all over. Who the hell is she singing it to? Creepy sidewalk cat guy, I think?

Dear mother, who art in heaven, you'll like the girl who likes this dumb-looking boy.

Summer lovin', had me a blast.

Joey made a fist and punched somebody in the queequeg. Ok.

Party time, he married Rosabella somewhere in there, and they were fighting at some point. Game over. At least the princess wasn't in another castle. That's something, I suppose.

Nope, no freakin' clue. Wiki time. Ok, so there's like 20 more songs that didn't make the record, and the plot is all over the place to begin with, but I did manage to get the gist of the pen pal romance turned to happy wedding part right. That's something.

If nothing else, at least you see what I'm grappling with when I talk about trying to figure out the concept of an album. This one was a workout.

The Rolling Stones – Let It Bleed

I did it. I listened to Let It Bleed from start to finish. It hurt. A lot.

Let's go back and remind ourselves what my personal problem with the Rolling Stones is. Their albums sound like garbage. The mixes are bizarre, they full-pan things for no good reason, parts that should be loud are barely audible, parts that should be subtle are 12dB louder than anything else, Mick's vocals sound like they put a microphone next to the air holes in the Plexiglas coffin they keep him in, the harmonica sounds like they put a contact mic on a garbage can and filtered all the highs off. Bill Wyman's bass is the only good sounding instrument in the whole ensemble, but even that gets panned hard right half the time.

Notice how half the title track lives in the vinyl death zone? Some bands can get away with it, but the Stones try to pack every single sound inside the 200-400 hertz range, so it's like listening to the full band broadcasting through the copilot's walkie-talkie. Also notice that this thing is pristine. There's no dust or grime, no groove wear, no surface noise at all, this is how it sounds.

There is some real truth to the notion that mixing and mastering for vinyl is a special art form. I would never expect the casual listener to notice, but hundreds of albums from the mid/late 60s later, I feel pretty confident stating the Stones on vinyl is an absolutely miserable listening experience.

Is Let It Bleed a great album? Absolutely. Their raunchy country-blues infused rock and roll is fantastic. The playing is phenomenal, the songwriting is great, I love it, but even the EQ smiley face of doom can't fix the low mid cacophony that is this album. Sure, you can hear most every part, but that's like saying you can still identify all 30 cars in the aerial photograph of a nasty highway crash.

That's a shame, but it's true. Actually listening to their albums on vinyl is pure misery.

p(nmi)t – The Long March

Hi, everybody! Hi, Dr. Bottle!

Oh, thank you so much for finishing my Simpson's joke for me. I know you expect some silly album review from me, but it's Sunday, so there has to be some reflective component to round out the week before the lights flick off and p(nmi)t rearranges all the furniture. I thought today we would turn the tables, so to speak.

Now, you've watched me ascend Mount Hilarity, wade the tumultuous currents of the River Rant, even swan dive into the empty swimming pool of some long-forgotten ghost suburb for the better part of a year. It makes me wonder...can you do it? Can you sit down and waste 30 minutes of your time to listen to p(nmi)t's The Long March and write an essay?

That sounded antagonistic. I take it back, it's not a waste, it's an experiment. I simply mean, can you force yourself to do it? Can you carve out 21 minutes to listen to it, and 9 minutes to write something about it? You might hate it and say it sucks. Awesome! You might like it and say, that's pretty cool. Great! You might be really confused and wish you could have that 30 minutes back. In that case, sorry. You might say, oh how intriguing, an elaborate commentary about the absurdist reality of defining our lives according to the agendas of our two-party political system. You might say "aaarg, it burns, make it stop!" The point is that I don't know. I like that guy for some weird reason. The goal is simply to have done it, to pick up an object and let it use your words to tell whatever story it can. It doesn't have to be good, it doesn't have to be anything, it just has to exist where it didn't exist before. And, as always, no is an acceptable answer....

[Tacit]

III. Bottle vs. The Compiler

Prologue

As I sit here amidst the technological spider webs of my personal catacomb, I become aware of a light scratchy sound in the direction of the door. 'Tis but a scratch, and nothing more I say, but there it goes again. When I can't stands it no longer, I open the door and peer down the dingy fluorescent hallway, but no one is there. Peculiar. Then, when I return to my desk, I notice the odd addition of a CD next to my keyboard. Not odd that it's there, mysterious things appear out of nowhere all the time. No, what's odd is that I didn't make it, and one glance at the cover tells me it's not a new p(nmi)t EP, either.

I run back to the door and peer around to the front; no "Closet" sign. This isn't GREGORY's handiwork. This is something much more frightening. Blue Sharpie? There is only one man who would dare give me the blue sharpie: The Compiler! What nefarious goings on have waked him from his slumber and shattered his prison? Tingly goose bumps and a rumble from my spleen, my heart races as I put the CD into the disc-o machine. Three words flash in front of my eye-sockets like the yellow lights at a particularly nasty blind intersection:

MUSIC. THAT. SUCKS.

Abandon all hope, ye who enter the information sewer highway of The Compiler. Melancholy Monkey, Angry Oracle, I'm not ashamed to say that the man is a madmaniacle genius, but this? This is the 2002 compilation that even I have only heard about in secret whispers attached to nervous laughter. It can't be real, it shouldn't be real. Yet, here it sits, radiating its sulfurous stench into the already dank and dismal air that feeds us basement dwellers like sickly sweet nectar.

Dare I? The Auditors would surely never know. I can't resist. Turn away as I work my secret magic, and when next we meet, I shall come bearing a new saga. Be afraid, be very afraid, as I attempt to publish this holy grail of terribleness. Until I return, safe tidings my dear hapless victims…

… Curse you, Compiler! What evil have I unleashed into the world? Oh well, I did it. Let's see where it leads us.

Chapter 1

E: Bottle, you bastard!

B: Whoah, whoah, whoah, there, Skiparoo. Is it my fault you thought we were exaggerating? King Calamity has his cyclothymic moods and I'm just really sensitive to the barometric pressure. You see my productivity ramp up, you know the storm is on its way. Every office has its own gyroscope, only the outer shell moves like a Rubik's Cube. Look, you're here, this place is weird, deal with it.

E: What? Seriously? The fire sprinklers came on, my door is now sideways, there's a terrifying scratching noise whenever I least expect it, it's madness.

B: Ok, ok, ok. Let me guide you through this. Did any of your stuff get wet?

E: Well, no.

B: Did Carl come squeegee the walls and wring out the carpet this morning?

E: Yeah.

B: Is your actual office sideways on the inside?

E: No.

B: See? Other than your blood pressure, everything is exactly where you left it. I'm ok, you're ok, we're all alright, right? The scratching noise may be terrifying, but I assure you that's my problem to deal with at some point. I'll tell you all about it sometime other than the time that is now. Now is the time for the season of something different. We need a new project. Any Ideas?

E: What's the scratching sound?

B: Still too much like now, Skiparino.

E: Tell me.

B: I don't wanna.

E: Tell me.

B: Fine, the hffnfllg.

E: What?

B: The complffgder. Oh, sorry, my allergies are bad today.

E: What?

B: Calm down, I said your words. Maybe not every single tiny little syllable, but close enough for a guy who doesn't need to worry about it. I said I'd explain it, and I will. Eventually.

E: That's the book, then. Write about that. Just don't make me actually put footnotes in it this time.

B: Ok, fine, but don't tell Sandra. She'll get antsy. Not like mad, or like she'll try to stop me, I just mean it's a bit personal. Touchy. Pinkie swear?

E: Are you a 12-year-old girl?

B: Of course I am, Skipatron. I'm every woman. It's a sacred bond, a reminder that we're only as strong as the weakest among us. Some monsters might try to ditch the dork, or leave him in the woods to be witch food, but I just walk a little slower. I'm in no hurry to catch the leprechaun. Nasty piece of work he is.

Chapter 2

A long, long time ago, in a parallel timeline 3 lanes over on the highway of doom (it's shaped like a figure 8, in case you were wondering), we had this little club. We called ourselves the League of Useless Super Heroes. The Pluralizer, The Effeminator, Ubiquitous Jones, Mathematico, Inside-out Steve, some other less relevant people, too. All imaginary, of course. Dream weevils, discorporate corporate functions, call us what you will, we're parasites. We feed off the electrical currents of peoples' dreams. Some of us are benign, some of us are so malignant your teeth fall out. Tell me more, tell me more, you chorus. No. I mean, yeah, of course I will, but in my own time. I work chronological, but my stories don't. You'll just have to read it all and make sense of it later. I'm not your mom, but it might help to reread my Explanatory Pamphlet of Doom.

Now, you have to understand something. What's the worst thing that could possibly happen to an imaginary guy like me? Sticking my finger in the electrical socket and getting sucked into the real. A fate worse than death, if you ask me. Don't get me wrong, some of us love it; taking over the host and living large. Not me. Why? Because you actually have to go live it, that's why. Sit there in a room full of 200 people who know your thing better than you do with only a styrofoam cup of coffee flavored bilge water to protect you, thinking I'm just a girl in the world, where did all the spider webs come from? Doesn't matter what you did, either. A book, a painting, an album, an essay about the diet of the vampire Muskox during the Pleistocene, whatever. You threw it together in a weekend and now it's alive, walking around making new friends. Next thing you know, everybody's squealing for the follow up, the Auditors are stealing your French fries, and it all gives me the heebie-beegees.

Hi, Bottle. Big fan. My name is Milton. In the EPD you say you can't remember if you imagineered Sandra or if she was always there, but now you imply that she has some connection to LUSH. Is this a plot hole, or just a sign of the unreliable narrator?

Aaaaaaah! I didn't pack those brain cells in my carry on for this alter ego trip, Milton! Mon Frere Doom got it spot on: send other people out on stage to suffer for you because that's exactly what a madvillian would do. Brilliant.

Chapter 3

E: Where did all these stories come from, Bottle? It's just a giant mess of half constructed plots, character sketches, nonsense poetry...

B: Oh crap, oh crap, oh crap, I didn't think he'd mess with you guys.

E: Who?

B: Not important, forget I said anything. Just don't edit them.

E: No, clearly it is important. Tell me.

B: Aarg, fine. The Compiler. You don't know him, he goes to school in Canada, but his family has a vacation home here for the Summer. I was going to write that chapter eventually, but I probably have procrastinated too long. Seriously though, don't edit them, don't even read them. Invent a shelf or a garbage can to store them in, they are too dangerous.

E: What do you mean dangerous?

B: Skip, you're getting all 5 o'clock news on me, but you know I'm a story at 11 guy. Chill out. They're just full of bad ideas that look good right up until you're locked in the bathroom wishing you hadn't combined all those obviously incompatible ingredients. It ain't gonna kill you, but maybe you'll wish it had. It's not like they'll grow teeth or wings (geez I hope not).

Chapter 4

Every Superhero has a nemesis, right? They battle on the rooftops for the salvation/damnation of the metropolitan area below, until the hero figures out the fatal weakness of his enemy in a dream sequence with Uncle Chester on a farm with a shotgun, and finally saves the day. But here's the thing, they all have useful superpowers. What if they were normal people with useless superpowers? The Pluralizer, able to replicate everything except meaningful relationships. Adding "s" to replicate whatever you want is totally useless, so poor Chad just ended up fighting sheep and mice, and every Christmas he'd get drunk and suddenly we have to make a plate for every character Anthony Edwards ever played. Imagine the unspeakably aggravating irony of Ubiquitous Jones. Sure, he was literally everywhere, but his seats were always behind a pillar, or a car horn blared just as the killer was about to reveal his true identity to a Golden Girl, or the conversation was in Tagalog so the information comes out like a 30-person game of telephone. "The bird-dogger ran a red light" isn't exactly damning evidence, now is it? And poor sweet Mathematico. Sure, being able to calculate running compound interest in your head sounds awesome, but anytime some jackass says a number? He'd get three simultaneous streams going and his eyes would cross. You'd have to hand him fake checks at 10-minute intervals for three days to gradually snap him back out of it. The real tragedy is that the finger counting system he invented turned out to look a lot like gang signs, and I don't think I have to say any more about that. It's enough to drive you to drink a bottle of bleach.

And yes, your old pal Bottle had his own nemesis. What's my useless superpower? I can store pretty much anything, but I ran out of labels, then distinguishable colors, sizes, you name it. Sure, the stuff you want is in there, but so is a bunch of other junk. Secrets, incriminating evidence against people I've never even met, horrible ideas, psychic poison, you name it and I can go much worse. You can't just pop the cork and take a swig, if you know what I mean. You gotta test it out in an inconspicuous area, a scrap piece of paper, or fabric. Even worse, some of those ideas taste great, but contain the essential oils of their own decomposition. It could take years before they oxidize into the 'splodey syrup they truly are.

It took *me* years to notice that the Compiler was secretly slipping me the sauce. Now, catching him again isn't hard, you just get him to drink from the flask of doom again. He's not smart, he doesn't remember any of the previous rounds, he's just a replicated worm in the tequila bottle that is the garbage folder, so to Sandra speak. The hard part is sweeping up all the shards afterward. You never catch 'em all, and a few years later you reenact the civil war all over again.

Like I was saying, the problem with your boring normal superhero isn't that he unintentionally wreaks havoc on the plebes by fighting the villain with an ultimately defeatable weakness, the real problem is that there's a cosmic battle between good and evil in the first place. Missy Elliot that situation in the Imaginarium. There's no winning now, the superhero is explicitly useless because the villain can't be defeated at all. You put him in prison, he breaks out of prison, you freeze him in carbonite, some yahoo thaws him out, and so on, and so on, so go on. Doom is an infinite wave my friends, the show that never ends. But, when you're really finally ready to call it quits, you realize that the bad guy is just the good guy in his own story, and you're the schmuck schmucking it up. Just negotiate with the terrorist. Half the time all he wants is a candy bar, and you were already going to write it off in the first place. How dare those poor people ask us successful shinola salesmen for some legit way to earn that money back, rawr!

I'm getting ranty again. My point is simply that everybody's the good guy *and* the bad guy in some story, so who even knows which book to throw at everyone anymore? Nobody, that's who, stop throwing books at each other, you lunatics. Try reading them.

Chapter 5

We weren't always enemies, the Compiler and me. We were a team: The Compiler and, you guessed it, the Bottler. He'd bring me all the great stuff he found, and I'd bottle it up, boom it from the speakers, and slip you the latest mix. Smooth operation, everybody got what they paid for without the fluff the Auditors cut their stuff with, we made a tasteful profit while buying it all above board and our audience wasn't going to buy from them anyway; 5 bucks for the cream of the crop vs. 15 for two good songs and a crummy creased up wall poster? No brainer. But he went too far, started farming out his own mixes to scabs. Cut rate junk too, going after a few extra pennies on someone else's turf, secretly taping bands in their own garages so he didn't have to kick anything back, straight up bootlegging out of market discs for a dime. The Auditors didn't mess with guys like me too much 'cause I could spin the occasional buyer back up to them if needed, but he was gonna bring me down like Bruce. Don't get me wrong, some of his stuff was amazing, but I'm the guy out there pushing play, you know? Play the bad guy with me and into the flask you go.

Chapter 6

E: Geez, Bottle, you make it sound like a sleazy drug deal or something.

B: Too much? I thought it was funny. Music *is* like a drug, though. You got uppers, downers, psychotropics, fake herbal placebos, imported exotics. Your neighbor knows a guy who knows a guy whose girlfriend cheated on him with the drummer from Styx. Your cousin got his hands on some way too pure Brazilian Mambo and now he walks funny and talks with a lisp. There's that face on your face again. You're supposed to be laughing, Skiptomyloo. Stop being so serious all the time. He'll go too far again, and I'll bottle him up again. Who knows? It would be pretty funny if GREGORY got to him first. I don't know how it's going to end, I'm just making it up as we go.

E: That's the scary part. Remember when you told me not to read any of his stuff?

B: You didn't, did you?

E: No, but the other day I saw a CD sitting on my desk. I thought it was something you were working on so I listened to it.

B: Ummagumma, what was it called?

E: Music That Sucks.

B: Er, uh, how did that make you feel?

E: Bad.

B: Oh, thank goodness. Plop, plop, fizz, fizz. It's supposed to. I'd be much more worried if you sort of enjoyed it. You had me trembling there for a minute. No, we'll be fine, I'll bottle him up again or GREGORY will make Maracas out of his kidneys, and we'll be brainstorming up a new project in no time. Skip away, I need some thinking time before the day shift takes over.

Chapter 7

Everybody had their own secret recipe for a great mix tape back then, but all the amateurs boiled it down to two silly categories: a bunch of copycat stuff from one general genre, or random stuff about the same topic. Rappers tended to do it better. The point was here's *my* new stuff and some other stuff from my friends. That's marketing genius, if you ask me. Why the Auditors didn't co-opt that strategy is beyond my dizzying intellect.

I prefer to think of it like a DJ set. It should be a continuous mix, there should be some musical journey, and it should be a complete grab bag of insanity. Why waste a good bottle on 3rd press pomegranate juice? I wasn't lying when I said The Compiler turned to the dark side and started peddling D-grade junk, but two of my best mixes came straight out of his back pocket. Seriously, they were fully formed masterpieces and all I had to do was stitch them together one afternoon. Melancholy Monkey got the Auditors in a tizzy (too much high-profile talent on that one), so you aren't just gonna find it on your best friend's bookshelf, but Angry Oracle is still out there in circulation, easy to acquire if you look hard enough (everything for a price…).

Flash forward, years after our final dust up, I heard a rumor. A little birdie told me he got his hands on some of the absolute worst of the worst. A mix tape so bad it did a Moebius flip and came out the other side with the most radioactively sweet lead paint flavor you could imagine. Some people heard it, said "ugh, this is terrible," and lived healthy, normal, productive, lives. Some people laughed so hard they pissed their pants and never spoke of it again, but a few people liked it; liked it so much that they shouted it from the rooftops. Apparently that virus was so infectious the RIAA and the CDC set up mobile containment zones in less affluent suburbs all across the country. I had long since retired to the basement of doom at that point, so I just passed it off as one of his more cerebral minions' attempts at rumor-hype. Music That Sucks, the audio analog of Montezuma's revenge. So bad it's good, so good it hurts. Damned if I didn't fall for it. Skip seems perfectly fine, but I can't lie to you, I'm afraid; scared to life, even. I want you to hear it, I want you to love it, it's gooooood. The kind of good that congeals in your arteries and makes you winded walking up the stairs. I'd break into your house, steal your little sister's mint-in-box first-gen Ferbie collection and hawk it for another fix. I'm praying GREGORY gets to him first, because I might forget the flask and give him a hug, Bunker of Beef be damned.

Chapter 8

S: Hiya, Bottle. Whatya dooin?

B: Hello, Nurse. Damnit. I mean, hi Sandra. Writing a story about the secret stupidly shortsighted peril I accidentally put us all in. Why?

S: I was thinking.

B: That's never good.

S: Shut up, Bottle. Can you imagine up something for me?

B: Like what?

S: Like maybe a tiny little window into the time vortex, but inside an isometric rendering of the Three's Company living room? Please?

B: Like at a 45-degree angle?

S: Nooooooo, the real deal, 30\120/30.

B: Why?

S: No reason. I'd do it myself, but you're just better at it than I am.

B: Kay. [Snap] Not even going to ask what peril?

S: No. Why would I care? I'm not a Beefette, my office is in another castle, remember? Don't get me wrong, I'd miss you if you weren't here, you're funny.

B: Want a reason to care?

S: About The Compiler? As if. Now, if My Three Mullets was traipsing around the place I might have a couple choice words, but The Compiler is totally your problem. Quiche vs. Raisins? Quiche any day.

B: Oh. Yeah, I guess I should have assumed he sent you a copy too. Ok, fine. Any particular wall you want it on?

S: West, please. Thanks! Good luck with the bottle battle, or whatever. Remember, Gladys is on vacation this week, so you'll have to fight him alone. Toodles.

Chapter 9

Well, that was anti-climactic. Crap, I guess that means I really do have to tell the whole thing now. I was kind of hoping to cheat and get Sandra to eyebrow him into oblivion.

Ok, Milton. Let me give you the run down. Sandra was the Effeminator, and Chad (The Pluralizer) was her ridiculously unlikely boyfriend. To make an SAT joke out of it, Sandra is to Chad as Paula Abdul is to that cartoon cat. As you might expect, he was always trying to cheat on her, but useless superpowers are like kryptonite to women. Tacking on an "s" isn't exactly a player move, so she just ignored it for way too long. Eventually, she went full nerd and left him for Gilbert. That didn't work out either, but their breakup was completely amicable. Nerds are actually pretty cool guys. Why do you think I like Skipernicus so much?

C: Pssst.
B: No, I'm busy, come back in chapter 10.

Long before we had a bowling team, I knew I was the Bottler. I could keep a secret so long it fermented, or I could ruin everyone's afternoon with a joke so dirty they'd hand out brillo-pad q-tips. Tons of storage room, too. Nobody's perfect, occasionally there'd be an apothecary fire, but on average I'm about as good as anyone. Not now, though. Like I said, I ran out of labels. Even I can't tell the nitro-glycerin from the mineral oil at this point. So, I retired to the balmy shores of the Basal Ganglia. It's a gig.

Chapter 10

C: Pssst.

B: That you, Compy?

C: 'Course it's me, Bottle. I got something I think you're gonna like.

B: I'll be the judge of that C-monkey. Where you hiding?

C: Where we always meet, in the Gallery.

B: Ok. Gimme a minute, I'm finishing up a mix where the third word of one line in every song writes out the Gilligan's Island theme. Dubbing The Boxer for the word "tour" right now.

Guess I've got a date with density. Joy.

Chapter 11

B: Alright, C-span, I'm here.

C: It took me forever to find you, Bottle. Nice digs, though. I wasn't sure which office was yours, so I took a tour. I think I lost my journal along the way. Did you get my gift?

B: Yup.

C: What do you think?

B: I think you're trying to cut me out, C-section.

C: No, no, no, Bottle. Can't a guy expand his own empire? I'm not weaseling, I'm just thinking you got the high road is all. I know you don't like rubbing elbows with the riffraff, but I want a little extra on my own, you know? Like you say, I'm not competing, just looking for my own niche.

B: Yeah, but you see, C-dog, you're putting me in a rough place. You wanna sell sea shells? Fine, but I got the Auditors to worry about. You accidentally leak an early demo of tomorrow's big hit, and they'll rock me like a hurricane. Rock stars practice in the garage like everybody else. I still got a thousand Morose Macarcasses rotting in the cellar. I'll take part of the blame, but you dug up them bones. Anywho, hand it over and we'll see what we see, C-snake. Just remember, first dibs. You hand me stale communion wafers again and we're gonna bug tussle. Come back somewhere around chapter 14, and we'll talk about maybe getting you your own office....

Chapter 12

Blech. I haven't lied like that in ages. It tastes like moldy pasta in a gloopy paper mâché sauce. At least he's still stuck in the end loop. I guess I'll explain.

I sort of created the Compiler. Sandra might call him a little subroutine that collects random bits and pieces for me to work with. I like the new, the crazy, the stuff some kid doodled then trashed and never picked up a guitar again. Dumpster diving is a full-time job all by itself, so *my* lazy self imagined up a little worm to do it for me. Really, the only thing you have to watch out for is accidentally slipping a soon to be mega hit out into the world. It's easy to forget that everybody sucks until the Auditors polish it up all sparkly. The trick is knowing who isn't going anywhere no matter how much glitter dandruff you sprinkle on 'em.

In other words, the Compiler has no quality control whatsoever. That's my milieu. Not everybody can handle that level of intellectual freedom. You gotta filter this stuff like 20 or 30 times, and you can't just flush it after you're done. You gotta rebottle the radioactive runoff and wait for some new context capable of neutralizing it. I probably put a decimal in the wrong place, or multiplied instead of adding, or some other dumbass mistake, and the C-monster just keeps hopping from one flash drive to another. More annoying than anything, really. Everybody wants their dumb idea to work, but they don't want the dirty job of stitching those incompatible ideas together in creatively absurd ways. I just don't have the heart to let it all fall to pieces like it probably should. That sounds mopey. Time to cheer up. It's a beautiful morning, I think I'll go for a walk. Hay foot, hay foot, hay foot, straw foot...

S: Hello, Bottle. Come to admire your handiwork?
B: Sandra, it suddenly occurs to me that 4 is indeed a crowd. How did you know?

S: Flagpole sitter, bird's eye view. That's why I tell everyone to walk this way, come and knock on my door. If you're lost, and you look...what's on your mind?

B: I've got this urge to be real again, shake it up, whip it good, but that might be overkill. I'm all shook up, nowhere to run to, like somebody's watching me. I'm not even sure which thoughts are my own anymore.

S: Is that necessarily a bad thing?

B: I don't know. Mopey time was fun, the album reviews were fun, writing wordy words was fun, but I've got that wicked Caddyshack slice on the follow through. I don't like being the death of the party. Nothing for money, 'cause the kicks ain't free.

S: I think you're just being a contrarian, but it's up to you. Bottle him up, or give him an office. Why not let Skip have a crack at him? He got you to stop swearing all the time, right? You're the only one selling the melodrama. What's it going to hurt to live a little?

B: Thanks, Sandra. We'll see how it turns out, I guess.

Chapter 13

Of all the things I miss, I miss Inside-out Steve the most. He loved wearing his clothes inside out because it made him impervious to pickpockets. He heard this rumor that if you made it all the way around on the swing set your body would implode on itself and he couldn't resist. It turns out that rumor was true, but somehow everyone completely failed to mention that the neighborhood playground was built on top of a centuries old cemetery. Profundo paradise, and before his feet even hit the ground 100 skeletons were all over him like Beethoven at a synthesizer convention.

My point is ideas are only dangerous if you actually go and do it. You need to take some time with a hot cup of good coffee from Africa or South America, and imagine what it feels like to be clubbed across the temple with a femur. Think about the roundworms lurking in that pretty pink steak. Think about getting a bug up your nose and riding the asphalt slip-and-slide for half a mile. It doesn't have to stop you from doing it anyway, you just have to come to some mental equilibrium about the potential consequences. You can't cross the line on purpose until you draw it in the sand, anything less is an accident waiting to happen.

Now, about my personal decision. I should just bottle him up and plan an actual plan for the C-serpent, but you and I both know I'm just going to wing it.

Chapter 14

B: C-note! You in here?

C: 'Sup boss?

B: You ever heard of GREGORY?

C: The real skinny guy? Laughs a lot? I thought he went underground.

B: I've got him. You ever heard of Arséne Face?

C: The pancake song! A legend! He just disappeared before I could get any more out of him.

B: He's here too, he just doesn't want his stuff public. How about p(nmi)t?

C: PT? No, never heard of him.

B: Not PT, p(nmi)t, nobody *ever* pronounces it right.

C: Oooooh, the loopy guy? You're got him? You're a busy bee, Boss-man.

B: You have no idea. Now, I'm probably gonna regret it at some point, but you wanna step up? It means you gotta play nice. It means no more jumping fences and crashing pool parties. The pay stinks, but you got nothing to spend it on anyway here in the Imaginarium. Maybe a lot more reading than you're used to…

C: I dunno, Bottle. I like rummaging through the trash cans.

B: Oh, there's plenty of garbage. You'd be amazed at how much I got stored away down here. All I meant was you got to get along with the other interns and stick to a plan. Wanna give it a shot?

C: Ok, Bottle. I'll bite the lime. What's the gig?

B: Well, I'm gonna hand you over to Skip the Editor, and you're gonna make me a list of all the movie and music references in my Explanatory Pamphlet of Doom. After that, we're gonna tackle the big fish, but one step at a time.

C: When do I start?

B: Let's see, it's lights out in five, so through that door on the left, find an office quick and I'll catch you on the flip side….

…Slowly, but slowly, the empire assembles.

IV. Scenes from the blog II

Katie Perry – Prism

Waaaaaa! Russell Brand left me and now I want to kill myself because I just love that sleazy British guy more than myself. I mean, I could get all Britney Spears about it, but my fans wouldn't like it. I could get artsy and make my 4th album a real musically interesting statement. Nah, too Bjork. Let's remake Whitney Houston's first album and maybe I'll find my own Narada Michael Walden (hello, Orlando Bloom in 3 years). Welcome to Prism, the Katie Perry album that sadly isn't secretly a Canadian rock band.

No joke, she wasn't allowed to eat Lucky Charms as a kid, because Satan. Columbia dropped her while she was literally in the studio in 2006, and this is her 2013 dance pop album with half a dozen producers. Shocking as it may seem, it's actually a good album. I don't mean good in the sense that I like it (though there's nothing I specifically hate on it). I mean good in that it's exactly what her character should make. She got dumped, she wants to feel empowered, she defines what kind of girlfriend she'll be in the future, hooray for fake feminism?

I mean, if you're searching for a new identity without bucking the system in any way, then every track should be off the wall different but completely and boringly generic. It reminds me of Fever Tree, to be honest. Whether or not I think the goal is worthwhile in the first place is completely beside the point. The beats are really good.

And let's not forget that she's recording it in 2012, 4 years after Brittany's meltdown, and 4 years before Bowie came back from the metaphorical dead to actually die. Pointing out that I'm not her target audience is like pointing out Rush Limbaugh is a lunatic. No one cares what my opinion is, they tickle that ridiculous "taking our jobs" brain cell malfunction. All those foreigners stealing our lawn mowing, sheet metal bending, roofing in the middle of the summer dream jobs.

Here's the problem: "core conservative values" are what people are rioting in the streets about right now. They are also the heavily squashed and manipulated version of the non-intuitively super liberal ideas this country was founded on: individuals should have the right to own private property (if those individuals are White Anglo-Saxon Protestant men). Remember kids, liberal and conservative are reciprocally defined adjectives, not nouns. You're liberal when you want things to change for the better, but the moment you've got it all running smoothly for yourself you flip on that conservative switch and play the victim of those greedy, poor, working-class vampires.

Also remember that my opening paragraph is the Katie Perry, Inc. PR character, which isn't the same thing as Katie Perry the person. That doesn't mean her feelings aren't real, it means that she only gets to use the ones that sell.

But, here's the difference: Katie Perry's message is feel empowered and define your own value for yourself regardless of your circumstance, Rush Limbaugh's message is that letting women and minorities step above their appropriate place in society will destroy the American way of life. Hers is sappy and a tiny bit too Stockholm Syndromy for my taste, his is flat out pandering bullshit.

Also remember that while Katie Perry was recording this album and Limbaugh was saying the same garbage he's been saying since the 90s because he refuses to actually digest new information, I was working in the mail room of a major newspaper with the Black, Middle-Eastern, and Asian people who do the actual work behind the scenes. Here's the thing, Limbaugh's daily verbal diarrhea brings in a whole lot of money for Rush Limbaugh, while Katie Perry's songs bring in a whole lot of money for people like Rush Limbaugh, and you'd have to be really bad at basic math to end up making that equation into an equality.

I dunno, maybe Sitsinachair McRamblesalot really believes what he says to his 15 million listeners (we'll very generously round up and call that 5% of the population), but that would mean that he doesn't actually have a grasp on the other 95% of the real world that takes place outside his radio booth. Presumably he reads something loaded on a truck late at night by immigrants, but he certainly doesn't research any of it until he has to publicly apologize on air a week later.

The ceiling for gain in the actual real life everyday world is approximately 20-30%. Said another way it costs $1000 to make $250 on a good day, and my personal end of the month balance hasn't been 4 digits since around 2005. I'm not entirely sure how I got from Katy Perry to the point where I am now, saying that of course HSAs are every Corporate Republican's wet dream, because it means that money doesn't actually stop collecting interest for your company until you actually physically go to see a doctor for something your insurance won't cover. Yay, creative accounting!

Limbaugh pays every one of his staff as little as legally required to listen to him regurgitate 1850s political philosophy, the same way Perry pays every musician and engineer for her studio/stage time. I know which one I'd rather listen to on the radio if the only other options are country and evangelism....

V. Skip the Editor and The Compiler proudly bring you this appendix of references from The Explanatory Pamphlet of Doom, with annotations as necessary.

Hello, fellow travelers, Skip here. My temporary assistant and I have compiled this annotated list of Bottle's haphazard approach to borrowed language. We hope this discorporate appendix provides you some illumination into the curiosities of his thought processes. I suppose it might be helpful to tell you that my real name is Marvin Gardens, though none of the clowns here seem to care. Take it away C-man, and I'll chime in when appropriate.

Prologue
1 – Beacon Street Union, The Clown Died in Marvin Gardens
2 – The Doors, Five to One and Waiting for the Sun
3 – Ministry, Thieves and Liars

At this point, Compy assures me that I made a reference to The Princess Bride in my second footnote. Having never seen that movie, I suppose I'll have to take his word for it.

Chapter 1
1 – Guns 'N Roses, Welcome to the Jungle
2 - It can often be difficult to conceptualize the larger framework of Bottle's writing, but given Bottle's penchant for Albums, we feel pretty confident that Modest Mouse's We Were Dead before the Ship Even Sank is shaping the conversation in the most general sense.
3 – The Presidents of the United States of America, Peaches.
4 – Charles in Charge
5 – Rage Against the Machine

Chapter 4
1 – Cover Girl makeup
2 – Ernest P. Worrell

Chapter 7
1 – Compy tells me the directions to Sandra's office are an oblique reference to secret areas in games like The Legend of Zelda, or cheat codes in general. He's much better at this that I thought he would be. All I hear is Beethoven's 5th Symphony.
2 – Pink Floyd, Ummagumma. That's the one where Wright suggested they don't help each other at all. It went wrong.
3 – Imagine Dragons

Chapter 8
1 – The Refreshments
2 – Compy tells me there's a whole lot of Terry Pratchett hiding in here. Putting in footnotes, GREGORY the skeleton, using all caps. And even the phase "clear as mud" is a reference to the massive and complex Discworld Multi-User Dungeon.
3 - Compy again, for the win. "Reticulating splines," is what the voice-over says when you're redrawing an initial map in Sim City 2000.

Chapter 9
1 – Third Eye Blind
2 – Metalocalypse
3 – Boomtown Rats
4 – Gorillas
5 – Mr. Rogers' Neighborhood and the Rolling Stones
6 – Bozo the Clown
I'll defer to Compy again. There was a real backlash against the elaborate performances and concerts of mainstream acts in the 90s, and a lot of people just wanted bands to get up on stage and play again without all the theatrics.

Chapter 10
1 – I was right, Bottle has a tendency to reference English culture, and the Stuckist Movement led briefly by Billy Childish plays a big part in his world view.
2 – The Shaggs
3 – Metallica, The Unforgiven Too

Chapter 12
1 – Billy Idol, Eyes Without A Face, and The Wizard of Oz

Chapter 13
1 – Will Smith goes solo.
2 – Harry Nilsson
3 – Bottle is referencing all the ways skeletons have been portrayed in pop culture: Cartoons, Army of Darkness, Clash of the Titans, They Might Be Giants, The Nightmare Before Christmas
4 – The 5th Dimension (the band, not the movie, though I have heard him mention the meat popsicle joke.
5 – Portlandia
6 – Tiger Lillies, The Gorey End

Chapter 14
1 – The Jackson 5

Chapter 15
1 – Compy tells me The Bushwhackers were tag-team wrestlers, and it's quite possible that Gladys is the personification of how much little old ladies seemed to love the whole Professional Wrestling spectacle.
2 – The Beatles, Come Together
3 – Gary Wright, Dream Weaver

Chapter 17
1 – That damned Grey Poupon joke
2 – MC Escher

Chapter 18
1 – Buddy Hackett, Shipoopi.
2 – The Teletubbies and Friday the 13th.
3 – The Weekend Update sendoff from Saturday Night Live.

And there you have it. It's entirely possible that we missed a few, and I'm sure we could go more in depth in terms of context and setting, like the Bunker of Beef being reminiscent of the hallway from House of Leaves and Hell from Bill and Ted's Bogus Journey, but Bottle just wanted to see if we could nail down the basics. A sort of official answer sheet for the game of identifying the most obvious ones. If you want a real challenge, try doing it yourself for the strange story about how Compy joined our little crew. Now, if you'll excuse us, we'd like a warm glass of miak and a nap. Iwrestledabearonce, but Bottle is exhaustipating.

[Grrrr. I wasn't done with part 4, ya jerks! Way to interrupt, and make my roman numerals look ridiculous.]

IV (Again). Scenes from the blog II.

20$ Adventure Time with Bottle

B: I have a new idea. Let's make up a new thing called $20 Adventure Time with Bottle. I'll send C-student into some place that has used records, he'll buy as many as he can for $20, and I'll write about them. What do you think?

E: Will this be a self-contained essay, or the normal facebook/blog thing?

B: Both. See, the problem with a book is that there's no instant gratification, and that means I get real uncomfortable, like I'm lying. On the other hand, facebook posts are useless for my ramblin' gamblin' style of verbal gunfighting. I'm thinking C-spray hands me a small collection of records, I run my mouth about each one, but also talk about what it's like to do the whole thing. Sumo-wrestle the whole experience, you might say.

C: So, I get to rummage through stacks of stuff other people threw away?

B: Yeah, totally.

C: I'm in. $20 bucks makes it a challenge for both of us.

S: Excellent point, C. I think I speak for everyone when I say you are making an excellent addition to our little crew.

B: That'll do, C-pig. Mr. Jackson says Christmas me up a conundrum to crack.

WHOOOSH!

B: He's way more enthusiastic than I expected. I still think it will backfire and give us all head lice, or something, but what do I know?

E: I think you're being too self critical, like Sandra says. He knows how you think, and he certainly passed your secret test with flying colors.

S: Skip is spot on, Bottle. You have to remember that you work backward from a moderately unfathomable level of speculative reasoning. Not everybody sees the world as a Markov chain of hypothetical cause and effect the way you do.

B: Why not?

S: Shut up, Bottle. He's back.

C: Ok, Boss. 20 on the nose. Read 'em and weep.

B: Ooooh, interesting. 2 juniors, a 5-spot, and something I've never heard of at all. You working from a theme, or just adding up the price tags?

C: I thought the point was for you to figure that out.

B: Alright C-shanty, what do I know? 1) you are just a part of me, 2) I'm certain you read my year's worth of reviews in about half an hour, 3) it's all rock and roll to me. Here's what I really think:

You had about 6 albums on the short list, all under $10. Prism was a no brainer, because A) I loved their first two albums, and B) last night's Katy Perry album was Prism. Modern English is that delicious fluke of a one-hit wonder band that never should have cracked the top 40 but is actually amazing, and my collection is woefully lacking in new wave/post-punk gloominess regardless of quality or notoriety. Camel is probably the most famous cult prog-band this side of Klaatu, and you're never going to find one of their albums on a junk shop floor again, and if I had to guess I'd say you mistakenly thought the last one was "Agent Circus," and thought with a name like Smuckers…. It turns out that adding an "R" to make Argent doesn't help me at all, but it's a pretty safe bet it's still some sort of prog. How'd I do?

C: When you're right, you're right. Good luck.

B: If wishes and buts were candies and nuts, we'd all be diabetic. Here we go.

1 – Prism – Armageddon

So, I listened to Katy Perry's Prism yesterday, and I jokingly lamented that it wasn't the Canadian rock band. What are the chances C-salt found their 3rd album today? 100%

Here's Armageddon, the album they made right before their personal label declared bankruptcy. Man, it's fantastic. It's overwhelmingly arena rock, but not cheesy or dumb or drenched in pointless machismo. There's some real adventurous stuff too, synths and horns and brief flirts with near-prog. The best part of this album is that it's explicitly about "a final and conclusive battle between good and evil." Everything is: love, jealousy, going on tour, politics. If borderline personality disorder was a rock band, this would be their album. Awesome! 5/3 stars, ridiculous and delicious. Find me their next 5 albums, C-Shore, I love these lost-in-the-shuffle weirdos.

2 – Modern English – Ricochet Days

You shouldn't know any song by Modern English. You know one, and only one, because the entire song appeared in the movie Valley Girl. Yes, you read that right, a Nicholas Cage movie gave Modern English a #7 hit. It's a love song written from the psychological perspective of falling in love while being actually terrified of nuclear holocaust, because who didn't love the Cold War Era?? What you don't realize is that I've already told the story of Modern English in the form of The Cars. Post-punk band makes album that nobody cares about, second album skyrockets them into public/critical awareness, critics slam their 3rd album, and band responds "who gave you a copy of it?" I haven't heard their 3rd album yet, but I know the first two pretty well, even though I don't own them. What I don't understand is how you can listen to Mesh and Lace and think this is a New Wave band. That first album is borderline Industrial, not Joy Division copycats at all. I mean, they're both British and not at all happy about being alive, but Joy Division sounds sad and lethargic while Modern English sounds like they got their arms mangled by the pasta extruder; similar mentality, completely different execution.

For their second album, the band basically says we never thought we'd make a pop album, but to be completely honest it was a hell of a lot of fun, and we still managed to give it our own peculiar nihilistic brand of irony. Then they moved to New York and disappointed everyone, thank goodness. What a bunch of posers writing extremely well crafted, broody but approachable synth-rock and living normal human lives afterward. Pfffft!

Ricochet Days is phenomenal, and you don't have to pretend it isn't. You don't have to hear their evolution from pseudo-Industrial to the synth side of New Wave as anything other than them enjoying the whole process of making music. This isn't Scritti Politti bubblegum ideo-irony, it's the melancholy after the anger. It's got that same kind of noir-ish darkness as Thomas Dolby without the agitated neurosis. It's more like The Cure than anything I can think of while listening to it, and there's more than a couple big surprises if you go into it expecting mindless neon dance floor fodder. Maybe the problem was that they weren't actually weird or downtrodden enough, and making a great sounding record is anathema to the cause. I've probably been guilty of flaunting that sentiment in other contexts, but not with this one. It's genuinely fantastic gloomy ennui from start to finish.

3 – Camel – Rain Dances

Camel is one of those confusing bands you've never heard of because they don't write verse-chorus pop songs. Yet, the moment you sit down and ask "what's this prog-rock thing I keep hearing about, then?," you see them pop up everywhere. Rick Astley says they were his first concert experience and they "blew his mind," and Opeth of all bands lists Camel among their influences. They are in fact that golden goose of a middle-ground band that achieved the weird level of success that let them live off playing actual music without going bankrupt or tripping into the Bermuda Triangle of corporate economics: enough money to live reasonably happy lives, not enough money for anyone to bother siphoning away into their own quagmire of cut-rate merchandising. Even their brief encounter with copyright infringement went away when they agreed to not publish a complete synopsis of Paul Gallico's story, The Snow Goose.

Critics who bother to mention the band at all say "Mirage is great, everyone should buy it, please don't make me listen to their other 13 albums." Bugger that, here's Rain Dances. Hello, Brian Eno, I assume you're bringing some melancholic atmosphere to this garden party.

Prog can mean a lot of things to a lot of people, but it boils down to a single philosophical idea: a rock band is a legitimate musical ensemble, and we should play musically substantive compositions instead of 3-5 minute lullabies. No one agrees with us, so we'll figure it out on our own and be perfectly happy with the 12 people in every town who actually enjoy listening to it. Your old friend Bottle is one of those 12 people who loves getting lost in the sound garden, because it doesn't remind me of anything (badum ting).

There are some lyrics, by the way, they just aren't sing-songy rhyming couplets all the time. It's from an original idea by Bert Ford (whoever that is). I imagine that idea was a kid looking out the window on a rainy day and imagining androgynously naked women performing a synchronized gymnastics routine, like any other normal kid would do??? I'm probably being too literal. It's almost certainly more along the lines of Willy Wonkan pure imagination.

Music is the only way to tell me how you feel. Yeah, I'll buy that. We are sailing in a ship that has no sails, after all.

Now, this isn't the in your face, EL&P kind of prog, or your Moody Blues type of prog-folk, it's that Steely Dan-ish light jazz/funk adjacent daydreamy type thing; super melodic and more wistful than spastic. More importantly, whether you like their style or not, it sounds incredibly fun to play. Most people might relegate it to background dishwashing/housecleaning music, but isn't that exactly the same kind of pleasurably functional escapism Bert was clearly trying to channel with his concept? Have to pass the time somehow, am I right? If you like whimsical meandering solos and melodic electric guitars like I do, then this is a little slice of pure pleasure. Put on your galoshes and come dance in the rain with me.

4 - Argent – Circus

One more album to go before I try to sum up this 4-album Markov Chain of rumors. I still don't know anything about Argent other than the obvious concept for this album: life is a circus. I assume it's prog because what else could it be, but I'll do the not so interesting real time jot down notes kind of review for this $2 naked high wire routine.

Yep, it's the in-your-face kind of proggy weirdness: spooky. IN THE CIRCUS!!!!!! So far this is great. It's 70s hard rock with the added deranged modulations and abrupt style changes you'd expect from conceptual music. It's not drive-time radio material, even by AOR standards, but quite enjoyably amusing. That guitar/synth duet near the end of Highwire is awesome. Ha! The Phantom of the Opera chromatic descent, with almost Gilmour-y vocals. Clown really is very Pink Floydy to my ears. What's Side B have for us?

Ooh, that kind of Klangfarbenmelodie approach is cool, and I loves me some ham-fisted keyboard banging. 70s ballad that doesn't seem to fit the album at all. Hello, weird stereo organ chorale thing. The jester only plays for himself, you know. Very Freddy Mercury.

Yeah, this is great stuff. And, I apparently paid 2 dollars for it. King sized Snickers bar or Argent on vinyl? No brainer, I'll take that tragically underappreciated prog-rock concept album over a sugar rush most any day of the week, thanks.

What a great album. It's completely coherent, stylistically focused with only that one obvious non-album single as time filler. It's not cheesy or preachy like it easily could have been. Rod Argent was an actual member of the real Zombies. Oooooooh! He's the God Gave Rock and Roll to You and Hold Your Head Up guy, and he went on to actually work with Andrew Lloyd Webber. Niiice.

To paraphrase the words of my hero DJ Lance Ramone, let's go back and remember what we did in the last two days. Yo gabba gabba, Hey!

I compared Katy Perry to Rush Limbaugh by saying I have no idea if either of them actually believes the messages they sell or if it's just the only things they know how to sell. Then, C-bgb handed me basically 4 random albums, and I proceeded to talk out of my ass. I called Roar fake feminism but defended it as a contextually appropriate message, then randomly ended up finding out Argent was responsible for the real feminist chorus "Hold your head up, woman." I also can't fail to mention that today is Labor Day, and she recently released a facebook exclusive music video while pregnant (congrats on the baby girl from all of us at BoB) dressed as a clown playing a video game about life being a circus. So, it turns out all four albums were bands who eschewed fame and fortune for honesty, the whole thing is a ridiculous battle between good and evil, we're all stuck in a fight we can't win for the benefit of someone else, and it's all just a Fleetwood Mac song: you can go your own way; you can call it another lonely day. Define your own purpose, do what you think is meaningful, and stop measuring yourself against the psychopathic tendencies of people whose only goal in life is to own the machinery of existence like humanity is just an ant farm on their bookshelf and you can just go collect more ants when they die. I think all those big-business anti-trust evading corporate guys are lunatics. Who cares if Katy Perry believes her own message, I clearly do.

    C: I'm impressed.
    E: Are you a homicidal maniac?
    S: How do you find all these coincidences by just randomly looking at wikipedia articles?
    B: Pinkie swear, I don't put any effort into it at all. It just so happens that I can't stand the cognitive dissonance of the Republican party because Teddy Roosevelt said screw you guys and they secretly morphed from being the progressive voice of American politics into the right-wing money hoarders they are today by just constantly lying about it. I'm not a Democrat either, but at least they naturally became more and more liberal over the last century as the Southern white-supremacist Democrats increasingly said sign me up for that elephant ride to corporate town.
    S: I'm sure we'll all regret my asking, but what non-sequitur of a song lyric sums up your non-intuitive solution to the problem?
    B: Go on, take the money and run? I got the pistols, so I get the pesos?? West End town in a dead end world??? I don't wanna be buried in a pet cemetery????
    S: Shut up, Bottle. Meeting adjourned. Everybody take Monday off.

Alice In Chains – Jar of Flies

It has been one of those days. We played awesome games like "forklifts in the rain," "logistics with morons," "will the substitute UPS driver come back at our scheduled pickup time?," and my personal favorite "suffering manager, aka no overtime for Bottle 'cause he costs too much." Somewhere in the middle there I got stuck explaining the truly bilious concept of the Friedman Doctrine, aka Shareholder Theory through absolutely no fault of my own, and it's times like this I usually remind myself what true suffering is by listening to country music. Not today. Today we're going to suffer with my least favorite technological advancement ever: piezo pickups. Plus, I said "ant farm" the other day, so heroin up your hypodermics, it's Jar of Flies from Alice in Chains.

EP my ass, it's 30 minutes. 15 minutes per side, album on your lunch break, no garbage inner-most tracks to tolerate. Their original bass player couldn't handle Guns 'n Roses levels of heroin anymore so they replaced him with Ozzy's bassist of the same first name. Something really familiar about a touring musician for Ozzy being credited for contributing to an album but somehow having their parts played by someone else... Mike Starr went through the normal treatment prescribed by doctors who don't care, but then said hey Dr. Drew, methadone is actually just as addictive, but without the fun part of actually being high, will being on your fake reality TV show help?

Hello Mike Inez, let's just jam on acoustic guitars for a couple days. My tinnitus is really acting up after being on tour for so long. Columbia actually wants to put it out? Ok, whatever.

Some people like the sounds of piezo pickups, I mean legitimately love it. Not Bottle. You know what would be even better? Piezos on the dead-inside sound of whatever hard plastic industrial waste product Ovation uses to make the salad bowls on the back of their guitars. Again, some people love them, famous people like Robert Fripp, even. You can have all of them, I literally have to stop myself from smashing them over the store clerk's head Animal House style whenever I forget how much I hate the way they sound and feel and dumbassedly test one out. That's just me.

The music? Oh, sorry. Awesome album, all the songs are great, singing's great too. There's even a lovely instrumental with strings, and some glorious fret buzz on Don't Follow. But goddamnit the piezos are everywhere and it sounds like they're playing rubber bands and I hate it! The last track is the absolute worst.

If you have no idea what I'm talking about, then great for you, just know that it sounds like playing a nylon string classical guitar ponticello with a jagged rock from the parking lot for a pick, and I'm in tangible agony over here. Maybe going back to work tomorrow isn't as bad as I thought....

Sevendust – Next

Stocking Stuffers, Rosie Ledet's Zesty Zydeco, or Sevendust? One of these things is not like the others, one of these things is good. Spoiler alert, it's Rosie Ledet playing the accordion and singing songs chocked full of innuendo! So, instead we'll listen to the underwhelming fifth album from Sevendust.

I didn't compare Fire from the Gods to Sevendust for no reason. Lajon Witherspoon doesn't rap, this is straight up alternative metal with alternating scream singing. It's djent before Meshuggah inspired Misha Mansoor to coin the term djent.

It's not a bad album because the band did a bad job, it's a bad album because they were lost in the universe and writing track after potential radio/soundtrack/anything track because it's 2005.

They had lineup changes, and left TVT for Winedark's promise of Universal's distribution channels. They recorded this in the same house Creed used for Weathered. Winedark was secretly already folding, stopped funding anything without telling the band, the band was maxing out every credit card they had trying to keep their crew fed, and then they found out their accountant hadn't bothered to pay their taxes for them either. Million dollars in the hole and fans were actually asking when this new album was coming out (it was already out) 'cause no advertising whatsoever from their label. It's actually much better than I remember, but no it's not fantastically amazing, or magically delicious. Better than Allmusic's 2.5 stars, Allmusic freelancers are terrible after all, but not by more than 1 additional star. Again, songs for the sake of songs is a crap concept. I will say, you could pick any song from it as a great representation of Sevendust in whatever mix you're making, but as a full album it really is "Next!"

Ric Ocasek – This Side of Paradise

Hey Bottle, is Ric Ocasek's second solo album any good? No idea, what are you expecting it to be? Most of the Cars are here, Emotion in Motion was a #1 hit. It's Ric Ocasek acting natural, whatever that means to ya. The real question is "which side of paradise" are we talking about?

Love bites, love stinks, love is a bunch of synthpop songs about how complicated love is. It's a very 80s album, and by that I mean the overwhelming vibe is a drizzly 1AM on the 14th floor of a downtown hotel with the neon from the street signs flashing through the window blinds while you pace back and forth smoking a cigarette and wondering how you ended up being caught in all this noirish intrigue. Oh, and some ripping 80s guitar solos from Steve Stevens and G.E. Smith.

I'm intrigued by Ric's outsider perspective on his relationships, particularly how he manages to never come across as stalkery. I don't have an answer for that, his inner-poet monologue just seems sincere to me. It's better than Heartbeat City (I haven't reviewed that album, and I haven't listened to it in a while, so I might have to take that statement back at some point).

Sorry, this isn't a particularly clever or ridiculous review. Partly that's because I'm just so damned tired of talking about politics and death and drugs and economics, and partly because he died 13 days after my dad in 2019. You might say my emotions are in motion (and not at all in a bad way).

But is it good? Yeah, it's great. Ric is a really good songwriter. Nothing dumb or cheesy, musically/thematically/stylistically consistent, nobody gumming up the works, making him include crap songs for filler, or ruining his ideas. If anything, it's proof positive that synthpop can be emotionally complex, introspective, and quirky at the same time. Give it a whirl some time. Cheers.

Spoon – Hot Thoughts

Hot thought: "Took time off from my kingdom, took a break from the war...."

I don't think Spoon belongs to any particular sub-genre, this is just 21st-century rock. They went back to Matador for this last album, so I guess it's indie by default, but it's also psychedelic noise timber collage wrapped up in an 80s neon adidas track suit, but not in a joke kind of way. If pop-rock could be a free-form scrap quilt of sparkly sound gems from every single piece of equipment in the studio, this would go in whatever you call that genre. Not really baroque or psychedelic pop, not really garage-indie, more like testing out all the sound effects on your synthesizer while everybody's pogo-ing on the dance floor.

This is a stellar album. It sounds amazing and the songs really do have a tip of the tongue, exploding mental kaleidoscope feel to them. They feel like pop songs, but Britt Daniels doesn't use formulaic catchphrases or mindless repetition, or any formulaic poetic structures. I don't mean it's rambling, I just mean it's not overtly formulaic. They aren't quite stories, more in the moment feelings or auras. And the whole thing ends with this beautiful midnight in the city type sax/percussion/ambiance experimental soundscape thing called "Us" that turns the whole experience into Britt's internal monologue of an urban love story.

I have They Want My Soul as well and I want to explore their whole discography at some point. As for Hot Thoughts, if I had more than two thumbs, those would also be up.

Evans Blue – The Melody and the Energetic Nature of Volume

I was going to do Spoon's They Want My Soul, but I heard "Cold(But I'm Still Here)" by Evans Blue today, so I'm going to listen to their debut album instead. It has a good title, The Melody and the Energetic Nature of Volume. See, told you it's a good title. But, it's from 2006.

It's no secret that the mid 2000s to the mid 2010s is like Bottle kryptonite, the audio equivalent of dunking an Oreo in ketchup. I've mentioned a few bands from that time frame, and I'll mention a few more. I like some stuff from that period of rock radio wilderness, but there's a Harry to my Hendersons, a giant brown bear in my cabin in The Great Outdoors and it's the hard side of rock. Emo, biker rock, nu-metal, you remember. We did the grungy flannel, we took a shower, then we just kind of walked off into the woods and started screaming nonsense at the trees about how much our high school manbearpig boy/girlfriends were terrible people and we're sad. I like quite a lot of it actually (well, except the hardcore crotch-rocket stuff and low-grade nu-metal garbage).

Did Evans Blue get really big and popular? Unquestionably, no. This is Evanescence, Flyleaf, Chavelle, Breaking Benjamin, Avenged Sevenfold territory, and EB are B (possibly C) team backups with Hawthorn Heights, Skillet, Three Days Grace, and Shinedown.

That's not fair, I literally only know the 1 song. They could be greatly underappreciated. They could, don't look at me like that.

Ok, fine, they could be garbage like Finger 11 or Our Lady Peace, or Seether. Cold sounds like Tool/APC crossed with Chavelle. Only one way to find out...

Not a great opener. It's not a bad song, just not a good opener. You might have to get used to Kevin Matisyn's voice. Ahhh! Don't do that stupid falsetto note at the end of a phrase. Rewrite the whole song if you have to, just don't do it.

The music is fine, but it's impossible to ignore the Maynard comparison. What's with that warbly thing, Kev?

I know it's hard to tell, but I'm liking it quite a lot. For starters, they've nailed the aesthetic. This is serious depression, scared to say anything, emotional plane crash type stuff. It's supposed to be whiny and a bit deranged because it's that non-objective kind of emotional insanity at the edge of a panic attack type thing.

Oh yeah, I remember Beg, it got quite a bit of radio play. It's all just pop-rock with massive low-end and high gain crunch, by the way. The one thing they do way too much is the cut out, anacrusis to the last chorus. On the whole, though, the first half is great.

Oh no, is the second half going to be all her fault and his justification for turning into a douche bag? If Over is that turning point, I'm gonna be mad. It's fine if you're part of the problem, it's even fine if you fail, but you lose me when you twist it around and forget you're the insane loser in this story.

Ok good, Possession gets us fully back into the me me me frame. Nice save, guys. Dark That Follows is interesting, he's arguing with himself about it. Believe me, you don't get that psychological complexity very often from this stuff.

I'm impressed, this is great. I'm going to let you into a really important aspect of good emo that you don't get from surface listening. Really good emo has total pronoun confusion. It actually takes work to remove all the signifiers for which character says what. "You" often refers to the character singing, and "I" actually represents a quote from the other character. Bad emo comes across whiny and selfish because it's very clear that the singing character is a self-absorbed lunatic with at least one restraining order and possibly even a parole officer. Good emo is impossible to tell if you're hearing a conversation with a mirror, or if everything is in quotation marks.

They changed singers in 2009 and Dan Chandler is much more tough guy than Jonathan Davis crazy, but albums 2 and 3 with Kevin might be worth checking out.

Overall, I'd give it a "yeah, this is good." 4-ish stars on the scale of 1 to crying on the sidewalk. Check it out if you like this dark, negative emotion stuff like I do.

Welcome to Moron Manor

I like to type nonsense into Bandcamp's search. Today's word is "morkon." Moron Manor Media? Yeah, let's review an indie internet label from Syracuse, NY. What have you morons got for me? Ooooh, acousticy emo songwriter type stuff. We'll skip the two big things at the top and go for the innards.

First up, it's Bridge Under Fire from AD80. Scratch that, other way around. Gargly garage indie. I like it, but I wish they took the three minutes to type the lyrics. Think I heard the word "die" in there somewhere. Really nice 2.5-minute song.

Ahnest! Ft. Rob Button gives us Rainclouds. Hey there's "die" again! I smell a theme here. Lovely mopey little ditty that morphs into a p(nmi)t style dissonantly amorphous synth seascape and devolves into noisy noodling. Creepy. Love it!

Looking through the small list of tracks that follow, this is Ahnest!'s label. My kind of guy.

Ten Years. Sweet, a 3 track. Nick Burger. I like him. Dare me to send him an email with nice things in it? He's really good, and he has a friend who plays cello.

Anthony Musior's turn to split a 4-track EP with Burger king. Yay, lyrics! Geez, this is great stuff.

The rest is more tracks from Nick and Anthony. It kind of looks like they went cold in the summer of 2019. Anthony stopped posting on his facebook page in 2014.

That's too bad. This is really good stuff. Maybe I will send them a note, might be fun....

Genesis – Invisible Touch

I'm supposed to hate Phil Collins. I'm sure of it; turning Genesis from loony prog to synthy sellout dad-pop. Drum machines and ending sentences with prepositions. What a loser.

No, screw you guys, with your mohawks and bolo ties, or whatever dumb fashion combination you're into. I love Phil Collins, and if Disturbed can cover Land of Confusion, then I can say this is the best Side A of the entire 80s. It's not, but I can say it Tonight, Tonight. I'm already In Too Deep, so roll that 15th album.

They wrote the whole album and more just jamming in the studio after a 2-year break for solo projects. Everybody wrote lyrics to a song or two. It's all over the place in terms of mood and themes and style, he even sings a quirky new wave song to a pin-up girl. Then Domino shows up. I agree with Mr. And the Mechanics, that's an awesome ADD track even

Adderall couldn't wrangle into the shape of political commentary (yeah, it's supposedly about politicians and unintended consequences).

You know what, it's prog-pop. It is. Pop songs with out-of-nowhere orchestrated interludes, love songs that turn a corner and get mugged in a dark alley, a protest song, said photograph of a scantily clad woman, bizarre synth parts, an actual drummer unashamedly programming a drum machine, and surprisingly raucous guitars. I mean, I was only six at the time, but this is totally the 80s I remember. The closing instrumental is insane, by the way.

This is a great Genesis album. Go freakin' love it, or I'll invisible punch you.

Gershwin Plays Gershwin – The Piano Rolls

My dad had a lot of CDs too, and here's an interesting one. It's called Gershwin and friend punch holes in paper tape for money...

Joking, it's Gershwin Plays Gershwin, but it's really Artis Wodehouse recording Gershwin's actual piano rolls of his pieces. Seriously, Gershwin was a piano roll arranger from 1916 to 1927. He made about 130 altogether, arrangements of pop songs and his own pieces. When my beloved vinyl records and the Great Depression killed player piano sales, he just switched right over to studio recordings and radio broadcasts. If you remember your history, Bell invented the needle in water thing in 1876 (they were terrible), Carbon mics in 1886 (slightly less terrible but crap for music even after Neumann's improvements), Wente gave us condenser mics in 1916 and Neumann kept making them better. Then in 1924 Schottke and Gerlach invented ribbon mics and yay we can record music that sounds like it wasn't played inside a trash can! Neumann came out with dynamic mics in 1931, but Gershwin didn't live long enough to see them blossom into actual usefulness (he died in 1937). Point is, player pianos were THE THING, and the story is that George actually learned to play the piano by following the keys at a friend's house. The Gershwins bought a piano for Ira, but George stole the show.

If you thought that explanation was complicated, wait until you hear how this recording was actually made. Some were simpler than others using a Pianola operated by Artis to play a 9-foot Yamaha Disklavier that recorded each performance, but for the hardcore ones they took Gershwin's rolls, scanned them into a computer, actually programmed a simulator to translate them into midi, and played them from floppy discs. Like any recording session, they did a bunch of takes and used the best segments. It's freakin' awesome. It's on youtube if you need some 20s light jazz player piano in your life. Of course you do, and you're welcome.

Premiata Forneria Marconi – Per Un Amico

I built a table today. Yes, obviously I deserve praise for my magnificence, but so much more importantly my friend Steven Stark shared some Italian prog I've never heard before, and sweet baby Yoda it's amazing. Tonight we're listening to Per Un Amico by Premiata Forneria Marconi (it's on youtube).

Your old pal Bottle isn't completely in the dark about Italian prog, I love Goblin and I'm well acquainted with the insanely enjoyable symphonic death metal that is Fleshgod Apocalypse, but I've never heard PFM. All I can say is wowzers, because this is about the wackiest blend of rock band with flute and violin I've ever heard. You know what it sounds like? It sounds like Ian Anderson gave the Grateful Dead and Dave Matthew's Band 'shrooms and they all just winged it for half an hour.

Then at 21:38 it turns into like a deranged Atari-core adventure game soundtrack that then morphs into a rainy jazz piano solo, and it's amazing! Go give it a listen because you didn't even know which parts of your pathetic existence needed filling until this album overflows all of them with joy and happiness.

For a friend, indeed. Now everybody pretend it's personal and say "thanks! I needed that."

Pete Seeger

I unbottled so much stuff today, I just want to listen to some of Pete Seeger's earliest recordings dubbed from the original 78s. Just Pete and a banjo (or guitar), and old folk songs from the 30s and 40s. Lovely.

But does it have songs Lead Belly personally taught Pete? Yes, of course it does. Now shush.

More of Roy Orbison's Greatest Hits

Hey Bottle, wanna review an Amy Winehouse album today?

Good gravy, no.

Tonight we ask the toughest question ever asked by people who understand the concept of questions. Who's prettier, Jason Priestly or Jennifer Connelly?

I suppose we need to back up a little. See, Billy Steinberg and Tom Kelly wrote "I Drove all Night" for Roy Orbison. He totally recorded that song in 1987, but that was the culmination of his 2nd wave of popularity and it just got lost in the shuffle and he unfortunately died in 1988. Not to rag on Steinberg and Kelly, but in 1989 Cyndi Lauper recorded it and they were like "sweet! She's not dead and people will finally hear our awesome song." Finally in 1992, some guy pulled up his original and gave Roy yet another posthumous bout of stardom. Strangely bizarre non-sequitur fact, Roy Orbison and Glenn Danzig were friends.

Is Roy Orbison's sampled and augmented original version awesome too? You betcha, but just like our actual question, we're comparing apples and whatever the opposite of apples happens to be. I'm a rum and coke swilling record lover, and I think Cyndi's and Roy's versions of that song are equally awesome. So, was teenage Bottle rewinding scenes from The Labyrinth or feasting on 90210 reruns?

Mwahahaha. I'll never tell. Here's Roy Orbison's 1964 best of album with "more" in the title. How many people deserve that? He's amazing. Anyone who doesn't adore Roy Orbison is a pathetically wretched soul indeed. I have the Hendersonville, Tennessee pressing if you're a weirdo who cares.

As far as alternative masculinity goes, he's about as non-toxic as Elmer's glue or Crayola crayons, both of which I've eaten in my lifetime (no explanations). Ok, honestly Jason Priestly is probably prettier, but I'd be hard pressed not to Tyler Durden him up a little if he got too fresh for her liking......

Peter, Paul, & Mary – Album 1700

I knew I had it in here somewhere. It's Peter, Paul, and Mary's 7th album named after the Warner Brothers catalog number it was going to receive. It's got a song by Leslie Braunstein, the Chevy Chase/Pete Best, of Blue Öyster Cult's history. For those of you who don't know that story, Chevy was the drummer in The Leather Canary with Fagan and Becker (who later became Steely Dan). There's a song by some Colorado guy too, or something. More interesting is Weep For Jamie. That song is downright macabre for whatever image you had of this beloved folk trio. If you live outside of chronological time like I do, there's even a song named after Green Day's Whatshername.

Sweet Kristofferson, I just got to the Great Mandella (sic) at the end of Side A. If there's an anthem for right now, it's that song without question.

Obviously, you're going to bring up the answering the door naked and hitting on a fourteen-year-old thing, and I'll remind you that Yarrow served his sentence exactly like you describe he should do without further incident, and I counter with Jimi Page, who served no time for his much worse crimes against humanity at large.

How could you not like PP&M? Look, as soon as you bring politics into it we all lose because the liars lie about the lying they lied about yesterday, and as soon as you let the moral righteousness go for one tiny second you realize that we want the same end result and my way of accomplishing it is frighteningly quick and effective. Counterintuitively, nobody has to die, you just have to suck it up and admit that you're wrong. I do it all the time, it doesn't hurt a bit.

These lovely people are the liberal left, the building lighters on fire are totally of your own making. It is indeed the theater of the absurd. Knock me down, I just come back running, as my friend Maynard says.

Sorry, sometimes I like to just rant at the overlords (who can totally hear me). Ignore my silliness, and enjoy Warner Brothers' 1,700th thing (assuming they started at 0001, that is).

I really don't want to "just pet" you

I dunno, what do you guys wanna listen to? We could do more Moon Hooch, or Spoon, or...

No! Tonight you suffer like you've never suffered before!

Geez, what did I do? Oh, yeah, that working overtime 'cause the man's too dumb to do it properly himself. Alright, what not so terrible Country album is it tonight?

OH, EVIL DEITY OF PESTILENCE AND SUFFERING!

Petula Clark? Seriously? Elvis wanted a three-way Petulant Clark? I can't read that title in the nominative, "just pet" is a really uncomfortable verbal non-sequitur! I'd rather revisit Barbara Mandrell's house at Christmas, at least that was hilarious. Alright, bombs away.

    Aaah! It's horrible. Please don't drop a dime, I can't stand your voice as it is, let alone over a pay phone. Things Bright and Beautiful is the most ghastly audio abomination ever, and I'm the guy who likes Throbbing Gristle and Merzbow. Even if you're the kind of person who hates everything about the Beatles, you can't begin to imagine the depths of hell where her version of Hey Jude plays 24/7. It's only Side A and I need the kind of break where the dogs run away and I have to chase them down in the dark, lose a pack of cigarettes for half an hour, and facebook restarts itself, deleting the first attempt at this essay so I have to rewrite it from memory before suffering some more...

    ...That's better. How much worse can Side B really be? Blaaarg! Why did I ask? It's like whitey white English Mariachi with completely needless jazz sax. Yuck, poor butterfly. Poor squashed butterfly in my clenched fist, what the ever-loving hell was that Chicago-esque interlude?! It can die? I want to die!

    Oh, ok, the fake sitar thing is actually refreshing. If I Only Had Time is actually fine. I don't like it, but it's objectively better than the previous 8 tracks. At least the guitar solo sounds like an obnoxious guitar solo. More sitar? Another terrible Beatles cover? At least it's impressively terrible, I'll give you that. It's like she's trying to mimic Eartha Kitt, but she's a D student on the best day of the week.

    Ok. How do I really explain it? Ok, you know her version of Downtown right? Of course you do. That's fine, that song can handle shitty horns and weird vowels. It's supposed to be garish. Now imagine that you perform every single song in existence that way. Every piece of clothing in your closet has rhinestones bedazzled on it. You walk around the Dollar Tree strip mall looking like fat, sweaty, muttenchop Elvis on a Tuesday. That's Petula Clark. I just might pull out the best of

Nancy Sinatra album as a palate cleanser. Even Crystal Gayle is better than this. What's that expression about gagging me with a spoon? Oh, yeah, *GAG ME WITH A SPOON!*

I promised you a palate cleanser

Pretty bold f-ing claim, Bottle, that Trump is a good and proper authoritarian Communist like he was trained to be....

Oh, sorry. That was one I decided not to publish. I meant that Nancy Sinatra was waaaaaay better than Petula Clark.

Yeah. We lead off with her greatest hit, Boots. Already, the horns and strings are infinitely better. Who's the dude? Oh, that is actually Lee Hazelewood. Nancy's voice is way better than Petula's, by miles. For starters, she doesn't do that weird dipthongy vowel garbage. I mean, it's all still way too uncomfortably sexualized, and it's really just a best of Lee Hazelwood album. It's like he produced it, or something... There is the duet with dad, Something Stupid (it's international daughter's day in case you didn't know), and how can you not enjoy that?

Seriously, you thought I was joking last night, but Nancy Sinatra is fantastic. I'm obviously not a fan of real thematically relevant Country, but Nancy's occasional twang isn't at all bad or displeasing.

Now, you all know I'm a diehard Marty Paich aficionado, but Billy Strange (you know him as the hall of fame guitarist of The Wrecking Crew) doesn't ruin many songs either. Oh, yeah! Her Bond theme is on here, and man that's amazing. Things, like I talk about. Things, like a Brussels' sprout. Thinkin' 'bout the apostrophes I like to use.....

And the cacophony of Lightning's Girl is the good kind of cacophony. A song that gets even better with the increasing inner-grove entropy of age? Surely a coincidence, but nevertheless delicious. As far as greatest hits albums go it's perfectly fine, and her voice is totally not at all like an Austin Powers sex-bot belting into the microphone like she who shall not be petted. And Nancy thinks Trump is an authoritarian nincompoop. There's a great story about how Trump was mad about how much Frank wanted for an appearance at Taj Mahal with Sammy Davis Jr. in 1990. Like Frank needed the "exposure" or some nonsense. "Loathed Trump" was the expression, I think.

Anywho, the moral of the story is Pet bad, Nan good. Clear as mud?

Radiohead – Ok Computer

Speaking of the next world war, and waking up to find that you're not dead and have to live like a stranger trapped in your own world where everyone is out to drain you dry and you just wish aliens would abduct you so you'd have an interesting story to tell....here's the monolithic 1997 album from Radiohead. Ok Computer, remind me of what every waking moment feels like right now.....

Did Radiohead invent time travel? I honestly don't remember 1997, other than that was right about the time when my high school adopted "core curriculum" and I wasn't allowed to take calculus. Really, scheduling conflicts meant I literally had to choose between advanced math and science classes and orchestra. I chose orchestra and wasted 2 years reading newspapers in classes below my level. I had many nice chats with the principal after doing a week's coursework in class and reading the newspaper until the teacher just told me to go somewhere else. He agreed it was dumb and unfair, and incidentally his favorite adjective was bitchin'. I'm an "awesome" guy myself, I saw him at a Barnes & Noble one time after high school and he insisted I call him Jerry.

I said The Black Parade was an exhausting listen, and that The Downward Spiral left you starving for nutritious food but too nauseous to eat it, but Ok Computer sounds like emerging from an opium den after a 3-month coma (or so I imagine).

It's been called a "reluctant concept album," as in it resists being constructed. Wrong, this is the inside mental state of the character that sings The Bends, the lost child.

The title is from Hitchhiker's Guide to the Galaxy, and the paranoia is exactly what we expected the age of instant connectivity to everything was going to do to us. Listening to this album today is exactly like a really bad morning on your facebook scroll: everyone you know is a raging lunatic and you're just bombarded by everything all at the same time, and you try to go back and comprehend some of it but it's just too much and you say *SHOOT THE HEROIN DIRECTLY INTO MY EYEBALL AND THERE BETTER NOT BE AN AFTERLIFE!!!*

You forgot that there was a time before the modern internet, a mystical land of bulletin board systems and AOL home screens, and modem noises, and people who really didn't want to live to see right now, because it's awful, right? Yeah, sure all the good stuff is still hiding under there somewhere, but every waking moment of the day is like watching crazy ladies sell unicorn jewelry on QVC, and you're sure at any moment one of them will pull out a hatchet.

This is still just a gorgeous album from start to finish with so many sounds and shapes and colors, and if you've never really sat down and experienced the whole 53:27 onslaught, then you really, really should. It was mind-blowing back then and it's still mind-blowing today, albeit for slightly different reasons, or maybe because now you have a lot more experience with the kind of mental state Radiohead was channeling 23 years ago.

How I learned to stop caring and avoided the thing
I had one goal in mind tonight, avoid the first presidential debate. I had to leave the basement of doom twice, but 99% of my nose hairs are unsigned. Here's what I did instead.

I think I know my geography pretty damned well. I also have Modest Mouse's first album on vinyl, recorded by Seasick Steve a year before Ok Computer. It's called This Is A Long Drive For Someone With Nothing To Think About.

I've talked about a fair amount of indie rock, and I talked about their masterpiece We Were Dead..., but this first album is just gloriously disheveled pathos.

Plus, the entire enterprise of the band literally comes from Isaac Brock's bedroom. I'm not entirely sure he's ever even been in an actual office building before, or that anyone would let him.

If you're one of those people who only knows their bizarre moment of fame with Float On, then you might not be prepared for how truly awesome they are. Obviously, if singing in tune or playing in tempo is at the top of your list of musical requirements, you won't enjoy this at all. It's not even a metaphor, it really is about how boring and lonely it is to live out in the country and have to drive long distances to find other humans. I totally disagree, but then I chose to live like this. Isaac was just born out in a field and moved to Portland as soon as possible.

Modest Mouse isn't one of those bands you can coerce people into liking, they very definitely live on the side of the tracks that most people think sucks. I, however, adore them, and have also been known to talk shit about a pretty sunset.

Next on the list of "I'll listen to anything except presidential candidates," we jump ten years to The Bottle Rockets' 2006 album Zoysia. My heart's a little bit broken, I'm a middle man, there's only so much I can take too.

I didn't know this until today, but "careerist" is a really prevalent insult in the rock criticism world. That was the exact pejorative everyone in Seattle leveled against Pearl Jam, and a quick rundown of The Bottle Rockets produced it again. Pfffft. These posers are trying to make a career out of it. Damn right. They're great.

They've been called a lot of things like alternative country, or roots rock, but this album sounds like if southern rock had a garage scene. It's crunchy, it's Midwestern, it's thoroughly enjoyable. It's like if Drive By Truckers and Tom Petty played a couple songs together.

I can't neglect to mention the song Blind. This is great, and I never would have found it on my own, so everybody go check it out and say thanks to Kris Karr for suggesting them.

UUUUUUGGGGHHHH. I made the mistake of surfacing for more pirate juice and heard Trump say "let me tell you about the stock market." Time to start hitting the hard stuff. Here's Accept's rather famous album Balls to the Wall.

Udo Dirkschneider could have and would have gladly joined AC/DC, who incidentally sent them some of Bon Scott's demos after he died and said "we aren't going to use them, but feel free if you like it." Instead, he did a Syd Barrett. Seriously, Udo was fired from Accept, decided to go solo, and the guys and lady manager/songwriter from Accept happily wrote his first solo album for him. You can't make this stuff up.

What you can do is write kick-ass metal about real people being oppressed and marginalized for their race, sexuality, hobbies, etc. Liberal German Metal sung in English at its finest. Awesome.

I'm gonna have to brave the overworld again, because every album deserves a freshly poured beverage to sip, but I think you'll be really happy with our next one.

Jean-Luc Ponty finally cracked the mainstream with Enigmatic Ocean, and people were all like "whaaaaa?! you can't play jazz on an electric violin." You're old pal Bottle's like "pffffffffffft! Stephan Gappelli, Regina Carter, Boyd Tinsley, Leroy Freakin' Jenkins! plus like a thousand other people from all across the spectrum. Jazz violin is everywhere, you're just a loser with no culture and an airplane window's view of the universe.

Sorry, that was mean. Jean-Luc Ponty is probably the most "electronic music" of the bunch, and it's not at all hard to hear what made everyone latch on to this album in 1977. It's damned near prog-rock, so close you can legitimately forget it's a jazz album at some point in every single track. It can be hard to recognize the effects heavy violin next to the equally soggy synths and guitars, but that's kind of the point. Go ahead and start without me, I've heard this album a time or two, and I need to freshen up....

I just heard James Carville say "I'm getting paid, and that was a struggle to watch," so if you did watch it, I expect you were either upset or you don't understand how bad this is, and that's the perfect reason to revisit my night of great music.

Instead of whatever you heard, I listened to albums by Modest Mouse, The Bottle Rockets, Accept, and Jean-Luc Ponty. Who won?

Type O Negative – Bloody Kisses

You like Gothic Metal, right? Who doesn't? Let's go back to probably the only platinum selling Goth metal album, or at the very least the first. It's Type O Negative's 3rd album, Bloody Kisses. The Drab Four are known for three things. 1) there will never be another Peter Steele, 2) they were hilarious, and 3) the scandalous cover of Bloody Kisses.

First, there shouldn't be another Peter Steele, the first one was more than you deserve. Last, the notion that two girls kissing on the cover in 1993 was scandalous is ridiculous compared to the Voodoo-U cover in 1994 (full on cartoon lesbian devil orgy). On to the humor.

Romance, sex, death, and a straight cover of Summer Breeze, because Seals really didn't like Peter's parody lyrics (reprinted in the liner notes). I think their humor is best summed up by the video for Black No. 1, where Kenny is playing doom riffs on a 12-string acoustic and Peter has an actual double bass hanging around his neck. There's sitar on this album too. Everyone pretty much agrees it's like Black Sabbath meets the Beatles and we're all dead, or undead, or about to die, or haven't noticed that we're dead and keep talking. Goth really just means aesthetic appreciation of the mysterious and dark, or occult. It comes from the dark side of post-punk like Bauhaus, Joy Division, The Cure, etc. But this is metal, so crank it up 7 notches. Loving you is like loving the dead, I guess it's too late to apologize now that you're dead, we're all just mopey vampires here, am I right? Why don't we put a psych-rock jam in the middle of this song?

I have the second release where the band cut out the interludes and filler. It's still a whopping hour and seven minutes of sludgy doom, so don't make plans for the rest of the evening. Or, put it on while you're dying your hair black, can't go out with your roots showing....

Spoon – They Want My Soul

They want my soul. Critics say "meh, it's a Spoon album. Sure, great, if you just want more songs by Spoon, but that's not exciting. I mean, sure they sound better and write better songs than their peers, but..."

[Bottle clears his throat] Uggghhmmmhmmm.

What kind of garbage pseudo-structural dribble drabble is that? You got paid to write that? It's 2014, four years since their last one, and you're hating on a rock band successful enough to even afford to put out a record?

I'll give you that it's compressed to shit, but Howie Weinberg has heard that criticism a time or 700. His million Grammys and Juno awards don't care. Look, this album wasn't really made for vinyl, Spoon has so much noise and middle-ground fiddlyness that it all needs to be about the same volume to tie the insanity together, and that means the guitars are pretty much brick walled and the snare sounds like it was ripped right out of an industrial metal album. Still, though, the songs are awesome and it sounds better than any Rolling Stones album, so suck it up buttercup.

Variety and experimentation is great if you're a group of Cheeto-eating 20-year-olds, but Spoon is an avant noise rock extravaganza squeezed into the candy coating of a 4 minute rock song. Consistency is their calling card, and I can't think of any filler that ever made it onto one of their albums. Maybe you disagree, but being great is pretty exciting as far as I'm concerned. If you can sing and dance along without feeling embarrassed, then it's a great rock album. Don't listen to them, Britt. They may want your soul, but you certainly don't have to give it to them.

Sandal-core

This one's been brewing for a while, so it's a bit of a read, even by my standards.

Let's talk Sandal-core. It's a term I made up to describe contemporary guitar instrumentals by Andy James, Lee McKinney, Angel Vivaldi, and all the other guys hanging around the Kiesel booth at NAMM. When they aren't out terrorizing the universe, they call Sumerian Records their home.

I'm not out to just blindly criticize them for churning out douche-tudes like line work at the candy factory, I'll freely admit that this isn't my scene and my general dislike for the highly specific and refined style is an unfair bias. I'm a champion of context, and in context these guys are phenomenal. In context, I can fully enjoy and appreciate their musicianship, creativity, and nuance. In other words, it ain't the chef, it's the recipe.

That recipe is beyond human drum cacophony, standard lowest-open-string Morse code djent rhythm guitar (bass is pointless since we're using 7/8/9 string mantelpieces with nuclear powered pickups and 6-octave ranges), an amorphous sea of synth/guitar orchestrations, and on top of all that we float the audio equivalent of a $27 tiki drink with chunks of 12 different exotic fruits, urban renewal scaffolding, and a tiny parasol on top. They drive it out to your beach chair, park the dune buggy, and strap the flexible hose helmet rig onto your head without even waking you up.

Every piece has an elaborate tapping section, simple diatonic melodies in riff form, and the kind of Grand Canyon-esque echo even Eric Johnson or The Edge would find a tad indulgent. Clean tone, high gain, clean tone, high gain, wax on, wax off, tappa tappa tap, and a saxophone! It all sounds like a magic space-peacock on acid.

But hold on, Bottle, you're the champion of all things guitar, you love avant-jazz, and all sorts of weird stuff, how can you say all these terrible things?

Because musically speaking, it's crap. I don't like Paganini, or Dragonforce, or the gods of shred either. All this stuff is just hacked together noodling Rondo forms with no trajectory or purpose. It's not *about* anything, just one drunkenly indistinguishable daydream after another. In a larger context that would be perfectly wonderful, but to quote Thom York, please could you stop the noise, I'm trying to get some rest.

Obviously, my opinion is of no consequence at all, so we have to dig deeper. Is it really ambition that makes them sound pretty ugly, or is it something else? We need some historical perspective on how this punch bowl of fluorescent bath water with bits of pine bark and goldfish crackers was concocted.

What are we really dealing with here? 1) virtuosity itself, in the form of shred guitar, 2) the anti-metrical rhythmic foundation of prog-djent, and 3) the peculiar friction between rock band vs. orchestra. Believe it or not, there are direct structural ties between this music and the cultural turbulence we are experiencing in the world at large; exceptionalism vs. collectivism.

We'll start with shred, fastest is bestest. Van Halen, Gilbert, Satriani, Vai, Batio, Malmsteen, Hammet, Becker, Friedman, Buckethead, and so on. The cream of the crop, so to speak, the guys who elevated electric guitar to the level of a virtuosic solo instrument. Some of it's great, some of it's vapid noodling.

I'm not saying this is true of every guitar extremophile, but this overemphasis on mind blowing technical mastery has a tendency to inflate an ego into "the band's not good enough to play behind me" or "I can't find musicians proficient enough to keep up" territory. Remember, these are all lead guitarists doing solo instrumental albums, so the douchebaggery is easy to accidentally step in and ruin your $1,000 designer boots.

Sweep-picking and tappegios are quite cool, and they can do amazing things in the context of transition, breakdown, build up, flowing from one thought to another, ending with a flourish, and all those real structural functions of melodic expression. That, however, is not their purpose in sandal-core. They are the primary melodic material here, pattern repeated 4 times and on to the next one. Riffs strung together with only their relative similarity to bind them.

And in between all the cracks in the sonic facade, the synthetic orchestra of misery drones out triads for eternity.

If we took a more philosophical stance, the notion that melody is an extension of the voice/mind, what would these pieces be saying? I'm awesome, I'm awesome, sometimes I'm sad and make my "I'm thinking" face, ooh a pretty butterfly, I want to die, life is misery, I love you, don't leave me, it's so cold here in the emptiness of my fighter jet. What is that low, twangy, epileptic seizure meant to express except rambling, incoherent, Tasmanian devil ferocity, the guitaristic presentation of a Jonathan Davis sermon on incomprehensible misery? What should a lilting diatonic melody in a major key mean against that mechanical stylized putrescence? A flower left untrampled on the battlefield of the biomechanical apocalypse?

Nevermind, I'll just sit and sip my pina colada while the palm trees blaze into ash and dust and wait for the tide to rise above me and sweep me out to my watery grave. Sandal-core, even the locusts say "oh, gosh, I couldn't. It looks lovely, but we had a late lunch, and my doctor says I need to watch my cholesterol. Thanks though, I'm sure it's delicious and everyone else will want seconds. I'm good."

This isn't a personal attack. These guys are phenomenal players just like Petrucci, Guthrie Govan, John 5, or even Brad Paisley. It's not really an attack on the genre either. Like I said, I can completely enjoy it inside its acute contextual limitations. What I can't do is give the overall expression itself much esteem. It is an absurdist stylistic mash-up with absolutely no joy or soul at all. Whatever soaring transcendence might be intended (surely that must be the intent, or else why reach for the emotive power of long legato phrasing in the first place) comes across hollow and glass-eyed, an empty soliloquy about pointlessness.

No, not every track is like that, only the majority. Not everybody does it either. Tosin and Javier don't do that, Ola England doesn't do it, Petrucci doesn't do it, and even Andy James's most recent stuff is significantly better in terms of the piece itself doing something. Maybe it's just a brief hiccup along the path from mindless self-indulgence to actual musical meaningfulness, but for me it's moderately awful. Unless I'm in the right mood, then I'd say "meh it's fine."

Well, that got us nowhere. What do you think? Do you know what I'm even talking about? Do you have some interpretational insight I can't grasp? Need specific examples? Have your own examples? Want to argue about it? The floor is yours. Obviously, I can't hear you because this is a book from the past, but still, have at it.

Born Of Osiris – Soul Sphere

Because I ragged a bit on Lee McKinney for making sandal-core, it's only fair that I give a Born of Osiris album the full treatment. I now randomly pick Soul Sphere. We'll ignore their evolution and just accept their wikipedia genre designation as Progressive Metalcore.

I really don't want to get fussy, but we need some expectations going into it. "-Core" means hardcore punk. "Metal" means an extreme version of it. "Progressive" means plus a bunch of non-metal/hardcore embroidery. Put it all together and it equals screaming, blast beats, fast noodly stuff, some metaphysical component, and probably some explicit digital manipulation (i.e. the computer it was recorded into is just as much an instrument in the band as the actual people). That's not good or bad, it's simply the world this music lives in, and we have to approach it that way. If you need a simpler context, perhaps "brutality." Not necessarily gore, or death, or the occult, just a general perspective of violence as the basis of existence. Also keep in mind, I'm interested in why Lee needs a super solo spectacular of his own.

And right off the bat, we get a screamin' great guitar solo that doesn't belong here. Well, not off the bat, third quarter guitar solo, you know what I mean. And, the tappy fast squiggly stuff is right where it should be, acting like the synth arpeggiator, the technological hum of our futuristic cyber-prison.

I don't want to do a play by play, or be super longwinded about it. We'll just listen to it and debrief at the end...

... I dare you to tell me I'm wrong, *this* is awesome. It seriously grooves, the kaleidoscopic glass shrapnel is exploding everywhere, all the buzzy mechanical wasps are swarming around the enemy, it's a glorious cacophony, and most important it's minor and diminished and completely insane. Don't tell Between the Buried and Me, but I might like this more than Between the Buried and Me.

That, my friends, makes my dislike of sandal-core all the more justified. "Guys, I just need some alone time where I can really showcase my squiggly noodling and Zakk Wylde-esque non-sequitur shred superiority." Fuuuuu...nny how that works.

I also need to mention that the string programming is a real part of the ensemble here, not just harmonic filler like the solo work. You can hate the genre outright if you want, but you don't have to put together a 1,000-piece jigsaw puzzle to form an opinion about it. It is what it is, and there's a "we're not trying to sell you anything you don't already want to buy" honesty to it that I demand from my cyborg-soldier space warriors.

I do in fact like it, and I don't have to squint and tilt my head sideways when I say it. I like it because the music says something more meaningful than "I can play fast and my vibrato is pretty." Those things are true for a given value of truth, but it's aesthetically pleasing for its intended expressivity, not gaudy or showboaty. Sure, it's fast and ultra-technical, but they aren't Doom, and they certainly aren't vaporwave adjacent sandal-core. Haunting, terrifying, brutal, mechanical, not a hot dog or ice cream trike in sight, unless it's on fire or currently melting. If I gave albums stars, this would get several.

Achilles & The Tortoise – Maccabee

Today, for your lunch hour dining pleasure, I bring you the delicious and nutritious tale of space-time explorer Maccabee who finds himself crashing toward some distant planet and longing to return home. Enjoy.

Moon Hooch – Red Sky

We should listen to an actual record. Should we say mean things about Oliver? Peruse the wider world of British Blues? Revel in the creepy strangeness of more Classics IV? Nah, let's just enjoy some high-octane dance saxophone from Moon Hooch. Red Sky is their 3rd album, and that's about all anyone has to say about that. Who doesn't love dancejazztechno? Not me, I definitely don't not love it.

There are a few reasons why nobody has anything to say about this album. 1) this is an incredibly niche genre, 2) there's nothing to criticize because it's objectively great, and 3) this is an album for people who already love Moon Hooch. Much like Spoon or AC/DC, you know exactly what you're going to get, and it's not really meant to command your full mental faculties. It's feel-good, pure and simple.

Yeah, I feel good. Mission accomplished.

The B52's

No one ever dies on Planet Claire, because they don't have heads.

The year before I was born, the B52's made their first album. Damnit, this is amazing. Sure, you can call them New Wave, but that's sort of like just saying Rotary Connection were Soul, or The Incredible String Band was Folk. You're stretching the limits of generalization is what I'm saying. These bands were fucking weird.

These are technically songs, they have words and guitars and drums, sure, but it's more like performance art than music. It's GWAR. No, no, hear me out. GWAR is fantastic, but it's the costumes and storyline that really make them tangible, interesting, legitimate. The actual hairdo, the 50s surfabilly, the pure camp, Fred Schneider being himself, Kate and Cindy making crazy animal noises in the background, boys in bikinis, volcanoes erupting, there's a moon in the sky called the moon, and their version of Downtown can only be described as "special."

It's one of those albums where you just say "I'm speechless." It's better than Lord Sutch and Heavy Friends because clearly everyone involved loved every moment of it or had no sense of embarrassment about anything ever.

How do you reach the level of genius where you shorten Uranus with an apostrophe?

If you've never really listened to their debut self-titled album, then have you really ever said the phrase "what the hell am I listening to" honestly? Have you?

Sylvan Esso

I was gonna do an in-depth thing about this weird genre called deathdream, but then I was like nah it doesn't really have beats and you can't dance to it, so I'd much rather listen to Sylvan Esso's third album, Free Love.

... but I don't like super hooky electronic dance music that makes me feel good, waaaaah!

That's what a doofus says. How does this not make you smile, and your arms twitch, and your feet shuffle? If I had money, I'd give them some of it. I don't, so I gotta put up with the same 4 Ernst vs. Greenfield ads between every other song. Politics is a big waste of money, we should collectively decide to stop supporting it and pay people for being awesome instead.

Maybe tomorrow we'll wade back into the pool of despair. Tonight, we enjoy the Free Love, and wiggle around a little. Join me, won't you?

$26 Adventure Time

Tonight on Disasterpiece Theater, we bring you a delightful dialogue from B and C.

B: Alright, C-spot, run and fetch me another $20 adventure time. Don't put too much thought into it though, I just want new old interesting things to listen to.

...several short eternities of muzak later...

C: Ok boss, I went a little over this time and had to pay sales tax, but I had a few bucks to chip in.
B: How kind of you, let's see what we hear with the smell of our thoughts.

Gather 'round kiddos, it's $26 Adventure Time with Bottle. This time it looks like we're judging the books by their covers. Phoebe Snow looks like she has something important to say, let's let the good times roll.

If this album is any indication, then we're going all over the place. There's a clear blues/jazz foundation, but she veers off into every direction at any moment. One moment it's jazz, then country, then Doobie Brothers or Neil Young type soft rock, southern twang to soul style glottal stopping to almost yodeling. She's a phenomenal guitarist to boot. Part of that eclecticism is that she recorded the songs anywhere with anyone who was around, and she and Dino Airali spent ages rearranging and editing and adding stuff like string arrangements and chorus, and there're jazz sax solos everywhere. Christgau calls it a cult album, and I'd say sure, this is a nice little secret to have amongst friends. You wouldn't want to pull it out for just anyone to hear, but your fellow aficionados will surely give an approving nod when they learn you scooped it up for $2. Alright, where to next on this mystical adventure?

Oh, of course, I should have known, it's Mystical Adventures by Jean-Luc Ponty. I didn't really say much about Enigmatic Ocean during last weekend's youtube binge, but Ponty deserves some serious credit. One, he really did elevate the status of violin in the jazz world, and two he made jazz-rock just about as popular as possible. To my mind, jazz and prog are kind of two opposite directions that smash together in the middle, Ponty being a jazz musician writing big epic rock show pieces. Zappa and Elton John both loved working with him, and Zappa was the guy who convinced him to emigrate to California. I actually haven't heard this one, so I'm really hoping it's as spooky and intriguing as the cover art leads us to believe.

We interrupt this broadcast to bring you the following confusing statement. Couldn't you technically argue that Phoebe Snow is jazz fusion, albeit on the soft side of the spectrum (folk styles as opposed to rock and funk)? Sorry for the interruption, on with the adventure.

Oooooooooh. Yeah, that's a little mysterious and dangerous. What an awesome album. And yes, it's that Randy Jackson just killing it on bass. You thought he was just some schmuck Simon Cowell dredged up from the ocean, but the dude is Wooten/Pastorius level phenomenal.

Next is The post-Graham Nash Hollies, I guess. For a moment there I thought we were going to keep the jazz going. You really didn't put much thought into it, did you C-cucumber? I mean, it does have Sandra's theme song on it, she is a cool black woman in a long dress. I like it a lot, I just wasn't expecting the complete 180 from jazz to swamp-pop. Yeah, the Hollies are the British approximation of swamp-pop: that murky, twangy guitar reverb, ever so slightly more yelling than singing, blues filler licks, it sounds like they're wearing hip-waders. It just does. I mean, I'm positive you picked it because the artwork has trippy upside-down portions to it, but all three albums so far have a kind of general murkiness about them. On the surface they are one thing, but behind the scenes there's a whole lot of everything going on. I'm a little bummed that the gatefold is ripped off and lost to the universe, but you only paid $2 for it, so whatever. Where we going next?

Canada? Red Rider's third album named after Pablo Neruda for no apparent reason? Not the album with Lunatic Fringe on it? Red Rider is technically a 1-hit wonder, right? Oh well, bombs away. After all, I love Prism, and The Guess Who, and Lighthouse, and Steppenwolf...I apparently love Canadian Rock, so why not?

Yeah, that's a hell of an intro. Even more mysterious than Ponty's. This is so 80s you can taste the neon, but I can't lie, I freakin' love it. It is metaphorically about Neruda, though if it were a movie it would probably star Michael Douglas and Kathleen Turner. It's not a "yay, Communism!" album, it's just one man standing up to the corruption of power, whatever form that power happens to take. If you demanded I compare them to some other band, it would have to be Golden Earring; it's the same kind of spooky hard rock nefarious nighttime espionage aura, but with the added value of grammatical comprehensibility. I gotta find more Red Rider albums, this is fantastic.

B: Alright, c-monkey. How did you do it?

C: Do what, boss? You told me not to put too much thought into it, so I picked interesting covers from the under $10 albums.

B: Yeah, but you picked an east coast singer-songwriter, a European violinist who emigrated to the West Coast to play with Zappa, an English band playing American rock styles, and a Canadian band singing about a Chilean poet. Sunrise, sunset, upstairs, downstairs, women and men, black and white, everything all the time, none of it sucked. Do you know how frustrating it is when everything's awesome?

I'm a smack talker! You have to give me one-sided garbage, so I can bludgeon it with a baseball bat.

C: Are you mad that you're happy?

B: *OF COURSE I AM!*

C: I got one more album, if you think that might help...

B: So help me, if it's an ironic 80s genre avoiding album in the form of a corporate motivational seminar, I will enjoy it so much my intestines explode and I will haunt you in your nightmares for eternity!

C: Oh. Um. Nevermind. I misplaced it, I guess.

B: You didn't?! You did! You found The Completion Backwards Principle by The Tubes. You bastard. Fine. Ruin my perfectly miserable day. What are you waiting for? Roll it.

The Tubes were just a silly rock band from Phoenix/California who kept hiring roadies from other bands and out of nowhere hooked up with Journey's manager and sold out enough shows to open for Led Zeppelin (manager's choice), and were almost too much for anyone to handle, what with the throwing cocaine and pills (flour and candy) at the audience. They were somehow a legitimate representation and complete mockery of the 80s at the same time. Their mascot is a schedule 40 PVC tee, 3/4" if I were to guess based on my knowledge of photographic scale and perspective.

They were art school kids who played in biker bars, and even more unlikely, Pointer Sisters shows. 5 albums later, they made this. After living through a bunch of unnecessarily pointless corporate shenanigans (including having to work really hard to get fired from A&M during an actual recession so they could sign a new deal with Capitol), this album is a satire of Reagan's "Morning in America" campaign. If you mistakenly think Trump is a good liar, you should go back and look at the nonsensical infographics Reagan broadcast on National Television. People still believe that garbage after decades of watching it get "taken away from them" like it existed in the first place. Why is my retirement fund in the same bank account as the CEO's severance package? Oh. That's why.

But Bottle, you say, you're just a useless commie Indonesian woman, and your opinion is a thing I don't like.

That's a fair rebuttal, but let's agree to pretend that I'm a 40-year-old white guy with a bushy red beard who has 3/4 of a brain and constantly asks people "why do you keep demanding that I lie to you? Do you really like being constantly surprised how reality works?"

You see, C-scape, I'm an absolute asshole. The happier you make me the meaner I am about all of it. Someone probably took this personal, and damnit that's not fair. I run and run and run and they just keep chasing me. Dividing money doesn't make more money, and "investing" is just double-speak for loan sharking. If we put it in terms of Republican and Democrat, the Republicans are selling fizzy lifting juice, and the Democrats are saying if you're gonna fuck us all over like that, then at the very least pay the $40 for our office visit so the doctor can tell us to stay home and not lift such heavy things for a while. I mean, just think about it for a minute. Your employer can fire you for any reason they want without telling you, but they don't just to prevent you from collecting unemployment. Said a different way, it's cheaper to keep paying your salary than to be a complete asshole. If you would just stop lying and be an asshole, I'd get a raise and have time and energy to find a better job.

Again, someone's going to take that personally. I assure you it's not personal, it's systematic incompetence.

I'm equally amazed that people don't understand the congeniality clause that rules the Senate. At least 80% of the nonsense you hear on TV is mandatory doublespeak because there are hefty punishments for calling each other "fucktards." Just stop lying. Be wrong, say "I'm sorry," and do your job, which is telling the asbestos salesman that he can't market it as a "weight loss supplement."

I haven't ranted like that in a while. It feels good. Real good. Thanks, The Tubes. And thank you for reading. I put an entire Saturday afternoon's worth of sheer joy into it.

Not Technically Adventure Time, but quite an adventure

I did a lot of stuff today, and in the process, I found 3 CDs hiding in the garage. It's pretty near impossible to do an Adventure Time with them, but the fact that they were out in the garage means they really do have something in common: I love listening to them. Not in the sense that they are fantastic albums, or that they are the best, or anything like that. Just pure unadulterated joy of hearing them play while I work because there isn't anything crappy enough to distract me.

Come to think of it, that's actually a pretty short list, and I can list them in no particular order:

> The Offspring – Ignition
> Breaking Benjamin – Phobia
> Chavelle - Wonder What's Next & This Type of
>   Thinking Could Do Us In
> Mastodon - Leviathan & Crack the Skye
> Avenged Sevenfold - City of Evil & Hail to the King
> Bad Religion - Recipe for Hate & Stranger Than Fiction

By pure coincidence, that's 10. Top 10 albums Bottle can listen to without cutting his fingers off with a circular saw. Exclusive club. Where's my check, Buzzfeed? Even better, I've only written about one of them so far.

I want to just binge and listen to all of them, but I love them so much (plus I did exactly that yesterday) I should really give each one its own post. Decisions, decisions...

... when we listened to Smash, I told you A) Ignition was my favorite Offspring album, and B) I was worried that mice ate it. Awesome news, they didn't!

If you've ever wondered what a character study of your old pal Bottle sounds like, then pay attention. We slip in and out of irony like it's a jacket we brought along in case the weather suddenly changes, and anyone who knows what they're talking about is clearly lying, so burn it all to the ground, or don't, just don't look to me to decide what you think I think you want me to think, 'cause hell if I know. That kind of thinking could do us all in...

... speaking of...

How the goddamned bloody hell is Chavelle Nu-metal? Yes, obviously you can make comparisons with Korn and Deftones in terms of singing in falsetto for no good reason and turning the treble on the bass all the way up, but just playing in dropped-C isn't Nu-metal. What other genre are they incorporating? I wouldn't even call them metal, except for maybe the extremes of mopyness. Even Deftones predates nu-metal, and not in any "proto" sense of the term. Is Faith No More or Mr. Bungle Nu-metal? Is Chavelle on the same playlist with Linkin Park and Coal Chamber and POD and Limp Biscuit and Papa Roach? Proto-emo maybe, but not nu-metal. Is Flyleaf Nu-metal? Sonic profile does not a genre make.

Don't worry, it gets even worse. Chavelle only has 2 albums. Pre-major label doesn't count, and the last 10+ years don't count either. Chavelle and Hanson are the same band.

Whaaaaaa?!

Seriously, three brothers. The only difference is that Hanson are a functional family, while Pete and Sam are like "why the hell did we let our crazy brother Joe be our bassist for so long when he clearly didn't like being in our band?" I don't know, but I stopped caring when he left. It doesn't mean you suck now, it just means it's not the same band anymore.

Does giving amphetamine adjacent stimulants to children help? No. Does heavy melodic rock music help? In my case, absolutely. Pete's right, BoB your head to this. And no, I don't have any idea where the jewel cases for some of these are currently hiding.

If you were wondering what's next, then wonder no more, it's Wonder What's Next, the prequel to this kind of thinking. Shove all the pain down inside, forget closure, and ask yourself if you're alone in here. This might be the rawest album I've ever heard. Not in terms of sound quality, it's so over produced it shimmers like lips after a Botox treatment, I just mean it aches with the kind of existential pain even Kierkegaard couldn't quite put his finger on. No catharsis, just accept that we're doomed and snowboard off a mountain or murder your entire anger management class. Who cares?

If you're wondering what's next, then you didn't read the last three pages. I'm afraid you're in for quite a lot more existential angst. I'm afraid, Phobia, ya get it? Nevermind, just enjoy the complete emotional anguish that is Chavelle, and rest assured the next album will break you.

You're listening to KBTL, nothing but rock. Nothing but butt rock. This next one goes out to Ben, who's scared of becoming part of the human centipede. I'm sure you'll find your place in the diarrhea chain eventually, but for now enjoy this album as much as we do; it's not a guilty pleasure if you don't feel any guilt. Here's Phobia from Breaking Benjamin....

Well, that was some kind of fun. I don't know about you, but now I'm thirsty for a rock band who loves their rock band predecessors so much they made an album adopting the styles of all those awesome rock bands. An album so good their fans said "waaaaiiiit a minute, you're just copying all those old metal bands us teenagers think are even more passé than heroin"

A Dandy Warhols reference? Has that pot smoking art teacher been letting you listen to KBTL without my permission?

Relax, not-my-mom. Whatever garbage you throw out there, it comes back 7 times worse, or at least that's the explanation I made up for this band. We're dealing with a period in rock music when I was literally driving back and forth between Denton, TX and OKC to see my wife and newborn child on the weekends and live in an apartment taking doctoral classes and teaching aural skills during the week. Avenged Sevenfold and Breaking Benjamin were as good as it got driving up and down I35 in the middle of the night. City of Evil was a good album, but Hail To The King is amazing.

Yes, you could sit there and say this is the Metallica album we all wish they had made instead of Load and Reload, but it's not. It's Avenged Sevenfold not trying quite as hard to be super killer amazing mind-blowing technical shred kings, and that's what makes it super killer amazing mind-blowingly awesome. They said fuck it, let's just rock. It flat out rocks from beginning to end. Story over. Hail to the King.

Greatest Hits Roulette

In a dimly lit room, 3 fuzzy figures sit around a card table. A bare light bulb pendulates slowly above them as the muffled conversation becomes more animated.

.... oh no, I'm not gonna pick one. I did Adventure Time, remember? Look where that got us!

...but I can't pick one, he always knows it was me, and won't criticize it at all. It's your turn, Marvin.

I just fix the typos. I'm not qualified to make creative decisions. Do the thing I taught you, Mr. Compiler.

With what?! He's chewing through albums so fast even I can't keep track of what he has or hasn't written about....

Oh, sorry...uh...read that all again, but this time imagine that the picture slowly comes into focus and we can see Skip, Sandra, and The Compiler arguing over stacks of records strewn about the table. Cinematography is hard work, and I'm not even sure I know why I'm doing it, or where here is, or who I am. I must be dreaming. Oh well, back to work.

S: Over there, that stack of records from the water damaged collection that aren't actually damaged. He definitely hasn't listened to any of those. Do it with your eyes closed so you have plausible deniability.
C: Hhhhhhh, fine: Eenie meenie miney mecord,
That's how we will choose a record.
From this slightly dingy stack
Will Bottle have a heart attack?
Skip told me to hurry up and just pick one and I guess if I must this one is it... are you sure this is a good idea? I don't know what it is I picked, but there's no way he's gonna like this.

Just then, Bottle appears at the door and belts out a greeting:

B: Hi, everybody! What are we listening to today? Reggae? Gregorian Chant in Pig Latin? 90s Yoga-pop? I could keep going on my list of favor...

Bottle is quickly interrupted by a resounding chorus of NO!s. After a brief pause in which the group sheepishly side-eyes each other, The Compiler slowly extends a cardboard platter with a face on his face that could only imply fear of an impending explosion. Meekly he says "here you go, boss." The whole group simultaneously inhales as they await their uncertain fate....

B: Elton John's Greatest Hits? That's an odd one. Any particular reason?

"Totally random. Top of the stack......" Sandra hesitantly asserts.

B: Oh. Ok. Who doesn't like Elton John? You guys are acting weird, like it could have been something terrible like Anne Murray or Lee Greenwood. I mean, greatest hits albums aren't particularly exciting; it is the 2nd most boring concept, considering that's what almost every major label album is in the first place (scale of weeks or months as opposed to scale of years). You'd have to try really hard to mess up a bunch of songs everybody already liked in the form of dollar bills....

As Bottle walks out of the room, the group finally exhales in unison. Fade out...

Fade back in to Bottle at his record player...

Alright. Sing us a song or 9, Mr. Piano man. Sorry, wrong short guy. Interesting fact, this record was manufactured in Portugal. Seriously, all the label specific writing is in Portuguese.

Let's check out the track list. Yep, that's every Elton John megahit I can think of.

... several moments later...

Man, this actually sounds great. A little quieter than I expected, but completely lovely. I was almost expecting a K-Tel extravaganza of faulty equipment and not giving a shit, but this is great if you don't mind a huge dynamic range. I don't have the original mixes in my head to compare it to, but in terms of just leveling everything so it's listenable, this is perfectly fine. They even cut the volume a bit to compensate for Saturday...Fighting being waaaaay too hot for the innermost track of Face A. It still distorts right at the end, but that's just me picking my nose at it. Face B is a little rough on my copy, but here's a dirty little secret from one record collector to all of you. Brand new records can skip, some beautifully shiny pressings are complete crap because the dies wear out by the end of a run, nobody bothers to QC or adjust machine settings, and some plants aren't as picky about the quality of their raw PVC to being with. This one is much better than I expected, other than physical track placement.

Like I said, who doesn't like Elton John? I don't know what the Beefettes were so worried about.

Biohazard – State of the World Address

Biohazard invented rap-metal. They didn't mean to, it just happened. Inner city Brooklyn doesn't sound like much fun, the way they tell it.

I have no idea what you think about Biohazard, but they're literally screaming "stop being terrible to each other! It really sucks!"

Best state of the world address I ever heard.

Cake – Motorcade of Generosity

Let's talk about Cake. No, I take that back, let's talk about Robert Christgau. He is one of Bottle's mentors, after all. There're great albums, A. They are rare. There are good albums, B. They are less rare. There are also various levels of hilariously bad albums. In between lie the honorable mentions 1, 2, and 3-star. Why? Because these are albums that people predisposed to like them probably will. I like the idea that most albums fall into the 3-star system between good and bad albums. I also like that he will listen to anything and make an honest assessment of it within his established likes and biases. I'm the Todd in the Shadows version of that.

I honestly don't know what to say about Cake's first album, Motorcade of Generosity. It's unique. I mean, yes there's irony, but it's not IRONIC. There are some sarcastic lyrics, but it's not SARCASTIC. Christgau calls it "unambiguity from the near side of cool."

Oh, I got it. The banality of hyperbolically ironic modernity. A Bob Newhartian chronicle of hipster ennui. Seinfeld on Xanax.

I always get the sense that John McCrea thinks the whole thing is dumb. Yes, we're a band. Yes, I'm a songwriter. Yes, music is important, *BUT STOP DEMANDING TO LIKE EVERYTHING ALL THE TIME!*

How dare you enjoy this? We're wasting a lot of money and making the world more horrible in a desperately ironic attempt to convince you to stop wasting money and make the world a little better. I get that. I'm like that. I think I'm an idiot illustrating how to try to not be such an idiot.

Cake is like Spoon, there ain't no surprise evolution taking place. I like Motorcade and Fashion Nugget, the rest is someone else's problem. My Grandma Mildred really liked their version of Perhaps, Perhaps, Perhaps.

Oh yeah, Cake, don't they like want you to stop building nuclear warheads and plant trees and stuff?

No, they want you to stop fixating on the pointless conundrums of artificial ceremony. The more you do it, the dumber you get, and the harder to we have to try to snap you out of it. Then that becomes work, and now we're dumb too. Look at us, we're a band being pointless to try to get you to go do something. That's retarded.

Now I kind of feel guilty for enjoying it. Help, I'm a sheeple.

Shhh. It's a secret

B: Wanna know a secret?
E: That's a bit of a loaded question coming from you, Bottle.

B: So, do you?

E: Ummmm.

B: Noooooo, don't try to Pink Floyd your way out of it. Wanna know a secret?

E: No.

B: Ok, then I won't tell you.

E: Damnit, Bottle! Fine, what is it?

B: No. You already decided you didn't want to know. I won that game.

E: Yes, but now that means I really want to know what it is.

B: Exactly, I'm better at this game than you.

E: Tell me.

B: No.

E: Grrrrrrr!

E: Ask politely.

E: Hhhhhhhhhh. Please?

B: No. Ask properly.

E: Hhhhhhhhhhhhhh. Bottle, do you have an interestingly confusing confession you'd like to share?

B: Funny you should ask. As a matter of fact, I do. I've never told anyone this, so hush hush, ya know? Sometimes, late at night, while the Beefettes aren't looking, I sneak away to my super secret office, lock the door, and...and....listen to Yanni. He's awesome.

E: What the hell is wrong with you?

B: Nothing, Yanni's awesome.

Bad Religion – New Maps of Hell

I love everything about tonight's album, except the way it sounds. I hate more than half the mixes, I hate the god-awful louder than thou mastering, and I hate the overemphasized low-mids.

I love the songs, I love the melody/harmony, I love that we're back with Brett and Epitaph, but it's 2007 and how many times have I mentioned how much I hate everything from the early 2000s to now? I'm positive it's because of ear buds.

Yes, my dislike is heightened by how much vinyl I listen to, but I like how those mixes from the 60s to late 90s sound. That's what I like. I like shitty cassette dubs of recordings in barns and garages and bathrooms with cars and crickets in the background redubbed back to CD. I'd rather listen to scratchy poppy moldy vinyl than the 300hz drone of a sonic vacuum cleaner. Yeah, it sounds like a vacuum cleaner to me. The world has moved on and I don't feel any need to keep up. Two or three days of nothing before 2005 and I can relearn to ignore it, but some of my favorite bands bridge that gap and it blows.

New maps of hell, indeed.

The Old Map of Hell

Here's the old map of hell, Ministry's 3rd album, The Land of Rape and Honey. One of the first industrial metal albums, it sounds like it was mixed and mastered through a broken megaphone.

Don't be too put off by the title, that was the actual slogan of Tisdale, Saskatchewan in the 80s because their entire economy was based on rapeseed and honey. Rapeseed is part of the mustard/cabbage family, and it's a major source of vegetable oil and biodiesel. It's literally second only to soy beans in terms of world protein consumption. I may not like Branstad's legacy of selling the whole state of Iowa to corporate agribusiness, but the fact that Trump took a dump on his entire life's work of selling Iowa soy to China instead of letting Brazil cut down even more rainforest to farm it for them is pretty terrible. True story, Branstad supported Trump, was handed the Ambassadorship, and then Trump started the trade war and ruined the whole thing. Brazil's chopping down trees double-speed as we speak.

Where was I? Oh yeah, Al thought seeing the phrase on a coffee mug was so hilarious he switched from synthpop in a fake British accent to attaching a power drill to the meat grinder and running his vocal mic through a distortion pedal.

Sounds purdy to me.

Thelonious Monk Quartet with John Coltrane at Carnegie Hall

Shortest album review I've ever written:

On November 29th, 1957, Thelonious Monk, John Coltrane, Ahmed Abdul-Malik, and Shadow Wilson played a double header at Carnegie Hall.

SHUTUPTHISISIMPORTANTANDIWANTTOHEARTHEMS PEAK!

Stuff, from a time people like! (Pricewise "The Best of the 60s")

Color me confused as hell. How is this record this good? I don't mean the tracks, they are generically 60s in quality, and I don't mean the mastering, it's way too hot across the board, I mean the physical record.

As far as I can find, Pricewise was a Scepter imprint that has a discography of 5 albums. They lasted about a year. This is the 3rd record they put out from 1965. Obviously, the quotes are cautionary, they're saying "don't worry, the next 5 years of music will be crap."

Let's be real, this is the carryover of the 50s, it's dance crazes and prom fodder. And no, it's not pleasant to listen to, these are dubs of dubs with nasty clipping and the sounds of the transfer machinery thrown in (I lowered my master volume and it's still there), but the gaps are pretty much silent with only the tiniest bit of dust popping. If I cleaned it, it would be near perfect. It's immaculately VG+ garbage!

I often wonder when I read record reviews, because half the time I think people have no idea how terrible these recordings were to begin with. Hahahaha! The corporate blurb on the back is all about the best music at the best value. "We know you will agree with us that we are fulfilling our objective" of seeing if we can milk as much money as possible out of you in a short amount of time for the absolute minimum investment possible. Are you tired of paying lots of money for good sounding recordings? Want to see if this is a tolerable middle ground? Pricewise, at least we didn't hire scabs to re-record them.

Skid Row

So, what's the deal with Skid Row? They were a functional band for two albums over 3 years, but it took another 3 or 4 years to finally fall apart. Unlike Christgau, I think Slave To The Grind is waaaaaay better than their debut. But is their debut bad? Again, Christgau thinks they are both bad, but given his preference for catchy tunes with a minimum of sexism and cliché, Skid Row is obviously the better album. So, let's tear it all apart.

I don't think we really need a historical rundown of the band, but it does help to understand that we're in New Jersey, and Bon Jovi literally owns them. Rachel and Snake signed away their royalties in exchange for Bon Jovi's publishing support. Standard pyramid deal, and eventually they got a little bit of their own money. It's much more complicated and intricate than that, but like I said we're in 1988 New Jersey, and we're talking about rebellious teenagers whose only available hobbies include bar fights and sex.

Are some of the songs borderline sexist? For a given value of degenerate teenagers in New Jersey, I suppose. They aren't singing about your neighbor's daughter in college who volunteers at the nursing home and takes care of birds that fall out of backyard nests. There're at least two actual prostitutes and one now divorced adulteress. These are the girls who like breaking the balls of dangerous guys, who then turn around and confess how much it hurts to have your heart broken. Also note, the narrator isn't the one in prison for beating up "a queer." It's a macho act for a tough world sung while wearing dude heals and leather. The key point is that it is an act, a survival skill when your friends are bigger drunken lunatics than you, Ricky being the wildest one, of course.

But damnit, Janet, the songs are phenomenal. Forget the lyrics, focus on structure. Story telling verses, huge sing along choruses, proper setups for the wailing guitar solos. Bolan has every right to brag about his songwriting prowess, these things are killer. The riffs are catchy and grooving, the transitions are so tight and effective, they don't recycle gimmicks or riffs, and it all paints a picture of teenage love on the sleazy side of the tracks. Booze and broads and bravado. Toms River, NJ isn't exactly downtown Brooklyn where our friends in Biohazard aren't having nearly as much fun, if you know what I'm sayin'. This is glam metal.

People didn't like the more aggressive second album, but I'm not people. Are Skid Row the best? No. Is it good? Yeah, it's not silly party time music, it's much more realistic in terms of actual feelings, and the characters are believable if not actually likable. More importantly, they aren't calling themselves the good guys here. They have nasty habits, they are wild, and forget the corporate ladder, they can't even reach the bottom rung of the fire escape standing on top of the dumpster in the alley. Park Avenue really does lead to Skid Row, and it's only a block or two away from your office.

2004 According to Bottle

I was trying to figure out what album to write about next, and I somehow ended up realizing that I have 11 albums from 2004. Maybe we don't do just one. Maybe I put some effort into it and do an Adventure Time? No, that has rules I can't break. For starters C-biscuit has to participate, and I'm not gonna stoop to lying about it just to give him credit for work I did myself. Next of all, I've already written about a few of them (and I still haven't found the cases for my Chavelle CDs). So, yeah, 2004 according to Bottle. What could possibly go wrong?

Here they are in all their glory. Actually, there's only one I don't like. I wouldn't call it bad per se, I just don't like Incubus's A Crow Left of the Murder. The other 10 are awesome. So, I'm not going to write about an album tonight. Instead, we're going to listen to the parts of 2004 I paid for, in order, and you can get a head start. Here's the whole list for anyone who wants to hear it *before* I write about it.

1) Incubus - A Crow Left of the Murder
2) New Found Glory – Catalyst
3) Skinny Puppy - The Greater Wrong of the Right
4) My Chemical Romance - Three Cheers for Sweet Revenge
5) Mastodon – Leviathan
6) Green Day - American Idiot
7) Chavelle - This Type of Thinking Could Do Us In
8) Brian Wilson – Smile
9) A Perfect Circle – eMotive
10) Rammstein - Reise Reise
11) NOFX - The Greatest Songs Ever Written (by us)

That's an ADD list if ever there was one...

Incubus – A Crow Left of the Murder

Welcome to 2004. Highlights include landing fancy dune buggies on Mars, finding out the US was wrong about weapons of mass destruction and that we have a secret torture prison (don't worry, we'll find out we have many more in the future), Reagan dies, and 4 goddamned more years of W.

Musically speaking, it's turning to shit. Don't get me wrong, there are some amazing albums from 2004 that I don't own, but mostly it's bands that aren't popular yet, best of albums for no reason, the first trickle of albums about how much we hated W, and the rest of the world is pretty sick of us as well. Bottle's collection begins in February with Incubus.

I don't like A Crow Left of the Murder. It's too long, it's completely unfocused, the concept evaporates after 3 songs, and how can you be nu-metal if you aren't in some identifiable way metal? Turntables and occasional fast words? Is Beck nu-metal? He had two of the damned things, and he's closer to rap than most actual nu-metal bands.

Incubus is noise rock. Not heavy/sarcastic alternative noise rock, but rock songs with sound effects in the background. They are quite good at it. I like Incubus a lot. That's why I don't like this album. I should like it. It has all my favorite ingredients, but we start off with Megalomaniac (a fantastic opener), and every single second after that feels like mind numbing drudgery. Why did I spend the last 58 minutes listening to it?

I think Incubus is a one song at a time band, they write interesting, often great songs, but their albums feel like found object collages to me. Maybe it would be fine if there wasn't a clear concept for the album, but no indication whatsoever which character is the estranged crow with a hole through his body, we just assume it's Brandon.

Was 2004 more like 1984 than now? Was it more like 1984 than the other times we said it's like 1984. Does the sort of inverted Philip K. Dick reference even matter? Or Caesar? Or history repeating? It's not like this is a "paranoid" album, or even an album about hypocrisy and delusional contentment. It's nonsense actually, when you combine it all together, they cancel each other out. How can you be outside the group if the group is defined by the false facade of the self-righteous pursuit of comfort? If you're raising android sheep in an attempt to appear like you're participating in clinging on to humanity, then it's safe to assume that everyone else is too, so why even pretend? So again, why even make this 5th album?

I'm totally not like those people who aren't like those people who it turns out are all the same because we're all just pretending. The group kills the individual, the individual either turns into a power-hungry monster or a wastoid. Either way we're doomed, right? 2004 is a big year for that, for some reason.

We're off to a slow start, I know, but the next 10 albums get much better.

New Found Glory – Catalyst

I'm sure you're not surprised to know that the punk revival of the late 90s spawned a whole lot of little brother bands playing pop-punk. Obviously, the big brother bands that started that wave are going strong, Blink 182, Sum 41, and the granddads who are Green Day, but there's a whole second tier now with Paramore, Yellowcard, Simple Plan, and this band, New Found Glory. I didn't care much, mostly because I was in the middle of getting my Master's degree, and the whole scene isn't that great. They also belong to that wave of Christian bands who found bigger success by not pounding their faith over everybody's heads like leftover 2x4s and folding chairs at Wrestlemania. Tonight's album is awesome though.

You wanna talk about catchy songs? Catalyst is chocked full of 'em. Awkward lyrics are par for the course (Incubus had tons of 'em I didn't mention), and New Found Glory has a very particular thing about relationships being difficult when you're always on tour. It's a consistent theme across all their albums. This one has awesome artwork though. A complete visual world of sleazy creatures and wide-eyed big-head children-people in a cartoon world of fame, failure, and lies. It works really well.

It's easy to misunderstand the concept here, because it actually requires knowing the definition of "catalyst." Chemistry wise, a catalyst is a substance that initiates a reaction without itself taking part in that reaction, but more generically a person or thing that causes a series of events by just existing. Trump, for example, is a catalyst of belligerent stupidity. I had no idea who the crow was supposed to be, but here the catalyst is intentionally a variety of characters: love, the person you love, fame, the person promising you fame if you just follow them through the spooky forest of lies, you get the idea.

Is it going to voice those deep -eated existential feelings you grapple with on the rooftops late at night? No. Is it as whiny or self-absorbed as their peers. Also no. Is it listenable? Yes, and dare I say enjoyably so. Then again, I'm best known for failure, so you might find it whiny and juvenile.

Skinny Puppy – The Greater Wrong of the Right

Speaking of strained relationships, Skinny Puppy made an album in 2004. Making The Process in 1996 kind of killed them. Hard drugs and just plain being sick of each other sent cEvin and Nivek in opposite directions (I'm pretty proud of that one). But, through the process of not taking hard drugs anymore, working on each others' solo albums, and working with bands who were inspired by Skinny Puppy in the first place, they decided to be friends again because they were a huge part of each others' lives. The greater wrong of the right is corporatization, by the way. They sent an invoice to the Pentagon for using their music without proper authorization to torture people in one of our other torture prisons. I suspect they got stiffed on that one.

Everybody nowadays imagines 27 shades of left/right, but it's only 2: social hierarchy on the right, social equality on the left. That distinction is not the same as

Republican/Democrat, or conservative/liberal. Corporate hierarchy is just about as right wing as you can get, and Skinny Puppy is just about as shocking a reaction to it as anyone could imagine.

Who's a good little bloodthirsty mongrel glitch-demon? You are. Yes, you are.

More importantly, are these the actual androids at war with their stupid barnyard animal raising human oppressors? Yeah, I like that; I don't care if it makes any sense, don't care if people weren't really thrilled with its commercial feel and total midi/vocorder approach to the human condition, I'm just happy these icons of industrial depravity got back together and started making music again.

Are we all completely useless? Sometimes it sure feels like it. All I'm saying is, this isn't torture for me at all. I love this stuff.

And with that, we end the loosely based on a Philip K. Dick novel portion of the year. Time to get emotional....

My Chemical Romance – Three Cheers for Sweet Revenge

Christgau is just wrong about the sophomore album from My Chemical Romance. Three Cheers for Sweet Revenge is phenomenal. The concept for the album was the demolition lovers from the first album are killed in a gunfight, but the devil tells the one who looks like Gerard that Helena is still alive and they can be reunited if he harvests 1,000 souls or whatever, but then their grandma died (hence calling the first song Helena) and it sort of devolved into more general loss and depression than proper narrative. It's emo with a self-deprecating sense of humor, what more do you want?
It's also a non-stop aural assault that can only be described as cinematic. Every track is a self-contained scene in this weird horror fantasy western crime dramedy. Even the credits are laid out like a movie poster. Best of all it's 39 minutes, with more meaningful content than any of the 50 to 70 minute

monstrosities I've been constantly complaining about. This is a serious contender for best all-around album of all time, whether you enjoy listening to it or not.

I love it. My only complaint is the mispronunciation of ephedrine, but since there's no way to rewrite the entire song to pronounce it properly, I will deal with it like a big boy.

3 albums I already wrote about

I've already written about these next three albums, so I'm not sure what to say about them. Mastodon, Green Day, and Chavelle. I suppose if the first 3 albums were loosely based on the book that Blade Runner was loosely based on, then these are not unlike that. You got your Moby Dick meets Norse mythology, the anti-W/America is actually horrible statement of teenage malcontention, and the straight up depression of living inside an electronic coma. It's almost like everyone just picked one thing about that Incubus album and ran with it.

Leviathan, American Idiot, and This Type of Thinking Could Do Us In, check 'em out before the plane crashes somewhere out in the Pacific.

Brian Wilson Presents Smile

Then in September, a thing happened that nobody ever thought would actually happen. Brian Wilson finally released Smile. You know, the album that finally snapped him and led to lifelong psychiatric therapy.

I'm cringing as I say this, but I don't actually like it. Sorry for accidentally lying at the start. Well, half a lie. I'm thrilled he was finally able to finish it, I'm thrilled Van Dyke Parks rewrote it with him, I'm deeply sad that Brian's life was such a struggle and that his dad was a grade a hole that feces falls out of, but it's not my thing. I'm not saying it's bad or dumb or that we don't need a break from the sheer emotional misery of the last 7 albums, but I know what's coming next and you picked kind of a bad time to pull it together and use that verse as the chorus for that other song and tell me about eating vegetables and the great Chicago fire of 1871, Brian. All I hear is the rhythm of the war drum, and those vibrations aren't so good. Maybe someday 30 years from now I'll find a way to properly enjoy it, but not in the context of Trump running for reelection while we listen to albums written about Bush running for reelection.

Be mad at me if you must, but meh. I'm a lean into the pain and suffering and dare anyone to tough it out with me kind of guy. And boy howdy, are we about to lean into it....

A Perfect Circle – eMOTIVe

Friends of the show will tell you that I've called myself heavy-handed on several occasions, but I don't have Maynard James Keenan money. He's Wreck-it Ralph. He straight up paid to have A Perfect Circle release an entire album of covers of protest songs on election day. That's what "executive producer" means.

Jesus fucking Christ! Toy piano and whispering for the opening Crucifix cover. It's your choice, peace or annihilation. Imagine the nuclear wasteland version of Imagine. It doesn't let up either, just one gut-wrenching soliloquy from the barren wasteland after another, and we end on the Maynard Choir's version of Joni Mitchell's Fiddle and the Drum. I dare you to smile. Obviously, we're not dead. A whole lot of American soldiers and people from the Middle East are, though.

Would this album still be as downright soul crushingly depressive if Kerry had won? I don't know. Probably not, it might feel like wearing one of those World Series losers t-shirts they have to make and then ship overseas because manufacturing isn't a spontaneous convenience like we delude ourselves into thinking. Still though, an album of protest songs during a war (even if you don't call it that) is rarely inane. We do a whole lot of stuff we should protest all the time, and now is as good/bad a time as any to pull it out and lean into the pain.

This is as tough as it gets. The next two albums are pretty down on our country, but in a more digestible form. If you can get through eMOTIVe then you can deal with most anything. Oh, you'll be totally and permanently messed up by the end, but you'll have a great story to tell. My favorite part is the reinterpreted propaganda posters by Steven R. Gilmore. Relax, everything is fine, we've got it all under control....

Rammstein – Reise Reise

And so we move on to Reise Reise, that flight recording of an album that takes us all the way to the scene of the plane crash. Amerika, ist wunderbar.

Last time I picked a fight with another critic, if I remember right. This time we'll just call it like it is. America is just jacking itself off while Russia watches. Ignore the rest of the world, wall up the ugly parts so you can't see them anymore, say "I just don't feel like it," and claim that's the nature of the beast.

Oh, did I get eMOTIVe and Reise Reise out of order. Sure did. Oh well. Accidents happen.

NOFX – The Greatest Songs Ever Written

Last but not least, here's The Greatest Songs Ever Written (by NOFX). They even remastered them with better equipment like George Lucas and Steven Spielberg. Whatever Didi Wants isn't on it, but most of the rest of the best of are, so I can't really complain. I am moderately pleased at the coincidental splash down on the cover.

Well, that was 2004. Just about the only thing we didn't get was a summary of how terrible LA is. One major metropolis is pretty much like any other, I suppose. I'm back to being a foul-mouthed, unpatriotic adult surrounded by spoiled children hoarding someone else's paycheck. Please don't vote for Trump, it wasn't funny the first time, and I can't afford enough guitars or albums or rum to survive the sequel.

Supertramp – Even in the Quietest Moments

Interesting fact. The piano on the cover of Supertramp's Even In the Quietest Moments is actually covered in real snow, and the sheet music isn't Fool's Overture, it's The Star Spangled Banner. They left an empty piano shell outside at a ski resort overnight (the same resort my friend Reiner skis at), and this is the album before Breakfast in America.

I don't completely agree with Christgau, but his sentiment is pretty great: most prog-rock is pretentious background schlock that's all too hard to ignore, but this album is modest background schlock that sounds good when it slips into the ear.

I'm biased because 1) I just like Supertramp, and 2) this is what Breakfast in America is actually about. I pointed out that album was about Hodgson and Davies having very different world views but making and playing this music gave them a common purpose. They wrote most of their songs separately and then fleshed them out as a band in sound checks and rehearsals. Their styles are quite different, Davies is very specific and tells a story while Hodgson is more vague and open to poetic fancy like the hippie he really is.

Christgau is right that this isn't the wackadoodle type of prog-rock like EL&P or Kansas or Jethro Tull or Early Genesis, the songs are bigger and more interesting than simple verse/chorus rock songs, and that's not schlock in my book. For starters, who are they pandering to with what clichés or stereotypes? Ugh, all those dreadful people who like songs about the complexities of love and life, and feel skeptical about buying those experiences from a magazine, or learning how to love from a book. At its core, this is music for listening. It's not supposed to be background at all, it's supposed to be the art medium. No, In The Quietest Moments isn't the theatrical production most people might expect, but it's quite an enjoyable listen for anyone who appreciates the humor in calling the last song an Overture after all the various fools already gave their monologues. I do.

Uriah Heep – Wonderworld

It seems like nobody but me likes Wonderworld. Critics and fans found it underwhelming, the band wasn't happy with it because they were burning out, fighting, and recording in Germany (a disruption to their standard process rather than a refreshing change of pace), and everyone says it lacks conceptualization.

Not shockingly, I disagree. I think it's a good album. Maybe we just need to better understand what Uriah Heep really is. So, here's my completely non-intuitive appreciation of the history of Uriah Heep, and why Wonderworld is actually one of their best albums.

Uriah Heep didn't become Uriah Heep until Ken Hensley joined in 1969. They were called Spice, and Spice was Deep Purple's lovingly adopted little brother. Hard Rock, Heavy Metal, and Progressive Rock. Not three separate genres, all three genres at the same time. Why? The simple answer is that the band thought adding a keyboard player would work really well, and once Ken was there, they all quickly agreed that they should just be Vanilla Fudge. Hard rock jams with no hesitation to hop a train to Noiseville or get off at Soft Rock Junction if they changed their minds halfway. Uriah Heep is an ensemble, every instrument is equal and interesting.

People say there's no concept to this album, but of course there is. The concept is that we try to live out our fantasies because real life is no fun at all. What's a bigger escapist fantasy than an internationally renowned rock band playing to thousands of people there to see the show? Especially considering you're falling apart, you're going to fire your soon to overdose junkie bass player, you're bickering about royalties and credits instead of making music, and you're jealous of each others' flamboyance. The cover is you posed as statues mid rocking out, for crying out loud.

Most people falsely equate "concept" with "plot." Telling a story is one kind of concept, probably the easiest to understand. Being the concept is a little less obvious, but no less meaningful. People also falsely assume that you have to do it on purpose. No, you don't. I like it better when you do it by complete coincidence.

Do the tracks flow from one to another? No, absolutely not. Every song is pretty much the same, structurally speaking. But inside each attempt at recreating that monument are some fantastic moments of musical bliss you couldn't make in a different context. That's the concept. The fantasy is the big crazy rock band on stage, the reality is just doing it over and over and over while it gets a little bit harder each time. Reality blows, so the fantasy gets bigger and bigger until it finally explodes and shrapnel flies everywhere.

This isn't an album "for listening." It's one of those albums you have to hold in your head and visualize. You have to treat it exactly like a statue or sculpture, walk around it and see it from as many angles as possible, hear all the components in counterpoint with each other, recognize the beauty of how it all fits together in the midst of it all falling apart. That's not something you can really do until you've heard it 20 or 30 times, and it may take quite a while to get there. It might actually be harder if you really like Uriah Heep, but for me this is much more enjoyable than their earlier albums. Plus, there's some grade A Halloween level spookiness in there thanks to Ken's organ and Mick's rampaging guitar bashing.

This album will eventually grow on you if you give it a chance. I'm not promising that growth won't turn out to be some horrible skin fungus, but so far I'm not feeling any worse for it....

Massive Attack – Collected

I need to feel good again. Obviously real life isn't going to make that happen, so we'll have to turn to the glorious world of headphones to soothe the savage beast. Now, your old friend Bottle doesn't really go for the sunshiny beach volleyball type of feel good, he likes to dive head first down a dark alley and say "oy! Mate. Show me something worth my time."

Trip hop isn't really a genre. It's the name everyone gave the downtempo DJ scene in Bristol in the early 90s. Believe it or not it's an evolution of House more than anything. Trip hop is really just 3 groups: Massive Attack with or without Tricky, Tricky on his own, and Portishead. Sure, lots of other groups make Trip Hop, like Groove Armada and Sneaker Pimps, even Bjork and Poe dabbled in it. Homogenic is widely considered a sort of Trip Hop masterpiece. Bottle says yes and no on that one. Trip Hop is just slow break beats, jazz or soul sampling, and atmospheric electronics. You can fit Bjork inside that description if you're desperate, but like I said at the start, it really isn't a genre, it's a scene.

You know Massive Attack because the TV show House used Angel as its theme song. If you had to boil it down to one word, that word is probably "haunting." It's not daytime music, it's probably raining, there are occasional ghost sightings, dark smoky club in a cobblestone alley. Massive Attack is much more overtly Hip Hop than Portishead, and also much more stylistically diverse.

Interesting fact, Robert "3D" Del Naja is a major contender for secretly being Banksy. Tonight, we're listening to their 2006 best of album Collected. It's fantastic. Tons of people all over it, even a Sinead O'Connor appearance hiding

in there. You can definitely hear what Bjork was influenced by in their later work (especially strings over beats).
    Critics like to point to Tricky in particular for "transcending the gangsta rap ethos." That's grade a BS, but Tricky and 3D both manage to be neither confrontational nor corny, so I can see what they're trying to say, sort of, if I squint just right. There're thousands of rappers like that, but they don't have real money backing them up. Personally, I just love the aural aesthetic of lo-fi hip-hop and EDM. As two thirds of the thing that is Trip Hop, Massive Attack is glorious and Collected is pretty awesome if you don't have thousands of dollars to spend on reissues and imports.
    Give them a try, I think they are truly fantastic... Oh yeah, that hits the spot. Karmacoma here I come.

Nine Inch Nails – Pretty Hate Machine
    You know, I gotta tell you, I'm just so tired of all of it. I'm tired of BH, and Microsoft, and Amazon. I'm tired of the idiotic bipolar politics. I'm tired of the ridiculous notion that corporations are people. I'm tired of dressing up modern mercantilism as some kind of global ambassadorship. I'm tired of listening to people use "the economy" when they mean "the stock market." I'm tired of people blaming each other for shit happening instead of making that shit less painful for everyone. I'm tired of the wealthiest Americans acting like they shouldn't have to pay full price like us poor people do. I'm tired of robo-calls and b2b sales. I'm tired of everyone shirking their responsibilities and trying to sell me marketing tips. I'm tired of insurance companies being an investment front instead of the social safety net they were intended to be. I'm tired of tradesmen fighting with urban planners when they have freakin' face-to-face meetings about it and could easily just cooperate for the betterment of everyone. There's a reason why none of these systems work when you're honest, go ahead and try to guess what it is.....

So, in honor of that tiredness, we'll just fire up the Pretty Hate Machine and let it mangle our souls into nutrient rich organic mulch.

Trent wasn't functioning well in society, and neither does this debut album. The drums are sampled from his own record collection (he planned on recording them with real drums, but in the end they just equalized his samples and ran with it), he intentionally used an E-mu Emax because it sounded terrible, and didn't put much effort into the vocals. I totally agree with Tom Breihan that this is an Industrial-aware synthpop album. My memory tells me I hate Side B compared to the universally acknowledge masterpiece of Side A, so we'll have to rum me up/down enough to compensate for that unfair presupposition. And away we go...

NIN really only has one aesthetic goal: make electronic music more human and aggressive. Now, that invariably involves Trent Reznor's actual personal psychology, and that means it comes from the perspective of actually being miserable and feeling existence as a terribly abrasive surface you have to rub your face against, or like a mental brillo pad. If you've ever listened to p(nmi)t's music and thought "geez, this is just so overwhelmingly depressing," that's kind of the same thing. It's real work for us depressive personalities to be functional humans all day.

Side A is a bit all over the place, but I think you just need to approach it as internal thoughts. More than anything, these are thoughts and ideas you wouldn't say out loud. They can seem juvenile or disorganized or melodramatic because they are. This isn't a "craft" album, it's a completely instinctually slapped together during studio downtime experiment by the 24-year-old assistant engineer/janitor. Bart Koster literally said what the hell, it's only costing me a little wear on the tape heads, and the floors do look all shiny and waxy....

Yeah, Side B isn't so bad now. You have to let go of the future NIN, accept that they're just making it up without a map or compass. Depeche Mode on rage-o-hol, semi-directionless aggression with a ladle full of hyperbole. It doesn't really sound small or claustrophobic to me, just uncluttered and atmospherically hostile. Not violent or evil, but caustic and snarly. Quite enjoyable, actually. I should really listen to it more often. Enjoy the rest of your evening. Tomorrow might turn out to not be horrible.

The Band – Stage Fright

Who's ready to talk shit about a pretty sunset? No, I don't have any more Modest Mouse records, but I do have The Band's third album, Stage Fright. Critics were confused by the contradiction between the jaunty, not at all nostalgic roots rock, and the not particularly jaunty, borderline cynical lyrical content. Good.

I'll fully admit, I didn't like it much the first 5 or 6 listens, but that's because it wasn't relevant until now. Tonight, it's perfect. When it's all said and done, I'm going to have more than one write-in vote for several offices in Calhoun County, IA, because it's unelect everybody season. They should just change the county slogan to "we're tired of people living here and wasting valuable pig farm acreage." I'd probably get assassinated 3 hours into my political career. You don't know the shape I'm in.

I think I like The Band better than the Grateful Dead. Like I said, it took me a while to like it. The sticking point for everyone seems to be the hard to conceptualize "confessional" quality. There's a lot of heroin, they're burning out, most of the songs are Randy Newman-esque here's literally what I see type things, and that's not what anyone was ready to swallow from the imagineers of the reinvented American Myth. And we end with probably the most pessimistic song I never wrote. Some of your neighbors would so muchly prefer any lie or rumor over having to care about and/or embrace each other. All you can do is hang your head and hope it will get better soon. And vote against the incumbent, even if you have to write in my name. I don't mind, as long as I don't win. That wouldn't help anybody.

Red Hot Chili Peppers – Freaky Styley

I still have hundreds of albums we could listen to, but not really anything to say about them. Since that's my problem, not theirs, we'll just listen to the crazy second album by Red Hot Chili Peppers, Freaky Styley.

George Clinton produced this album. No, you heard me right, *the* George Clinton agreed to produce the album for 25k, let Anthony get through his heroin withdrawals at his house, helped write and arrange the 30% of the album they hadn't written yet, and let his drug dealer do the interjections on Yertle the Turtle as payment for all the cocaine they were snorting. He's the one (Clinton, not the drug dealer) who said take Africa by The Meters, but rewrite it about *your* Africa, aka Hollywood.

This is pre-Frusciante/Smith funk fusion. Not rock with a funk background like the Chili Peppers you know, but funk with a punk attitude and style. Flea and their manager contacted Clinton because a) they hated the way their first album turned out to be watered down and superficial, b) McClaren wanted them to be a watered-down commercial rock band centered on Kiedis (you know, like they turned into 30 years later), and c) their fans constantly compared them to Parliament Funkadelic anyway, so why on earth not humbly request the services of the Funkfather himself?

In my mind I keep mistakenly assuming it sounds dated and corny. It doesn't. Juvenile sure, but not at all throw away garbage. I'm surprised every time I play it, it's actually fun.

On a personal note, I can't help but make a connection between Catholic School Girls Rule and the Catholic School Girls In Trouble scene from Kentucky Fried Movie. I warned you not to watch that movie if you haven't already seen it. RHCP constantly sings about sex, I assumed you knew that, but not in a particularly offensive way. Thirty Dirty Birds and Yertle The Turtle are the real highlight of the album, but you really need the previous 35 minutes to fully appreciate them. 40-minute album, right in the sweet spot.

I have their other two huge albums too, but this early 2nd album is pretty spectacular in my book. Give it a try, if/when you get the chance.

Delaney & Bonnie – Motel Shot

Delaney and Bonnie captured the imagination of America with their brutal string of robberies and murders, and their almost titillatingly secret unmarried sex life. I'll be voting against everyone on Tuesday in Knierim where they robbed the State Savings Bank...

... no, I'm sorry, I'm being told that I've confused my Bonnies again. I must have misunderstood the title for a headline. Motel Shot appears to be a concept about the kind of late-night jam sessions traveling musicians would have with their touring companions after the gig. Duane Allman, Gram Parsons, and Leon Russell appear courtesy of their own handlers, and Christgau gives it an A, for whatever that's worth. I've never heard it before, but I do know that they had a reputation for being spectacular in concert and underwhelming on record. I have no basis for comparison, so roll that beautiful bean footage (I also know I've used that joke before, but the image of eating canned beans on the lam was too great to resist given that we did actually have some variety of Bush's tonight).

Oh, yeah, a bunch of people in a big room making all sorts of racket. Obviously it's all miced up fancy, but the aesthetic is really nice. Ooh, Rock of Ages is deliciously terrible. It's all a little more Gospel than I was expecting, but I'm not complaining at all. If that confuses you, maybe I can help explain. I do not believe in religion, but I do believe that every person has to build some purpose for themselves. Quite a lot of my self-constructed mental universe coincides with general "Christian" values, but without the authority of a god, or his kids, or his revolving cast of Press Secretaries. Complex causality by coincidence, C is for Cookie (that's good enough for me if you're a little slow on the draw). If you're a fan of quantum theory, everything moves in electromagnetic waves until you try to look at the place it might probably be. Go ahead and talk about Jesus, he's a pretty interesting character just trying to make his immediate surroundings less terrible for everyone to occupy. Who can't relate? Personally, I'm a lot closer to Stoicism than anything, but you gotta do you. The only line I draw in the sand is don't prey on me 'cause I'm the big mangy dog you mistook for a sheep.

Yeah, this is really enjoyable. It's ragged, but not in the "we secretly hate each other and want to die" kind of way. Most importantly, it sounds like people playing music because that's what they do. It's authentic. I can't dissect that one any further, I just know it when I hear it. What a great album. Definitely give it a listen some time, I think you'll enjoy it too.

Bottle's hastily assembled Halloween Spooktacular

E: What horror show of an album do you think Bottle will bring out tonight?

C: I dunno, Skip. He's never really been a fan of holidays in general. I mean, he'll play along, but you can always tell he's thinking "every day is [insert holiday] in my head, why's this one special?" Plus, he hasn't sent me out to find anything in a while, so it'll be a surprise to all of us. Maybe Sandra has a guess, try calling her.

Skip picks up the phone and dials Sandra's extension, 4446. Ring, ring, click...

S: You have reached the office of Sandra D. I'm currently in another castle, but if you'll leave your name and a brief message, I'll deal with it later...
E: No luck. She's probably out painting mustaches on all the garden gnomes.
C: I doubt it, Skip, it's too windy to do anything out there today. Guess we'll just be surprised. What's that scratching sound?
E: Oh, it's just GREGORY decorating the hallways with cobwebs and rodent entrails. Halloween is in his bones after all.

The Compiler's head whipped around so fast it almost fell off.

C: That's the first joke I've ever heard from you, are you feeling alright?
E: I am kind of tired. I mean the news feed is spitting out so much nonsense lately it's impossible to filter all of it. My brain feels like a colander with swear word sized holes in it. I'm sure we've all noticed the decline in quality....
C: Yeah, I hear you. How am I supposed to compile any of it into a coherent experience? It's like there's a horrible disease in the air that everyone forgot about, or something. Best not to worry too much. Let's go for a walk, I found a couple new hallways off the gallery that might be worth exploring.
E: You mean that creepy hallway with all the stock photo families and faceless ghosts running in and out of doorways? No thanks.
C: What? You're scared of Bottle's band portraits? Oh yeah, I forgot you have no imagination. Yeah, I guess it is a

little creepy for the uninitiated. You just gotta walk it like you own it and tell anyone who gets in your way that you're with the opening band. Nobody knows who they are anyway. Everybody gets a little disoriented their first time backstage. C'mon....

Little did they know that Bottle was indeed planning something. Perhaps not an elaborate Oingo Boingo concert in Rodney Dangerfield's dorm room, or the spectacle of his surprise Triple Lindy at the end, but maybe a suitably impressive dive on its own terms...

B: Good eeeevening. I am count Bottle von Beefenstein, your host for this evening's entertainment. Though I am sure you are aware of my personal peculiar postulate that every day is Halloween inside my head, I will play along and give you the guided tour of three truly terrifying albums from my personal collection. A trifecta of terror, from the unlikeliest of ululators. A ghastly group of greatest hits.

We begin as we surely must. Halloween, after all, is the only time I can really talk about Classics IV. Luckily, Spooky is the second track on this one, so you simply have to suffer only one set of sappy saxophone solos before it begins. They might not be the first thing you think of when it comes to terror, what's really scary about this album is the band photos.

Call me crazy, but there's something truly terrifying about them, a Texas Chainsaw Massacre vibe about running into this band of secret psychos out in the country. They sure miss a lot of ladies they used to know and love. Give it a bloodbath in that twangy guitar, massive vibraphone, cavernous reverb, and I get a Buffalo Bill, lotion in a basket, kind of terror that send shivers down my back and goose bumps all over.

Traces of love that didn't work out right? Strange changes taking place on a dark foggy night? Maybe try not murdering all your girlfriends in the basement of an old abandoned farmhouse, Yost, am I right? I guess you don't have to hurry on a soul train ride, you got eternity to go....

"Out of the way, dweeb! Skullthrasher's on in 10." Like a deer in the headlights, Skip stood transfixed by the oncoming steamroller of an effects rack barreling toward him at ludicrous speed, propelled by two behemoth yellow shirted roadies with matching face tattoos. Luckily, he was dragged out of the way by C-man just in time to avoid imminent pancakery. Still shaking, he was ushered into an empty room.

C: Stop sputtering, Skip. You gotta keep walking, like I told you. You can't clam up with stage fright just 'cause you're out of your depths. They'll eat you alive. C'mon, I want to see what's around the next corner...

Onward with this ride into the danger zone. It's Loggins and Messina On Stage! A double doozie of delirium. No, there's nothing particularly terrifying about Loggins or Messina, this is more an esoteric indulgence in the sheer agoraphobia one such as myself might feel at the thought of actually attending a Loggins and Messina concert. See, I used to love going to concerts, right down in the pit with the other gyrating lunatics, but there was one experience so terrible it still gives me nightmares. You don't know real terror unless you've spent an hour and a half surfing the Brownian motion of hundreds of bodies pack together like sardines at a Marilyn Manson concert, the only thought you can possibly have being "if I lose my footing I will literally be trampled to death." I saw Marilyn Manson in concert and all I got was this lousy Merinthophobia. No surprise bear-hugs for Bottle, please. I might get a little stabby after you let me go.

"Stop! I can't take anymore," Skip suddenly screamed. "I'm suffocating on the stifling sorrow of this sappy soft-rock séance!"

Just then a crackly voice, not at all unlike the Wicked Witch of the West, boomed from the loudspeaker with pants wetting ferocity:

"Oh, you mean your Air Supply is getting low? Here, let me help you with that. Gag on THEIR greatest hits."

E: What is that dreadful noise? Why am I feeling woozy all of a sudden?

C: More importantly, Skip, why are you humming "All Out of Love" under your breath? Maybe this was a bad idea. Even I'm not feeling so good now. We should get back to the office, quick.

But no matter how fast they ran, how many corners they turned with comic strafing, those two shadowy figures kept getting closer and closer and louder and louder until our two hapless victims collapsed in a puddle of sobbing gibberish on the linoleum floor.

Then, when no man of conscience could watch them suffer a minute longer, and right before Russell and Hitchcock could sink their vampire fangs into those sun starved throbbing jugulars, a sound much like snapping occurred, and they magically woke in their office with the lights on, only a faint wisp of fog machine smoke slowly dissipating in a halo around them.

"See, Skip, I told you we wouldn't die," said the compiler with a hint of nervous laughter. "I mean, I kind of thought we would for a moment, I need to change pants for reasons I won't talk about, and I'd like you to remind me not to get the wanderlust next Halloween. On the plus side, at least I'm not curious about potential albums anymore. Let's never speak of this embarrassing episode to anyone...."

B: You don't think we were to cruel, do you Sandra?

S: It's Halloween, Bottle. They secretly loved it. See, they are pinkie swearing not to tell anyone as we speak. I know I had fun watching them suffer, and I'm pretty happy with my Air Supply joke.

B: Yeah, that was pretty good. I'm not thrilled we actually had to listen to it, but it is objectively the most frightening album I can think of in my collection. I'd call this Beefoween a success.

S: In my official capacity, I hereby outlaw the word "beefoween," but yes, I agree, totally worth it. Now if you'll excuse me, I have some garden gnomes to bemoustache.

Beastie Boys – Check Your Head

It's time to Check Your Head. It's the third Beastie Boys album, and it's their return to being a band. It's not really hardcore like they started out, it's not alternative rock like everyone calls it, this is a specifically hip-hop band. That's surprisingly unique, and there aren't any others I can think of off the top of my head. Lots of collaborations, but nothing so self-contained.

Believe it or not, this is a golden age structured album. A mix of songs and interludes, a real back and forth between the sampling and band, silly and serious, all of it designed to get your head bobbing. The album is an audio block party, something for everybody to enjoy.

Christgau called it a great concept with "half there execution," like they were Sexual Chocolate or p(nmi)t's Audiodetritus or something. I disagree for the simple reason that he is only comparing them to an idealized image of big-business mainstream, and his judgment is based on the supposed idea that they aren't good at the New Orleans Jazz style they try to emulate. I've said it before and I'll say it now: who told you you aren't allowed to suck, and why can't I enjoy it? Beastie Boys being a band again was seen as a nod to their little coterie of die-hard punk fans instead of the first attempt at actually doing it. Like I said a long time ago, there's a lot of love/hate because on one hand they just straight up peaced out on Simmons and Rubin for Capitol's money machine, but on the other they didn't become anything radically different from what they had always been. He's essentially reading the band as a board meeting gimmick when they aren't. They were a punk band that liked hip hop and invented being both at the same time. It's like ragging on Uriah Heep for being near-prog, you're missing the obvious point that that's what they're doing on purpose.

What does that have to do with anything? Well, 3/4 of the concept for this album is about the lunacy of Bush and Schwarzkopf and Desert Storm. I won't weigh in on that topic, other than to remind you that 10-year-old Bottle watched the largest coalition of nations since WWII hurl depleted uranium at Iraq while Saddam Hussein threw the biological weapons we sold him back at us on live television. Yay, sports team!

Ok, I checked my head. Still pretty terrible in there. At least I have Biz Markie singing about the Beastie Boys coming home to cancel out the air raid sirens.

VI. Capital with Bottle (an adventure in its own right)

$23 Adventure Time

I gave C-lab2021 very explicit instructions this afternoon, and boy did he deliver a doozie of an adventure time. Those instructions were "pick albums by title that Bottle would say "I don't care what it turns out to be, I can't not buy that." $23 dollars later he somehow picked a freshman, a sophomore, a junior, and a graduation montage by total coincidence.

Now, I'm not one of those people who won't tell you they voted for Biden because A) that's not shocking at all and you knew I was going to, B) I've been begging you all to come assassinate me for years, and C) I didn't want Trump to be president the first time, but Bruce Willis still hasn't traveled back to correct it (yay! a 12 Monkeys reference).

I also don't want to just blow through them all in one go, even though we all know I totally do want to, and also not be near a TV or radio from now until next Thursday. We'll compromise and do the next 4 posts as a serial. If you want to get a head start on me, or just want to know what I would have listened to, here's the list of albums:

Life's Hard and Then You Die
Cargo
Pretzel Logic
Der Kommissar

Look for part one later tonight as I adamantly not care what percentage of precincts have reported. I still have to go to work and receive freight either way.

P.S. you're totally allowed to watch it and care, but I can't function like a human being if I do. I know my limits better than anyone.

It's Immaterial – Life's Hard And Then You Die
To paraphrase the poetress of our modern age, we are living in a material world, and I'm an immaterial girl.

B: Life's Hard and Then You Die is the first album by It's Immaterial.
M: But who's it by?
B: It's immaterial.
M: No seriously, tell me who made it.
B: Good gravy, Milton, the band's name is It's Immaterial.
M: Oh, ok, thank you for grammatically clarifying that for me.
B: You're welcome.

These gentlemen are from Liverpool, and the back of the jacket has a photo of a man spraying a flammable liquid from his mouth onto a flaming torch in front of another man with a bucket on his head. I don't care what it turns out to be, I can't not buy it and listen to it.
Get in your car? You betcha! 30 miles or more seems kind of arbitrary, but I'm in for the long haul and I don't mind ridiculous. It's suspiciously Talking Heads-ish, but it's only the first track. Perhaps a bit of an ellipsis is in order...
... song about quitting being a Tupperware salesman ... there's some Pet Shop Boys things going on ha! "Turn off the TV" that's a nice coincidence ... well, Side A is just lovely. You could certainly hear them like a Talking Heads meets Pet Shop Boys rip-off, both musically and thematically, but they have their own personality for sure. It's wildly eclectic in terms of instrumentation, but there's a tangibly mundane quality too. It's about how truly weird and oddly unfulfilling "normal" actually is. On to Side B.

Hello, new-wave take on mariachi. I think what impresses me most is how natural this all feels. It's objectively bizarre, but it feels completely logical and coherent. I think it's the production, because all these radically different instruments from one track to another aren't jarring at all. Oh, Dave Bascombe. Yeah, he did all the big British stuff in the 80s, Tears for Fears, Depeche Mode, even modern stuff like Goldfrapp and Lady Antebellum. I wouldn't have been able to tell you this sounds like him, but as soon as I read he was the producer I could definitely hear it. He does have a very distinct approach to the audio spectrum and how vocals sit in the mix. Think of how Everybody Wants to Rule the World sounds, then imagine any other song sounding like that.

Well, this was delicious. I can't really describe it better than I already did, but it's well worth a listen or 12. Weird, but tangible. Here's what life is like, I'm not sure how I'm supposed to feel about it. No explanations, no hyperbole, no ideology to speak of, it's quite a strange experience to be honest. I really enjoyed it, go give it a try for yourself.

Addendum: sweet! My copy even has the Driving Away From Home bumper sticker still inside.

Men At Work – Cargo

I'm a man at work, I deal with cargo, Lance may not want it anymore, but I can't not buy it.

Cargo is the second Men At Work album, the one they made after the first one we listened to a year ago. Is Colin Hay still quirky? Only one way to find out.

Oh yeah, just wonderful. Men At Work is the Australian equivalent of The Cars (even a couple of Elliot, sorry Ron Strykert, songs), but with a definite Elvis Costello quality all around (critics would say Sting/The Police, and sure I can hear it too, but it's way more Elvis Costello to me).

This album has the standard bipolar critical response. Some say it lacks the punch of the big debut singles but the album as a whole is better, others say it's an REO Speedwagon album (two hit songs and a bunch of pointless filler). Ummmmm, yeah, I'm gonna totally be that guy and remind you it's called Cargo, as in "here, I brought you all this stuff, get it off my truck and deal with it yourself. My job is done here, have a nice day. Or, don't. See you next time I have more stuff to bring you."

They actually had to postpone its release because the first album was still selling so well that they would legitimately tank their own profits. Has any other band ever had that problem, ever, at all, anywhere? Put that second album in your back pocket guys, we're still pressing additional runs of the first one.

Man, this is great. No, it's not in your face like the first album, but listening to it is absolutely fun. Seriously, I could just put this thing on repeat and be content for days. It's paranoid, sure, but not exhausting or fleeting. I can't imagine actually tiring of any of it, it's not cheesy or cliché or annoying, these are just objectively great songs. Ha! Bid my devil friend goodbye. One can only hope.

We're 2 for 2, both for tonight's albums and Men At Work's discography, go on and love it as much as I do.

Steely Dan – Pretzel Logic

If we were playing the standard Sesame Street game One of These Things Is Not Like The Others, you wouldn't even need to know the fourth album to know that the lower left hand corner is the answer (coincidentally where I seem to fall on the political compass; I'm quite a bit more anarchic than Gandhi).

Steam Powered Dildo is an awesome name for a band, but ABC is not Bottle of Beef so Becker and Fagan went with Burroughs' name for it, Steely Dan. Here's their 3rd album,

Pretzel Logic. It's a 5-star album across the board. The only criticism of the album is that most people don't have a clue what any of it's about, but when has that ever mattered? The point is that this is one of the few jazz-rock albums where no one can find any sort of pretension or insult lurking beneath the surface. They certainly aren't trying to call you an idiot for not "getting it." Jay Black famously likened them to the Charleses Manson and Starkweather.

I, of course, am a big Skunk Baxter fan, especially when he's going head-to-head with the saxes or imitating a muted trumpet (seriously, East St. Louis Toodle-oo is amazing), but he certainly isn't stealing the show from anybody else on this album. It all just works so well. Jazz rock is kind of a misnomer. I can't think of a better term for Steely Dan, but this isn't at all like Chicago, or Lighthouse, or the Prog of The Moody Blues or Ponty.

This is one of those honest albums I mentioned. There's no gimmick here, this sounds like everyone involved said "yep, that's perfect, that's exactly what we wanted to do, and you can't deny it's great."

It doesn't matter if you don't understand it, they feel the monkey in your soul, and how could you possibly call them liars? He's not gonna stop you from buying the more expensive peanuts and chestnuts, be mostly he sells hot fresh pretzels. Buy two pretzels and split the difference, that's Pretzel Logic.

After The Fire – ATF (Der Kommissar)

So, what do we do after the fire? We listen to After The Fire's compilation album Der Kommissar. In the US it was simply called ATF, and very confusingly reused the cover art from their 3rd album Batteries Not Included, but the whole point was to release their translated cover of Falco's Der Kommissar in album rather than single form.

This isn't my normal album review, it's more a "meta" interlude in a much larger train of thought. See, 3/4 of the albums C-the-ball-be-the-ball picked happened to be synth heavy new wave. Plus, I'm about to take a break from album reviews, and invite you to actually read Das Kapital with me.

Everything alright, officer? I assure you it won't be as unpleasant as you think it might be, much like this album. If you think After The Fire is a one hit wonder, you might be surprised that there's absolutely no reason why they should be, this is lovely even if it is a compilation for the sake of that one hit. They started out playing prog rock, but transitioned quite well into new wave. It's much more pop than either It's Immaterial or Men At Work, but definitely not in a bad way.

Sure, we still have to wait until the smoldering rubble is cool enough to touch before salvaging what's left, but all this stuff is just stuff. But wowzers it's great stuff, and except for Alzheimer's nothing can take that experience away from us.

Capital with Bottle

A couple days ago I shared a link so all my friends could download Capital and read it for free (I'm naughty). I've casually read chapter one, and I assume you ran out and found a copy as soon as I mentioned it in the last review. Of course you did, you guys are inquisitive and not content to just recycle third-hand catch phrases from the last hundred-something years. So, you're probably thinking "why am I reading this boring treatise on classical market economics by an old dead guy in a library with nothing better to do than read history and politico-economic discourse and then write about it from his own point of view?" The answer of course is that that's what scholars do; that's what half the country thinks is a waste of time. It's why facebook and twitter and wikipedia aren't valid sources of academic knowledge.

So, chapter one. What's a commodity? It's a useful thing people make/produce specifically to trade for other useful things. That's a loaded definition, and chapter one presents a reasonably thorough explanation of how the concept of value is embedded inside a commodity. If it seems boring and pedantic, that's because it is; you have to define all of your terminology or else no one will understand what you're actually talking about. A pretzel doesn't just magically equal 3/5 of a roasted peanuts (that's a Steely Dan joke if you somehow skipped the last 192 pages).

It can be a little hard to really understand what we aren't talking about in chapter 1: no money, no different types of labor, no profit or loss, just the simple mechanism by which we determine the amount of different things being equivalent. Marx says that equivalence comes from human labor, whereas people before him said "I dunno." Not specialized labor like you're thinking about, but the abstract notion that there is an average time and energy required to complete any task, and that we can determine equivalences from the sum total of the labor involved. He uses weaving linen as an example.

He also uses that infamous word "bourgeois," but he uses it only in the contemporaneous context that his audience understands it to explain why it makes the whole thing really confusing.

Are you confused yet? Yes, it's a book that many people have used to justify killing each other, but so is the Bible, and so too are nonsense Beatles lyrics. The only purpose of this endeavor is to actually read it so that you can use the fact that you have actually read it as basis for your future feelings and opinions about Marxist theory, whatever they may be.

Marx is not simply a crazy guy in the woods like the Unabomber. He is widely considered the inventor of modern sociology. Capital is by all definitions a scholarly text on economics (albeit cutting-edge 1800s economics), whether you agree with his theories or not, and I believe in complete intellectual freedom. I will obviously weigh in with my own opinions, but it makes no difference whether you or I agree with Marx or not, only that we understand the subject matter. I can't stress this enough, you must let go of any preconceived notions and simply listen to another person express their ideas.

Chapter 2 of Capital should kind of smack you in the forehead like you could have had a V8. You have to A) understand that people own their wares, and B) mutually agree to exchange them. You trade things that aren't valuable to you for things you want (aka are valuable to you) in proportions you both agree are equivalent.

There are some important points here. First, the value or equivalence of commodities is not magically apparent on the surface, it only comes into existence at the moment of trade, and each and every trade redefines those values. If you try to escape that exchange in some way, then there is no value of equivalence anymore. Second, money is itself a commodity, but it functions as a universal equivalent because everyone accepts the exchange of money as a commodity. The confusing part is that as soon as you accept this universal equivalent as money, you tend to forget all of the complex relationships that gave it comparative value in the first place. Third, you have to again remind yourself what we are not talking about. We aren't talking about the intricacies of haggling, bargaining, and negotiation. We are looking at a functioning system of trade after the labor/production is over.

That last distinction is important. We aren't promising to do work in the future, or guessing about the usefulness of the commodities at hand. That usefulness is constantly being evaluated in the process of exchange, and we the observers are not actively participating. The active participants load up the useful things they have but don't need, and head out to exchange them for different useful things with other people doing the same. That's "the economy" as far as this book is concerned at the moment.

I should also mention that we aren't really concerned with the end notes of each chapter. They serve as documentation of the ideas he is including or arguing about, but they don't really do much for the kind of naive reading we are doing. We aren't sitting around a table plotting world domination, or studying for a test. We might disagree with his descriptions or assumptions, but we have to remember that we're listening to Marx express ideas. We can't start debating those ideas until after we understand what he's trying to say.

Chapter 3 begins the introduction to precious metals as the basis for monetary systems. We're getting close to our modern understanding, so it's easy to let your imagination run away with you. The important thing to keep in mind is that we imagine a "gold standard" for the equivalences of precious metals. We can use any such metal as money so long as its own value remains consistent to the value of gold, which is in turn based on the labor of obtaining it. The actual price of buying gold does not affect its status as a universal equivalent because that characteristic is based on units of weight. An ounce of gold is an ounce of gold no matter how much stuff you can trade for it.

All this stuff is, to my mind, basic economics. Certain aspects of it may be more or less understandable to you, but I think we can all mostly agree that it is a reasonable explanation of the historical development of Western Economics, or at the very least the things you were taught with regard to economics in a "common sense" kind of way.

It's easy to get carried away if you try to give a present-day example, but I think I can do a reasonable job. Let's say I have way too many records that I don't want to listen to anymore, but I don't have any potatoes that I want to eat. I know from all my trips to the grocery store that I can buy a bag of potatoes for around $3, and I know plenty of people who would give me $3 for one of my records. In this ideal model of economics, I go sell a record to that guy for $3, then go buy a bag of potatoes for $3 and presto change-o, economy accomplished. Yes, that's simplistic, but I think you'll agree that it's a tangible example of real-world activity.

We can let our minds wander a little at this point. With regard to labor, it's easy to justify why used records are cheaper than new records, computers cost more than a bag of dirt, boiling up a pretzel isn't quite as costly as roasting peanuts, a day spent driving a bus isn't really that much different than a day spent entering receipts into a spreadsheet. We all have a mental checklist of things that are roughly equivalent and we exchange the results of that labor frequently enough to keep those relationships relatively stable. We might wake up to find that my potato/record exchange cost $4 or $2, but I would instinctively try to compensate because I haven't changed my mental equivalence between a record and a bag of potatoes; that would take several instances of failed exchanges to adjust. From an observer's standpoint, I'm still selling some quantity of records and using that money to buy some quantity of potatoes, or some other equivalent commodity. So long as there are people who buy my unwanted records, I will exchange them for things I do want in a similar fashion. Got it? Good.

The rest of section 1 is a historical synopsis of the development of fiat currency. Regardless of your feelings about it, it has repeatedly happened throughout history and it's where we are today. So long as nobody jumps ship or tries to get too sneaky, it still works well.

When we continue reading, we see that my example is exactly what Marx describes; his example is the weaver selling

20 yards of linen and using the money to buy a bible of equal price. We aren't reading anything into those specific items, by the way, the weaver is simply trading what he has for what he wants via money the same way I did in my example.

Continuing to read we see that Marx addresses exactly the same problem I raised. I'm looking at pages 136 and 137 in my PDF copy. He talks about all those scenarios where the guy gets surprised by not being able to effectively trade, and points out that so long as he is able to make some trade for his wares the system is functioning properly. One bad day doesn't mean the system is broken. One day he might not get much, the next he might get more, such is life.

What follows is a lengthy description of the process of buying and selling commodities where each purchase removes a commodity while the money continues toward infinity, enabling further purchases. That continual drifting away only stops when someone "takes the money and runs," or less humorously has no intention of spending it. To put it bluntly, if you stop buying things, the economy dies.

The rest of section 2 is kind of an information dump, but it's easy to follow the progression from coins of gold/silver/etc. to paper money that represents only the circulating portion of exchange (the infinite chain of buying things), until finally we get the novel money (currency) issued by "the state" as an abstract representation of bullion. That fiat currency only exists inside the state itself for the obvious reason that anyone outside that state has no understanding of these funny coins and papers as representations of money. There is still a universal form of money at the highest level, but inside a particular community we can use technically worthless representations without any problem, so long as the amount of currency in circulation represents the sum cost of all commodities.

And now, on page 169, we get to hoarding. I don't want to drag this out, so hoarding money is simply not buying things you want. There are good reasons to do it and bad reasons to do it, but what follows for the rest of chapter 3 is a description of the growth of local hoards (think of banks in general), and the growth of credit and debt to such an extent that the whole system becomes unstable and wildly unpredictable save for the fact that when banks have way more money than normal it is obvious that the exchange of commodities is stagnating.

Hold on Bottle. This is all starting to sound like what the people who are somehow vehemently against Marxism are saying.

Well, you know, we're only on page 200 something of a 2,000 page multi-volume work. He could make a u-turn. He could dive into the empty swimming pool head first and not prove me right. I don't get the sense that the first 3 chapters are written in the form of sarcasm, but I'm also not opposed to the idea that I'm the one who has it all backward. He hasn't told us we're wrong for participating in common-sense economic activity, but maybe I'm missing something. Maybe this is just a faulty bizarro copy of Capital and Marx really thought that manipulating currency streams to generate new forms of economic slavery was super awesome. Look at those schmucks making stuff and trading it for other stuff, what a bunch of losers.

Now, I'm not going to make any real predictions, I'm just commenting on reading the book. I am reading the book, and so far he has outlined classical economics, elaborated on the ways that people attempt to manipulate that system for unfair advantage, and given us clear examples of how that historically played out. It appears to be backward from what everyone claims Marxist theory to be, and actually coincides with what explicitly anti-Marxist talking points say we should be doing instead. He could be trolling us, and I'll have a nice hearty belly laugh if he is.

I'm going to take a break and give you all the chance to digest both the book and what I've said so far. If you're just now joining us, we're reading Capital by Karl Marx and I am shocked you managed to open the book to this exact page. Go find a copy and read it. The only real danger is that we might learn something in the process.....

Today is kind of a refresher course. I just want to outline what happens in the first 3 chapters of Capital. At a fundamental level, we humans barter, that is face to face exchange of commodities. Obviously, bartering can only work in a highly localized community, and it is an explicitly social activity. On top of this barter system, we superimpose the concept of a universal equivalent, aka money. Money is an intricate concept, both a commodity in its own right and an external measurement of comparative value, but we all understand it as a useful way to facilitate exchange over longer distances, between very different communities, in exactly the same social exchanges of commodities that constitute barter.

But, this is only one side of economic activity. There is a mirror image, so to speak. While one person trades a commodity for money then trades that money for other commodities, his counterpart trades money for a commodity then trades those commodities for money. We can use whatever terms we want for these two people, but "worker" and "merchant" seem the easiest to my mind. The really important part is that we distinguish between the two frames of reference: C-M-C and M-C-M. We might be participating in one or the other for any particular exchange, so we have to understand which one is taking place.

Similarly, there is a difference between the regulating of money as a commodity in its own right and using that money for its intended universal equivalence. For now though, we simply assume that a person is engaged in one or the other at any particular time.

You will also notice that Marx has a, shall we say, Bottle of Beef quality to his writing. You can tell there are things that make him mad, and ideas he thinks are stupid. I gloss over that stuff because it doesn't really change the theoretical model he is describing. He's mad about certain ways this system has been manipulated and our task is to understand why he thinks those things are terrible.

I've given you an example of how it might apply to my own life in a limited context. Though remedial, I think most of you can see how the C-M-C side of this model describes some basic principles we all accept. It may not represent your actual day-to-day life very well, but we are reading a book from the 19th century here in the 21st century. Maybe the closest modern-day phenomenon is a theoretical "garage sale" based economy. People sell their unwanted stuff, take that money, and buy your unwanted stuff; old records, clothes, cookware, chicken waterers, toys, useful things being exchanged through the universal equivalent of our modern form of money. The overall prices are extremely small (much smaller than buying these items new) because the amount of work spent acquiring them is miniscule compared to making them in the first place. Swap meets and pawn shops might also be reasonable examples of finite commodity markets; the more useful or desirable an item, the more money we all expect to spend. Furthermore, if we all stop participating, then the pawn shop will go out of business.

Everybody happy so far? Questions? Things about the model that don't make sense, or things you completely disagree with? Too bad. As I've said before, I think I understand it, he hasn't said anything illogical or false, it's a reasonable basic foundation for economic activity distilled from studying the history of Western civilizations. Still though, we should leave some time for it to percolate in our minds before going on to chapter 4.

We have to be very careful when we read chapter 4 because words are tricky little things that twist and distort. So, rather than reading his words from our own internal dictionary, we have to read them with what Marx tells us those words mean to him. He's going to define "capital" and "capitalist" in a very specific way. It's a fun little game show: Bottle of Beef presents You're Not A Capitalist. You almost certainly participate in the thing we all call "capitalism," but probably not in the way you thought you did.

Capital comes from the markup of a commodity, and it exists only in the act of obtaining a commodity in order to sell it at a higher price for a profit that you do not intend to spend. In his own words, you invest $100 in some commodity you don't actually care about simply to get back $110. Then take that $110 and do it again to get back $130, and so on, all the while refusing to spend any of that profit for things you will consume. A capitalist is a person who practices this type of money hoarding at the expense of the market, draining the market itself for power. In other words, a capitalist intentionally destabilizes the market itself for monetary gain. That is a radically different notion than our modern-day usage of the term capitalism. For us regular everyday people the hoarding of money as Marx describes it is a perfectly acceptable practice because we are 1) saving in order to spend for much more valuable commodities than simple barter can support, and 2) we have no intention of radically damaging the market itself for personal gain. Scrooge McDuck is a capitalist, Papa John is just an extravagant doofus.

Jokes aside, we have to understand what is and isn't capitalism according to Marx. The simple fact that each person who handles a commodity adds value to the final price of that commodity is not capitalism, per se. Rather, it is simply the accumulation of labor. Fruit from 1,000 miles away that came on two trains and a semi should obviously cost more than fruit grown 2 miles away by a local farmer (the difficulty of growing fruit in your specific location notwithstanding). That's because there are many more people exchanging their labor for money along the way. That is what Marx lumps under the term "coincidental," because the consumer cannot reasonably predict those fluctuations on a day-to-day basis. So long as they eventually even themselves out, everything is as good as it can be.

In contrast, a Marxian capitalist is someone who intentionally manipulates that entire process in order to pull the commodity of money out of the system for purely monetary gain, say pocketing the difference between the cost of labor here, and that astonishingly cheap labor available in that poorer country over there, for example. That is a large part of the reason he equates a capitalist with a miser.

Are you simply buying and selling things to amass more money than everyone else so that they can't afford to buy the things they want? No? Congratulations! You're not a capitalist, according to Marx.

B: You might be surprised that that's it. That's the end of Capital.

M: But, but, what about the next 2,000 pages?

B: There's no easy way to tell you this, Milton, but Marx is dead. What follows is at best Christopher Tolkien's loving continuation of his dad's notes about Middle Earth, and at worst Lenin telling his goons to go ahead and murder the Romanov's in the basement where they are being held captive under false pretenses of rescue. But, he died well before that. The Czaricide was totally Lenin's idea.

Volume 1 of Capital is simply a description of capitalism, what it is and how it develops. This is a materialist description, meaning that it focuses on describing the actual historical events that lead to a particular situation rather than philosophies and ideals. It does not pretend to solve those problems, it simply elaborates how they come to be a problem.

So, Marx is describing the abstract concept of commodity markets and he breaks the whole thing down into two binary relationships. There are producers of commodities, call them workers, craftsmen, laborers, whatever. They stand in opposition to merchants, not because there is any conflict or animosity between the two, but because trading commodities involves both a seller and a buyer, both operating from fundamentally different points of view. The producer is interested in exchanging for equivalence and the merchant is interested in maintaining that equivalence in the broadest sense. The producer compares wants, the merchant compares values. This whole market stands in another opposition to the owners of the market itself, that is "the state." Whatever form that state takes, it has the job of not letting the commodity of money grow wildly out of proportion to the entire quantity of commodities, money being the universal equivalent.

Marx the person sees this as a form of internal conflict. That conflict manifests in antagonism between the participants in a market and the, shall we say, regulators of the market itself. Marx is obviously referring to workers and factory owners (the proletariat and the bourgeoisie). The closest modern equivalent, in my opinion, is the conflict between everyday people and major corporations. I don't mean the people in offices doing their jobs like you, I mean that imaginary human that we have come to associate with the corporation itself.

Kevin in accounting is no more a Capitalist than Helen punching rivet holes on the line. They are both trading their commodity (abstract labor) for money and intend to spend that money for other commodities. Their individual salaries are theoretically irrelevant. I think the confusing part is that we forget that Helen isn't selling those rivet holes to the company for their equivalent value of money any more than Kevin is looking to steal some part of Helen's paycheck. Instead, Helen and Kevin and everyone else are simply contributing to the total amount of labor in the same way that everyone in your family might have specific daily chores. The general price of an airplane is determined by the amount of labor involved in producing it compared to other commodities.

So, can we construct a scenario that will give us some insight into Karl's opinion of this situation? I think so, we just can't get too carried away.

Let's say they make airplanes, and for all sorts of reasons nobody wants airplanes anymore. They can't sell their airplanes, so there isn't much point in working there anymore and they close up shop and head off in separate directions to find a different thing to make. That sucks, but such is life.

But if instead, Barry the boss only cares about turning his 5 million investment into 7 million, he might invent all sorts of ways to manipulate the system. He might cut everyone's paycheck in half regardless of the final selling price without any concern for what that will do to the larger economy. That would make me mad, so I can see why Marx would be mad too. Marx would probably blame that terrible thing on Barry's Capitalist greed because there was no market reason to do it other than money grabbing. Helen and Kevin might be pretty mad too and kill Barry. Marx is saying he's seen it happen a thousand times and trying to describe why he thinks it happens. Obviously, he doesn't want people like Barry to do that, but he doesn't have any sure-fire plan to stop it from happening a thousand more times. All he's saying is that he thinks it is an inherent danger of Capitalism in general.

That's my interpretation of what we've read. Do you disagree with my interpretation? Have I unknowingly made some crazy assumption? Do we need to go backward and read The Communist Manifesto for historical perspective?

If you need some deeper explanation of why I'm doing this, it's because today's general daily banter about Marxism and Communism and lefty righty revolutions don't make any sense to me. People in general are saying things backward from how I understand them, and I think that's because no one has actually read any of this stuff. It's just empty-headed regurgitating of third or fourth-hand gossip.

If my reading of Capital strikes you as weird, that's because it assumes that we aren't hell-bent on burning the whole thing to the ground. Neither are we content to murder the bourgeoisie (whoever they are) and become the ruling class as a middle step toward utopia.

Marxism as a political philosophy entails doing away with markets altogether, removing the system that creates a Capitalist mentality. But, as I've showed you, his complaints are quite valid. He doesn't like child labor, the inability to have and use what you produce, the trophy wife oppression of women, the way that the exploited class revolts only to become the new bourgeoisie, in short exploitation.

The biggest problem with reading the theory is that it's very easy to just walk away and call it nonsense. But it's not nonsense. If there's enough food being produced for everyone to eat, let everyone eat it. If there isn't, produce more food. If there's too much food over there and not enough here, spread it out. Does that pretty shade of green come with a side of arsenic poisoning? Stop making it.

Am I a Communist? No. Am I angry about a lot of the same things all of you and Marx are angry about? Yes. The biggest difficulty in all of this is that we get so wrapped up in the ideology that we lose the meaningful dialog about the actual problems. We forget that people argued with Marx on certain points, and agreed with him on others.

We are constantly bickering about theories of how people will react in a given situation, but making no effort to plan for those situations. I'm willing to work hard for the rewards of that hard work, I'm not willing to grind away at a stupid task just so you can have a McMansion in a gated community and tell me I'm a loser.

There has to be some meaningful compromise.

Ok, so we've read volume 1 of Capital (and possibly revisited the Communist Manifesto in the process). Obviously, we could keep going in the understanding that Marx the person isn't there anymore. He spent the last few years of his life doing exactly what I do. Writing notes, essays, doing more research, but he died and Engels did all the assembling. Marx isn't there to debate his ideas, debate other Communists with different ideas, change his mind, watch the US do all sorts of terrible things all over the world, privatize prisons and throw drug addicts in there then capitalize on their free labor. Sure, he was alive and reading about our civil war as it happened, but he would have had a field day over the last hundred years.

The popular sentiment now is that we are in "late stage capitalism," that information dump I mentioned where it's all wildly uncontrollable and everyone overreacts and we burn it all to the ground. Some people think Trump was trying to prevent that, others (like me) think that he was bafoonishly going on national television and unknowingly reciting a bizarre mishmash of Fascist and Communist talking points. He inherited a capitalist fortune with absolutely no understanding of how he himself had been exploited to create it.

Regardless, we should be able to come to some explanation of what is or isn't Marxism with regard to his narrow definition of Capitalism in general. Remember, Marx has told us that capitalism develops on top of market-based economics through the manipulation of capital (obtained by draining the market of money by continually devaluing labor). Even though his theory is that this development is inevitable, we can see that the two things are quite different in his mind, and we know that his larger idea is preventing the exploitation. Marx the self-taught economic theorist has no idea how to do that, so Marx the Communist says unless you have a better idea, throw the whole thing in the dumpster and light it on fire.

Is Marx the Communist actually saying "kill Barry the Boss anyway, make airplanes to your heart's content, and fly them wherever you want," or is he simply telling us Barry doesn't own the labor of his employees and we should refuse to work for him without adequate compensation? We can't answer those questions.

What we can do is compare the blatant idealism of Communism to the blatant greed of Exceptionalist Capitalism as Marx might understand it. I call it exceptionalist because America (the idealized nation) believes itself to be unique, devoid of similarity to past cultures and nations, the exception to every theory of everything. Obviously, I think that's absurd, but that's not the point. The point is that Marx was simply building an opposite idea to the forms of Western Capitalism he himself experienced. Those forms are not exactly what we call capitalism in daily conversation, but more closely resemble what we call Crony Capitalism (not happy go lucky market risk, but political favoritism for certain businesses over others through lobbying or straight up bribery).

Arguing for a stateless society is actually a Marxist idea. The state before Marxism is the regulator of the commodity of money, the state after Marxism is the absence of the need for money because we collectively make what we all agree we want. Words are tricky little things, remember. "The State" can and does refer to very different ideas because it actually applies to the rule book not the referee. The conflict manifests between the participants inside the market and the regulators controlling the commodity of money. Marx says Capitalism creates a world economy in its own image; wealthy nations exploiting poorer nations for cheap labor and political power. That certainly seems to be what we are doing, and it's making the problem worse. And as for private property, grazing cattle on public land is only possible if it's "public land" after all.

Having the working class be the ruling class makes no sense, it is merely the closest analogy Marx could use to describe it. Saying that a heavily regulated market is Marxist makes no sense because there is no market. The whole thing is nonsensical because it has been defined as an irreconcilable binary opposition with pure greed on one hand and complete satiation on the other. Reality lives somewhere in the middle.

What I'm trying to get at is that defining your position in terms of this bizarre Capitalism v Communism thing is nonsense from both sides. The actual Marxist view of capitalism focuses on the common-sense things that we pretty much all agree are terrible, and the Capitalist view of Communism defends those terrible things while blaming Communists for forcing them to do it. Regular everyday people can't tell the difference anymore, so we get anti-Capitalist conspiracy theories from ardent Capitalists claiming that Communists want everyone to be homeless and steal your car to drive to their tax funded abortion appointment.

Too much Bottle on that one? Sorry, I just don't want to go back to being exploited, I mean work tomorrow.

[Sometimes you have to leave a page blank, you know?]

VII. Scenes from the blog III

3 random Bad Religion albums

Suddenly it came to me, we did the bookends of my Bad Religion collection, but what about the middle? Recipe for Hate, Stranger Than Fiction, and No Substance are my favorites after all. Why? Because the songs are great.

I don't think I could really tell a story with them, and I certainly can't review them. They are so ingrained in my brain that I can't tell the difference between them and myself. I could tell meandering anecdotes, I guess.

Nah, we'll just leave it at they are my favorite. I shouldn't have to explain why. I'm allowed to just like stuff. The sarcasm is probably a big part of it. And the abject refusal to recognize authority. Oh, and I really like that idea that we are all a microcosm of the human race. Plus, the idea that the real, ugly, mundane world is more important than idealism and ideology, that really seeing the terrible stuff is how you develop compassion, that life isn't striving for an image, it's the living it. No matter how much you disagree with me, we are of the same plague.

Yes, you can tell that Recipe For Hate is decidedly not major label while the other two are, and you can tell that Brett isn't there for No Substance, but none of that changes how much I like them. They are great albums in spite of all that. All three have clear concepts: the various ways in which all of this modern, urban, industrial, unthinking, corporate lack of individuality suuuuuuuuuuuuuucks!

Insane Clown Posse – The Great Milenko

Don't be mad 'cause I'm doin' me better than you doin' you. I got a raise today. Not a secret strings attached raise, a proper keep doing a great job for more money raise. So, obviously, I went on a great hip-hop binge. Childish Gambino, Run The Jewels, Geto Boys, Gravediggaz (I love horror core, no surprise), and then I thought "what's a great album from a terrible rap group?"

I have an album for that! Here's The Great Milenko from Insane Clown Posse. No, we aren't going to learn how magnets work, but we do get an intro from Alice Cooper. I'm sure you all know ICP is a concept group like Coheed & Cambria, or Mac Sabbath. They are insane clowns in an evil carnival from the Netherworld. Each album is centered around the arrival of a new character from the carnival. Milenko is kind of like the Ghost of Christmas Future, all the songs are sort of getting what's coming to you fables. Obviously, the whole thing fizzled out into nonsense by the last album, Shangri La was heaven and they turned the whole thing into a weird pseudo-Christian joke, but in the early days, the marketing gimmick about the world ending was fun.

I've heard most of their other albums, I have The Ringmaster hiding around here somewhere too. They aren't as good. We could analyze it from all sorts of perspectives, but mostly it's the juvenile humor used as a foil for calling out hypocrisy that I like. That doesn't mean they aren't terrible, it's just the reason I can thoroughly enjoy it. Even if you think the whole this is completely stupid and grotesque, you have to admit that this album does an amazing job of it. It's an in-depth exploration of that rage feeling of wanting revenge for injustice, like Offspring's Bad Habit.

Slash, Legs Diamond, and Steve Jones are on here too. They make fun of themselves, you get band mythos and testicle jokes, the beats and samples are great, classic hip-hop funny spoken interludes.

I can't help it, I'm laughing out loud, it's so awesomely ridiculous, I absolutely love it. It's a great album for every reason I've ever called any album great. Yes, it takes a strong sense of terrible humor to appreciate, but I've got exactly the terrible sense of humor necessary, and I'm not ashamed to enjoy it. Cheers.

Meat Puppets – No Joke

No joke, I'm at a loss as to what to write about anything. So, we'll just listen to Meat Puppets. Too High To Die was their mainstream breakthrough, and with No Joke they happily crawled back underground. I never have much to say about stuff I really like anyway, so just enjoy this bizarre country meets stoner metal approach to mid-90s alternative noise rock. It's Meat Puppets, you should just expect weird and all over the place. Great songs though. Go enjoy it while I figure out who to be anymore. Toodles.

Roger Miller – Dang Me

S: Serious? That's it? You're just gonna flip the switch and walk away? Leave it all behind? Look at all the awesome stuff we accomplished, Bottle. What will Marvin and The Compiler do? We're all just supposed to sit here and wait for GREGORY to eat us?

B: Dang me, Sandra, I don't know. I was just chug-a-luggin' away from the orange nightmare. I assume he cornered p(nmi)t in a dark alley and chopped his head off or something. I don't think Bridbrad and Gladys are coming back either, and I've used up most of my rage-o-hol. Who's gonna worry if Bottle doesn't come home tonight? I'm pretty terrible, you know. You squares make the world go round, not Bottle.

S: It takes all kinds to make a world, Bottle. That's why we love you like we do. We all feel lonesome and miserable sometimes, I mean not usually because things are slowly improving again, but we get it. You can't give up for real.

B: Sure I can, but I hear you. I just don't know what else to do now that he who shall not be mentioned is on his way down the drain.

S: Everybody needs a break now and then, but I'm sure you'll think of something. It's not like the escalator suddenly started moving the other direction, now did it?

B: Alright, I guess if you want me to....

As Bottle slowly meanders away from Sandra's office with his hands in his pockets, kicking a conveniently appearing rock for that genuine lovable loser authenticity, he suddenly stops, cocks his head and looks over his left shoulder.

Slowly the confused squint morphs into a smirk on its way to what might possibly qualify as a smile if your family name is Addams.

B: Ha! I've got an album for that!

Cypress Hill – Black Sunday
Yes, I am fully aware that you are loco, and no I don't particularly want to eat a bowl of dick up. Is it wrong to listen to Cypress Hill's Black Sunday on a Friday?

Now, most rappers will try to diversify and rap about all sorts of stuff. Not Cypress Hill. Gun fights and legalizing marijuana, that's it. They are on message all day, all night, 100%. Looped bass line, simple drum pattern, one or two great samples, rap about pot and getting shot; one, the other, both at the same time. If you like variety, Cypress Hill is not for you.

But here's the thing, the songs are good. Sen Dog and B-Real have great flows, they aren't cruising for trouble, life's just stupid violent in southern California. They're the first famous Latin American rap group.

Will it make you like hip-hop if you don't? No. Is it better than all the other Cypress Hill albums? Probably yes. Does it have anything to do with the actual 1935 dust storm of the same name? No, unless you've got a super-secret method for growing plants when the dirt is moving sideways instead of not moving at all. Maybe all the bullets are like a devastating dust storm, sending migrants looking for places to live that don't have flying dirt. That seems like a good pothead metaphor.

I heard a story once that marijuana was the reason Bob Marley could keep touring while he died of cancer of the everything. Willy Nelson is doing fine on his ranch in Texas. I think we all recognize that its classification as a schedule I narcotic is pure nonsense, it has more to do with the devastating effect it has on the economies of cotton, paper, and tobacco corporations than it does anything else. Don't get me wrong, a city full of marijuana dispensaries isn't much fun, but neither is a city without them so that's a pointless distinction.

Am I a hypocrite for liking this album when I neither smoke pot nor shoot people? Some questions may just be too big for us mere mortals to answer.

Red Rider – As Far As Siam

Red Rider again? The album *with* Lunatic Fringe? Ok, blame Canada, I guess. With a name like As Far As Siam, it's not going to be amazing. It will be undeniably 80s, but if Neruda was what they made after their one fluke hit, then there's no reason to expect the album that random one hit came from to be consistent...

... and my goodness that's a bit too much country for a Canadian rock band. But, I expected it to suck, so it's a tiny bit better than I expected. Here's the thing, you honestly had no idea that Lunatic Fringe was about the appalling wave of anti-Semitism that resurged in the 70s. Knowing that kind of makes the concept of "Cowboys in Hong Kong" seem a little ironic. Not ironic in the Alanis Morissette coincidental ennui sense, or the Celine Dion "ironical" sense, but in the Iggy Pop/David Bowie China Girl sense. Luckily, the rest of the album is terrible enough to render that tumor completely benign. Terrible album, throw it on the "recalibrate my rifle scope" pile.

I don't think I'm being unfair when I say these songs are playlist filler. Each on its own is generically fine, but they don't add up to an album, especially not a "war" album (either they're named after that particular horsewoman of the apocalypse, or they misspelled Daisy's flagship BB gun to avoid trademark infringement). Believe me I've tried, but I can't find a consistent frame of reference for all of it, it's just stereotypical stuff.

If you fell down the escalator here at Bottle of Beef and handed me the demos for this album I'd probably say "you guys are great, why are you doing such a shitty job of assembling an album? Lemme hear all the stuff you thought was bad and then maybe we'll talk." It's not even AOR, because that would imply you were trying to make a coherent album. Remember what I said about Uriah Heep coincidentally being their own concept? Yeah, that doesn't apply here because these guys are clearly lost at sea as to what kind of band they actually are, just flailing at anybody's style to see what sticks on the Canadian airwaves.

I don't necessarily hate it, I still like most of the music, it's just not a good album. Somebody must have said something similar to "shape up or ship out" because Neruda is muuuuch better. Can't win 'em all, I suppose.

While we're up here though, we might as well check out what everybody says is Prism's worst album....

Prism – Beat Street

The story of Beat Street is mildly confusing to me. As far as I understand it, Henry Small showed up to make his 2nd Prism album (Ron Tabak got fired somewhere in the past), only to find out that the rest of the band had already quit. Their producer owned the name Prism, so they just made a Henry Small solo album with session musicians. So, bizarro Pink Floyd.

Call me crazy, but standing on the corner at night with an electric guitar slung across your back seems like a great way to get mugged. Then again, we're in Canada. Maybe they don't have muggings up there. I don't know.

Critics say "hey, wait a minute, this isn't wacky synthy arena rock." Again, I don't know, I haven't heard it yet. What I do know is that I'm not good at picking out random records. There's probably a good reason why I imagineered the Compiler up. Welp, time for Darth Bottle to get what's coming to him.

Huh? Nightmare doesn't suck. The title track is pop, but then we're right back to rockin'. Side A does have a decidedly Foreigner feel to it, but considering no original member of Prism is on this album, who cares? We just lump it in with all the other bands who turned into completely different bands. I seem to recall half of Pink Floyd's discography not being Pink Floyd albums, and we won't even go near the Geoff Tate/Queensrych quagmire.

Yeah, I can totally see it. The whole band quit, so Small and Carter said screw it, let's make a murkily paranoid Foreigner album. This is great. If you were expecting prog you'd be totally disappointed with the straight pop hooks, but even if you tried to hear it from a sellout perspective you couldn't call this bad. Every track could be a legit radio single, just not all on the same station. I'm fine with Prism being two completely different bands.

I picked out one more album I know doesn't suck, but we should leave picking handfuls of random albums to the professionals like C-3PO. I've learned my lesson. The Empire assembled for a reason, and I keep waking up, so time to stop being so picky and just go with it. We'll assume I'll wake up again tomorrow, and worry about it then...

Jethro Tull – Aqualung

See, told you I'd wake up again today. Remember that time Metallica lost the Grammy to Jethro Tull? We aren't listening to that album, we're listening to Aqualung, but that particular injustice led to finally separating the hard rock and metal categories and there was eventually justice for all. It was great, Jethro Tull took out a full-page ad proclaiming flute a heavy metal instrument and Metallica added a sticker saying Grammy Award LOSERS, and the academy was completely embarrassed. I'm not a voting producer because as Groucho Marx so eloquently put it, I refuse to join any club that would have me as a member.

Before all that, Jethro Tull made a few Prog albums and Aqualung was the first. They weren't trying to make a concept album, but they ended up putting the concept right there on the back of the jacket.

The two sides are subtitled Aqualung and My God, and the whole thing is a contemplation of society creating both its dregs and gods. Intended or not, that's a more coherent concept than most actual concept albums. Why? Because the concept grew from assembling the songs, all of which come from a narrator standing in the middle and observing the best and worst of everything at the same time.

Aqualung asks "who would choose to be the dregs of society, and who could possibly justify buying salvation?" My God explores the hypocrisy of creating a god to justify your own selfish desires.

It's not an album about religion, it's an album about humanity's selfish motivations, and using religion as a justification for greed. God isn't a mechanical wind-up toy for your amusement, that's the message at the end.

Did I mention how much it rocks? What a great album.

Violent Femmes – Add It Up

S: Why do you dislike Greatest Hits albums, Bottle?
B: Because it's a dumb concept. You know that band you love? Well, here's most of the songs you already know you like! Or, we can't afford to keep publishing their back

catalogue! Or, you've heard *of* them, they're famous, here's all the songs you need to fake a conversation at a party you didn't want to attend! They never flow, they sound like a slapdash mix tape, any new songs aren't strong enough to build a new album. This isn't the 50s, Sandra.

    S: But you do have a lot of them.

    B: Of course I do. I either couldn't afford to buy all their albums the first time around, or I wouldn't want to. You could argue that's how they get you, but just because the concept is dumb doesn't mean I can't like their hit songs. Most of the time, though, it feels like channel surfing, so you have to be picky.

    S: Ok, what's your favorite?

    B: The best of the worst of the best? It just so happens I can honestly answer your question and cheat at the same time! It's Add It Up, from Violent Femmes. It's tons of different versions of their best songs from 1981 to 1993. I'll buy that. That's a scrapbook worth making.

Bottle Takes a Break

    S: Has anybody seen Bottle? He's not in his office, or his other office.

    C: No, I thought he was with you.

    S: Two days ago we were listening to greatest hits albums, but I haven't seen him since then. New reviews, Skip?

    E: No, my inbox is empty. He shared that Ebow on Dobro thing last night, so he was near a computer, but nothing new to spell-check. Maybe he saw a butterfly or went for a jog or something. He does seem restless lately.

    C: Check the Gallery. Sometimes he just paces the halls and admires his braindiwork.

    S: I think it's more serious than a nostalgia trip can cure. Search party. Everybody pick a hallway and always veer left. Shout if you find him. And check the electrical sockets for scorch marks. He's been casually mentioning being real again.

C: Oh, that's just what he says when he's not feeling on top of everything. I wouldn't worry. Then again, that thing you're doing with your eyebrows tells me a walk would be good for my health. We'll see what C sees, so to speak.

As she watched Skip and the Compiler amble off on their uneventfully not worth describing spiral to nowhere, Sandra stood lost in thought. "Where would he go? I guess the Gallery is as good a place to start as any."

As she rounded the corner, there arose the unmistakable crunch of glass under foot. Slowly she raised her head, surveying the sparkly path until her eyes landed on a familiar pair of dingy tennis shoes and a broom head sweeping shards of broken glass into an equally dingy old snow shovel.

S: Carl, have you seen Bottle?

J: Which one?

S: What do you mean, which one? There's only 1 Bottle.

J: And if one of those bottles should happen to fall? Thousands of the little buggers, bouncing off the walls like flubber. I'm gonna be here all night. Then they swarmed and headed off into B-space.

S: Thanks, Carl. Remind me to get you a new shovel for Christmas.

J: Old shovel works fine. I'd take a case of Abba-Zabbas, though. Only friend a janitor needs, if you ask me. Still, I'd keep your shoes on, if I were you.

You might be familiar with L-space, and you might be familiar with the theory that reality splits with every conscious decision, and if you put those two things together you get

Backstage, B-space. It gets really hectic on the weekends. Most bands don't notice as they're passing through, but all the grisly old road warriors will tell you that all back stages are connected by poorly lit hallways. How else would you get all of those one-off cameos in the headliner's set? Why's the band an hour late? They lost sight of their tour manager and ended up crashing some other gig three cities over. A few bands get really lost and end up camping in vacant green rooms for the rest of their careers. Sometimes, late at night in the middle of the week, you'd swear you could hear Jim Morrison or Elvis warming up.

This particular Tuesday night it was dead quiet. So quiet you could hear the faintest echoes of staplers pinning hand scribbled "CLOSET" signs to thick wooden doors. Profundo Paradise, as Bottle might say. As Sandra surveyed the endless hallway, she caught just the teeniest whisper of a sad little melody on the stale breeze. She took a few steps forward and listened. There it was again, miles away, but definitely something resembling singing. Too far away to walk. She bent down and felt the floor. No, not enough wax to skate, even in stockings. Nothing for it, she'd have to fly.

Wicked Witch of the West, Bottle liked to joke. "I'll make him wish I'd turned him into a newt," she thought as she suddenly clapped her hands together with the ferocity of a springing bear trap. A bright light slowly seeped out between her fingers, and she started pulling her hands apart. She pulled and pulled, making something from nothing with the energy of a thousand suns, until finally she was done, slightly out of breath and holding an anti-climactically boring looking broom. A quick glance around to make sure no one was here and she wriggled up on it and zoomed off down the corridor.

Back in the bunker, Skip and the Compiler had finished their own look-sees.

C: I take it you didn't find him either?
E: Nope. I saw some pop-tart crumbs at the foot of the escalator, but that's about it.
C: Good. Can't say we didn't help. Sandra's problem, she'll deal with it.

Thousands of doorways and a few startled skeletons later, Sandra could definitely hear the melody. She couldn't make out the words yet, but it seemed vaguely familiar. Not a big, flowing melody, but a little jaunty thing on a constant loop. It might or might not be Bottle, but eventually we'll all find out.
Closer and closer, faster and faster, louder and louder, she could almost make out the words.

Do. Dee do. Do.
Do. Dee do. Do.

And suddenly she was at a complete stop. Not like she hit a wall, but magically not moving anymore. Momentum should have propelled her another 200 yards, but clearly we've gone metaphysical. One moment she was zooming at mach-3, the next she was at a standstill, suspended mid-air like nothing had happened. Zoom the camera out a little and we see a bony hand firmly clenched around the broomstick just before the bristles. Before she could even catch her breath, a voice like a lead weight pounded in her ears.

I'M SORRY SANDRA, BUT YOU CAN GO NO FURTHER.
S: GREGORY? What are you doing here? Where's Bottle? Where are we? We're further out than even I knew about.
TURN BACK. IT IS TIME FOR YOU TO HEAD HOME. HE IS BEING MENDED.

S: What are you talking about? Who's being mended? Is that the Winnie the Pooh theme song??

HOW WOULD HE SAY IT? OH, YES. OUT THERE IN THE COLD, GETTING LONELY GETTING OLD...AND THE WORMS ATE INTO HIS BRAIN. BUT, THE SILLY OLD BEAR CAN BE MENDED. YOU MOST OF ALL KNOW THAT ETERNITY IS A MOEBIUS STRIP. NOW, HOME WITH YOU.

And so, without any ceremony or crazy special effects, Sandra was back in her beanbag chair watching the time vortex slowly pulsate inside the isometric rendering of the Three's Company living room that Bottle had imagineered onto her west wall. No answers, no explanations, all she could do was sit, and wait.

To be continued....

... and continue we shall, in 3, 2, 1...

As she sat staring into the swirling glow of the vortex, Sandra wondered what would happen if Bottle never came back. Who would write anything for Skip to edit? What would Compy compile in the first place? Would the escalator reverse directions and let us all go free? Not that she wanted to go anywhere in particular. Not that she was actually stuck here in the first place, but that infinite hallway irked her to no end. It hadn't registered at the time, GREGORY does tend to occupy all your brain cells at once, but they weren't in the hallway for that conversation. The memory was still fuzzy, but it was more like a cul-de-sac.

But there isn't an end to an infinite hallway. She pulled out the world map to make sure. Right there, headed off at a diagonal with a note in some anciently gothic script: Hallway, recursive. The map can't lie, it's distilled from the universal code itself. Unless...aha!...of course! Time is a Moebius strip!

But, time must exist to even have a boundary. So, the space in which time exists must be boundless but unoriented. A Klein bottle! Space is a Klein bottle. Leave it to Bottle to go back to where it all started and fall through the hole he created from the other side.

"The empty Bottle needs a refill. How droll. Of course he'll be back." So, with the faintest hint of a smirk, she settled back down for the remainder of the wait for this little pocket of eternity to pass before another adventure begins.

"Op!" One more thing she wanted to do. "Skip! Compy! Make me a list of Bottle's favorite albums. Not the ones he says are his favorite, the ones he unintentionally adored."

She didn't need to hear a reply, the clatter of keyboard and shuffling of paper told her they got the memo.

Bottle Returns (Down On The Upside)

CCR: Ok, I've finished gluing all the pieces back together. Let's see if he holds water. Glug, glug, glug, glug. So far, so good. Yes, I think he's ready. We'll just put the top back on. There. How do you feel, Bottle?

B: With my fingertips.

CCR: See, good as new. Should be fine as long as you keep him away from high heat. Anything else I can do for you Mr. GREGORY?

NO. THAT IS ALL. THANK YOU, MR. ROBIN.

B: Sorry, I must have dozed off. Where's this bus headed?

CCR: Do you remember what you were doing before you don't remember being here Bottle?

B: First, who the hell are you? Second, why are you asking the right questions? Third, are we in the THX 1138 white room prison?

CCR: Now Bottle, those are obviously rhetorical questions, and you asked them in the wrong order.

B: No. Skullboy will back me up on this, I asked them in order of increasing importance to me. I don't respect authority, I'm super confused when people who aren't me have a firm grasp on implied reality, and I want to know if there's a beat down in my imminent future. Who? What? Where? Don't care why, just want to know what to expect.

YES, DELIGHTFUL. YOU'VE DONE AN EXCEPTIONAL JOB. WE WON'T KEEP YOU ANY LONGER, MR. ROBIN.

B: Mr. Robin? Mr. Robin?? You're Chriscrosstopher??? Hold on a moment. I'm in a white room with black curtains, Kenny Loggins playing in the background, and instead of just letting me blissfully shuffle off this mortal coil after whatever dumbass thing I did (I know me, it had to be spectacularly stupid), you had Criscrostopher Robin glue me back together?

YOU AREN'T FINISHED.

B: Finished with what? I was joking about the eternity part; killing time until we got back to some enjoyable part of the infinite loop.

NO, YOU WERE NOT JOKING.

B: Ok fine, no I wasn't, but you could have let eternity end with an ellipsis. That hardly qualifies as cheating.

NO. ARE YOU READY TO GO BACK NOW? THE OTHERS WILL BE GLAD TO SEE YOU.

B: Hhhhhhhhhh. K. I still say you should have just let me die, but what do I know? Incidentally, what did I do?

CCR: I believe you were trying to do everything all at once, and spread yourself so thin that you collided with yourself going the opposite direction in an explosion that would make the team of scientists at CERN pee their pants.

I COULDN'T HAVE SAID THAT BETTER.

B: Me neither. I can totally see me doing that. I don't remember what I was trying to do, but I've also wanted a few fewer brain cells, so win/win I guess. I may not like what you got me hanging from, but it's too bright out here in the outside world. Turn it back around, I mean lead the way, Bones....

What a bizarre sight indeed to watch Bottle and GREGORY walking down the empty corridor toward the Bunker of Beef. One might liken it to Arnold Schwarzenegger and Danny Devito, or Gandalf and Bilbo, or even the obvious Christopher Robin and Winnie the Pooh, but let us not romanticize the image too much: a bumbling short guy and a 6+ foot tall anthropomorphic skeleton don't really need any further contextualization to fully inhabit their peculiar proximity.

B: You really think they missed me?
OF COURSE. WITHOUT YOU THEY HAVE NO DIRECTION, NO PURPOSE, NO RAISINS TO EAT.
B: Hey, that's my line. Anyway, I still don't know what to do next.
HAS THAT EVER STOPPED YOU BEFORE?
B: Touché. I guess I'll just keep winging it like I always did. I assume you'll go back to just snarling and hiding in the closet?
OF COURSE, THAT IS MY FUNCTION.
B: Well, it's been something, I'm still working on that piano for you. Can you try banging up some drum beats for me?
I'LL SEE WHAT I CAN DO.
B: Thanks. Well, time to face the music, I guess. Albums don't review themselves...

And with a snap of the fingers, Bottle was back inside the bunker, ready to say wordy words about soundy sounds, and possibly make someone giggle in the process. Who knows what surprises lie in wait to ambush our brains in the night? I certainly don't. Narrating this nonsense is hard work. As Bottle would say, cheers.

Joe Cocker!

Welcome to the inevitable downside of the reopening of 'Merica. How fitting that I find another Joe Cocker album for the occasion. It's his sophomore exclamation point. I mean, Feliciano wore it first a year earlier, but we aren't here to cat call the catwalk. We're here to listen to a spastic British curmudgeon belt out his versions of other peoples' songs. Yeah, no, how interesting that the Cuban Jazz guitarist and British Blues singer both yell their names at you.

But, you know what I hear? It's a word I've used before. That word is "authentic." Disregarding the self-titled second album (a fashion faux pas to be sure), there is nothing questionable about it. You might ask why he chose that particular song by that particular songwriter, but you definitely can't say that there is any other way that Joe Cocker could possibly sing it. Joe Cocker is not Barbra Streisand, he's not making choices; Joe Cocker walks up to the microphone and has an unpremeditated audio-epileptic seizure at it. It's glorious.

Christgau called him "gruff and vulgar" and they printed that on the actual jacket for the back-handed compliment it is. Remember, 49% of what Eric Burden does is copy this guy. Your old pal Bottle might rival Gloria Steinem on the scale of Dude to Feminist, but I think she and I would both agree that any woman knowingly climbing into Joe Cocker's bedroom window signed the liability waiver by default. That's a purely musical joke, Joe Cocker was an angel of human being. McCartney and Harrison loved the royalties his biggest hit brought them so much that they said something like "she's all yours, Joe." Again, I joke, they were super happy that he made "Friends" into a legit Soul masterpiece.

What's hilarious is that he refused to go back on another US tour and broke up the Grease Band, only to find out the tour was already booked and that he'd have to hire a new band and tour whether he liked it or not. If only he'd read my book "How to confuse people and not be popular."

But there's an even more interesting thing we can say about Joe Cocker. There isn't a millisecond where he doesn't mean it. It's not for show, it's not contrived, it's 100% if it kills me 100% of the time, compared to say Ian Curtis's 99.9999%. If Joe Cocker sang your song, you got to hear that it meant something, and that exclusive club that includes Linda Ronstadt, Weird Al, and that's it. If we were enrolled in Cultural Appropriation 101, this would be the lesson plan for "this guy gets it." Like I said, authentic.

Coheed & Cambria – In Keeping Secrets of Silent Earth 3

Dear my friends,

I imagine everyone's first impression of Coheed & Cambria is something along the lines of "what the bloody hell am I listening to?" Then you learn that the whole thing is Claudio's comic book sci-fi-saga, and you're still like, "no, but this isn't how words work. I can't tell what's a noun vs. a pronoun or even a verb, which character is talking at any given moment, how the hell does he play and sing this prog-tastic insanity at the same time?"

I've read a big chunk of The Amory Wars, and I still don't know. It's insane, the first album is part 3, there's a prequel hiding in the middle of their discography, they write a little note at the end of Three Evils reminding you that it's a story not an actual suicide note.

They write some super-freakin catchy stuff and that totally belies how brutal and terrifying the whole thing is. What's a Newo? Who/what are the Prise. Those interludes sound ghastly.

And when the answer that you want is in the question that you state, you just give up and enjoy the 71-minute deluge of rage and fear and emotional anguish in Claudio's bizarre hyper-tenor.

I guarantee by the end you'll be saying "that was certainly some kind of adventure, I hope this eye twitch I suddenly developed goes away soon."

I'm totally in, I've got most of their albums, but I won't call you bad names if you scalp your tickets after this first 3rd episode. It's not a trip everyone will enjoy, but I'm a huge fan.

What are some of your favorite non-sequiturs? Mine are "your face and a door between," and "over and out Connecticut."

Queens of the Stone Age – Songs for the Deaf

Speaking of interesting concepts, here's Songs For The Deaf. It's the one with Dave Grohl sitting in as drummer (they met when Homme was still in Kyuss). Lots of people do the changing radio stations thing (Rob Zombie, for example), but Josh Homme brought in celebrity guest DJs to narrate this conceptual drive from LA to Joshua Tree.

This is kind of the biggest and lastest first stage Queens of the Stone Age album (Homme calls them a trilogy of not being Kyuss, doing more of that, and finally getting it right). It's heavy and creepy. Not so much evil, but creepy. Desert stoner rock/metal. A lot of the songs came from Desert Sessions (that's the side project where Homme just invites friends out to his studio to just create music for music's sake).

The radio concept is nice because it means different things for everybody. For Homme it's the way all the disparate styles they were going for fit together fluidly, for Oliveri it's making fun of how radio stations all play the same stuff (which definitely isn't Queens of the Stone Age).

Whether you like them or not, the whole point of the band is to be completely unconcerned about writing hit songs and instead writing what they wish they could listen to but doesn't exist yet. My copy of their latest album Villains got eaten by the make funny grinding sounds receptacle in my car. I really should disassemble that thing some time.

If you didn't know, we're listening to a few of my actual favorite albums. Obviously, I love all albums like they are my children or dogs, but this particular batch doesn't have off days, they are amazing no matter what frame of mind you're in. I've got a few more before I start veering off into the woods again, so enjoy.

Bernstein does Venice, I mean plays and conducts some random Vivaldi Concertos

I don't have wordy words about things and stuff, I just wanted to hear some Vivaldi Concertos. He was music master of the Ospedale della Pietà for orphaned girls in Venice. Thus, Vivaldi wrote all sorts of stuff for random and now long-gone instruments, and for varying abilities.

This recording is interesting because Bernstein plays Harpsichord and the violinist is another famous composer, John Corigliano. Quite lovely.

I'm thankful for Arlo Guthrie

Touch your nose and blow your toes, it's Thanksgiving. It's on a Thursday again this year, what are the chances? I could obviously just repost last year's blurb about Alice's Restaurant, but I thought it might be more fun to do a proper analysis of the album. Not the song, the album. It's actually quite fascinating, because the whole concept of the album is that you only care about Alice's Restaurant, you only bought it to hear Alice's Restaurant, and that's as good a reason as any for Harold Leventhal to tell "the story of Arlo Guthrie."

It's a great story in its own right, a little biography, some evidence that he's a lovably funny character, a nice little mention of the practicality of what an agent actually does (send letters and call people to get real gigs for musicians). And the moral of the story deserves a quote: "This record will give many people a chance to hear some of Arlo's other talents. I think they'll be impressed...."

Lurking deep under the surface of Bottle's Taxonomy, we see this is actually a here's a thing and some other stuff album, Like Tarkus or Inna-Gadda-Da-Vita.

But I don't wanna pickle, you say. Well look, I can't help it that most Mayors and Governors are terrible communicators, nor can I help it if you think basic science is demon magic, but I can tell you that wearing a mask and not breathing directly into other peoples' faces does in fact help limit the spread of a virus which appears to be highly contagious during its incubation phase. The point is to try as best as possible to not flood our horribly disorganized and perpetually mismanaged healthcare system to the point that babies can't be delivered, broken arms can't be positioned and put in a cast, etc. I can also tell you that listening to everyone whine about it for the last 10 months has elevated my not giving a shit to epic proportions. I don't like that about myself. I'm supposed to be the happy-go-lucky guy who just takes life as it comes and shows you that none of this mass psychology gobbledygook is helpful for everyday life. I don't mean that Psychology is bad, I mean that walking around reenacting the showdown between Vissini and dramatic irony Wesley every moment of the day is stupid and unfulfilling. I can't even write an album review without veering off onto that tangent.

My point is we as a collective people in geographic proximity to each other seem to have lost the ability to listen to another person without arguing about geopolitical power dynamics. I myself have argued for bombing the living bejeepers out of us several times (a KMFDM reference in an Arlo Guthrie review on Thanksgiving, seriously? Sandra would surely say "shut up, Bottle"), and repeatedly told you that these essays are meant to be funny (if it isn't funny, you're reading it wrong), the same way that Arlo's story about the draft is funny, 8x10 glossy photographs notwithstanding. Obviously, my incredibly dark and macabre sense of humor isn't for everyone. I perpetually publish preposterously perplexing pieces of prose on this pointless platform. I'm also a fictitious character, designed to be intellectually challenging by my creator, whatever implications that might have for you.

So, whether it's Festivus or Christmahannaquanziccah you're in the mood to celebrate, I'm thankful that I have the ability to tell myself that I'm being a dumbass and try to do better. It doesn't mean I'm doing an awesome job at it, it just means that I'm still willing to love all of you even when you say terrible things that I don't agree with, let you rant when you need to rant without responding with too much childish moral outrage, and keep waking up with my best compromise on my sleeve.

Remember kids, if it makes you so mad you want to burst, find a way to throw it in the metaphorical dumpster, but try really hard to not accidentally light your neighbor's house on fire in the process. Insurance is simply one fancy front-end for the stock market and your agent is technically and legally your broker. See how I tied that all together like I had some plan at the beginning? I assure you I didn't.

And so, the sincerely apropos conclusion to this silly string of loosely connected stories:

Thank you for taking time out of your own day to let my brain thoughts attack your brain cells. No good deed goes unpunished (wink, wink).

The Offspring – Ixnay on the Hombre

Welcome to the disclaimer. We all remember The Offspring morphing into the cheesy pop-hop prankster image ensemble they became, and Ixnay on the Hombre has the first hints of that transition, but it's still a good album. It's structured the same as Smash, and the concept is somewhat similar. Smash was wrapped in the humorous enjoyment of the album with an adult beverage as an intellectually stimulating art experience (you know, like I do), and Ixnay extends that to another thing I like to do: lecture on the experience of life from a personal perspective. It might be completely disagreeable to you, and you are welcome to go away if you can't find some way to engage with it.

It also tests your irony muscles. The beauty in The Offspring is that they neither telegraph their sarcasm, nor clarify afterward. That's actually hard to accomplish. You can listen to the whole thing either way and it gives some rewarding perspectives. It also has a bunch of my own personal philosophies and sentiments on it, but I won't beat the dead horse you represent in this scenario.

Part one is a nice little story. It starts with the realization that everyone is out to push their own agenda on you, a recognition that he doesn't want to live that way, and a final statement that ultimately you choose to participate in whatever situation you find yourself. Life is a nightmare, but you can in fact just walk away if you want to do so.

Let's take a brief pause to thank our sponsor, coffee. Coffee, stimulating brain cells and making you go to the bathroom more often since Kaldi watched his goats tweak out after eating those particular berries.

Nobody wants to "be controlled." Yet, at the same time, if you find yourself stuck in the same miserable cycles of making being human terrible, you should listen to advice and break out of it.

Now obviously the title is a Pig Latin based pun, and there's a certain level of juvenile humor involved, but really the total message is pretty coherent. Whether you're sad, or angry, or perpetually lazy, or fatalistically depressed, or pretending you're out to change the world for completely selfish reasons:

Stop being such a douche bag.

Fall Out Boy – Under the Cork Tree

Fall Out Boy certainly has a lot of things they do that could technically qualify as gimmicks, but is their sophomore album Under The Cork Tree middle of the road, forgettable pop-punk?

No. I get that there were tons of bands flooding the market at the time, and I get that critical response has more to do with looking good in 6 months than having actual opinions, but this is way better than Brendan Urie, or the favorite comparisons Jimmy Eat World and All American Rejects. The latter bands had two good songs each and disappeared from mainstream consciousness like they should have.

Here's the thing, you don't realize this is 2005 Fall Out Boy, not 2013 Fall Out Boy. This is some standout stuff from the decade of dismal.

I know I've talked about this before, but the mid to late 90s so totally warped everyone's perception because fringe rock was the mainstream. It went back to the fringe in the 00s. You hear big radio hooks now, but this wasn't in standard rotation back then. This was the occasional bright spot in between past their prime Matchbox 20, Nickelback, Gorillaz, Hinder and terrible middle period Weezer.

Unlike Christgau, Bottle's tastes are decidedly anti-mainstream with a healthy dose of credit where credit is due. You see any of those bands in my collection? If so let me know and I'll destroy them in humorously inappropriate ways. I kept a few of the absolute worst as showpieces and mementos, but it's the bad old middle ages as far as Bottle is concerned. 2001 to 2009 is a barren wasteland because the majors straight up dropped everyone who couldn't pop out for a TRL taping tomorrow morning. Long gone are the days of artist development, be sellable in 20 minutes or drink drain cleaner.

Fall Out Boy was in it for fun, but Wentz's suicide attempt was as much a result of the pressure to not screw up their deal as anything. Narcissistic sure, but not completely his own fault. I'm sure I said it before, it sounds like clumsy teenagers because they're just barely not clumsy teenagers anymore. Wentz is the oldest and he's only 7 months older than me (and I'll remind you that I myself moved out into the corn fields). Life's been a tad rough for the class of '98, plus or minus a couple years.

Regardless, this is a great little album for a bull that would rather smell flowers under a tree than fight a matador, and as far as emo concepts go it's quite serviceable. Its case is long gone, but that's no reason to throw it out, all things considered....

Iron Maiden – Fear of the Dark

There are great Iron Maiden albums, there are terrible Iron Maiden albums, and somewhere in the middle they made Fear Of The Dark right before Bruce Dickenson quit for a while. I'm not sure I feel either way about it. It doesn't suck, but it's a little too all over the place to be satisfying.

The title track is obviously a classic, and there are some fantastic instrumental sections (and the guitar tones are gorgeous in my opinion), but it's really just 12 random Iron Maiden songs about soccer hooligans, AIDS, the Gulf War, being framed for murder, dying and coming back as a ghost, you know random Iron Maiden stuff. I suppose it's all sort of loosely about fragile mental states, but not in any coherent way. It's too eclectic in my book.

Don't get me wrong, I thoroughly enjoy most every song (The Apparition gets quite tedious), but as an experience it's about 10 minutes too long and none of it flows. I feel like there's 3 EPs hiding in here, but I wouldn't even know where to start extracting them.

Mr. 76ix – 3 (Minority of 1)

I know what we should do. We should listen to some weird obscure stuff that I have on various dubbed CDs. We won't dive straight into the deep-end, we'll start with Mr. 76ix's 3 (Minority of 1). Truth in advertising, it's his 3rd album.

If you're totally new to electronic music, it doesn't tell you how to feel. This might sound like 52 minutes of gibberish broken into 18 completely arbitrary tracks, but what if it isn't? What if it's 18 pieces of electronic music that are stitched together to form a 52-minute stream of consciousness? No, no, I can see your face, it's clearly still gibberish.

Ok. For the sake of argument, let's say there isn't any rule that says the various sounds have to interact with each other in traditional ways. They can do their own thing, other stuff can interact and/or interfere, 3 or 9 different meters can be happening at the same time, pretty sounds and scary sounds and annoying sounds can occur in rapid succession.

This album has sampling, break beats, glitch noises, and all sorts of synths. It doesn't have to be good or bad, it can just be an imaginary playground. Whatever it makes you feel is completely valid because you are instinctively reacting to it. Yes, that means you're stuck listening to it for an hour, but what super important thing were you going to do instead?

Mr. 76ix is a complete mystery. You can't go find out more about him, other than that he has more albums if your brain isn't totally melted after this.

Don't worry, they'll get much worse....

KMFDM vs. Pig and Kettel

Hi, everybody, Compiler here. Bottle's working on a different album review, but I just learned it's KMFDM vs. PIG's 24th birthday today. I have that album, let's listen to it.

I'm not good at the word things, I'm more of a smash things together and let it speak for itself kind of guy. This EP is like that, it's Raymond, Sascha, and Svet Am making a few songs together.

Now, Raymond Watts may or may not show up for any KMFDM thing, but it's pretty great when he does. The bad word counter goes crazy, and the sleaze becomes palpable.

My favorite sample is "witchcraft has invaded the government...." Bottle's favorite sample is "America, you can change the laws to suit you...."

Most people won't rank this very high in either discography. Bottle might say that's because most people are brain-dead backwater hillbillies, but he'd be joking. You wouldn't think he's joking, but he is.

I'm rambling too much. How does he do this every night and still manage to sound coherent?

20 minutes of head bobbing industrial dance music with samples that will offend your delicate sensibilities. What's not to like? Trust me, I've heard the album he's reviewing next and this is like Vivaldi compared to that mind melting nightmare of electronic flotsam and jetsam. Thanks for your time, I'll C myself out....

... Fee, fie, foe, futer, someone's been sitting at Bottle's computer.

Seriously, the chair's all messed up, and the screen's crooked. Ew, gross! Is that Cheeto dust in a puddle of Mountain Dew?! I'm looking at you, Corkscrew, you filthy animal. I demand Justice!

On second thought, we'll save Justice for tomorrow night. Let's pour the Hi-C out of the frying pan and into the Kettel. This'll make everybody Whisper Me Wishes. Or, shiver me timbers.

Kettel is Dutch, if you couldn't tell by the nonsense of a track list for this gem of an album from 2007.

You're still gonna get samples and synths and tasty beats, we're just gonna turn the knob labeled "discombobulator" up 7 or 8 notches, sprinkle on some jazz, a dash of glitch, make a field recording of people eating at a fancy restaurant, tweak the filter knobs like things that want to be tweaked, invite some actual instrumentalists to play stuff, change tempos and meters for no reason, pretty much every possible way to create music as far as I know.

Regular people get all uppity if you call him a contemporary classical composer, but that's what he is. He creates music for ensembles of various instruments, some of which are traditional orchestral instruments and some of which require computer sequencing and synthesis. It's like a Classical/EDM fusion. It's much less frightening than yesterday's Mr. 76ix, but equally technologically chaotic in places. I find it quite soothing and happy, actually. It's sub 50 minutes, so it's got that going for it. Plus, you can imagine people dancing to most of it. Go on, give it a spin, you know you'll secretly enjoy it.

Justice – Cross

Speaking of 2007, let's hear the debut album Cross by French electronic duo Justice. Are they secretly Daftpunk in different costumes? No. Are there about 400 micro-samples of everything from Michael Jackson to Slipknot in this bizarre thing they call an Opera-Disco? You betcha.

I do actually like Christgau's review of this album because he clarifies it from his own context. As a dance album it's not for everyone, but as a work of electronic pop-art it's way more fun than Kraftwerk. His words, not mine. I'm not convinced Kraftwerk is supposed to be "fun" in any context, but that's still a compliment, backhanded or no.

In spite of all that, this *is* a straight French House album. The experimentation here is completely related to sound sources rather than structural discombobulation. Yet, there is a certain gobbledygook quality to all of it, hence its inclusion in this weird electronic music segment of my collection perusal. Justice has indeed been served.

I don't know about you, but I'm enjoying this little sojourn into not so well-known electronica. I don't actually have any Aphex Twin, Autechre, or Amon Tobin albums, even in dubbed form. What I do have is some more relatively obscure stuff, I just have to fire up the other computer they live on. No promises, though. We'll just have to wait and see what tomorrow brings.

Harry Connick Jr. – 25

Ladies, and man-ladies, it occurs to me that this time last year I was right in the thick of saying mean things about Barbara Mandrel and The Oak Ridge Boys. Sure, I could just repost some of those essays while I battle through this winter funk of not wanting to live in a world where Capitalism, Socialism, Marxism, and Communism are so nonsensically tossed around that even the Brookings Institution can't figure out what the hell people are talking about, and Denmark says "please stop calling us a Socialist country, because we aren't one." But, that's the universe you all apparently love to live in now, so I actually went and found 3 more Christmas CDs hiding in my collection. We're gonna save those, and instead go to crazy town. I also have three Harry Connick Jr. albums.

No Bottle, please, don't do it!

You can't tell me what not to do, there's an entire crate of records I deemed unacceptable to review last year. If brain damage is what you're serving for dinner, then I'm bringing potluck!

I wish I had his best-selling album because... yep you guessed it, it's a Christmas album, but I don't, so I can't, and I won't. He's from New Orleans, he's technically a person, let's find out if I can survive three nights in a row of whatever kind of jazz adjacent music he sings.

First up is his 1992 album "25." You know I was joking earlier, right? I not at all secretly love crooners, and he's lovely. Repeatedly naming your albums after how old you are is about as questionable as the opening of track two (the first 40-ish seconds are little more H. Jon Benjamin than anyone could be prepared for, [how many of you will actually get that joke?]), but it's pretty hard to say he's ridiculous or terrible, but also equally impossible to call him a subtle or nuanced piano player. Harry is a piano smasher through and through, but a charming one.

This is 99% solo piano and singing (with a few guests and a full combo track at the end), and a lot of it was seemingly impromptu and unrehearsed.

I know I ragged on the reused "here's how old I am" concept, but it's actually a good concept for random stuff. Here's what interested him when he was 25, I can't hate on that too much 'cause at least it's honest.

See, that wasn't so bad. We can do 2 more nights of Hairy Croonick. I mean, it's not like he made a funk album or anything.....

Harry Connick Jr. – She

... Oh no. He did. He did make a funk album. He made 2 funk albums, and I don't have the one about the space turtle. I have the supposedly worse one, She. She screams in silence, a sullen riot penetrating through her mind (thanks, Green Day).

What should we expect? Will it be surprisingly tolerable, or will it make me puke? Plus, there's two different kinds of Funk, you know? There's your James Brown Soul you can dance to, and then there's your outer space weed Funk a la Hendrix and George Clinton. I can't see the Con man going the Average White Band or Rare Earth route, mostly because he'd have a whole lot of high caliber hometown heavyweights busting his chops if he did an actual terrible job. New Orleans has a pretty substantial Funk history, after all. I think most people would be willing to accept a certain level of lyrical dumbness, but musically it has to be at least mediocre. Lots of Chinese people were confused when he toured the album there, but who wouldn't be confused by a Jazz singer showing up with a whole set of bass grooves and wah-wah? Clearly it wasn't terrible enough to make preemptive soup out of the Star Turtle, but there's only 1 way to find out...

...m'kay. Let's not sugar coat it, the opening title track is Adult Contemporary Funk, and I'm not entirely convinced the chorus is a compliment. The cool down of Between Us is way too early, and there's absolutely no reason for those funky guitar licks to be anywhere near this middle-age Clapton-like ballad. It doesn't sound smooth or sophisticated, it sounds out of touch and weird.

Here Comes The Big Parade and Trouble are much better. This sounds great, actually. I'm not sure we really needed the extended snare solo, or bongos, but at least these are reasonable Harry Connick Jr. jazz funk songs. Some of that trademark questionably flap your hands against the keyboard piano work. Track 5 is great. I'm thinking the first two tracks are the fluke stinkers that most people don't even bother getting past. I'm not crazy about that guitar tone for the solo, but that's a personal problem.

And then we go straight to crazy town. I don't want to ruin the experience for you, go check out Follow The Music and Joe Slam and the Spaceship (tracks 6 and 7). They are unique, to say the least. JSATS sounds exactly like something I would publish.

And then back to the boogie. And then the important question "why is Honestly Now... on this album?" And funky robot sounds. Ugh, 4 more tracks. If we must.

Hello again, honky-tonk piano and brass. Nothing quite as unsettling as a monotone chorus of the words "funky dunky" punctuated by a gunshot and that god-awful slowed down spoken voice again.

What the hell is this album? Clearly, it's structured to mean something but I don't like going to parties like this. Is That Party supposed to be social commentary, or just his version of Tom's Diner?

And we end with life is a prison, and we're all on death row, so play some honky-tonk piano, I guess.

Ok, there are more than a few truly enjoyable musical moments here, but this is like the worst album ever created. 1) no, I don't, I have absolutely no goddamned idea why Booker died of a broken heart, but that outro guitar solo is disgusting in a good way. 2) what does it even mean that Fieldfines Samantha Rambardi played "woolen squeak trinket," let alone Harry himself taking on "dog chain" duties? 3) it took like 4 tries to figure out the bizarre folding of the booklet and now that it's finally back in there I'll write a sticky note to never take it out again. 4) who is that old guy staring at me on the actual disc? Is this album a hallucination at an airport terminal? 5) the little intro text by whoever that was seems to tell us that "she" is actually New York City, but that makes no sense at all so clearly it must be true.

The first two songs are obviously throwaway radio singles, then the true bizarrity of this album begins. It has structure, but what that structure means is a total mystery. Maybe it's because I wasn't born on the banks of the Mississippi, or maybe because it's actual nonsense. I have no freakin' idea. Is that ridiculous spoken voice an homage to the interludes more common in hip-hop? Is there some meaning to the on again off again honky-tonk out of tune piano? Is it meant to be a reflection of that dichotomy between the hustle and the real life of the people who actually live in the French Quarter? Again, I don't know, this album is the weirdest thing I've listened to in my whole life, let alone the last year.

I'm finally at a loss for words. It's your turn. Is this garbage, or genius? I can't tell anymore.

Harry Connick Jr. – Every Man Should Know

Now we'll jump the better part of 2 decades later and open his 2013 album Every Man Should Know. You have the assurance that Harry wrote all the music and lyrics himself, and they didn't even fire up the auto tune plug-in.

It's a musical journey down a back road of Harry's desire. It's gonna be a bunch of pop-jazz ballads. Everybody gave it a mildly bad review, but I expect it will be quite nice. Let's go for a walk.

Well, the first 4 tracks are fantastic. Yes, he's genre hopping, but they actually flow like consecutive thoughts. You could actually have these thoughts in that order with the associated mood portrayed in the music.

Then it breaks. Come See About Me is stylistically fine, but irreconcilable with the previous 4 songs. Then we go all over the place.

Ok, I think I see why people don't get it. This isn't a pop album or a jazz album, it really is a concept album. It's not a story per se, but a series of situational experiences. It's not a linear album even though large portions actually flow quite well. Love and loneliness are the central themes, and the contextualizations of each song explore how those themes manifest both lyrically and musically. That's tough to engage with because all the actual work takes place in between the songs, so to speak. You have to let go of the sense of control you want from the sequencing. The concept of a solitary walk through the alleys of your mind is a good concept for that. He's thinking of a particular experience (real or imagined) that popped into his head and expressing that complete experience in song. Obviously, it's not his last album ever, but it ends like it is because that's where the solitary walk through reminiscence leads.

You might disagree with me, but this is actually a fantastic album and every song is wonderful. It's properly bookended as a coherent experience, the songs are good both in and out of that context, and I'm certainly not left with the feeling that listening to it was a waste of time. Shock and awe, Bottle says this is awesome. Go check it out.

The Best of Eric Burdon and The Animals, Vol. II

I'm feeling saucy today. What does the second best collection of songs by Eric Burdon and The Animals sound like?

Oooh, it's their psych rock stuff. Growly tubulous bass lines, nasty reverby cheese grater guitars, noisy noises, and like 80-proof Eric Burdon (not the full-strength ethanol, but more than enough punch to get the job done). It's a great collection actually, and I think Tom "Adamantium Testicles" Wilson is all the explanation we need for that. He knew what he liked, and he was rarely wrong.

Plus, it actually sounds good. It's really dark and cavernous like early Iron Butterfly, and very snare and bass heavy, but that's totally alright in my book. I don't think it's possible to listen to it without closing your eyes and bobbing your head everywhere. It's like some deep reptilian instinct takes over and you just can't feel mopey or bored.

There aren't any hills or valleys to this collection, the intensity is consistent from start to finish, and you'd have to be a serious weirdo to say "aw man, I hate that one" and reach over to skip it. This is just about as good as trippy tunnel vision 60s rock and roll can be. I have an extra copy, by the way, if you're willing to part with 3 times what it's worth to ship it to you....

$26.75 Adventure Time, Gladys Edition
Slam!

E: What was that?

Slam!

E: Do you guys hear that?
B: Hear what, Skipasaurus?
E: The slamming, Bottle.

SLAM!

B: I hear it now. *CALM THE HELL DOWN GLADYS!!* Wait. Could it be? Is it really? It's been like a year, and I just assumed....

SLAM!

G: Why won't this infernal door close properly? *SLAM!* There, I'll have to get Carl up here to fix that.

B: *CALM THE HELL DOWN, GLADYS!*
G: I'll calm you, Bottle!
B: It is you! I thought you got lost or dead or something. Did you win?
G: Win? Win what? Oh, the tournament? That's a doozie of a tale, that one. Steven and Sven had the highest points total, but the president of the host club refused to award them saying that they played fewer hands than his

team so it wasn't fair, but the first-round bye is always randomly selected and always counts as a win. It's printed right there in the tournament rules, and even those crazy old codgers who've been lobbying to change that rule said that those are the rules even if they don't like it (which they don't, but they agreed to play under them), and there's no actual evidence that anybody cheated anywhere close to enough to influence the outcome. Everybody just wanted the whole thing over with, so the team that supposedly played more hands with a higher average than anybody said "who cares? Claim victory 'til you run out of air, but the SS Pinochle clearly gets the prize money," and that made everybody start bickering, so nobody actually won by the time they kicked us all out, and the bus drivers they supposedly hired to take us back to the motel weren't there, and poor Sven caught pneumonia from walking back on foot, so we got him to the hospital, but apparently there was like some plague of cooties and people were drinking disinfectant and dying left and right, and once Sven finally got better we still couldn't leave because of all the cooties in the air or whatever, and I ran out of yarn but obviously we had no money to buy more, and finally we hitched a ride with this nice truck driver, but apparently he was a psycho and got arrested for driving through a crowd of people in a parking lot while we were asleep in the back, so....

    B: Slow down, Gladys.

    G: Catch up, Bottle. I haven't even made it to the part with the wildfires and the crazy people hoarding maple syrup so they could sell it for $100 a Yousir after the trees burned down. But right now, what I'd really like is a hot shower and a nap in my chair, so I'll just put your presents on the escalator and worry about whatever you've been doing much, much later.

    B: Oooookay. You do that. Glad you're back.

Ooh! She brought me some records. Never heard any of these, maybe C-diver can give me the low down on some of them. I see she kept the receipt (like I'd need to prove she bought them?), so file this one under $26.75 Adventure Time, Gladys Edition.

Speaking of getting lost in the shuffle, here's the totally obscure 1978 self-titled debut from a band that formed 10 years earlier and never got famous anywhere outside Santa Cruz, CA: Snail. A sarcastically cynical marketing man might say "well it is Snail, by Snail, with a Snail on it, so we aren't exactly hooking 'em with the intrigue, are we?"

My research assistant Compy Compilerson tells me diddly squat except they aren't Disco (doing better than late 70s Three Dog Night on that count at least). Some say soft rock, some say country rock, the band talks about being psych rock/borderline heavy metal a la Deep Purple. They have several recordings, but only 2 proper albums (according to my standards) on a super small label, they don't have a wikipedia page at all, so who knows what we're actually going to get. Amazingly enough, it is on youtube if you want to hitchhike along with me.

Welp, lie down on the table and rotate. Yep, just as I thought, it's all of those things all mish-mashed together in a way that can only be described as a bunch of songs by a band called Snail on an album called Snail, and the worst thing I can say about Side A is Music is My Mistress is a bit cheesy, but there again, of course it is. You're gonna think this is weird, but it's 70s country rock with string arrangements, a bunch of crazy guitar effects, tasty riffage, jam session style solos, some psych-noises, not terrible lyrics. I wouldn't want to listen to it 3 times a week, but it's totally good if not flashy or mind-blowing. Solid from start to finish. Did I mention the guitar solos are fantastic? They are. So are the string arrangements. Clark Gassman, never heard of him, but he has the second best name on this record. The winner is obviously their bass player,

Jack Register, but I imagine Chet McCracken would feel cheated if he didn't at least tie for second place. This record does sound fantastic, but I'm not sure how much praise the Aphex Aural Exciter actually deserves for that. Is some crummy studio engineer out there screaming "no fair! They used the Aphex Aural Exciter, those dirty cheater fraudsters!?" I only bring it up because it's presented less like Harry Connick's "I don't need no stinkin' auto tune" and more like "warning: expensive tube hardware in use!" or "love it? Hate it? Either way it's the Aphex Aural Exciter's fault."

Regardless, you know what they put me in mind of? The well loved and cared for lovechild of a fling turned marriage between Black Oak Arkansas and Prism; that so close to prog feeling, but this time leaning decidedly to the hard rock side of the spectrum. If like most people you've never heard of Snail, you might be surprised how much they don't suck.

From the obscure Country Rock of Snail, to the not in any way obscure New Wave of The Motels (which I admittedly didn't remember I totally know and love at first glance). The obvious connection between them is the dig at politicians, the more subtle connection is a his side/her side interaction, but who cares? The Motels are just amazing, possibly my favorite American New Wave band ever, and I wish I could afford their whole discography on vinyl right now (I can't 'cause shipping would be like $9,000).

They had two big hits and Suddenly Last Summer is on this album, Little Robbers. Motels vs. Hotels, you ask? I believe it was Ludacris who delivered the definitive distinction to use when deciding which one to stay at while accompanied by a lady friend. I won't weigh in on that one, the more traditional difference is whether you enter your room from inside the building or from outside the building.

But is it a good album? Indubitably. It's a fantastic album, are you daft? Little Robbers, songs about intricate details of modern life that steal your sanity, purple and yellow, duh.

$8 might seem a little pricey without the continental breakfast or heated chlorine bath, but I'd be willing to pay upwards of more than that because Martha Davis is awesome, plus it's not like you're trying to stay long enough to surreptitiously acquire tenant's rights, and it's statistically unlikely that a random stranger will break into your room and murder you no matter how paranoid you are about it, so close your eyes and enjoy.

I repeat, amazing album. Sleep tight.

Rise and shine! It's day two of Adventure Time with Gladys. Remember how I unintentionally commented on how strange it was that Snail mentioned their fantastically exciting vacuum-tube based studio gear? And how I mentioned that motels have fewer amenities than the place you might take a "ho"? Well, Gladys also bought me an album by The Tubes, because what else are you going to do in your room on the road in a town you don't know except watch basic network TV?

A concept album about a TV addicted idiot savant produced by Todd Rundgren? Who even cares if the songs are any good when this is clearly the grand prize winner of the Best Concept Album of the 20th Century Award? They will be because it's Todd Rundgren wrangling The Tubes and that means Todd Rundgren made an album that The Tubes played on, but does it matter? No. Again, what else are we gonna do except thoroughly enjoy it, have pizza delivered, and drive 600 more miles tomorrow?

You know what else I just noticed? We're hovering around San Francisco. Now that I've said it, the 4th album will be totally not anywhere near San Francisco, but it was way too obvious to be anything but coincidence anyway.

Oh, man, The Tubes are great. It sounds silly and fun, but also meaningful and like it actually matters. It sounds like they are putting on a show with a proper story, and that show sounds super entertaining.

Critics said "this is meh," then said "it'll be hard to top how awesome Remote Control was" when The Completion Backward Principle came out. No sarcasm on that one by the way, just straight up "I don't feel like liking this album today, but rest assured I'll pretend like I just said it's fantastic in a year or two. I don't need no stinkin' consistent criteria!"

Another ludicrously stellar pick from Gladys to start our day. One more album to go on this particular adventure. Hope it's interesting....

Uh... er... oookay? I'm not entirely sure Gladys bought this album for me specifically. The phrase "eye candy" comes to mind. Oh, see, I told you we'd be who knows where, and it appears to be Georgia (the state, not the former Soviet republic. They both have about the same amount of beach front, so it's easy to get confused).

I feel like I should go back and mention the actual driving distance between San Francisco and Macon somewhere in there, but then I'd have to delete this paragraph and the time vortex would collapse like an abandoned apartment complex. It also seems like we've rounded out this trip with another on the nose album cover: Cats on the Coast, by Sea Level. Funky, sweaty hippies on a beach notwithstanding, I expect we're in for some Jazz Fusion, but probably not the mysterious long range concept kind (hippies on a beach withstanding); more likely Steely Dan style pretzel logic I presume, but probably not as delicate or refined. Calgon, I mean ellipsis, take me away...

... ok, first things first. This is awesome, as in legitimately wonderful. Screaming guitars, funky grooves, complex harmonies, mood shifts from one end of the rainbow to another. There are hints of southern rock, blues, gravely vocals, some salty sax solos, a full buffet of delicious delicacies delivered deliriously. Did I mention the awesome guitar solos?

How are these guys not more famous? Oh, because they were previously known as The Allman Brothers Band, Gregg being particularly unangelic toward them after the breakup (damned fine joke if I do say so myself). Pretty sure Gregg and Dicky quit, not the other way around.

Well, that was invigorating. If you're at all apprehensive about an album by a group of half-shirted dudes on the beach, all I can tell you is this one turned out surprisingly awesome.

Now that my friends was an adventure. Best of all, it's not quite lunch time here in the bunker, so we have the whole rest of the day to unwind from our journey. Sadly, we do have to wake up tomorrow and go back downtown for the Monday Shutdown, but at least we have some awesome mementos to remind us of all the fun we had. Even more sadly, today marks the beginning of the 12 days of Christmas. I suppose I'll have to do something for that....

12 Days of Bottlemas – 1. Jethro Tull

Last year I was still testing out my useless superpowers when it came to Christmas Albums. For obvious reasons, we have to listen to 12 of the damned things, but it's so hard to pick. Do we do 12 good albums? 12 bad albums? Repost my 12 favorite reviews from last year (good or bad)? 12 new albums we've never heard? I have 3 more, but youtube has thousands...

… That all seems like real work, so we're just gonna keep winging it.

I have questions. Were Christmas albums ever actually lucrative? Has any self-respecting band ever really wanted to make a Christmas album? Do you actually want your favorite bands to make Christmas albums? I submit that the answer to all of these questions is "no."

Jethro Tull made 20 albums. Their 21st album, the last one to date, is Christmas Album. Why? I'm not sure Ian

Anderson even knows why he did it. What I do know is that it's both terrible and completely fine at the same time. The everyday normal person in your brain says "oh hell no, not Christmas at Aqualung's house!," but it actually just turns out to be an hour of Celtic adjacent Folk music about the fact that it's beginning to look a lot like Christmas. For lack of a better term it's an actual album, not just schlocky standards.

Sure, it's terrible for a Jethro Tull album, but perfectly boringly tolerable for Christmas. Do we need to go find the third Oak Ridge Boys Christmas album for comparison? Yeah, didn't think so. Please enjoy this strange thing Ian Anderson produced in 2003 for some unknown reason. It will be our baseline for this year's collection of corporate Christmas calamities, and it's actually surprisingly tolerable.

2. A Celtic Christmas
BULRYOR

I got nothing, that's just a nonsense license plate. Maybe if the O were a D, but I'd still read it "Beullery Door" on purpose. What I do have is A Celtic Christmas. Because when I think Celtic Christmas music, I always turn to a random independent label based in Brentwood, Tennessee. Obviously, my first inclination is to question the superlative adjectives used in the naming of the musicians involved, but the fact that the googlemaphone actually delivers their respective teaching studios, discographies, bios, etc. is pretty strong evidence that they are not in fact a bunch of random weirdoes and do have the expertise they rightfully claim (I'd normally let these jabs go full surreptitious, but the Republican party thinks etymology is the study of bugs, and started desperately attacking Jill Biden because other people called her "Doctor" out of respect for her actual PhD). It also sadly means this album will be perfectly enjoyable and I won't be able to make fun of it at all. The one glimmer of hope is the phrase "performed in Lilting Celtic Style" like they're winging it, but I have my doubts. Either way, down the hatch it goes.

Yep, Balderose can play the bagpipes. The janitor of my first elementary school was a Piper. I like bagpipes. Oh, thank goodness, they're just gonna string tunes together without any transition at all, and McCullough is gonna portamento the living snot out of everything.

You know I was joking earlier, right? Ernie Hawkins is pretty well renowned and it actually sounds like he's just playing guitar on this album. There's fret buzz and he's definitely using a noisy brass slide, and other mechanical noises. I'm actually starting to enjoy this quite a lot. You might have a raging migraine by the 10-minute mark, but I'm in heaven. If you gave me a record store, I'd crank this up in August just to drive out the riffraff.

So to recap, terrible album of completely random and disorganized Christmas Carols played on what most people would consider the most annoying musical instruments ever created this side of a hurdy gurdy, and I love it. Skip's right eye is twitching like he's got metal shards in it as we speak. Maybe we'll see if I can slip it past the Auditors later this evening 'cause I'm not finding it on youtube, but everyone should have the chance to enjoy the level of mirth I'm enjoying right now. I like it a lot...

... and now you can too.

3. Rudy Ray Moore – This Ain't No White Christmas

I really should save this for actual Christmas, but it's been a helluva day.

There's no preamble I could give you, there's no commentary I could make. It's crude, it's dirty, it's probably illegal in three states, it's the only Christmas themed stand-up album I know of, it's the legendary Rudy Ray Moore's This Ain't No White Christmas. It's an experience. Not suitable for work, home, children, public broadcast, or pretty much any occasion involving conversations with other people.

Enjoy.

4 & 5. Brian Setzer v Rev. Horton Heat

S: We need to have a talk, Bottle.

B: Is it about last night's Christmas album? I had a rough day, so I was just letting off some steam. Don't be such a Sandra, Sandra. Nobody actually goes and listens the stuff I talk about. They read it, it's either immediately humorous or they just ignore it.

S: No, This Ain't No White Christmas is a completely egalitarian album for its time and cultural milieu. The women are definitely empowered, and the racial content isn't actually insulting in either direction. I can't help it if some people are prudes. I'm actually referring to an argument between Skip and Myself. He's adamant that Reverend Horton Heat's Christmas album is better than Brian Setzer's Christmas album, and I had my hand on the straight razor I carry in my purse before I realized how inappropriate that was. Please settle this issue out of court, if you see what I'm saying.

B: I'm guessing you don't want to know I like Reverend Horton Heat better in all contexts.

S: No, I don't want to know that at all.

B: Kaaaay. Will you accept my final judgment on this issue if I put on my objective hat and make silly comparisons like I did for the Bangels and GoGos?

S: Yes.

B: Are you lying?

S: No comment.

B: That's my line. Put those eyebrows back in their holsters, I haven't heard either of them. It will be as fair as any other comparison I've made. Deal?

S: Ok, but no tricks. I'll accept losing if it's legit, but you know I'll know if it isn't, and Gladys is back to back me up.

B: Yes ma'am. Please allow me to fire up the youtubulator. I have Dig That Crazy Christmas but I don't have a copy of We Three Kings...

I'm Doug Llewellyn, and this is the Bottler's Court. He's no Wapner, but he is as fair as they come. Today's case involves a sort of domestic disagreement between Sandra D. and Marvin Gardens, more commonly know by his stripper name, Skip. Mz. D (sic) contends that Brian Setzer Orchestra's second Christmas album is better than Reverend Horton Heat's Christmas album from the same year, 2005. Both litigants have agreed to submit to Bottle's advisement and are forgoing their right to plead their own cases. A straight third-party adjudication.

Let's now join Bottle halfway through listening to Rev. Horton Heat's We Three Kings. He doesn't know the mic is on, so take a listen to his true inner monologue:

B: Jesus Christ (no pun intended) she's gonna slice an ear off, if not something more sensitive. This thing is just amazing. Catpiss McPompadour better not be fooling around...

...Ahem, well that's probably enough eavesdropping for now. Sit tight folks, we're ready and waiting for Bottle's verdict, and we'll be as surprised as you. In the meantime, you're more than welcome to hear Skip's preference for yourself. Ah! The chamber doors have opened, and Bottle emerges to vanquish the dais. All rise!

No, no, don't get up. This is more like Night Court than anything. Skip is probably Markie Post, and Sandra and Gladys together equal Marsha Warfield. Actually, I'm probably more Marsha than Harry, but that's not the point. We're here to compare Big Band Swing to Psychobilly, or something.

If I understand it right, Skip isn't particularly impressed with Setzer's shtick, but Sandra's a stickler for shtick, it's her shtick. We all know I'm inclined to side with the good Reverend, but I've been politely asked to stay impartial.

So, let's go about this logically. What are they both doing that's equal? Well, they're both playing Rockabilly guitar, and they are every bit equal on that score. Next, it's Christmas music, and they both play it straight. No tricks or parody, these are legitimate adaptations. Rev chooses to go completely traditional and let the music be as experimental and off the wall as possible. Setzer has some more interesting selections and some originals. Showmanship, rather than surprise is his goal. Last, we all expect Setzer to be smoother, less raspy, and have a horn section. You might like the stripped back trio better, or you might love the horns so much you just can't do without them. All of that makes choosing one pretty impossible.

Unwad your panties everyone, these are both legitimately good albums. The concept is Christmas songs, but neither group compromises what they do just because these are Christmas songs. Both albums are legit parts of their respective discographies, unlike some Jethros I've tulled you about (no, you're right to cringe at that one), and I could not jokingly listen to either any day of the year.

Final verdict, it's a real tie. You can like one better than the other, but you can't claim the other is less in some way. Be honest, if I Faro shuffled all the songs, you might not even notice except for Setzer's horn section. Case closed.

Doug here again. Well, there you have it, both albums are actually good. Not just for Christmas albums, but as albums themselves. Who could have predicted it? Let's get a word with Sandra and Skip. How do you feel about Bottle's decision?

 E: To be honest, I hadn't actually listened to the Setzer one, I was just trying to get Sandra riled up. Sorry if I offended.
 S: No, I'm the one who should apologize, I overreacted. Bottle's right, the two are trying to do opposite things and they both succeeded in their own ways. My preference probably has less to do with the music than I care to admit in public at the moment. Care to join me for an adult beverage while we alternatingly listen to both of them?
 B: Skip and Sandra sitting in a tree...
 S: *SHUT UP, BOTTLE!*

 Filmed at the Barristers of Beef Ballroom in balmy Bethesda, all judgments and appearance fees paid for by the H. R. Trustandstuff Fund for the Temporarily Insane. I'm Doug Llewellyn wishing you a good night and some form of tomorrow.

6. Rotary Connection – Peace
 Believe it or not, I put so much effort into last night's review that I sprained my epic imagination muscles. My back hurts too, but that's unrelated.

 So, instead of a zany corporate adventure about a new album, we'll go back to last year and relisten to Rotary Connection's 3rd album, Peace. Actually, now that I think of it, I didn't actually mention the zany corporate adventures involved in this obscure Christmas absurdity. No plot, just some random stuff.
 First, it turns out Rotary Connection really is a Cadet Concept concoction. Marshall Chess was tired of pumping out

boring old blues and rock albums for his dad, so he started a new subsidiary with one of the secretaries as the female vocalist. Minnie Ripperton was her name, and you have her to thank for Mariah Carey's career as the dog whistler. Not up on your list of whistle register divas? Ok fine, Maya Rudolph's mom was the lead singer of Rotary Connection.

Marshall really did just invite a bunch of avant garde (for the time) musicians and let them do whatever they wanted. I think you already know they are insane and it's awesome.

This isn't your normal throwaway Christmas thing, this is a bunch of crazy hippies who woke up and said "you know what this whole nasty Vietnam thing makes us was to do? Make a Christmas album."

Yeah, about that. Another corporation really put a damper on everyone's Christmas cheer.

Some historical perspective: back in the day it was totally normal for corporate executives to walk through the lobby about 9:15, flirt with the receptionists, and then head up to their office for the long day of drinking and phone calls that constituted their "work." One such drunken executive at Montgomery Ward was flipping through Billboard and mistook an anti-war political cartoon for the album cover and angrily cancelled all shipments of the album. What a douche.

If there's one Christmas album you should definitely check out it's this one. It's not the holly jolly happy dappy show tune kind of Christmas, it's a pretty deep look at the realities that breed the escapist corporate Christmas contraption.

What would it be like to live in a world where peace was all there was? Not that we had no concept of tragedy, but that our goal was to ease the pains of those unforeseen tragedies as they arise. What would that be like? Seriously. We have no idea. We're all at least twice as cruel and uncaring as 5 years ago. I know I am. Piss on earth, ill will toward man.

I'm sorry, that wasn't fair. You haven't done anything wrong. We're all making the best choices we can in the face of an actively and intentionally dismantled world. I'm not talking about the corona virus, by the way. Nor is it a conspiracy theory, he did every part of it over the table on national television and half of you applauded.

I only bring it up because 7 shitbags in Waterloo got fired yesterday for gambling on how many people would get sick (insert Toy Story 3 joke here). Tyson itself should cease to exist for all the other horrible stuff they've done in the last two decades, but I'm the radical anarchist chopping off chicken heads in my own backyard, so don't look to me for answers.

Someday we'll find it, the Rotary Connection, the lovers, the dreamers, and me.

7. J.J. Hrubovcak – Hellish Renditions of Christmas Classics

B: Kiddos, I don't think I can do it. 6 more? 4 of 'em were great albums, and I still don't care.

K: But Bottle, if you don't listen to them no one will, and the twinkle fairies will be trapped under the evil witch's spell forever!

B: Fine. Can they be *any* Christmas albums?

K: Sure, the grimoire simply says "and the bottle shall pour forth the 12 bounteous yulebums, lest the princess Zanzibar shall weep and drown the kingdom of man in her tears.

B: Ok then, I don't want to make the princess sad. I'm not a complete monster. I know of a couple death metal Christmas albums. That should be moderately entertaining. Snuggle up kiddies, tonight it's J.J. Hrubovcak and his Hellish Renditions of Christmas Classics from 2013.

"Yay!" the townsfolk rejoiced.

Best parts include A) it's only 5 tracks long, 2) his rendition of Dance of the Sugar Plum Fairies would certainly put a smile on Azrael's face, and Honorable Mention) his version of Greensleeves is completely insane.

I realize 99.93% of you are like "what the hell is wrong with you, Bottle?," but c'mon this is legitimately awesome and enjoyable. I feel giddy joy listening to it, because it's wonderful.

Give yourself the gift of 20 glorious minutes of Death Metal Christmas songs, and long live the Princess!

8. The Killers – Don't Waste Your Wishes

The Bunker of Beef is gonna get a little bit of a makeover tomorrow, so you know just in case I chop a finger off, or drill a hole in my thigh or something, here's Don't Waste Your Wishes, the compilation of a decade worth of holiday singles by The Killers. The sub plot is that Santa is coming to murder Brandon for being naughty, but finally has a change of heart and doesn't actually kill him. It ends with him doing a duet with his 4th grade teacher. Fun stuff.

Pirates of Darkwater

Ug. I can't. I just can't. There's 4 more days counting Christmas, 4 more albums to make 12, but I don't wanna. I'm using my get out of Christmas free card on this turn.

Thankfully, I don't have to. That courtroom skit bought me an extra night, and the ghost of Bottle's past bought future me a present I'm sure to like: a self-published CD from the former band of a bassist in a now more famous band with a name very similar to another bassist from an even more famous band using the title of a TV show. Did you get all that?

Here's the real story: the bassist of The Sword, Bryan Ritchie, found a box of 30 copies of his previous band's self-titled album Pirates of Darkwater, and I snatched up the copy right before the preantepenultimate copy. It's got some impressive track titles.

Obviously, you can't buy the CD now that it's sold out, but you can listen along on Bandcamp. I want to open it so bad, but I won't. I'll delicately place it upon the shelf and listen to it on Bandcamp as well. That's the kind of nice guy I am.

It's a lovely mix of stoner rock, metal, and whatever "math" supposedly sounds like. There might be someone screaming occasionally, but I can barely hear it and I certainly can't make out any lyrics, so we'll just call it an instrumental album.

Gorgeous.

9. Bad Religion – Christmas Songs

Alright, back to my public service obligation to the universe. Here's such a thing Mrs. Bottle didn't know existed.

This year's theme is loosely "why did they make a Christmas album?" Some are unexplainable, some are actual albums that just happen to be about Christmas, The Killers took the unique approach of compiling one single a year over a decade. Tonight, we step through the looking glass and wrestle with the Jabberwocky. I'm convinced it exists only because it shouldn't exist.

What's truly baffling is that Bad Religion's Christmas Songs isn't actually sarcastic (except for the sucker punch of American Jesus at the end). Maybe we need a refresher on irony.

It's not dramatic irony. They know how bizarre it is that they are intentionally singing Christmas songs.

It's not situational irony. The intended effect is clearly to point out the contradiction of overtly religious ceremony as performed by an erudite punk rock band.

It's not verbal irony. There's absolutely no indication of disbelief. If it's verbal irony, it's drier than Bob Newhart with tuberculosis.

It's not cosmic irony like Alanis Morissette likes.

It's not classical irony, 'cause who reads ancient Greek treatises on rhetoric?

It is in fact romantic irony.

M: Hey, Bottle. I didn't know that Romantic Irony was a thing, and now that I do I still have no idea what that could possibly mean.

Ok. I'll try to explain it. All irony is an interruption of discourse, a sudden change in the rules of communication. Now, imagine that Peter Falk is your grandpa and he interrupts the story to remind you that you're listening to Bad Religion sing really great punk versions of Christmas songs. They don't believe in angels, or that some baby let his dad's friends kill him because he didn't think it was fair to punish everyone just because some ancient lady ate an apple and realized she didn't have any clothes on, but they aren't making fun of it either, now are they?

What they're really doing is asking you if American Christmas is somehow any different than American Jesus, and wondering out loud who's getting taken advantage of in this situation. Remember, there's an entire army who will blindly follow along, and even though you try not to be, we are of the same plague.

Plus, you can enjoy the Yule Log version, where Greg silently reads a gigantic book filled with pictures of animals and makes faces at the camera while the album plays.

A desperate plea for recognition from my facebook friends: French hens, I mean 3 albums to go. Any suggestions, or are you just going to let me drive this bus wherever I feel like?

10. The Vandals – OI to the World!

Are there any obnoxious and sarcastic punk Christmas albums?

Yeah, of course. Here's OI to the World! from The Vandals. It's every bit as terrible as Erlewine thinks it is, if you have Erlewine's taste in music. Why'd he even listen to it? Was he surprised he didn't like it?

I love it. I think it holds up even outside the holiday. Remind me to test out that theory next April.

Why would The Vandals or their fans care about mainstream rock criticism? More importantly, why would anyone who values Erlewine's opinion go listen to the Vandals Christmas album whether he liked it or not? Did Christgau even bother to listen to it?

I don't need to synopsisize it. It's great. By now you all know that means it's sloppy, unpolished, and not concerned about your tastes and preferences in any way. Plus, there's a song about being nice to grandpa even though he's a miserable grump. That's the kind of mundanity I value deep in the cockles of my heart.

Thumbs up, quite an enjoyable Christmas concept album for no reason other than it presents some uniquely interesting situations for The Vandals to write silly songs about.

Do I have to do two more? Can I just republish the Oak Ridge Boys reviews from last year and call it a wrap? I guess we'll find out when it happens. Happy Christmas Eve Eve everybody. Four-day weekend, here I come....

End Scene – Marty Friedman's Scenes
'Twas the night before Christmas and all through house, Bottle was fidgeting, figuring things out. Gladys in her kerchief, and Skip in his chair, Compy Compilerson combing his hair....

You know what? No. Not gonna. Go find two more Christmas albums if you want to on your own, but I'm moving on to something else. Time for a new direction, a new age...new age...new age......

You're thinking Yanni and Enya (both excellent choices), but I'm thinking something more unexpected. Marty Friedman made a new age album. Yeah, his second album Scenes was produced by Kitaro and it's a full buffet of sappy, cheesy, soaring melodies, wandering tonality, the kind of exotic appropriation that makes you wonder if Kitaro was secretly giggling inside the whole time, and then you remember it's Marty Friedman. He happily chose to relocate to Japan where they love him more than Germany loved Hasselhoff. They love Mr. Big too, so Paul Gilbert's hanging around as well. Anywho, Marty Friedman does whatever Marty Friedman feels like doing, and this album is pretty bizarre for a shred guitarist. Whatever else I end up saying in the ensuing paragraphs, the overwhelming intention of these scenes is "mystical."

It would be easy to dismiss it as corny or emotionally sappy, but that would belie the fact that it freakin' awesome. It's not the standard neo-classical infused wankfest you expect from a super famous lead guitarist's solo album. It's not an exercise in impossible guitar theatrics for the sake of being a guitar god as though it's an infinite billiards tournament in an episode of The Twilight Zone. It's melodies Marty Friedman liked at the time strung together in various creative ways. Sure, there's shred and screaming noodles here and there, but he's clearly composing music, not trying to win the talent portion of the pageant.

The album itself also flows surprisingly well. Not just a bunch of random tracks, but an intentionally plotted journey. What it means is your problem, but its construction is certainly not slapdash.

None of this means I hate all of the others. Satriani has some amazing pieces, Gilbert is fantastic, Buckethead is pretty great. I don't like Vai or Yngwie, and I'm meh on Petrucci, but that's me not them. The line dividing those groups is actually fairly simple, but ridiculously difficult to put into words. Melodies, for me, are monologues. Guitar solos in particular are little lectures, rants, poems, sermons, etc. Ok, here comes the guitar solo, what's he got to say? Listening to a Zakk Wylde solo is like watching the Swedish Chef scream and throw kitchen knives at the wait staff; great if that's what's necessary, distracting absurdist nonsense 85% of the time. A lot of these guys just sound like "Motormouth" John Moschitta reciting a Micro Machines commercial script. This entire album is sumptuously Largo by comparison. Plus, Friedman's melodic writing uses harmonic tension and release, emphatic statements with conjunctions and introductions and segues, body language, shape, direction, you get the idea. The perceived meaning might come across as simplistic or naive in these particular pieces, but the expression itself is what I'm interested in here. The magic of guitars, synths, drums, and oxford commas.

So, diverging timelines. One Bottle finds another bizarre Christmas album tonight (how about Bootsy Collins' Christmas Is 4 Ever) and pulls out Jesus Christ Superstar tomorrow. Two Bottle (the one I'm gonna be) says "buggerit, let's build bookshelves in the Bunker, binge watch every episode of The Adventures of Pete & Pete on youtube (totally there), and get ready to make some new bizarre music next year."

From all of us crammed in the headspace of hamburger, Merry Christmas. And, as we all anxiously await the arrival of another adventure, enjoy.

Boxing Day with Bottle

B: Why's there a box on my desk, 2*pi*r? Are we refilming the final sequence of Se7en?

C: It's Boxing Day, Bottle. We're fresh out of Gwyneth Paltrow body parts, and Sandra vetoed taking turns punching you in the stomach, even though I thought that would be exactly what you'd like. So, they sent me on a little scavenger hunt.

B: You guys got me records?

C: Yeah. You keep imagining us, we keep feeding you. Seems fair.

B: Adventure Time?

C: No, no, no. Adventure Time only works when you send me because you're bored and out of ideas. These are albums we each thought you should have in your collection; one from each of us. Well, not GREGORY, he was hiding when we came up with the idea, but he'd definitely approve of at least one of them. From Sandra, Skip, Carl, and Gladys to you. Enjoy.

B: I'm speechless. Wait, you didn't pick one yourself?

C: No, I picked all of them from their contextual instructions. Plus, the face on your face says I got the sucker punch I wanted to give you, so I'm good.

B: I, uh, er, I really don't know what to say.

C: When has that ever stopped you? Don't open it now, they want to be as surprised as you. They each wrote you a little note about the instructions they gave me, but they don't know what specific record that turned into. Shelves are looking good, by the way. Cheers, Bottle.

B: Well. I guess at least I know what I'll be doing for the next 4 albums. Until the night, then. These bookshelves aren't going to build themselves.....

Black Sabbath – Paranoid

Alright, ibuprofen administered. I've got my rum and coke. Let's see what the heartiest of minions got me. Oh, there's an envelope on top with "readme.txt" scribbled on it. Hilarious.

Welcome to the box. We each got you a little something we think you'll enjoy. Seeing as you tirelessly imagine our existence, even when you're grumpy, we thought it apropos to base our choices on our perceived functions in this interesting universe you've created for yourself. As for me, I gave Compy the following instructions:

He doesn't have very many truly classic albums. Preferably rock/metal, but anything as long as it's a true classic.

I'll be as surprised as you are by what he actually picked, but I have little doubt it will be thoroughly enjoyable.

Sincerely,
Sandra

A classic album from a classy lady. Yes, I suppose that is fitting. Well, here we go.
Ooooh. The second Black Sabbath album, Paranoid. No argument here, it certainly is a classic album. There're tons of stories about it, but my favorite two are that the execs said "guys, your suggested title is ridiculous, but that song Paranoid is a real potential hit, so let's call the album Paranoid," and that they were really nervous about putting Planet Caravan on it, but famously had so little material that there wasn't much choice. Also, Ozzy didn't know what a Leslie speaker was, I think he called it "a refrigerator with a knob on" or something similarly ridiculous. Paranoid turned out to be a massive hit, and they all agreed to never do singles again just to keep the randos from annoying their actual fans at their shows.
The other awesome thing is that this is basically a jam album. Iommi kept coming up with riff after riff, Geezer and Ward would just groove under it, Ozzy would come up with

melodies and Geezer would write some wordy words. Literally making it up as they went along with only working-class anger/depression to guide them.

And the stories, my word the stories. War mongers are the real Satan. Date night in outer space. A time traveler from the future who gets so mad that no one will heed his warnings that he creates the Armageddon he witnessed. Nuclear war as their response to the hippie flowers in your San Franciscan hair. The Vietnam/heroin problem I'm sure I've mentioned somewhere before. A drum solo just because they had to chew up all those endless 45-minute sets at their early gigs. Cap the whole thing off with Ozzy's encounter with some skinheads, and this is the absolute heaviest thing imaginable for 1970, let alone here at the end of 2020.

It is Heavy Metal. It's Doom. It's literally saying "look at the world, no really look at it, it's horrible. It sucks. We haaaaaate it."

Just an amazing album, the concept being not really knowing or noticing the difference between paranoia and depression, but definitely feeling both when you look at the harsh realities of England and America's politico-economic systems.

Is it even a record collection if you don't have a copy of Paranoid? I submit that it is not, and now I don't have to worry about it at all. Thanks, Sandra. You were right, Compy has pretty good taste. If the other 3 are half as good I'll be ecstatic.

Kansas – Point of Know Return
Who next? How about Gladys? What's her note say?

Poke him in the ribs, but make sure it's delicious. Find something from a band that surprised him. Prog rock maybe. I know he wants a copy of Brain Salad Surgery, but we'll just pretend like I don't know what that means and settle for Kansas, or Argent, or something like that.

Just like a grandma, isn't she? Oh, wow! There's no joke here, I freakin' love Kansas and every other opinion is crap. Point Of Know Return, the one with Dust In The Wind and an unnecessary pun. That's a total Gladys move right there.

This one has the same stupid criticisms as Leftoverture: b-grade English prog blather, too crazy but not crazy enough, Dust In The Wind is the only good thing they ever recorded. Even the movie HI Fidelity took a jab at Kansas for this album. Too obvious for a lead off title track?!? You're all idiots, this is glorious. A song about Einstein, one about Howard Hughes, life is literally an adventure. How does this sound dated? Do you mean it sounds like 70s prog-rock in pop song form? It is the mid-70s in case you missed that memo. Sure, yeah, it's a stark contrast to the doom and gloom of Sabbath, but it is coming from an intentionally different mindset. It's not garbage just because it's fantasy, and it's not cheesy just because it's optimistic.

This is fantastic. If cantankerous Grandmas made albums, they'd have surprisingly raunchy guitars, Animal-esque drums, and wacky synths just like this one. More violins and other stringed instruments in rock music now! I don't care how long it takes, sign me up for that voyage off the edge of the waterfall!

Thank you, Gladys! Compy's 2 for 2 on this journey. What's Skip bringing to the party? Tune in tomorrow, and we'll find out together.

The Boomtown Rats – A Tonic for the Troops

I'm slightly trepidatious about Skip's pick. Not that I won't like it, but he's surprisingly difficult to figure out. I guess that makes sense, if you could guess what the editor is thinking you wouldn't need an editor, would you? Alright, bring it, Skip says:

Get him something that's missing from a band's discography. Fill in the gaps.

Oh, yeah, totally how an editor would think. I was worried for nothing.
Oh. Oh no. The Boomtown Rats. Compy found their second album, A Tonic For The Troops. Oh boy.
Ok, I haven't heard it. I'm fairly sure I will like it, but I haven't been exactly forthcoming when it comes to the two albums I did review and the one I haven't reviewed. I loved The Fine Art of Surfacing, and their first album was great too, but there's a reason The Boomtown Rats aren't famous, and it's because The Boomtown Rats are offensive. I don't mean they use bad words (I love those), I don't mean they have questionable subject matter (I obviously love the dark side of everything), I mean Bob Geldoff is in your face repugnant, smarmy, vicious, and completely uncompromising. Jello Biafra is all those things and likably famous, so is Henry Rollins, even Maynard and Les Claypool live across the line from civilized conversation, but Bob makes them look like the cultured antagonists they really are. Johnny Rotten can't hold a candle to Bob Geldoff. Bob Geldoff is an offensive personality even the Thin White Duke would have to tip his hat around. I agree with him 4/5 of the time (that's 80% if you're fractionally challenged) and I'm still like "he said that, I didn't say that." Whatever it is, Bob Geldoff is being nasty about it. I haven't reviewed their 4th album because it's terrible, but I know this one isn't. It is, however, tough to talk about.
Hitler, suicide, euthanasia, the sheer terrible of being fully aware of your surroundings. Now, I'm rarely accused of

being a shiny happy person because I'm totally as cynical, sarcastic, and introverted as anyone, but I also make a show of tempering that bile. Not Bob. If "sheeple" was a word in the late 70s, he'd use it to death as an insult to the people who say "sheeple."

Regardless, as an album this is pretty great. They reuse a couple songs from their first album, mostly because the concept lets them. The concept is hard to condense into a simple tag line, but it's all about how public appearance is a facade, polite society is a joke, everything is a lie, a placebo of trashy entertainment in the guise of intellectual fashion.

The thing you have to remember is that this is 1970s Dublin, only a few years removed from the bombings and the nastiest part of The Troubles. Dublin was not a wealthy, fashion forward city, and it's hard to believe anything when you're quite frankly poor, dirty, hungry, and exceedingly tired of car bombs and paramilitary violence.

Irish politics is a topic too big and confusing for 3 of me, so we'll leave that alone and go back to the music. Jangly New Wave energetic pop-rock, cynically vicious social commentary floating on top like oily scum. A rainbow of snark and misery! More than anything this album puts me in mind of an Oingo Boingo album in a bizarro universe where Danny Elfman isn't quirky or macabre, but just downright mean.

It occurs to me we've done something pretty interesting. Compy says it's not an Adventure Time, but we're bouncing back and forth from the UK to America in roughly chronological order, and so far it's reality sucks, escapist adventure fantasy, no seriously reality suuuuucks.... Why do I get the feeling the last album will be America in the 80s? Why do I get the feeling it will be exactly the opposite of everything I just said, a tonic for the troops in its own way? I mean, I totally believe this is all coincidence, it's not like C-lector listens to them while he's crate combing. We're just going through the stack in order, and they don't even know what record is next. It's like we live in a perpetual spiral of the same old arguments with new technology and different but equally silly looking pants. Alright, Carl. Surprise me....

Alice Cooper – Raise Your Fist and Yell
Give him the chair, turn on the bug zapper, shock rock him. Something theatrical. He loves that stuff even though he doesn't have a lot in his collection.

How does he manage to get both insult and compliment in one little package? Carl's in charge, and also the janitor. I've seen the world from both sides now, so here's Carl's vicarious present, Alice Cooper's Raise Your Fist and Yell. Yep, that's the face Carl usually makes at me when I pass him in the hallway. It's also Kip Winger's second and last Cooper album.

This 10th album is supposedly from Alice's horror movie tie in period, Freddy Kruger himself makes a cameo on here somewhere. None of these songs are well known, no radio play ever, smack dab in the middle of the late 80s with Madonna on one side and England/Germany calling the stage show for the tour too graphically violent for public consumption on the other. James Randi (rest in peace, Mr. Skeptic) originally designed the guillotine set piece they brought back for this tour. Sounds like it would have been awesome. Too bad I was only 7 at the time. None of these songs were ever performed again, so it's like a time capsule of stuff that may or may not be totally embarrassing to revisit decades later. Will it be surprisingly great, or surprisingly terrible? Only one way to find out.

Yeah, this album really does need its full historical context to understand. It's a fantastic album, but it isn't a standalone kind of album.

Ok, the short short version. The band existed to shock audiences and really dive into the theatrical possibilities of stage shows, horror, and social controversy. Alice Cooper is a female villain. California didn't get it, so they went back to Detroit and just got bigger and more shocking throughout the 70s. Then in the early 80s, Alice pulled a Clapton and did so many drugs he barely remembered recording any of those albums. After a decade of relentless touring and recording they were just burned out on each other, and Alice sort of became a solo project rather than a steady band. He took a break, got sober, and came back with Constrictor and Raise Your Fist..., leading to his second wave of popularity and movie crossover stuff. These two albums are way harsher and more metal than anything before, and you have to approach them as mythos albums. They aren't really concept albums, more reestablishing the character in a contemporary musical setting; hair metal as opposed to garage rock.

Every song really does read like the back-story of an 80s horror movie, and you kind of have to just accept that that's how the character fits into the decade. There will always be a villain because there's always a nasty side to society, and Alice is back to haunt your nightmares.

Like I said, it isn't a standalone album, and you aren't going to be humming selections while you work (except maybe Freedom, it's sort of a lesser-known Cooper classic), but it's a chapter in the book of Alice Cooper you can't actually skip reading. If nothing else, it's totally worth checking out what Kane Roberts and Kip Winger were creating early in their careers.

Well, this has been a thoroughly enjoyable holiday after all. I hear we're in for some level of snowpocalypse next week, but as always, I'll deal with that when it happens. One more week of 2020 to go, here's hoping it's not particularly eventful. Cheers.

In the Aeroplane Revisited
We've reached that radian of the endless spiral of regurgitating revolutions where youtube pukes out covers and analyses of The Aeroplane Over The Sea. That's not me, it's totally youtube. Maybe Jeff Magnum felt like he needed some attention and paid someone to bump him up the algorithm rankings, I don't know. What I do know is the original is unimprovable upon.

Sorry, but you can't honestly tell me the meaning is transferrable, because this is 100% Jeff Magnum's inner monologue. You can understand *that* it means something, but you and I can't communicate in this language. I'm reluctant to make the comparison, but it's a bit like Cobain in that the words obviously fit together like that, but they don't mean what they say. They don't mean the same thing if *you* say them. Or, like, sure you can cover a Cake song, but you'll just come across as a douche bag if you do. All this lo-fi DIY gutter folk is like that, much more than any other genre. These aren't universal ideas, this is deeply personal and idiomatic stuff.

My wife was telling me about the Nashville Christmas explosion, and how it's incredibly disconcerting. It is, but the circumstances do point to the classic arc of depression and suicide with a tinge of luddite dissatisfaction, albeit confusingly grandiose.

Why do these things coincide? I don't know. Is it a fever dream romance with Anne Frank, or is she just one of the characters in this hallucinatory nightmare? Sure, why not both? The beauty of surrealism is that it means what you think it means. The downside is that most people want validation for their interpretations; it can't be meaningful unless you tell me I'm really on to something. That's nonsense. You know it's nonsense, because Magnum's literal reaction was "I'm not an idea. I'm a person who clearly wants to be left alone." Seriously, can you imagine if 10,000 people just suddenly started downloading my nonsense albums and went to town with the schizophrenia subplot lurking under the surface? I can, it's terrifying.

Haaaa, here's a fun image, Neutral Milk Hotel covering The Boomtown Rats' Living In An (Avery) Island.

No, people just want to be in a cult. They'll make up a cult if one's not available. I don't get it. It's a great album, but it's Jeff Magnum's album. Go write your own and let me hear Jeff sing this one. Then let me hear your album, in your words, with your personality. I'd like that better.

The Specials – Whoo boy, it's special

You know who lived 2020 for their entire career? The Specials. No seriously, from a structuralist perspective there is literally no difference between Thatcher-era England and Trump-era America. People are fleeing metropolitan areas in droves because A) they can't afford to live there, and B) they can't afford the actual cost of handing your city over to major corporations. Bottle version of their bio in 3, 2, 1...

What was the driving force behind Punk/New Wave in England? C'mon, you remember. Why?.... why are?... Ok, fine. Why are all you people so goddamned racist?!

Ozzy told you his story about the skinheads around Birmingham, Red Rider gave you their unhelpful synopsis of the lunatic fringe from a Canadian perspective, but let's hear it from the band with actual stab wounds. Side note, everyday Brits don't have the right to keep and bear arms, so they stab each other instead. The shape of the weapon is relatively unimportant when you've reached the bottom rung of killing each other.

The Specials became a band because A) there wasn't any meaningful work in Coventry, and B) night clubs paid their entertainers. One of their goals though was to be actively anti-racist, so they blended early Punk with Reggae, formed their own record label Two-Tone, and conquered the English pop charts all on their own. Then the skinheads started literally attacking them and wrecking their shows. The normal drugs and alcohol and touring broke them up, but they eventually got back together, with Terry Hall on a successful treatment regimen for his bipolar depression.

Thatcher, oh yeah, right. See, one of the things you can learn from history is that people generally feel like governments exist to take care of the important details of having a society; coordinating and developing infrastructure, planning for the future, negotiating trade and commerce, generally using the community resources as a means to keep everybody happy and allow everyone to be productive without killing each other. Government officials, however, tend to reinterpret themselves as the ruling class and capitalize on society for personal wealth and influence, then pass that down to their children with the warning to never let the plebes rise above their function as pure labor capital.

Now, markets fluctuate and industries boom and bust all over the place. That's reality. But, people tend to think that the profits and taxes and stuff that accrued in the boom times should be waiting there to ease the pain of the tough times. Governments don't work like that. Lord Governor Muckmouth isn't going to sell one of the seven estates he owns just because there's a grain shortage over in Theresville, and he certainly isn't going to pay one of his rivals to truck their excess grain over here either. So instead, he blames all those "greedy foreigners" that came over during the boom and lets desperation kill enough people to make the problem go away on its own. That's what Thatcher did in the 80s in every major city that wasn't feeding the purse at a satisfactory rate, foment racial antagonism then send in the troops to squash everyone back into complacency. One of Trump's babysitters was clearly reading the same bedtime story to him every night, he didn't even try to be creative the last two years.

Why do people take drugs, kill each other, and themselves? Because they are miserable, they have no hope that anything will get better, and no one will help resolve the source of that misery, only scold them for being ungrateful and entitled. So, they medicate their problems in completely unhelpful ways and end up going crazy.

Why do corporations kill communities? Because all the wealth and vitality gets siphoned out of the community to the point that its inhabitants don't have the resources or relationships necessary to help each other anymore. They're too busy competing instead of cooperating.

Anywho, back to Thatcher. "Swamped" is obviously the most famous word she used from our perspective, but the situation is even more complicated than a single sound bite. Her win caused the National Front to focus its attention on working class cities to regain its support, but she also specifically brought back the racist imperial rhetoric of her predecessors, weakened local governments as much as possible, decimated industrial centers that showed weakening profits, supported Apartheid and actually called Nelson Mandela a terrorist. If you thought Roger Waters hated Margaret Thatcher's England, let me introduce you to my friends The Specials. They hated her so much they created a whole new genre of music just to talk about it.

Which brings us to the ultra-confusing opposition between Economic Liberalism and Socialism (with which Mandela was certainly affiliated, but not to the point of tearing down existing policies, merely extending them into the realm of African Nationalism). Yes, those things are opposite. Social liberal/conservative is the opposite of economic liberal/conservative. Again, I'm not making any of this up. If you want to change a thing you're liberal, if you don't want to change a thing you're conservative. The problem is that those positions switch places each time we have a fight about it, so you end up with the absurdist nonsense of ultra Right Wing politicians extolling "freedom," State Socialists not realizing that's mostly still Right Wing politics, Capitalists pushing

Marxist policy, Marxists who aren't actually Marxist because no one has read Marx in at least 70 years (wait, you mean Lenin was only 13 and Mao was -10 when Marx died having not finished writing all those books he meant to write?), the majority of people not having any understanding that public corporations are a type of socialist institution created to feed capitalism in its most abstractly useless form (the capitalization of investment itself), and Political Anarchists like me being terrified of all the economic anarchists driving around with truck nuts on their pickups.

That's a lot of heavy-duty stuff for some rock and roll with a horn section, and I didn't even go anywhere near Terry's being kidnapped by pedophiles when he was 12.

Mastodon – Once More 'Round The Sun

As is tradition for New Year's Eve, we bring out the psychedelic space-monster and beg him to let us take one more turn on the doomy-go-round. If you recall, last year I said I'd try to be nicer. I failed on that one, didn't I? Extenuating circumstances, schmekstenuating smirkumstances, I lost my shit a couple times, as the kiddos like to say. I'm officially a grumpy old man, Graybottle the Beardnificent. But, you know what? I'm still going to wake up tomorrow. I'm still gonna put on pants and shoes and stuff, feed the chickens, play with power tools, and generally enjoy what time I have. If there was a suggestion box around, I'd probably write something like:

"I think it would be a great idea if we could all focus our time and energy on getting all the important things taken care of as quickly and efficiently as possible, instead of wasting at least 1/3 of our waking day doing pointless busy work for someone else. I have tons of my own busy work that needs doing, but all my minions keep exploding, remember?"

It's also today that MF Doom's wife announced his death back in October. Rest In Peace, Mr. Villain. I don't have any of your albums in my collection, but not for lack of appreciation.

I've often said that I can't make the world a better place. I can't, but I can make the parts of it I touch think a little harder. So, we'll tuck Bottle in to sleep and Tread Lightly as he hums his little mantra to himself:

Open your eyes. Take a deep breath and return to life. Wake up and fight. Fight for the love and the burning light.

Happy New Year. A new adventure awaits. Cheers.

Nevermind, in however many parts

<u>Prelude</u>

B: GREGORY. Come out, come out, wherever you are!

Crash! scurry scurry crash!

B: GREGORY! Don't be like that. It's a new year, a new adventure. Let's write a story in several parts that will get jumbled up in peoples' feeds so they can't keep track of what I've said in what order. It'll be fun.

Slowly a door opens. Bony fingers surrounded by a slight bluish aura grip the door one by one. A top hat emerges, followed by the gleaming skull of our very own Skeletonus Anthropomorphous Profundo. He and Bottle lock eyes, one set of which flares red and gives out a blood curdling screech.

B: Sorry GREGORY, it's just that you're frightening. I'm over it now, whaddya say?

To call the empty stare of a skull deadpan might be a little on the nose, but as luck would have it, skeletons don't have the necessary cartilage for one.

B: Nothing? Not even a head nod. Fine, if I must. Baa ram ewe. Open sesame. Whatever those words are to get you to talk to me. Use the boomy voice, I like that one.

DID YOU BUY MORE RECORDS?

B: There, that's more like it. Yeah, I got two records at Target, 'cause what else am I going to use a Target gift card for?

HOW DID YOU FIND THEIR SELECTION?

B: Lifeless? Bare bones? Lacking in substance? I got two of the three things they had that qualify as real albums, Nevermind and Bat Out Of Hell. The third was Abbey Road, and we all know I have the original.

MORTIMER.

B: Schwa? Baking powder?

MORTIMER. THE BAT OUT OF HELL IS NAMED MORTIMER. NICE GUY, IF A TAD ERRATIC.

B: I was not aware of that. I suspect you made it up, but it's humorous, so we'll go with it. Why don't you go freshen up, or whatever, and we'll meet up later for a phenomenological exposé of one of them. We'll have Sandra flip a coin, or something....

Alright, no need for a coin toss. Nobody has meatloaf on Saturday, tonight it's Nevermind on vinyl. Compy, what have I said about it in the past?

C: Not much, actually. Your official statement on the band is "Every single second of the whole discography is perfect, exactly what it should be, and it's glorious." You compared it to the Ramones with a budget, and marked it down as right place, right time, right message: I cannot possibly care about anything anymore.

B: Yeah, that sounds like me. I have a copy of it on vinyl now. Should I just put it on the shelf and wait 40 years to see if it regains value as a pristine, never played, Target special limited edition reissue pressed on silver polyvinyl chloride? Show of hands. No? No one?

E: You know, Bottle, it might be interesting to approach it like new. Analyze it as an actual experience from beginning to end, really go in depth.

B: Interesting idea, Skip. Why?

E: Well, most of your reviews are critical readings. You've already listened to it a few times, you pick out lyrics that connect with real experience, in short you tell people what it means to you at the moment you're reviewing it. Why not give it an outsider analysis?

B: The art experience treatment? Ok, that could be fun. What if it takes more than one essay?

E: Then I won't be bored next week, and you won't blow through albums so fast.

B: Ok. Any objections from the rest of you? Nevermind for as long as it takes, and you'll all pitch in? Sandra?

S: Yes.

B: Compy?

C: Righto.

B: GREGORY?

DELIGHTFUL.

B: *Gladys*!? Do you mind hearing Nevermind 27 times through the floorboards over the next week!?

G: Not at all, Deary. That one never gets old.

B: Oh boy, oh boy, here we go. Let's say I just wandered into a store and saw a photo of a naked baby in a swimming pool. Sandra, verdict?

S: Ok, I'll play along. Without any context, that's definitely obscene, but the fact that it's the cover for some recorded music on the shelf at a major corporate retailer at a time when the mainstream music industry is at the lowest point it has ever been since ever does hint at some level of cultural significance. Its apparent cultural value transcends any surface level outrage regarding its imagery. Plus, there's no "you won't believe what the Nevermind Baby looks like now" articles flooding anyone's news feed. Spencer Eldon has talked about how weird it is, but he's not gonna stake his life on exploiting his own coincidental involvement. Gray area.

B: You said it. Naked baby chasing dollar bill on fish hook means something. Irony check, Skiperdoodle?

E: No, I'd say that is pretty direct, coherent, and intentional social critique. Probably not songs about sunshine, lollipops, or anthropomorphically helpful forest creatures. I don't know where we're headed, but this is kinda fun.

B: Me neither, Skip-rope. GREGORY, dead or alive?

IN WHAT WAY?

B: Don't spin me right 'round you bag of bones, old band or now band.

I FIND IT QUITE DIFFICULT TO BELIEVE THAT ANYONE NOT CURRENTLY UNDER A BOULDER WOULD BE UNAWARE OF THE PAST TENSE OF THE BAND NIRVANA.

B: Couldn't have said it better myself. Look at all the pretty luggage we brought along with us, and we haven't even flipped it over to gaze at the worst photograph ever intentionally taken (no monkey with creepy electronics strapped to its back on this one).

Stickers on cellophane, what do they tell us? Sorry guys, rhetorical question, I'll take it from here, but feel free to chime in if something strikes your fancy.

Limited edition? Target exclusive? Silver? All marketing crap. You can dye anything any color you want. What you can't do is manufacture a bunch of crap no one will buy, at least not repeatedly. Target paid for this run of obsolete non-recyclable plastic, but only this one time to try to make some money. I bought it with money someone else already gave Target. We're ignoring the fact that I had it on cassette before I was a teenager, at least three copies on CD, my wife had a copy, etc. We're pretending it's a new experience. I vaguely know they were famous, this album was a big deal, it's Rock in the broadest sense. Not happy or party rock (from the imagery), but guitars and stuff. Maybe a friend said "you have to, have to, have to hear this album," and I said "ok, I'll bite, what's this thingamajigger all about?"

So, we open it. There's an insert with pictures and lyric fragments and credits. Yep, that's silver, and a poly-lined inner sleeve, fancy. Doesn't smell like deodorant. Take it away, play button and ellipsis...

... no, shut up, play the whole thing again...

... holy shit. You're serious? Just some random guys from Seattle making their second album? It's incredible. For one thing, it's a proper album for vinyl: big obnoxious songs first, end with the softest tracks with barely drums. You got 2 choices, move toward soft and sweet or move toward soft and sorrow. That's the thing about vinyl, the structure is determined by the medium itself 'cause the center gets too squished up for a wide signal. Polly and Something In The Way ain't sappy love ballads.

I have to break character a little and say this mix/master is phenomenal. I've listened to it at least 40 times in every format imaginable, but I've never heard the vocal overdubs sound so nice and clear before. It's fantastic. Who knows how it will hold up with age, but it's certainly not a garbage pressing out of the box (except for the tiniest bit of crackle from factory dust).

Now, this is a phenomenological analysis. That means it's mine, in the first person. I don't know what you hear, what it means for you. I hear a pieced together studio album, various takes sewn together, some weird and questionable overdubs, some of the stitching is clearly visible like a mended old teddy bear, there are tracks that "didn't make the album" due to redundancy or lack of interest or because they didn't quite fit the mindset of the people in the room. I hear that in spite of all the layering and tone sculpting it's blatantly a power trio. 1 guitar part, 1 bass part, 1 octopus of a drummer named Dave Grohl, and some of the I don't care-iest vocal-chord destruction imaginable. That's not cultured screaming, it's just pure abandon with no hope of sounding un-raspy tomorrow. It sounds like it hurts.

Skip will back me up on this one, Nevermind means "never mind, either you get it or you don't, and I can't give you any better explanation. I'm just a person who clearly wants to be left alone."

So, we'll take a coffee break, maybe take a nap on the couch, and come back ready to dig a little deeper, figure out what the hell he's trying to say....

How big of a deal is Nevermind? Weird Al big. The whole shebang, the cover, the song, the video, the voluntary royalties (Weird Al doesn't hide behind parody defense, he pays licensing up front and asks for permission. His execs lied to him and told him Coolio was fine with it, or he wouldn't have done that one; that's a televised apology from Al himself). Mind bogglingly humongous, and Nirvana was sincerely thrilled. They nearly imploded every week and Kurt killed himself 3 years later, but that's outside the scope of this analysis.

So, cover art. This is like one of the 3 most immediately recognizable covers in history. Sandra mentioned the infant, but let's really explore it. It's genius.

The story is even better. Kurt was interested in water births at the time, so some poor unsuspecting label intern had to sift through image after image of babies being born in bathtubs just to say "uh, sir, we can't publish any of this as the album cover." So, they hired an underwater photographer to go to swim classes, but that wasn't working either, so the photographer said to one of his assistants "can I just take a photo of your newborn baby? It'll take like 15 seconds. Thanks, here's $200."

Any person on earth would feel conflicted if they were that baby. The dollar bill on a fish hook was obviously added later, and it's obviously social critique. It's not hypocrisy, it's division of money. Geffen won that gamble, and the trickle is what the trickle is. It cost millions of dollars to make this album with no guarantee that it would sell. I don't hear Grohl and Novoselic bitching about all the worse albums they helped bankroll by hitting it big with this one. There's no sinister plot afoot, our economy is designed around rich people playing heads up poker in the televised final of a WPT tournament, no mention of who payed anybody's original entry fee. Some guys are there on their own private winnings, some guys are there on borrowed money with a whole line of people waiting to get back their investment with interest.

It's hard to call this photo exploitation, because it's not. It's coincidence. Should Spencer get royalty checks for this cover? Technically the answer is no. He could turn it into his livelihood if he wanted to prove the album cover right, but that seems pretty horrible. You can't ignore the fish hook.

E: Ok, ok, we get the image and the ethos, but what about the lyrics?

B: Mostly nonsense.

E: You can't just leave it at that, Bottle.

B: But Skip, nonsense is the point. The meaning of it is that all of it is stupid. Top to bottom, life is dumb because life has devolved to the point where we're all just chasing money, love, fame, happiness. If you define life as chasing all those things, A) you'll never attain them, 2) everything will be a competition with no winners, and last) it's all stupid and fake.

Nevermind isn't a story. There's no plot, every song is a series of absurd situations and descriptions of the participants. Even the kidnapper-rapist of Polly is clearly bored by the pointless mundanity of the grotesque situation; he has to feed and water and chase her when she escapes, exactly like a pet parrot.

What are all the images that make up this universe? In no particular order: macho bravado vs. impotence, guns, sex, codependence, homelessness, depression, and self-loathing. All the things that make really being alive a miserable experience for someone who feels like they don't belong. Scenes from the losing side of life. The real question you might ask yourself is "what's the point?" I think we all know the answer, there is none, existence is Absurd.

Then why is it a great album? It's an example of its own absurdity. In spite of its haphazard imagery and lack of meaning, physical reality forces structure and direction upon it. If Side A builds up cliques and communal relationships only to find them becoming pointless routine, Side B strips away those cultural definitions and the materialist greed only to find us redefining existence in the same terms again. If you search for meaning you never find it, if you tear away meaning you end up rebuilding it out of desperation.

S: You're getting too abstract, Bottle. We can't follow you.

B: You're right, Sandra. You can't. You have to do it for yourself. You have to hold all the songs and images in your own head, try putting them together in various ways like a jigsaw puzzle with no reference image. All I can do is try to describe how the parts I'm working on are starting to fit together. I can't tell you what it means for you.

I THINK, BOTTLE, IT MIGHT BE HELPFUL TO HEAR YOU DO IT OUT LOUD.

B: Ok, I can try. Track 1, Smells Like Teen Spirit. What or who smells like Teen Spirit? Is teen spirit a thing or an abstract idea? Or maybe that juxtaposition is the important idea. Teen Spirit was a brand of deodorant marketed to girls.

Do you know what that deodorant smelled like? Maybe it just smelled like baby powder, or maybe the scent image in your mind also involves the scent of sweat or masking the sweat, or the self-consciousness of your armpit odor, or the implicit assumptions of gender. Can you substitute Old Spice or Axe Body Spray? Does your brain have a clear distinction between boy smells and girl smells? Is that a good or bad thing? Maybe this deluge of ideas and associations is exactly the kind of muddled awkward confusion he's trying to express? Maybe we should press play.

A sort of trashy catchy pop chord progression (reminiscent of early punk), then stomp on the distortion pedal and everybody plays it while head banging and flailing around, then pull way back to a sparse cleanish texture for the first verse. That's a musical gesture: do a thing, do it again super exaggerated, everybody quiet, I'm about to say something. That's what the opening 20 seconds mean to me, it's an introduction, the "ahem" before a statement.

"Load up on guns and bring your friends, it's fun to lose and to pretend."

Kay, that means nothing.

"She's over bored (overboard) and self assured, oh no I know a dirty word hello (how low)."

Well, that's certainly a verse and a pre-chorus. Wowzers, that's a lot of grammar to parse: puns, obscured punctuation, 4 seemingly unrelated ideas, and don't forget all that stuff about deodorant and gender roles that encapsulates the whole thing.

Is "hello" the dirty word, or am I supposed to supply my own? If she's part of the group of losers with guns, maybe his saying hello to her is a serious cultural transgression. Is she excessively bored, or is she "in too deep/out of her element/etc."? It's a pun, so keeping both meanings of the homophone open is the intention.

Are they a militia? A gang? Police? Guys on a hunting trip? Just a bunch of macho jerks? Either way it's clear that he thinks they are losers. They probably also think he is a loser. That's an unresolvable binary opposition (two sides of the same coin).

So, we have a group of people, a girl who may or may not be part of that group, and an unspecified narrator, all under the umbrella of teenage experience/deodorant for girls. I'm certain everyone has some memory or at least understanding of participating in a scenario like that, some similar experience. That experience shapes your interpretation and gives the first verse meaning. The analysis shows us where all those gaps are, which parts are being stated and which parts you yourself fill in. Interpretation is about playing around with all those puzzle pieces, not to find the best interpretation, but to understand all the possible ways someone might interpret it compared to the way you yourself interpret it. I tend to think it raises the question of who does or doesn't belong to a group, how those groupings are antagonistic to each other, and how there is no resolution for that antagonism. Kurt didn't put that stuff there, he assembled a complex network of relationships without closing off all of those potential connections. The rest of the song may or may not clarify any of those relationships, we're still inside the world building stage, about to plunge into the chorus.

Calling it a chorus actually requires a lot of presumptions about pop music or music in general, so maybe we should just label them as sections. The first section was music, the second section was 4 lines of text and a build up to the 3rd section we're about to hear.

"With the lights out it's less dangerous,
Here we are now, entertain us.
I feel stupid and contagious,
Here we are now, entertain us.
A mulatto, an albino, a mosquito, my libido, hey!"

Is this "us" the same as the earlier group with guns, or is it a different group? Why is it less dangerous if you can't see each other? What do those descriptions actually say about the people in the group? Is the exclamation at the end intended to be humorous? Sarcastic? Accusatory? Angry? Is he saying it with jazz hands? There isn't any clarification beyond the relative aggression/calm of the musical textures so far. This section belongs to the more aggressive, loud, crazy, etc. side of that dichotomy, and that will influence your interpretation in some way.

I could keep going like that forever, but it's tedious to write. Instead, I think it might be helpful to do a kind of thought bubble analysis of the connoted themes. I mentioned some of them: antagonism, self-consciousness, aggression, confusion. Try to imagine how and in what way a particular line or image points to one or more of those themes. For example, a group of people with an arsenal of weapons can certainly point toward aggression and antagonism, but it also has an effect on how we categorize inclusion or exclusion. We saw a split in the potential meaning of "over bored" and "overboard." It might seem silly, but the smell of deodorant might signal her self-assurance and signal her inclusion in the group. Or, perhaps it is masking her fear or desperation to belong. Remember, the song isn't telling you, you have to either build that meaning for yourself or tear down assumptions you've already made. The process is the purpose, not whatever result you happen to get.

E: Uh, Bottle? I know I've asked this before, but are you a homicidal maniac? Do you seriously listen to music that way?

B: No and yes, respectively, Skip. Not all the time. I have dozens of listening strategies I can pick from. Closed eyed head bobbing, the air-drum approach, I can pretend I'm the one screaming it into a microphone in front of a crowd of people. I can hold a bunch of pictures up in my brain and connect them with thumbtacks and string like I'm hunting a serial killer. I can pretend to be offended, or turn it all into a joke, I can compare it to a TV show or movie, I can make it about installing a bathroom cabinet, or let it make some statement about what the President is doing. I don't have to pick one, I just enjoy the process.

It's only day two, are you tired of it? I expected to keep going all week: answer your questions if you had some, debate your interpretations, a collaborative experience for everyone. You might learn to like it, you might learn to hate it even more, Sandra might tell me to shut up. I don't know, it was just an idea. Why don't we take a break and let it simmer for a bit? We don't have to bash our faces against the brick wall, unless you want to. You tell me when you're ready, I've got lots of things I can do in the meantime....

Ok, here's a question. What are some of the standard criticisms or put downs of Kurt, the band, etc.?

Well, there's that old joke "I used to like Nirvana until I realized I'm a better guitar player than Kurt." That's just pure feel-bad narcissism, and you're a jerk for thinking it. The sentiment is that he wasn't a great guitar player. What does "great" even mean? Could he play the notes he wanted to play when he wanted to play them? Why isn't that good enough?

What else? The music is too simple, it encourages lazy sloppy copycat mediocrity, it minimizes virtuosity and the appreciation of excellence.

Zappa famously stopped playing guitar for long periods of time just so that he would sound clumsy and unrehearsed on stage. How many Joe Bonamossa albums do you and your friends own? Is Kenny Wayne Shepherd still relevant? I can't think of anything less enjoyable than listening to Angel Vivaldi or John 5, but they certainly qualify as exceptionally virtuosic. And since when does complex equal exceptionally great. I don't see you guys sharing links to Brian Ferneyhough tracks.

You may not realize it, but this is all a deep and heavily debated question in Aesthetics, brought into public awareness by some random band from Washington in the early 90s.

For you it might be a real sticking point, but for me it's a definite plus. I spent a few decades playing that game of chutes and ladders on the quest for excellence, now I'm the better part of a decade into really climbing up the chutes and sliding down the ladders because it's more interesting.

Good or bad doesn't factor into it for me. Sure, I like some things and dislike others, but my question is "why am I wrong?" This album is really tricky for me. As Compy reminded us all, I love it and there's no way to change that. So, I have to try to understand why people might hate it; not to change their minds, but to appreciate what effect it has on other people. Try to guess what it might mean for you with only the clumsy machinery of badly saying what it means for me. What I find funny, you might find grotesque, or tragic. Sure, that's not how most people listen to music, but I'm not most people. Time to listen to it again, me thinks.

Maybe we should do a kind of emotional ranking of the tracks. Everyone will have a different response to certain things, but it's useful to get a sense of the overall flow of an album. Mine goes like this:

Side A
1 - neutral
2 - whoa, nature is a whore and the I killed you part is something
3 - neutral
4 - neutral but funny (I like putting words out of order)
5 - depressing, but like seeing it not experiencing it yourself
6 - that's so bizarrely messed up

Side B
7 - just pure vicious sarcasm and anger
8 - this just feels disgusting
9 - neutral
10 - kind of a self deprecating thing, but neutral
11 - slightly depressing, but mostly neutral
12 - oof, just soul crushingly depressing
13 - hidden track included on second run versions (all mine are original run, so I don't have it as a hidden track, hilarious when you consider people traded in their first run copies just to have it on there)

That's an interesting contour to me. Side A is mostly neutral with a couple blips and an intellectually difficult ending. Side B is the exact opposite, it starts supercharged, levels out, and just crashes into misery at the end. Your reaction might differ, but clearly there's a long-range structure that resonates with me and gives the whole experience a feeling of completeness. Whether or not I can describe it to you, there's some tangible emotional response going on when I listen to it. That's a pseudo-psychological apparatus, but I'm not being dishonest when I describe it that way. If your response is just neutral all the way, or all over the place with disgust, anger, confusion, etc., then clearly we'll have a different response to the experience of listening to it. Mine is quite pleasing in the most abstract sense, I'm not bored, I don't get lost or feel impatient or need to skip anything, subject matter aside it's a completely lovely album to listen to from start to finish. You might disagree.

Some lyrics stand out more than others, In Bloom and Drain You have a lot of them. The squeak toys that sound like rats in a sewer tunnel is highly disturbing, and everything about Something In The Way feels like the guy in the alley next to the trash quietly sobbing on the cover of p(nmi)t's We Get Tired EP. Try to find your emotional trajectory for this album.

B: Alright, everybody had a nice breather? Ready to dive back into the swimming pool? What's your take C-world?

C: Uhh, nothing. I mean, I tried to compile stuff, I looked at various lyric interpretations, I tried to catalogue imagery, I'll admit I didn't look at keys or musical stuff, but it's all just randomly all over the place. There's a little bit of experimentation with poetic structure, but not in any meaningful way.

B: Why do you suppose that is?

C: Because it's crap?

B: No. That's a value judgment, not an analytical conclusion. It doesn't add up to anything for a reason. Let me help you out a little. Pronouns.

C: Huh?

B: Are there any nouns anywhere on this album? Names? Nicknames? Places?

C: Polly. Uh, yeah that's about it.

B: So, the only named character in this entire thing is the fictional female kidnapping/rape victim. Everything else is an unidentifiable pronoun, all you get for the entire album is he, she, I, you, animals, and people. What's that say about this universe?

C: Jeez, when you put it like that it's terribly lonely and frightening. I feel like I should go listen to it again...
B: Ok, go ahead.
C: ... but I'm not sure I want to.

B: Skip, whaddya got?
E: Well, you're not wrong, there's no story here. It's just one scenario after another. Some are plausible scenarios, some are absurdist juxtapositions, some are just sardonic reflections on intangible experiences. It's definitely egocentric, but not for any apparent purpose. No dialog, just stuff. Devoid of humanity, you might say.
B: Why?
E: Well, if you want to say there is a narrator, which is tough because he/she isn't really narrating anything, then that narrator must be an inner monologue.
B: Can you and I communicate in this language, whatever it is?
E: No. There's nothing to respond to. If you were talking like this, I'd be thinking "how the hell am I supposed to respond to that?" It's like screaming "everyone shut up, just shut up!" for 40 minutes.
B: Sure, I'll buy that. There's more to it than that, but it's certainly a valid interpretation. *You doing okay up there, Gladys?!*

Just because you're paranoid...

Sounds like it.

... don't mean they're not after you.

Hi there. I'm the narrator. I'm one of those discorporeal corporate functions that sometimes seem necessary. I often show up when some context is needed for understanding or interpreting the text. There're lots of ways I could do that, but the underlying purpose is to fill in the gaps. Here, I'll show you. Let's start the last snippet over and I'll do what I do so you can see the difference.

As Bottle sat contemplating the question of a narrator for Nevermind, he thought about Gladys. Better check on her. "You doing okay up there, Gladys?"
The response filtering back down through the floorboards sounded not surprisingly like a wizened old lady cackle-singing the lyric "just because you're paranoid...."

"Sounds like it," thought Bottle.

See how much smoother that feels? I give background details, clarify which character does what, close off some of the disorientation you might feel if I took a bathroom break while the story just plowed ahead all willy-nilly. And it's at the point we return to the story. I'll step aside for a while and give the floor back to Bottle.

B: Skip brings up a good point. If there's a narrator here, that narrator is a nincompoop. He's not giving any context to anything, just saying "I see stupid people" followed by "I'm stupid people too." At one point he doesn't even know if he has male or female genitalia, or so he just elects to have both veterinary surgeries at the same time. The one consistent thing is that people are gross, mean, and perfectly happy to shrug and say "whatever" and seek comfort over knowledge. This world is starting to look like no fun at all.

B: Ok, Sandra, your turn.
S: I don't want to.
B: C'mon, everybody gets a turn. Remember, we're trying to find a good reason for me to dislike it. Something I

can hold up and say "you know what? Here. This thing just doesn't sit right with me."

S: Hhhhhhhhh. Well, I just find it dull and pointless. I get that that's part of the whole thing, but I don't like it. It *is* too simple, it *is* a joke, he's not a genius, he was just a guy who was angry and depressed and enjoyed playing music and messing around with words. The fact that he's fully aware of it and suffering even worse from the corporate push to rake in a fortune from it makes me care even less, especially when everybody gets so adamant that he was some sort of messiah of mopyness. I'm sure that's out of character, but that's my reaction.

B: Out of character? You were about to shiv Skip for slighting your boyfriend Brian Setzer two weeks ago. Out of character? Pffft, I say, pffft.

Totally valid reaction. I don't have that reaction, but I understand it. You're comparing it to everything else in your head, like any one would do. I don't have to guess, you find The Pixies more enjoyable. So did Kurt. He loved the Carpenters, The Vaselines, Goth Rock, Bowie, hippie rock from the 60s and 70s. He just loved pop music. If he could have spent his time just playing covers he probably would have.

We'll have to step outside the album for a bit, and get a wider perspective. Nevermind is the anachronism in Nirvana's discography. It's not supposed to be this unwieldy behemoth of culture clash. It's not supposed to be this quintuple platinum best seller everyone knows and loves. It's just that it was so raw and unapologetic, and so blatantly a self-deprecating joke that all those guys who spend their days trying to capitalize on trends for big returns blinked a couple times and said "that I can sell. Ketchup popsicles my ass, I can play that for anyone and look them straight in the eyes and we'll both nod 'cause it will sell." All we have to do is get them to the show and wait for him to focus.

Bleach is not commercial, it's garage metal about TV-show characters and how dumb childhood is. Nevermind is about how dumb being a teenager is. Incesticide is what he wanted to do instead of be famous. In Utero was designed to make the general public in love with Nirvana hate them.

What does everyone say about the real-life Kurt? He was an ardent feminist, he was sarcastic, and he was funny. He was also in a lot of pain, real or imaginary. He was just a person, and he wasn't necessarily fond of that person. His songs aren't some countercultural manifesto, it's just how he felt, screamed at the top of his lungs a little different every time he did it.

So, back into the album. It's not special, it's weird that it's famous, it makes fun of itself, and that's the source of however you feel about it. I personally don't care about any of that, I like the way it sounds, and I like the way it makes me feel. I don't know why I feel that way, but I also know that I don't feel all those things other people say makes them dislike it. Something about it fascinates me, and I suspect that it's as simple as that I just get it. Not in a trendy way, or as some genius work of art, but just that need to get it out of my system whether it's good or bad or if anyone else cares. I think that's what's happening here, and I totally get it.

Are we closer to somewhere than we were before? Are we really chasing the Absurd like it's eating its own tail? Like everything, it depends on your goal.

I had no goal other than to just talk about Nevermind until I ran out of things to say. Mission accomplished. Took 3 days. 30 years of listening to it. It's mostly gibberish, and I'm perfectly happy with that.

And now, the exciting non-sequitur conclusion to our tale:

B: Oh, wait, wait, wait. We didn't hear GREGORY'S take on Nevermind. What sayeth the skeleton from out the closet?

I THINK WE SHOULD HAVE A VISIT WITH MORTIMER.

B: Really? Like listening to Meatloaf's first album will just magically clear everything up? Preposterous! Ok, I like a challenge, Bat Out Of Hell in 3, 2, 1...

This one time, Todd Rundgren thought he was making a spoof of a Bruce Springsteen album, so he did what anyone would do and hired half the E-Street band and Edgar Winter to play on it. And don't forget that play-by-play monologue from The Scooter. Lundgren legit thought the entire thing was hilarious.

Nobody wanted to publish this thing. I mean nobody. Every exec they pitched said "have any of you buffoons ever even heard a rock album before?!" That was kind of a problem considering they lied to Todd Rundgren, who had been paying people out of his own pocket this whole time.

You need some background on Meat Loaf. He had a successful band with tons of big label offers. He passed on all of them. Then he was in Hair. Motown begged him to be on their roster, then replaced his duet on the only song he liked from those sessions with Edwin Starr, and everyone just kind of treated him like the worst Sunday dinner ever. Meat Loaf is the nickname his football coach gave him. Bat Out Of Hell was a Peter Pan rock musical called Neverland (itself a reworking of a previous musical) Jim Steinman started at a writer's workshop. 3 of the songs were great (how many crap songs did that musical have?) and they decided to turn them into a Meat Loaf album. How can you expect anyone to take any of this serious?

Fast forward to modern times, it's still selling ridiculous numbers of copies for a 40+ year old album, but in the mid-70s it was a joke. The goofy werewolf intro to You Took The Words Right Out Of My Mouth is what finally got Steve Popovich interested enough to take it on.

Here's how this thing caught fire. Meat Loaf went to the UK and performed these songs. Next day this was the most underground cool must have album that could never be broadcast mainstream. 140,000 copies with no radio play later, Popovich called his former boss at CBS and said you guys aren't doing jack, start a marketing campaign in Canada and I guarantee they'll be flying like hotcakes after one concert. And they did. So, they pushed it into Omaha, and radio stations had to buy bigger phones to handle all the call-ins every time they played it.

Who would a thunk it? A teenage testosterone fueled fantasy world turned out to be pretty popular. Unlike Kurt Cobain, this is exactly what Meat Loaf wanted, and 40 years later he's still Meat Loaf. My favorite line from Popovich is you could publish this anywhere, anytime, and it would be the most bizarrely unexpected thing ever. It's a spectacle.

I agree. The only thing it's not is a great album. All the parts are fantastic, but it's a bit of a chore to listen to in one sitting. The songs don't flow, the narrator is as inconsistent as Cobain's is absent, and I'm completely confused by just how damned long these songs feel. They aren't really that long, but an 11-minute Tool song goes by twice as fast as the 10-minute title track. The 5-minute Heaven Can Wait takes at least half an hour, and I'm crying out loud for Crying Out Loud to end already before the halfway point. They aren't bad songs, they're just too much food on one little plate. I love Meat Loaf, but I don't need 7 servings.

No joke, I listened to the full Nevermind 4 times in the last 3 days, but I barely made it through Bat Out Of Hell once. I feel like I failed the 72-oz rib eye challenge at the Texas Roadhouse, and I've got the red and black splatter all over my turntable to prove it.

VIII. Have Fun Storming the Castle

Mahler 1 – No review, just Mahler 1

I don't know how you guys feel about it, but this 1987 recording of Mahler 1 with a Klimt painting for the cover is just the bees knees. I think I bought it at the Galleria in Dallas on a high school field trip.

Stone Temple Pilots – Tiny Music

E: Hey Bottle. I deleted some of your stupid hasty and inaccurate posts.

B: Thanks, Skip.

E: You wanna do an album tonight?

B: No, not really.

E: C'mon. I'm sure you've got one lined up.

B: Why? Why bother? I'm too angry. I say things wrong when I'm angry. Then I have to apologize, and get everything back on track, and I'd rather just nip myself in the bud before it gets worse. Plus, my copy of STP's third album has some horrible disgusting goo on it.

E: Spit polish?

B: I hadn't even tried.

E: Now Bottle, you were the one who said it's perfectly fine to be wrong or dumb as long as your brain didn't get messed up.

B: Yeah, I did.

E: Well, you got two thumbs, right?

[Lick, wipe, wipe, insert, press play]

B: Well, what do you know? It worked. Dear Sen. Lankford, I was wrong to criticize your speech this evening. I took the liberty of being grateful that my editor deleted it, but I said it and I was so eager to crap on you that I just spiraled into insanity. I still say the senate needs to pass a no Reagan quotes rule, but I'm eating the humble kidney pie this time. Chewy. However, I'm not wrong for assuming that it's really nothing more than lip service, and you'll go right back to undermining your own ideals.

Look, the people who storm-troopered The Hill today are the people Trump has been talking to this whole time: the crazies.

Also look, I'm a no BS kind of guy, and you have to realize that Trump owes more people more money than you could earn in your entire life. Nothing's for free. Does anybody know how that story really goes? Yes.

Aw, man, we crapped out at Lady Picture Show and I had to skip to Trippin' On A Hole In A Paper Heart. I'm not myself, I'm not dead, and I'm not for sale.

I don't know how you could say there's no personality, this is a DeLeo Brothers album. They aren't required to only play 1 type of music. They were just writing songs for two different bands. Later on, they sat down and decided which singer to use for which song. I haven't heard whatever the other album was, but this one is great. In part that's because Scott Weiland isn't being such a dick on it. He's still doing whatever drugs Courtney Love was doing on probation, but it's not like he's stealing cars or robbing gas stations for all that drug money. He got busted buying: probation not prison.

Yes, I know, Kurt's widow. Again, no victim, no crime. People are allowed to be pricks as long as they accept the consequences. Scott's consequences were Velvet Revolver and being dead, but he doesn't have to apologize like those Republican senators who had to change pants this afternoon.

Uncool joke, Bottle. Ok, fine. Sorry. It's been a week and a half, but it's only Wednesday. I never said I was great, in fact the opposite, but I'm my own worst enemy and the truth's getting farther and farther, and Bottle (hey that's me) keeps churnin', so maybe we just all take a moment to be thankful that a few more people have joined the side of quitting the charade. 5 years later, surely no one will notice the swimming pool, alligator, and shrine...

Real Life Intrudes

The biggest problem with all the opinions I've heard today (and it's too many to count this morning) is that it's second-hand repetition of reporting. I can tell the difference in your speech patterns if I've known you for a while. The second problem is that the train of logic starts off perfectly fine based on what people saw and heard, but quickly goes into the murky territory between intentionality and cosmic absurdity.

It's a very simple thing to come to the conclusion that the general shape of the day was planned and encouraged (it clearly was), but it's quite another thing to imply that a full acting troupe spent the last 3 weeks choreographing it like Ocean's 11. That's TV brain talking through a delicious dopamine fantasy.

The reality is that no one knows how to act in the current hypersensitive state we all live in. So, some people act erratic, make small bad decisions that snowball into chaos, and everyone slips into a pure reactionary (unpredictable) mode of operation. Some people are trained to deal with that, some are not and the clash of those two forces takes its course.

It's difficult to draw too many conclusions until certain basic timelines and facts can be established, and above all it requires patience. Now, shut up and let me get back to pulling orders...

...To continue: The Senate has confirmed the electoral vote and from a legal standpoint it is over. We're still 2 weeks away from inauguration and there is every reason to expect more problems. Censuring his facebook and twitter accounts is of little value, but it seems quite reasonable to do so. Everyone wants it to be over and done with the minimum effort required.

The scary thing to me is the change of rhetoric from the Republican party to "it's devastating that Trump's legacy has been destroyed," and "we have do it all over again." You can disagree with me all you want, but I feel that you watched Trump's legacy take place yesterday. How many times have I said I'm not good at explaining it, but this is how the plot unfolds? That's not an I told you so statement, really it's not. Call it my intuition for structural consequence if you have to call it something. Systems fail in predictable ways based on day to day working relationships, and there aren't any now because Trump fired all those people and replaced them with sycophants.

There is certainly a case for sedition, but the real question is how many more of these outbursts are going to happen? Hopefully none, or very few, but we have to be prepared for real people to keep acting out their frustrations in violent and counterintuitive ways. This is an era of "get what you want by threat and force." I can only hope that more and more people will come to the realization that it's a counterproductive way to live and think, but I still expect it to get worse. Hopefully I'm wrong in that somewhat pessimistic expectation.

Ives – Symphonies

Tonight, it's Ives. He proposed a Constitutional Amendment to let people directly draft legislation that Congress would cull and select for public referendum. Some say his first heart attack was brought on by a heated debate with FDR. Ives proposed issuing $50 bonds during the WWI effort and FDR, chairman of the committee, scoffed at the low value. He was going to hand out a pamphlet criticizing Too Much Politics in Our Representative Democracy at the 1920 Republican Convention, but the printer didn't finish them until the convention was over. He wrote music that no one wanted to perform during his life in his spare time, and paid for pretty much all his publications out of his own pocket. If it weren't for Copland, quite a few people would care a lot less today. He sounds like a kooky old lovable guy.

I won't bore you with descriptions of all 4 symphonies, but I will say that the world he sculpts in symphonic sounds is much more noble, playful, thoughtful, and downright pleasant than the world I see most of the time; not without its difficulties certainly, but steadfastly optimistic all the same. He gave his money to other composers and musicians because he cared. Slonimsky would have had half a career without Ives. If he were alive today, he wouldn't be because yesterday probably would have killed him.

Perhaps, if you're looking for a productive use of your time this evening, give the first famous American composer a listen. I know I feel better for doing so.

... and, you know, you could retrieve his biography from the attic, like I did...

Dave Matthews Band – Crash

Alright. I have to do it. It's the most controversial album in my collection and I haven't listened to it in a looooong time. It's controversial because some of you I know love it, and some of you detest it with every fiber of your being. It's the sophomore album from Dave Matthews Band, Crash.

No, that's not it. It's controversial because you gotta decide how to approach Boyd Tinsley and the sexual harassment settlement. Plus that, uh, unpleasant incident with his tour bus and a bridge and a guy who can certainly attest to the stink. I am Bottle, hear me squeamishly point out my past instances of separating the art from the person. I think it's fair to point out his coincidental involvement with the band from the beginning. Dave wanted a fiddle part on Tripping Billies, and Dave fired him many years later for said controversies 'cause Dave don't need that kind of headache.

Mrs. Bottle hates it because she was subjected to it on the level of college roommate torture prison. I get that. So, Boyd goes in the tread lightly crate while DMB gets the standard Bottle evaluation (the band doesn't get an automatic ejection for the violinist's questionable interpersonal relationships). Does it flow, is it coherent, or does it make me want to puke?

Most critics wished they weren't a jam band, but were at least glad they were talented. Christgau called it a dud. I guess we'll find out together.

Oh yeah, I remember what's so divisive. This is a character album. These aren't straight forward songs from a reliable narrator; it's not Dave singing these songs, it's various characters in various levels of, for lack of a better word, failure. These aren't mentally together people, they are "heading for a crash." Confusion, aggression, depression, regret, nostalgia. The narrator of Crash Into Me is a peeping tom. These are character pieces, and those characters aren't completely well adjusted, not necessarily bad, but unstable and emotionally fragile. Most people don't have that analytical framework at their disposal, so it just comes across as creepy, aggressive, even toxic. But, like all things, it could strike you as sincere and touching from the slightly skewed perception that this is "normal." Of course Christgau didn't like it, he consistently hates this kind of stuff.

Musically speaking, yeah this album is phenomenal, beautiful. I'll join your every other weekend DMB cover band. Dave goes in the Joni Mitchell/ Melanie crate for pronouncing words weird, but that's just idiosyncrasy. Bottle doesn't judge you for being you, unless you're not keeping you to yourself. I'm not exactly proud to say it, but if you did to me what James Frost-Winn alleged Boyd did to him, you might have a couple nasty stab wound scars.

Dave himself was born in South Africa and had a multinational childhood (South Africa, UK, and US), and he's not known for overt political statements, so let's just say it's highly unlikely he voted for his now publicly silenced Virginia Senator Chase. "Trump in heels," there's a mental picture I didn't need.

All things considered, a lovely album. It feels like a set list, like it was meant to be performed in its entirety. It's too long at 69 minutes, but there's no garbage filler so it doesn't feel exhausting. I don't want to listen to it again for a while, but only because this kind of folk jazz fusion isn't my native language, it's not crazy enough for my taste. It's one of those perfectly wonderful albums that I can highly respect and praise, but that I have to be in a certain bland and sappy frame of mind to enjoy. I imagine if I smoked pot I'd enjoy it a lot, but I don't so it's just kind of drab except for those deliciously minor chord progressions that surface every once in a while.

Well, that was a long winding improvisatory album review. Fitting, I suppose.

Sandra's Story – MLWTKK – A Crime for All Seasons

You know who needs a more fleshed out back story? Sandra. Take it away wordy words:

They call me Ubiquitous Jones. I'm sure I had another name once, but it's hard to remember things you don't have daily use for. It's hard to remember anything with precision these days. I should explain; they call me Ubiquitous Jones for a reason. I was there. Whatever it was, I saw it happen. I may not have had the best vantage point.

Obviously, I wasn't, but that's the easiest explanation this side of the Borg consciousness. There's a distinct difference between remembering something and describing what you saw. Memories are never singular; your senses coalesce and form a network of associations. Color and smell become a taste, ideas become people in the background . . . you get the idea. I don't have that problem. I simply observed what happened; a fact, to which I have no sentimental attachment. I guess I literally know what I experienced. I don't remember when it started (like I said, there's no sepia toned home movie in my head), but I do know it scared the hell out of everyone. Wispy old ladies thought I was psychic, psychologists were frequently convinced that I was an unaspiring pathological liar, one keen old Philippino lady (definitely not wispy) called me Balthazar, pretended to shave her head, and patiently waited for my little epiphany before laughing herself into cardiac arrest. Ironic, that the only person ever to know about my "special power" never told a soul; believe me, I learned Tagalog just to check.

    I was a detective for a while. Fedora? Check. Trenchcoat? Check. Side arm? Check. Big mouth and bad attitude? Check. I liked to play a mix of Dick Tracy and Archie Goodwin. I was good, of course, but it's so much damned work to keep timelines straight. Plus, whose gonna pay you for a crime they don't know or care about? I had some friends once. Chad, "The Pluralizer" (able to replicate everything except meaningful conversations with women), The Effeminator (some people called her Jill, most people called her Janet and marveled at her vast collection of upholstery samples), some other less relevant characters, and me, Ubiquitous Jones. I saw me standing there, as McCartney heard me say on the way back from Southport. Together we were the League of Useless Super Heroes, conquering the forces of sobriety one Gray Goose at a time. It was fun for a while, but it's hard to be friends with someone who knows that, to some extent, you know everything they say and do. When you start saying "I know, I was there" without an ounce of irony, people don't feel much like talking.

I was surprised when the phone rang. "UBJ!" (man, I hate that acronym). "It's Chad. Get over here quick."

As the phone went dead, I felt the little twitch, that rush of recognition some people feel when they remember something they haven't thought of in a long time. It used to make me queasy, but at this point it's barely worth mentioning. I remembered seeing Chad walking in the direction of the pay phone outside the bus station, but the evergreens that line that section of Maple Street (situational irony at its most droll) blocked my view of the whole north side of the building. Like I said, not always the best vantage point. By the time I walked the 4 blocks to the station Chad had worked up quite a sweat.

"Janet's gone, man. She's gone."

What do you mean gone?

She's just gone. She's not here. She called me from the Hellhound to tell me when she'd be here, but she's not here. Where is she?

She probably checked in then saw an antique shop across the street, or saw an ad for pink throw pillows, or something. She's The Effeminator, Chad.

No, man. Where is she?!

I realized two things at that moment. One, that wasn't a rhetorical question, but more importantly, I didn't know. I mean I really didn't know. I had nothing. That's never happened before. Sure, there have been times when what I "remember" is pretty useless, like overhearing a conversation and the only word you catch is "skullcap" or whatever, but there has always been something. In 37 years I'd never drawn a complete blank. I must have been zoned out for a while, because I noticed Chad looked about to beat the shit out of me. "I don't know," I croaked.

What do you mean you don't know? You're mister fucking "I was there!"

I don't know, Chad. Let me think. I remember hearing a guy in a diner say "Janet's going back tomorrow." I remember noticing the way the hack checked out her ass as she walked away from the cab. She asked the ticket lady where the pay phone was, I assume to call you, and then nothing.

What do you mean nothing?

I mean nothing. It's like she stopped being Janet on the way to the pay phone, or walked out of existence or something. There's no sight, no sound, no memory of Janet.

I was sweating at this point. I'm not kidding, there was no memory of Janet to have after she walked away from the counter. I didn't see her in the phone booth, I didn't think "hey why didn't that lady get on the bus?," I didn't pick up the paper to see a "Bus Station Kidnapping" headline. She can't have just disappeared. I mean she has to be somewhere...

Sure she can, boys. She's up in the beanbag chair drawing pictures of Lucifer's flowers. It's a dope doll jungle out there. Acid angels might come to the fangs of love, but some of us stare deeper into that blank mirror and say "you know what, I hate this vacant heart. I don't want to be Mrs. Bottomless Pit, anymore."

Who could blame her? Walking around screaming that Ting Tings song all day. Not quite as catchy as their "Happy Birthday," but 27 repeats on the old mental jukebox of doom and you're ready to hijack the laser from Real Genius and shine it in your own eyeball, popcorn party be damned. She didn't vanish into thin air, she just joined a slightly less dangerous Kult. We're groovy.

Feel better now, Milton? Sandra has a proper back-story with intrigue, previously mentioned characters lost in their own dramatic irony, a reference to a Val Kilmer movie, and most importantly: I've got an album for that.

B: Do you hear it, dead C-scrolls?
C: Hear what, Boss.
B: I'm not the boss of anyone, Cease and desist. The heels of those Freebirds pacing back and forth across the floor of Sandra's office.
C: Can I go with a no on that, B-man?
B: You can, but they're deafening.
C: You got a telltale heart or something? I don't hear anything.
B: No, no, no. 1) I didn't do anything wrong, 2) even if I did I'd say "I'm sorry, it was not my intention to cause whatever problem this is, how would you like me to clean up my mess?", and 3) Sandra wouldn't pace about stuff like that, she'd eyebrow me 'til I squirmed or else just nip me in the bud permanently. No, she's contemplating, and that's pants-wettingly terrifying.
C: If you say so. You did blab her back-story all over everywhere the other day.
B: I made at least half that up. Not the Janet part, accidentally call her Janet and you'll lose at least one testicle.

Chad made the mistake of using his useless superpower to replicate his lost lad after said serious fight and he, uh, briefly regretted it, if you catch my drift. No, this is something completely different, unexpected, impromptu. If I didn't know better, I'd say she's worried she stepped on your turf.

C: Whaaa?

B: Keep in mind I'm guessing, but I bet you she bought some records and she's trying to decide A) whether or not to even give them to me, and B) how to properly apologize to you.

C: To me? What are you talking about? Why would I care?

B: No, no, no, no. Classic mistake. It's not about you, C-spray, it's about getting it right in your brain. She's totally conflicted, 'cause frankly this is more fun than whatever she was planning to do out in the real world, but you're the compilation function and she has to justify it in her brain. I don't make the rules, I just point out how dumb they are.

C: Kaaay.

B: Oh, she's about 12 paces away, quick act natural.

C: How?

S: Knock, knock! Hi, C. Preemptively shut up, Bottle. C, I hope you don't mind, but I wanted to better appreciate what you do for us. I probably did a terrible job, and I probably went overboard, but I went record shopping today.

B: Told you.

S: I'm certain I said shut up, Bottle. How do you have the patience to sit there flipping through crate after crate like that? My brain started to fizzle and everything started to look the same after 5 minutes. Why don't people alphabetize anything?

C: Oh, that doesn't bother me so much. You get used to it, I guess.

S: Well, I certainly have a better appreciation for Adventure Time now, but I don't think I did anywhere near as good a job as you.

C: Thanks, Sandra. It's nice to be appreciated.

S: You're quite welcome. Now Bottle, I have one request.

B: Hmmm?

S: Don't be nice about them just because I picked them out.

B: When have I ever done that?

S: Every time. Stop it. If it's bad just say it's bad.

B: That sounds suspiciously like a terrible idea. Look, I'm all for blatant honesty, but like you always say, you're not a Beefette. Your office is in another castle, and I have a tendency to fling cannonballs.

S: I think I'd like to halfway change my mind.

B: Well, then I'll be half honest about your album picks. Skip's a Beefette and he doesn't seem to feel conflicted at all. Even C-weed doesn't mind it, do ya?

C: Yeah, no actually. Not at all. Beefette is a total improvement from whatever I was doing before this. It's all a bit fuzzy, really, but yeah definitely more fun in the bunker.

S: Hhhhhhhhh. Ok. Am I stuck here forever? Do I have to sign anything? How does it work?

B: Work? Contract? What are you, some kinda corporate narc? Nothing's different, except you're here. You don't have to be here, you just are. The only thing is you'll find it increasingly difficult to hide behind your own embarrassment. There might be a brief uncomfortable period where you have too many opinions, but you just talk yourself back out of the red zone before you 'splode. Plus, you wanna know a secret?

S: What?

B: You've been here the whole time, you just didn't want to admit it. And, I wasn't coddling your picks, that's all in your own head. Sometimes I don't know how to feel, so I reserve judgment. Now, let's see what kind of damage you brought me....

The Motels – All Four One

E: Now I'm confused, Bottle. What's going on with this story? Did I miss a memo?

B: I don't send memos, Skip. You guys are all on different time lines, and right now Sandra's in retrograde.

E: That doesn't make any sense. She clearly has memories of the stuff that has happened since I got here, or else she wouldn't know who I am.

B: Standard misconception of time lines, you're thinking of the River Song version from Dr. Who. That's not how it works down here. Down here is chronological, but up there isn't. Reality jumps around like when I pick random albums on consecutive nights. Someone has a brilliant idea, it catches fire like California or Australia, and when it's all said and done, I point out that it was a Hitchcock plot from the 50s. Down here she's having new experiences as they happen, up there she's slowly forgetting them in the opposite order. Up there is Devo, down here is the adventure.

E: No, that still sounds like nonsense.

B: So? It's my nonsense. Did Gladys stab you and throw you down the escalator, or did you volunteer to be interned? Sandra didn't come down the escalator. Those rules don't apply to her unless she wants them to apply. This is the island of misfit toys. The toys are misfits. People aren't toys.

E: I still don't get it, Bottle. This story is so confusing.

B: It's totally not confusing at all, Skip. Here, just go listen to her first pick (maybe not the first one she picked up, but the first of this particular journey). It's The Motels' 3rd album, All Four One. I mean really listen to it. I think you'll learn something.

Armageddon
4-4-4-6

[Ring, ring, click]

S: Sandra speaking, how may I assist?
B: We took the liberty of starting without you.
S: Pretty sure you know I know that, Bottle. You picked up The Motels first, and I figured you didn't need me there for that one. It's a tad "on the nose," as you like to say.
B: Pretty sure you know I know you did that, Sandra. Hurry up, I'm just about to light the indoor campfire hazard.

...Several eventful moments later...

B: Everybody here with all their facial hair? Good. We've had a few dress rehearsals for the next day of the rest of our lives, but today it's Sandra's turn. Everyone give her a round of applause, this is a big step. No, C-horse, not the slow clap, you jackass, a nice golf clap or even a coffee house finger snap is more appropriate. Our friend Sandra has decided to join us for this round of Adventure Time. Normally we'd be gentle on her, but she's dead set against that, so are there any questions about the first album by The Motels?

[Dead silence]

Ok, ok, I see we're all a little unsure about this. What's the problem guys? She's been here for every other adventure time, right?

E: Well, yeah, but it's different, you know? Before she was Sandra, now she's like Sandra Sandra.

B: That's the dumbest thing I've ever heard, Skip. Fine, I'll start.

What the fuck is the deal with that Carole King song? Now I'll tell you. That sentiment was legitimately expressed to Carole by her babysitter. You're supposed to be as dumbfounded as Carole was at that moment. Works every time no matter who sings it, but it's got a special place on this album for sure.

Skip, you're here 'cause I need a second opinion. Compy's here 'cause all this nonsense needs to be compiled into a coherent experience. Sandra's here to make sure I don't get too carried away and turn into a complete jerk. Bottle and the Beefettes, no album can escape unreviewed! This one's Story Time With Sandra, but it's sure to be an adventure.

Jeez lady, how much did you spend? There's like somewhere between 6 and 8 albums here. Good thing we're about to be snowed in at the Stanley, am I right?

Album number 2 is some seriously obscure stuff. Armageddon's only album, and self-titled to boot. They were a brief British super group of recently defunct famous bands formed by Keith Relf after The Yardbirds broke up. Keith died after being electrocuted by his guitar while working for the follow up. You know that third prong we have on all our stuff now? Yeah, tube amps didn't have grounding back in the day, and electric guitars and microphones plugged into them could totally Lawnmower Man you into eternity.

But my word this album is amazing. It's prog, but of the heavy metal persuasion. This is one of those hidden gem albums, only not super famous because they didn't tour. Dead front man didn't help on that front either. Still, if you run across it out there in the wild, it's a keeper. As for what it says about our new old friend Sandra, you'll just have to wait it out with the rest of us (or read the lyrics, they're moderately insightful).

The Eurythmics – Touch

B: I said across her nose, not up it! The Eurhythmics, Touch, the one with Who's That Girl, no less. Alright Mz. D. Are you playing a game here?

S: Of course I am, Bottle. This is fun. I mean, it's all coincidence and I expect it to fall apart any time, but you were making up stories and I can play that game. If it's going to be about me, I might as well be me. Oh no, Skip's gone cross eyed.

B: Skiperoni! Snap, snap, come back to the now.

E: I'm so confused.

S: We know. Bottle?

B: K, best explanation I got. Ready? We're inside a Klein Bottle. Well, inside is relative. The point is it's impossible to pin down which direction we're going. Now is now, obviously, but that doesn't mean you're living it that way. Try to give it a twist through the 4th dimension so that you're living your memories while reality fractalates around that stream of consciousness.

E: Whaa?

B: Ok here's a good example. Hello, Michael Kamen. It's great to see you again. You guys remember Michael, right? He did Metallica's S&M, then he died, then he helped Roger Waters build a wall to fence Bob Geldoff in, and now he's working on the string parts for this album by Dave and Buster, sorry, Ann(ie) and Dave. See? Completely chronological for us, but totally out of order.

E: Oh, ok. That sort of makes sense, I think.

B: Great news! Skip's here, everybody. I believe Sandra was giving us the rundown of the depression after a breakup, or something similar. 3rd album? That's quite a nice coincidence you got there Sandra.

How could anyone dislike The Eurythmics? This album is fantastic, it's complex, it's believable, it's the right blend of pop and wacky synth sounds. Killer bass lines, intriguing harmonies, and a full assortment of blips and bloops. Plus, the songs are good. You might not have all these emotions in this particular order, but you definitely have them.

You're 3 for 3. We'll see how it proceeds. I've been peeking at the stack, and there's this nagging suspicion you're pandering a little bit. Interesting eyebrow there, I haven't seen that one before, so we'll assume it signifies coyish ambivalence. Alright, keep your secrets. We'll get to the bottom of it one way or another.

Kansas – Monolith

I'm out of order? You're out of order. The whole trial is out of order! From day 1 everybody said totally fine if British people want to play this pretentiously juvenile and bombastic form of rock music over on their island, but this is America, damnit. Progressive, schmogressive, you'll write pop chord changes, and you'll like it! Gold and Platinum selling albums labeled as "commercial failures," the band feeling like the thousands of people there to see them in concert didn't like these songs. Kansas *is* prog-rock, not imitating prog-rock, or flirting with prog, they *are* prog. Reading anything about Kansas is like following a cookbook recipe but substituting every ingredient without measuring and then complaining to the writer that it tastes terrible.

Why is it Sandra's 4th pick? Well, clearly we're dealing with different interpretations of the same phenomena, trying to understand some perspective different from your own. Oh wait, did I unbag the cat too early? Was I supposed to lead up to that? Oh well, what's their 6th album Monolith sound like? I have a sneaking suspicion it will sound a lot like Kansas...

... man, there's just something so familiar about that Native American in a fuzzy coat wearing a space helmet with bison horns on it, surrounded by crumbling infrastructure, like I saw something similar recently. Something about the government and a bunch of heavily armed space cadets or something. Oh well, not important, press play.

Did you know Kerry Livgren was sort of in a cult for a while? He was big into this thing called The Urantia Book, assembled by a doctor who studied a neighbor with strange sleeping trances where he babbled about alien gods delivering religious sermons. He actually hired a stenographer to write it all down so his book club friends could have something interesting to talk about. That's a hardcore paraphrase, by the way, it's actually pretty interesting.

Oh yeah, the music, I almost forgot. You are not going to believe how much these guys sound like Kansas. It's uncanny. You know who loves Kansas? Bottle. Oh wait, I'm Bottle. This *is* Kansas? Oh ok, no wonder I was confused for a moment, I thought this was something totally different than what it's been the whole time.

Now that that sarcasm is out of my system, let's thumbtack some important nodes in this network of associations. Where's my spool of thread? There it is, wrong pocket, forget my own head next.

So, everyone has a bias, some prejudices, assumptions about how everything works. That's great when the reality you experience matches up with it, but what's a girl or dude supposed to do when it all goes haywire? Nothing's working right, everyone's acting crazy and confused, my instruction manual is in Portuguese all of a sudden.

Well, some people blame everyone else, some people go search for a revised edition, some people learn to read Portuguese, some people just take a break, hide in their own bunker, and wait for the storm to pass. You gotta be willing to pick whichever one of those options is most helpful at the moment, not whichever one feels easiest. Sometimes you have to look on the bright side, but sometimes you have to choose to suffer a little, or play a different game. If you're playing backgammon in the service box, you're gonna take quite a few tennis balls to the noggin and walk away a couple dice short of a yahtzee. But, who was wrong in that silly analogy? The whole situation was stupid, so maybe that's an important consideration....

Long story longer, I freakin' love Kansas, and no doubt about it, this is certainly a Kansas album about remembering the past, longing to return from the edge of catastrophe, getting back to helping each other, and looking at things from a different perspective. What's not to love about it? Standout tracks and obvious anachronistic commercial singles are terribly disruptive, that's REO Speedwagon's tragic approach. I think you've all got this confused with Three Dog Night, they went from awesome to trendy crap for lack of inspiration. This is just as good as any other Kansas album and you're the one who's being inconsistent as you get older and more crotchety.

Like I said, you're out of order! Kansas isn't saying "burn it to the ground!," they're saying deep in our souls we all know it will eventually crumble, and this won't be the happy part of future mythologies.

Prism – Small Change

Prism's 4th album, Small Change? You *are* pandering! No, no, no one will notice we fired Ron and changed from wacky, synthy arena rock to tastefully synthy adult oriented softish rock, then just gave up altogether. I already told you that story, this is the actual crash.

Luckily, I also told you it doesn't bother me a bit. I still like Prism, even this album. What I don't like is buttering me up. This is supposed to be what Sandra wants Bottle to review next, not what Sandra thinks Bottle might like to hear. What say you?

S: Ha! You're wrong, Bottle. I can say with complete honesty that I put no thought into it whatsoever. I had Compy give me a list of stuff that you liked by surprise, and just happened to find some albums from those bands. But, I picked them for no reason other than they felt like I should pick them all together. I was worried I went overboard, but I think I won.

 B: Yep, you're right. You did. The face on your face says it all. I have no counter argument, except for one tiny little detail...

 S: Nope.

 B: You didn't let me finish.

 S: Because you were going to say pronouns. You switch them all the time, so I can too.

 B: Oh, ok, um, well...Aha! You were pacing 'cause you were making sure you didn't leave any unguarded openings. You, you, you, clever intelligent woman, you. Nice job. Everyone agree? Sandra won, Bottle zero? Case closed. On with the show.

 Yeah, people change, bands evolve, you shouldn't be stuck anywhere you don't want to be, but you also kind of have to make the best of it when it happens. Prism's been bankrupt since Armageddon (another beautiful coincidence, gold star), so of course they gotta go commercial pop rock, or just quit altogether without even trying. Prism tried it both ways. It's totally fine. How it fits into your story is still a mystery until we get through 'em all, but the logic train seems to be chugging right along, no bandits in sight. Don't think I ever argued Chad wasn't a jerk, did I?

 Actually, since we're doing it all out of order anyway, do you guys mind if I take a peek at the last two? Well, that was a resounding chorus of yeses. Ok fine we'll just stumble through the dark like always.

 We've morphed from the harder side of synth-prog through pop to adult oriented soft-core rock. If I didn't know any better, I'd say this has the non-nutritive varnish of "growing up," not to be confused with the much more useful and healthy process of maturing. Maturing involves getting better and more refined, growing up is just a biological function. Grownups are pretty fake and terrible, as we just heard. Maturity is a balanced state of mind without any particular age restrictions. I know which one I'd rather be, and it certainly isn't a grown up. There's always a hole in paradise. If I didn't know any better than not knowing better, I'd say you picked this album as an attempt to see the story from Chad's point of view, but you said you were intentionally messing with the pronouns. It just so happens I do know better than knowing better. If both sides of an irreconcilable binary opposition feel exactly the same, then one of you is delusional. Quick check to earlier in this review, yep Sandra won and Chad was the jerk. She's learning to pout from a magazine, but we're listening to it from the knowledge that he's just as brainwashed to believe he isn't a fully participating part of that problem. This is Chad being a codependent, self-aggrandizing vampire. Please Henry, can you and Bryan Adams write us some commercial radio hits? Take whatever part of our souls you need, we couldn't turn a profit from them. Normally, I'd serve up my world-famous rat poison Rangoon, but something tells me a little bit of suffering through the thunderstorm alone is exactly what Chad needs to mature a little bit.

I'm guessing we'll get one more ironic nail in the love coffin and then go completely non-sequitur in a logically conclusive way. But first, one final thought. How dare the assistant engineer be nicknamed "Beef." That's my gimmick.

Steely Dan – Aja

Steam Powered Dildo invented Yacht Rock? The Motels was "on the nose?" Seriously, Sandra, you're gonna give me a heart attack trying cram all of this into one bottle.

Okay, Steely Dan made a because Japan album. Sandra's making that 'splaining eyebrow, so I better make like Lucy. I just mean that Japan takes its corporate capitalism very serious. The best, the newest, the marketable. Your value as a person is mostly interchangeable with your value to your company. Obviously, I have some deeply ingrained prejudices against that, so I set them aside for this album, which would otherwise be considered overproduced by Swiss watchmaker standards. Enough, get on with it.

Here's one of the 8 seminal Yacht Rock albums, one of the top test records for audio equipment due to its immaculate production, it's Aja. No, you're pronouncing it wrong, it's pronounced "Asia." Jeez, even the title is obtuse.

Here's the thing about Steely Dan, they are hard core ironic anti-heroes, their characters rival Jethro Tull for unsavory, their songs are always about booze, porn, crime, manipulation; the surface is all glitz and shimmer, but the underbelly is seedy as all get out. I think we all recognize those characteristics in Mz. D, don't we? Not sure exactly which one she was is real life, but it's the lifestyle she's lamming, removing the source of the problem.

S: Guilty as charged on that one [wink].

B: Shrapnel in your eye? Afraid you went overboard? My real question is how does this fit with the new sincerity of west coast beach bathers? They were perfectly happy to not have a manager and not sell millions of records. Oh, now that I say it like that, I get it. Ok, I'm good now. It is a pretty spectacular album. My third eye is blind this time, how's the last album of Sandra's Sojourn going to be?

Good Rats – Birth Comes to Us All

B: Hahahahaha! Please excuse my knee-slapping outburst of belly laughing. We looked at the bad rats, now we'll hear from The Good Rats. Beautiful. Admit it, you have no idea what this album is, do you Sandra?

S: No, I just knew it was the end of the story.

B: Well, let's review. I was making it up as we went along, we all know that for true. We established that you really did assemble them from some deep gut feeling it would tell a story about your character without contradicting the character I've already established for you. We started out in the sleazy underground industrial discotheque, worked our way up through the secretly more sleazy world of big business pop (sadly losing some friends along the way), with the delicious irony that business is class, people are trash, and crash landed in the pacific with the most Zappa-like album ever created from the complete opposite approach of Zappa, and found out you ran away leaving those sad rich losers feeling like sad rich losers (the riffraff) and couldn't be happier. All those dress rehearsals paid off, welcome to the first day of the rest of your life. Let's hear some obscure Long Island club rock. Like they say, Birth Comes To Us All. So, let's all find out together.

15 albums, everybody from the surrounding 5 blocks got a turn to be in the band before moving up to a bigger band. These guys were the Dead Hot Workshop/Canned Heat of the Long Island rock scene (Twisted Sister being their Gin Blossoms, but with a much better outcome than the analogy suggests for either of them).

You're gonna say, jeez this is all over the place, they overtly copy everybody, I don't get it. My response is, this is a 7 night a week, top 40 cover band whose fans started demanding original material. This *was* their idea of success. Also notice this isn't a pipe dream album, these guys are good at what they do. What they do on this album is point out that every one of us is born into the same bizarro world where everything is a lie and you reach this late teenage point where you realize none of this is the way you think it should be and there's nothing you can do about it. Some people grow up and lose, some people mature and make the best of it, but everyone is in the same rickety old boat. Nobody asked to be born, but what matters most is how you choose to live that life. I'd call that some real good philosophy. How you doin', Skip?

E: There is not enough ibuprofen in the world to ease the migraine of climbing through the convoluted Escherian staircase room you've constructed in the last two days. You've got responses to scenarios before you develop them, reviews from one album weaved into another, I can't decide if Sandra was a call girl or a professional assassin, or both for all I know, Al Pacino showed up out of nowhere. Somehow, it's a simple breakup and start a new life story, but man there's a lot of emotional baggage.

B: So, you're saying I did a good job of fractalating reality around Sandra's trip down memory lane?

E: But how do you even begin to end it?!

B: Spaceballs.

E: What in the hell is that supposed to mean?!

B: That was Sandra's industrial strength hairdryer, and she can't live without it.

E: I hate you so much right now, Bottle!

B: I didn't know you were a Kelis fan, Skip.

E: Aaaaaaaarrrrrrgggg!

THUD.

S: Maybe that was too much, Bottle.

B: Nah, he'll be fine. He might have a bump on his forehead for a couple days from slamming it against the desk like that, but we all have growing pains.

Coheed & Cambria – Year of the Black Rainbow

B: How am I supposed to review this thing, Skip?

E: Well, what are you asking Year Of The Black Rainbow to do, Bottle? Do you want it to be just another Coheed and Cambria album? Do you want it to explain the psychological climax that led to their fight against Wilhelm Ryan, the supreme ruler waging war to take over Heaven's Gate? Do you want it to be relevant to real life? Do you want to just crap on Atticus Ross' (over) production?

B: I don't know, Skip. I'm not a normal critic, I'm an analyst. I break it down into its component parts, them reassemble them to show how it works. You just did that for me, review over.

E: That can't be the whole story. You've got thousands of things you could say about it.

B: Yeah, sure, but why? Anybody can search for the synopsis and experience it for themselves. Does describing it actually influence anyone to go listen to it? Is it just fun to listen to me rant? Aren't I supposed to be dreaming up creative ways to sell people my useless junk? I'm supposed to be marketing and making deals and building my brand so everybody else can have 5 minutes of happy and forget it? What does anybody get out of it? Business is the childish, greedy, entitled side of humanity. The goal is to squash your competition and make everyone do what you want against their will without getting caught. I can't be rich and decadent and feel superior unless you're all toiling away on my command! How many different ways can we say "that's dumb and we don't agree with you!" When skeleton's live inside your closets... we're all afraid of the one thing we can't be; free from the shackles of someone else's ego trip.

That's the big secret, right? You can't become the hero by winning the war if there isn't a war to win. Nixon, Reagan, Thatcher, Bush, Trump, feed me, Seymour, feed me!

It's right there in the Conservative handbook. People won't work hard unless you deprive them of their liberty, read I can't capitalize on the hard work of others unless I convince myself they are inferior and force them to do my bidding. What a little shop of horrors this is, and I don't want to buy any of the things they're selling. I don't want to climb the ladder. I don't want to Huckleberry Finn you into whitewashing my fence for me, I don't wanna have to build more fences in the first place.

    M: Ahem, I believe that was actually Tom Sawyer.
    B: Yes, thank you Milton. May I continue?

Here's an example. Cars are great, they let you travel longer distances and accomplish things that used to take days in a few hours. But, time is money, so magically those accomplishments aren't worth the cost of keeping that car running anymore. Easy, peasy, we'll just use airplanes and spaceships to go further and further. Oh, you want to stay in one place and grow tomatoes? Tomatoes are crap for rocket fuel, so no. Plus, Steve over there is already growing enough of my patented schmomatoes, so really you're the bad guy here trying to steal Steve's hard work. And, since Steve's hard work feeds my pocket, that means you're my enemy. Now, if you think you can sell more of my schmomatoes than Steve then we might have something to talk about, but Steve's ready to kill you 'cause I promised to hand the whole empire over to him when I retire. Why are you here, Skip?
    E: Because you said you needed a second opinion.
    B: Well, where did I take a wrong turn? How am I misunderstanding it? How is any of this *not* lying to get what you want by tricking people with the allure of shiny objects?
    E: I'm not sure I follow.

B: Ok, what does the farmer grow? The farmer grows whatever we promised to pay for. What happens if we change our mind halfway through the growing season?

E: Oh, ok, so you're saying there's a reciprocal relationship here?

B: Yes, exactly. What I meant was are you here because you want to be here, or are you here because Gladys stabbed you and rolled your dead body down the escalator?

E: I honestly don't remember, Bottle.

B: Of course you don't, this place is a complete scattershot absurdity in someone else's dream. Is GREGORY a frightening monster lurking in the shadows, or is he an eloquent chap with a tragic dermal deficiency? Either way we're a record label with no bands, no money, and no interest in pursuing either of those things. I've been writing every day for no reason other than it was fun. I could just stop, there's no reason to keep doing it. No one would get hurt, the world wouldn't end. We'd all find something else to occupy our attention. No one is relying on me to review an album tomorrow. Actually, I bet deep down they think it's a silly waste of time.

E: But, you like doing it.

B: Yeah, I love it, but that doesn't mean it's worthwhile or valuable. Claudio's net worth is 3.5 million. He could just pay everyone what he owes them and watch TV 'til he dies. What keeps him going? Certainly not the critics saying "this prequel lacks all the ingenuity that made C&C Sci-Fi Factory fun to listen to. I'm bored, next." He made it 'cause the story called for it. They tried a non-story album and everyone including me asked "why?"

Year Of The Black Rainbow is their best. It's their heaviest, but also their most coherent and consistent album. If we've learned only one thing from this whole adventure, it's that none of these amazing bands did it for the money, but they needed the money to pay for it. If Claudio's worth 3.5, then somebody worth 7 paid for it, somebody worth 14 signed off on a new ledger called "Coheed And Cambria," and the whole thing falls under the umbrella of a business loan from Sony to Columbia. I probably paid $17 for it and it's freakin' awesome. Does that mean I owe them another 50k? Who cares if I like it or not?

E: Well, clearly you do, Bottle. You care a lot. You made this life out of nothing to cleanse your useless identity.

B: Nice try, I can't follow this damned story to save my life. Who's singing which songs? How does any of this prepare 2, 3, and 4? Liking it doesn't make it good.

E: So, you're saying it's not good?

B: No, it's fantastic. It doesn't make sense to me, but clearly it makes sense to them. Would it help to read the novel? I don't know, maybe. I just like the idea that Coheed, Cambria, and Inferno have no idea why they were created to fight someone else's war, then have to pass that war on to their children for equally no good reason. That part I get.

Steven Stark – Wandering Woven World

S: Jeez, Bottle. What crawled up your ass and died?

B: Huh?

S: Well look, sure we've been living through our own years of the Black Rainbow, but you're all wishy-washy all of a sudden.

B: No, no, no, Sandra. You're reading it wrong. Look, every review is just another thread in this wandering woven world. The Klein Bottle is just my version of a decent myth. We need every possible pathway. The suffering is awful and the happiness is real. I'm just trying to read the times. I'm not buying what they're selling, but I'm right here in the now doing my damnedest to really experience life.

Some people just don't understand, so they search for some magic wormhole back to "the better times," some people want to build teleporters and skip over all this terrible stuff, but some of us feel like this is exactly the right place to be. Obviously, we get upset when people try to steal it from us, but we aren't the ones out there wreaking havoc. We're the ones whose voices get drowned out by all the childish screaming and destruction.

What's the point of it all? To notice those voices of love and inspiration, and let them lead you through it.

John Lee Hooker

No story, just The Very Best of John Lee Hooker. His are better than mine, anyway.

Mr. Bungle

E: You ok, Bottle?

B: Yeah, fine Skip, why?

E: You just look beat.

B: You mean different from the way I normally look?

E: Yeah, a little.

B: Sorry, I'll try to fake it better.

S: Jeez, you are in a bad state. What's going on inside your brain?

B: I don't think you guys want to go there. It's like an evil carnival ride operated by murderously drunk clowns. The whole world sounds like John Zorn and Mike Patton made a deathmetal-jazz-funk-musicaconcréte album as the audio personification of a 1950s education propaganda film puppet.

S: That sounds horrible, but kind of intriguing.

B: Well, you know Sandra, that's why we just blackout while I go live it. Usually, I can tune it all out, but today just pushed all my elevator buttons and I had to stop at every floor.

E: Surely, you're exaggerating.

B: No, Skip, I'm actually putting it nicely. I have an album for it if you're just desperate to suffer along with me.

This is the part of experimental rock history that would make your guidance-councilor vomit. I wasn't lying about John Zorn and Mike Patton, either. If Warner Brothers wanted some of that sweet sweet Faith No More with Mike Patton money, some of it had to go to his other band (well, at least until Anthony Kiedis had a hissy fit and kept firing them from an entire Summer's worth of festival line-ups in 1999) Here's the 1991 self-titled debut by Mr. Bungle...

S: Oh god, I did just throw up in my mouth a little.

B: How ladylike. Skip, tasting notes?

E: It burns!! Make it stop! Make it stop!!!

B: Nope, start to finish I'm afraid.

E: Aaaaaaaaarrrrrrrrgggghhhhhhh!

S: Aaaacchhhlllffleggh!!

C: I heard screaming, is everyone ok?

B: Oh, hey Compy. I was just sharing my slightly more average than normal day with Skip and Sandra. They seem to be enjoying it, don't you think?

C: You made them listen to the whole thing?

B: Yeah, those are the rules.

C: Isn't that like a war crime or something?

B: Only if you force alive people to listen to it. We're all dead on the inside, remember? I find sharing it out loud helps exorcise some of the demons. I certainly feel better. Oh, they both fainted. Let 'em sleep, they earned it.

Bottle's Punishment

B: Oh, looks like they're waking up. How bad do you think they'll retaliate, C-ment mixer?

C: In Scoville units? Probably somewhere between Ghost Pepper and Carolina Reaper.

B: So, they're packin' heat, but just shy of pepper spray? Alright, I can probably survive. Wakey, wakey, rise and shine, bring me all the pain that's mine.

E: Huh? I had the weirdest dream.

S: Me too.

B: I'll bet. Why don't you two go for a walk, and when you remember what it was I did you can think up some suitable punishment. Off you go. Trash can on the left, Skip.

Barf!

B: There you go. Feel better? See you crazy kids later. What's the chances they'll goof and actually pick something enjoyable, C-wolf?

C: Did you leave any secretly good stuff in that pile you passed over the first time?

B: Maybe one or two, but definitely not 20.

C: Well then, prepare for Sandra's iron heel.

B: You been sifting through Jack London novels or something? I guess we'll just prepare for the call of the wild...

... alright, here I am. Rock me like a hurricane, or thundersnow me, or whatever.

S: We picked two albums. We aren't going to tell you who picked which one, and we aren't going to tell you what they are. Listen to both with your eyes closed and we'll deal with Mr. Bungle's damage ourselves.

B: Oh, execution style. Lovely. Ok, I'm ready.

Oh god no, not the comedown after Rocky Mountain High. What a miserable album this is. Farewell Andromeda, I'll just walk out into the wilderness and revel in my own misery, 'cause yep I suck and I'm not gonna make any effort to change that.

I'm not saying you're wrong for not wanting to be in a monogamous relationship, I'm asking why did you commit to one in the first place, you two-faced jackass. Please don't get drunk and ruin Christmas, dad. Again, not saying you're wrong for feeling that way, and not defending your dad's actions, but clearly he has a problem and the alcohol abuse is an additional layer of terrible on top of it. What's the backstory? It's pretty tough hiding out in these Canadian mountains. When I talk about running off into the woods and eating raw squirrels it's a joke, but you sound like you're serious.

I want to be independent as much as anyone, but that's because I want to make things happen, not just sell people a bottle of sugar water to make them grind a little harder. When it's every man for himself, we all fall further and further behind.

I love John Denver in small doses, but not this album. His character has exactly the same problem as Richard Carpenter. People thought he bathed in Windex for that squeaky, streak free shine, so they kind of glossed over all those moments of grit and gravel in your teeth. But, while Richard was funny, Bob (my mistake, John, I'd just rather listen to the Gilligan's Island theme than this album) is straight up D for depressing. The problem is that he and I are polar opposites. He's a ray of sunshine looking down, I'm a number 2 cynic demanding to break even (I have a complicated disdain for unearned pleasure, and a nasty intolerance for anyone who ignores how much actual work everything takes). He gave up the rocket ship flight so he didn't have to make an effort. I gave up the rocket ship flight 'cause I neither want rockets strapped to my back, nor to strap rockets to yours. Now, you could twist that around and say "that's what I'm trying to do too," except it doesn't work that way with money. You don't get to decide what I can or can't do *and* whether or not I can pay for it. Is Farewell Andromeda a good album? Yes. Do I want to live in a world like that? Hell to the no.

I'm sure I was just like him in one of my previous lives, but my time in the Trump-dumpster set me patiently waiting for the not at all surprising plane crash. That was probably uncouth. Sorry, I just can't understand why people list all the things they wish could be different, then elect people who intend to keep it that way forever. It's madness.

S: Uh, Bottle. You do know we have a new president as of today, right?

B: Really?

E: Yeah. And a female vice president who understands the conflict between large corporations and workers. I wish those roles were reversed, but it is a step in an actual direction.

B: Seriously?

S&E in chorus: Yeah.

B: So, I don't have to worry about what they're doing because at the very least they will be trying to make decisions that actually produce the results they say they are aiming toward?

Chorus: Yeah.

B: That's great! What's the catch?

S: You still have to listen to the next record.

B: Aww. That sounds like it will not be great. Alright, I'm a man of my word. Fire when ready. I'll write about it if I survive...

Eww. Sappy show tune country. Alright, it is what it is. We let all that go and just take it at face value. He sounds really familiar, but we all know I don't enjoy this, so there's no reason I should be able to pinpoint it. Not obscure though, he's obviously pretty famous, I just can't name him or picture anything other than a sequin vest and cowboy boots. It just sounds like a slow Thursday night in Branson so they let an up-and-coming country leaning rock band give it a whirl.

Schlocky as it is, though, I can't help but kinda respect it. This is like a complete 180 from John Denver. He's talking about how love excites him, even if it doesn't work out. It takes for granted that things aren't all rosy, but that connecting with other people is what makes life special. He doesn't want to run off, he wants to get back home to the love and happiness of a house that stays in the same place for more than a day at a time. It's corny, but sincere, like he wasn't searching out this ramblin' gamblin' life, it's just a fact he has to slog through to get to the good parts. That's way more my style. Not musically, I never want to hear this again, but not because I disagree with it.

B: Alright I give, who is this? Really? Mr. Chicken Roaster himself, huh? This is like early Kenny Rogers, right CB Radio?

C: 5th album in 3 years from 1970, B-man.

B: Ok, yeah, I can see that. He did emigrate to the infinite last year. Not my thing, but I definitely couldn't call him terrible. You know what you two did, right? You made a lovely little sideways figure 8, here. We had an album I hate by a musician I like, followed by music I hate from a world view I appreciate, a guy I can instantly recognize but disagree with followed by music I disagree with from a guy I don't have much negative to say about. At least it all drowned out the loop of Go Diego Go my brain's been singing all day. I don't feel too bad at all. We might get through this yet. Thanks guys.

The Compositions of Dizzy Gillespie

Yep, today it's The Compositions of Dizzy Gillespie, because Kris Karr mentioned playground merry-go-rounds, and I have an album for that.

Dizzy, Monk, and Bird are like the My Three Dads of Bebop. It took 20-30 years for the jazz world to catch up. Cab Calloway didn't like his adventurous approach to soloing, but I imagine it was getting stabbed after blaming him for blowing spitballs in rehearsal that really soured their relationship.

Friend: Hey Diz, how'd you get fired?

Diz: Stabbed the bandleader in his thigh. Wouldn't even let me apologize or nothin'.

Friend: Yep, that'd do it.

True story. Wanna hear another one? He declared himself a write in candidate for the 1964 presidential election and listed Phyllis Diller as his running mate. Man, I'd love to live in that world today. He got a 4-F from a MEPS during his WWII interview for saying that the number of times the United States kicked his ass might just lead to unintentional friendly fire. And you thought Arlo Guthrie's draft story was entertaining.

But more importantly, he wasn't content to let Bop be a secret, exclusive thing. He'd play anywhere with anyone and teach everyone what he was doing. He wanted people to hear it and join the adventure. So here we are with our tasty beverages, enjoying this 1962 homage to the man who kicked Jazz in the pants so hard it landed smack dab in the middle of modernity. If anything deserves it, it's certainly this. Cheers.

Are they? Are they really?

E: So, you're saying Conservatives are optimists and Liberals are pessimists?

B: Almost. Conservatism most definitely correlates to optimism, philosophical optimism that is, but I'm not happy with the opposition between conservative and liberal. Conservative and Progressive are the real opposition in my mind. Pessimism/optimism equals progressive/conservative.

E: So, if I understand you right, John Denver's optimism is irritating because that kind of thinking actually pulls society apart?

B: Oh, you were so close to a Chavelle quote there, Skiparticus. Let's give spastic children drugs so they can concentrate on the things we think are important, and save a lot of money on playground equipment in the process. Drugs are cheap by comparison, and isn't that why we manufacture drugs in the first place? They work great. That type of thinking could do us in. It might alleviate your symptoms of being a complete stick in the mud, but it certainly doesn't solve the underlying problem. Medicine doesn't cure anything, it just eases the symptoms. Unless the kid says "dependence schmopendance, I'm objectively way better off being high 24/7." If that's the case, then I don't really have an argument. Unlikely, but plausible.

E: Ok, so what about this album?

B: Ew. Where did you find that thing?

E: In the stack.

B: You mean the stack I just wasn't going to listen to at all?

E: I dunno, there aren't any signs or anything. You said Kenny Rogers was fine.

B: No, I said early Kenny Rogers out of context was moderately agreeable from a philosophical perspective. This is late 70s/80s Kenny Rogers, show tune country without any of that pesky "rock" to get in the way, the famous Kenny Rogers, and I think you'll notice that 99.95% of this garbage wasn't written by any form of Kenny Rogers. Show me a bar with a pretty woman... women are awesome, but I can't figure out why they keep leaving me... I didn't start that crazy Asian war, and I realize that I got my legs blown off in 'Nam, but that's no reason to cheat on me, I'd shoot her if my house was wheelchair amenable. And, we won't even go near all the things that are wrong with the atrocity of the song called Scarlett Fever. This is Prism's Small Change without the redeeming irony of not actually being Prism.

The one redeeming quality is that he does occasionally reverse the gender roles, but mostly it's "mopey time with grisly-man, sufferer of the wily winsome woman." I guess you could list his singing voice as a redeeming quality, but The

Gambler is really his only good hit. "Horny middle-aged faux cowboy" is not a good album concept. The lonely couple songs about race relations and toxic masculinity don't change the fact that this album mostly vilifies women, and that makes my insides try to get outside for some fresh air.

This isn't pessimism, it's misogyny, though not specifically Kenny's. Burning Something came from the perspective that he longed for a life he couldn't fully participate in, but these "greatest hits" are the exact opposite: love would be fantastic if it weren't for all these imperfect, heart breakers I keep falling for when I'm out on the prowl.

Where's the trash can, Skip? I don't think I'm gonna make it on my own, or with help. I don't need you barf bucket, but just let me use you until I can hold down something more substantial than a piece of buttered toast. Oh no, this version of Something's Burning is absolutely atrocious. Bring back the First Edition, and never do that glottal stop garbage ever again. At least the theme from Six Pack is coming from the right direction, 'cause Kenny actually participated in writing it. Maybe I can hold my dinner down after all, but man that was a close one. How's 'bout you never pick a Kenny Rogers album again, guys? I'm gonna have to chase that one down with Throbbing Gristle or something.

Flyleaf

B: Relax, I'm not actually going to make you listen to Throbbing Gristle again. I did, and it worked like a charm, but I fully acknowledge I'm weird. So instead, we'll listen to Flyleaf. It's the album of the extended EP of the EP of Flyleaf.

C: Aren't they Christian Rock?

B: Yes and no. Spoiler alert, nothing about this album is coherent, and it's unanalyzable. But, it's a completely honest album, so even though I think it's total nonsense, and I would almost certainly become suicidal if I thought that way, we have to take Lacey's word for it and agree to disagree. I love their sound, her voice, the way the songs feel, the melodies and counterpoint, and the almost primal misery that is the concept of the album. It starts at the nadir of human psychological misery and proceeds to build up the mythologies of a new functional existence. Spoiler alert again, it's Jesus.

What's the corporate marketing strategy version of Lacey Sturm, née Mosley? Drug addicted atheist lesbian's grandma makes her go to church where she finds God, gets off drugs and breaks up with her girlfriend, marries a nice boy, and eventually quits the band to raise her 3 sons, 'cause Jesus. Now, I've already told you I live in a completely opposite psychological universe, so if this is a Jesus album, he sounds a hell of a lot like the hallucinated boyfriend of a crazy lady.

M: Uh, Bottle? Imaginary record label with fictional characters running an album review blog, much?

B: Correct me if I'm wrong, Milton, but you know I'm making that up as a fictional context for the writing, not having a dream seizure and telling people it's real. As a contextual framework I have no problem with it, it's when you start telling me that I have an actual emptiness in my soul that only accepting Jesus as my lord and savior can fill that I say no thanks, I already had breakfast and I just need a box of screws to fasten a few pieces of wood together. Have a nice day.

This is a "you" album. We can all tell that Lacy's "you" is Jesus because that's the revelation in the last song, but it doesn't have to be. If it had to be Jesus, she'd just say Jesus.

Like I said earlier, this is a recreation of the bottom of the barrel. It's the same "here's what's gone wrong" album as Nevermind or The Downward Spiral, but with a different ending. Kurt said "welp, guess I'll just pretend this bridge is my house, eat fish and grass, and play with my road kill friends," Trent said "Garçon, I'll take that bullet to go, please," Lacey said "I could have had a v8, of course I'm miserable, I was doing a terrible job of making my own life choices. Here Jesus, you drive the rest of the way."

What you thankfully don't get from Flyleaf (or the other two) is any indication that you're supposed to do the same. This isn't how *you* get through it, this is how they imagine or experience getting through it. Bottle's version of getting through it is something like "who told you you weren't good enough? That's some grade a bullshit, right there."

So no, this isn't Christian Rock, it's just dark alternative rock/metal from a Christian mindset. I have a Bottlean mindset, which is muchly much much more complicated, but I think we can all agree you've been watching me do it for years and I don't appear to be homeless, or unemployed, or tangibly psychotic. I'm sad when things make me sad, and I'm happy when things make me happy, and I don't think that's any reason to treat other people like crap, or call my local supernatural deity for backup.

Judy Collins – Judith

Now here's an interesting album. Judith is the 12th studio album by Judy Collins, and even random people in their basements say it's 50/50. The highs are exceptional, the lows are indication that she's gonna make a bunch of albums that suck. Can I bring a different point of view to the table?

Yeah, I think so. What other mid-career 12th albums about dying are you going to compare it to? Seriously, 28 studio albums. Least effective Jagger/Richards cover ever? Admit it, you're assuming the original Salt of the Earth wasn't a sarcastic snipe at elitism, and you're not noticing that this is a farce in its own right. This is a two-faced album, and you're just ignoring the other face. You say half this album is great, half is crap, but you never bother to ask why the half you don't like is there in the first place. I'm not saying I have the right answer, but half Broadway musical, half honky-tonk isn't an accident.

Part of the reason self-titled albums should be your first is that it's really hard to say "I know you like all the albums I made, but they're not real, here's the real me, hope you aren't mad." This album is a great example. You can't accept the split personality, so you say she's doing a bad job. That's crap criticism. I don't like the overtly country cuts because they're country, and that's nobody's fault but my own. I'm prejudiced, so I have to recuse myself. Actually, no I don't. She's half countercultural icon, half entertainer with an entire crew to financially support, and even though she's paying for all of it at the end of the ledger, some rich white guy who thinks country schlock sells is putting down the money up front. Criticize the industry and the mainstream audience for that one.

So, while I agree that half of it sucks, it's the half that made it possible for me to hold in my hand this evening, and if that doesn't strike you as a little bit suspect then you need a turn in front of my funhouse shaving mirror of doom. This album screams "not allowed to write the whole album myself!," and that's about as honest a self-titled album as anyone could dream up.

Black Pumas

> S: Bottle, are you ok?
> B: Gnnnnhh.
> C: You're drooling there boss, you ok? *BOTTLE!*
> B: Hhnggff. Shut up, C-turtle, I'm listening.
> E: What are you listening to?
> B: I said shut up!

.....

> B: Oh, man! That was even better than I thought it would be. What an amazing album. Oh, hey guys, been here long?

S: About 20 minutes, just watching you drool and bob your heard back and forth. What are we in for tonight?

B: Glad you asked, Sandra. Well, previous Bottle heard a song by a band and thought "yes please, more of that!" So, he went over to the googlemabox and asked the nice people at Plaid Room Records to please send him a copy of Black Pumas. Those nice folks in Loveland, Ohio wrapped it in cardboard and handed it to some other nice people at a Post Office who planed, trained, and/or automobiled it over to the Bunker of Beef here in Iowaland. It arrived in tip top shape, and oh my it's so pretty.

I of course, being the unabashed audioglut that I am, took the first available moment to enjoy it in all of its glory. And, it is glorious. I may not be a lot of things, but knower of what I will like in the near future is not not not one of them. They also sent me a nice postcard with a picture of their dog and a thank you message on the back, and I certainly won't hesitate to send them more money at some point in the future.

See how pretty that red/black split looks sitting on the table? Now, please allow me to share it with you...

B: Skip?
E: Oh, yeah, that is good.
B: Sandra?
S: Mmmmmmmm.
B: Compy?
C: They produced this themselves?
B: Oh yes, the very much did.
C: Wowzers!
B: *Gladys!?*
G: *No talky talk down there, play it again and be deathly silent.*
WHAT WAS THAT?

B: Oh, hi GREGORY. Did you like it?

THERE ARE NO WORDS. PLAY IT AGAIN LIKE GLADYS REQUESTED.

B: Ok, don't mind if I do. I guess the verdict is 12 thumbs up. You're wasting your life if you haven't heard Black Pumas. Well, what are you waiting for? It's everywhere music can be played. Go hear it for yourself.

Black Pumas (Debriefing)

B: Alright, we all agree that Black Pumas is fantastic, right? Winner of the Bottle of Beef award for Best Album We've Heard Since the Last Best Album? Gladys is clapping, 4 head nods plus mine, op! GREGORY'S seems to have popped loose. C-d starter, be a dear and hand it back to him. Ok, where was I? Oh yeah, why? Certainly not simply because Trump isn't president any more. Sandra?

S: That voice.

B: Cucumber?

C: Quesada. He's not just some random guy from Austin, but he heard Burton and was like "yeah, you're perfect for this project I've been toying with."

B: GREGORY?

THE WHOLE PACKAGE. EVERYONE IS DOING THEIR OWN THING, BUT IT ALL FITS SO WELL TOGETHER.

B: Yep, all of that, plus fantastic guitars and keys, and it's totally devoid of trickery. Honest love, honest perseverance, and engagement with the actual world. It's old school, but right now. And lastly, the lyrics aren't stupid. That was my real criticism of Kenny Rogers, wasn't it? He was singing about stupid crap from a self-centered view of how everyone else makes the world moderately terrible. This is exactly the opposite, this is "here's what we're gonna do. We're gonna get dressed up, go to town, lift everybody up, and be the best. Not for prizes or bragging rights, but because it's who we are."

Sure, Colemine did limited color runs for the first press (I have 1 of only 750 of this red/black), but the next deluxe run is surely paid for by now. I don't care about that stuff, I just want more music with some passion behind it.

They call it Psychedelic Soul because of the guitar effects, but this is just honest to goodness modern day Soul to me. None of it is really trailblazing or wackadoodle, but it understands the evolution and cross blending of genres that happened between the late 60s and now. It knows hip-hop, it knows that "hide me from what's mainstream popular" ethos from the 90s, it knows the light and the dark, it's obviously a very Austin sound/style, but it transcends that local hipster vibe.

This, unlike industrial rock and nu-metal, is the appropriate place for that end of phrase rise to falsetto. Here it signifies bliss.

It's not a coincidence that Burton's folk-strumming self-accompaniment plays in counterpoint to Quesada and the band. It's one voice supported and lifted up rather than drowned out by the eclectic background. It's easy to drool and say "this is fantastic," but it's hard to put all of it into words.

GREGORY was right, there aren't words to describe how the combination of all that stuff feels. Whatever it is you feel is the experience, and for me this is sublime.

Lighthouse, with friends this time

B: Alright, pop quiz time. Why are we listening to Lighthouse tonight?

C: Ooh! Ooh! I know, I know!

B: I know you know, Cognate. You've got that unfair advantage of being eventually omniscient. I wanna see if Skip and Sandra can spot the coincidence.

E: Horns?

S: It's got horns and the same kind of authentic emotional content as Black Pumas?

B: Nope. They both have songs called Old Man like Neil Young, and we went from Texas to Canada. But unlike Neil Young, they're calling themselves "old man." I'm way more simple than you guys pretend I am.

E: Oh, binary opposites and Bottlean character traits, I should have known.

B: Of course you should have known that, Skip. You half-assed edited the book, for crying out loud. Now for the real test of Compy's acumen: drug of choice?

C: Oh, oh, I know this one. Same as another one, but from even further south. Oh yeah, got it! Stan Getz and Bob McBride, robbing drug stores for Morphine.

B: Very nice. Can the love of a woman get you higher than larcenously acquired opioids? Dunno. But, I do know this album is still every bit as freakin' awesome as it was two Novembers ago. Man, have I really been doing this for a year and a half or so?

C: 539, counting this one.

B: Wowzers! That's a great exclamation, Compy. I'll have to make a running gag of it. Oh, I just noticed the lyric "their greed for gold," and characters die along the journey.

Yep, music is life, you just have to be patient enough to remember how it all just endlessly circles off into infinity. I assume that's the doorway to the aimless drifting of the karmic cycle, the anglicized misspelling of saṃsāra.

E: Like reincarnation?

B: Ok, who am I to stop the aimless drifting if this essay? Different. Reincarnation is specifically the rebirth of an individual spirit/mind into a new physical body. Saṃsāra is the eternal cycle itself: birth, death, rebirth, and so on, or at least until you achieve whatever level of enlightenment the Auditors deem "ultimate." They say a proper case of imposter syndrome is a sign you're getting close, but I've decided that's the halfway point. You gotta flip around and realize there's no club worth belonging to before you really get somewhere. You can't join our club! Of course I can, you just don't want me to, and that's as good a reason as any to refuse. No sparkly lights or Theremin serenades? Guess there's still a flaw in my logic somewhere. Oh well, where was I?

Yeah, 70s jazz rock, Canada style. This is an album that's got the goods to merit that awesome Brad Johannsen artwork. Hopefully I won't let another full year pass before I listen to it again. It's lovely.

Bottle Does Stonks

E: Hey Bottle, what's a short squeeze?

B: That's a spicy meatball there Skip. Why? Have you been talking to Capsaicin again?

E: Well, he was just talking out loud, but I don't know what half the words mean, and it sounded more like a movie gun fight than anything.

B: Yeah, insider jargon is special. What's your conceptual framework of the stock market?

E: Huh?

B: Conceptual framework. You know, is it a normal boring market, is it gambling, is it connected to reality, are stock brokers providing a service to their customers or selling a product? Do you want to know about Citron and Melvin specifically, or do you need the schism between day traders and investment firms as background? Is this an answer your 2 questions humorously thing, or do I have to start from scratch?

E: Oh. I dunno. I guess I just wondered how they're still in business after losing 5 billion dollars.

B: Because a couple other billionaires bailed them out. Citron covered its position quickly for a mere 100% loss. Melvin tried to fight back, and some other big hedge funds helped cover the damage. Ooh, that face on your face. Where did I lose you?

E: Kind of at the beginning.

B: Oh, so all the way back we go. Ok, for you the stock market is a little black box that you put money into, tell it when you're going to come back, and when you do you might get more or less than you put in. It all depends on what actually happens inside the box. There're actually many little black boxes, but let's just pretend there's only 1. Basically, Compy's talking about some crazy stuff that happened inside the box recently.

E: Ok, that makes sense. So, it's not like real real?

B: Yes and no. If you aren't counting on getting any money out of the box, then it's all relatively unimportant. If you are, then you should know that inside the box is looking a lot like the 1980s at the moment. Good with part 1?

E: I think so.

B: Ok, then let's take a break, and we'll come back and talk about what's in the box.

Welcome to part 2 of Bottle does stonks! Let's step into the doorway and float a bit in the infinite ether of INVESTING (picture it like the doorway on last night's Lighthouse album).

Two people, both alike in dignity, playing a game with numbers. One person wants to sell a thing, one person wants to buy a thing, it might happen, it might not, the only real rule is you have to declare your position first, then see if they are compatible. It's like rock, paper, scissors meets musical chairs. I'm kidding, the stock exchanges quite boringly match buyers and sellers according to their terms of trade.

Now, the normal way trading works is the familiar "buy low, sell high." You buy things you think will increase in value by the time you come back and find out, you sell things when you don't want to wait any longer, either because they rose enough to make you happy or because you're afraid they'll go way down. There's lots of nuance and rules and information that goes into making those decisions, but that's the game they play on Wall Street.

With stocks, the normal framework is investing in stocks that will rise in value and selling them once they do. But, there's an Alice Through the Looking Glass version of that called "short selling." That's where you borrow a security and sell it, hoping that the value will drop by the time you buy it back to return to the lender, pocketing the profit.

E: Isn't that bad? I'm sure I heard that's bad.

B: Only if you suck at it. Remember my Romeo and Juliet quote from a couple paragraphs ago? No position is inherently good or bad, but some are inherently more risky than others. Short selling is super risky because the profit is capped at 100% but the potential loss is infinite. Traditional investment, a "long" position, is the standard, but "short" is merely its inverse. I think the stock market as a whole is garbage anyway. I'll believe my 401k when it's in my own bank account. Until then it's just gibberish numbers on trash can food, as far as I'm concerned.

E: So why is everybody so freaked out about GameStop?

B: Ok, that's trickier. Traditional investors think they are the good guys, selling relatively safe strategies for reasonable returns at a moderate risk. They have proven track records, consistent earnings, yadda yadda yadda. The hedge fund guys are crazy desperados robbing trains and orphanages in traditional eyes. Again, I think they're all wackos, but whatever. Let's do some actual research into this particular situation.

Citron. What's Andrew Left's actual business plan? He's an analyst/short seller. He tries to find stocks that are overvalued due to management fraud; he searches out companies that are straight up lying to their own investors and customers, and short sells them when he thinks they are about to crash. He's also guilty of being wrong and getting sanctioned for influencing trade with faulty research or outright false information on multiple occasions. Legit business model, not so legit person. Same story with fewer ethics complaints for Melvin.

Their position was and still is completely legitimate according to the rules of the little black box, and with regard to the specific stocks in this instance (the top ten most shorted stocks are legitimately not good traditional investments at the moment). That's why their friends bailed them out. However, they both made the mistake of leaving their ridiculously aggressive (however justifiable from a real world perspective) calls dangling in the breeze during a period of excess funds, loose day trading with low buy ins, and personal antagonism. Essentially, they took their guns to a gunfight and were somehow surprised that people who don't like them opened fire. If you're wondering why Elon Musk was giddy it's because he hates short sellers in general, and Tesla itself has crushed a few of them in recent years. But he also wants to 'splode people to Mars and has a child with Grimes, so both alike in dignity I remember myself saying. Any questions?

E: So why does any of this matter, Bottle?

B: Well, you see, half of our economy is tied up in it, and the executives of all those publicly traded companies are only there to increase shareholder profits. Out in the real world, companies are struggling. Why? Because people can't afford the stuff those companies sell.

E: Why can't they afford stuff?

B: Because the people with billions of dollars aren't reinvesting that money into wages and education. They make us pay to learn how to do a job they won't pay us to do. They aren't rewarding their employees with proper raises, funding schools or arts, or even throwing big parties. They hide more and more of their money in foreign banks, waste psychotic amounts of money endorsing laughable political candidates, and absolutely refuse to pay taxes to compensate for any of it.

 Look, I can't put a percentage to it, but most jobs are garbage. The crummier the job, the more people want to be paid to do it. A job is just a task the people around you don't want to do themselves. The biggest problem is that trying to figure out how many cantaloupes equal replacing an alternator is a stupid waste of time and energy. Have you ever considered paying people to be friendly and share their talents with their neighbors instead of sitting at a computer hoping for a spontaneous brain hemorrhage? Have you? It could possibly work.

 But back to the actual saga. "Borrowed stock" is a bit of a misnomer. It's only borrowed in the sense that it will be replaced in full at the end of a complete transaction. Borrowed in the sense of a money loan repaid with some amount of interest.
 Say you "borrow" $10 from a friend, go out and make $40, then give your friend $15. It's not the same physical $10 bill, but you both made a profit from "borrowing it."
 One of the underlying questions is, what did you do to turn that 10 into 40? Another is, is that system still fair when you elevate the numbers into the millions of dollars? A third is, how does this ethically operate when the original $10 was borrowed from yet another unknown person in the first place?
 Then you have to understand that Robinhood and Ameritrade are brokerages; the firms doing the actual trading. Did they break their license by stopping trades? (No) Is there a malfunction in their software, or was the whole process completely legit? (Legit) The whole thing is exponentially

more complicated than a hastily written one-sided facebook news story.

E: Ok, so some people made tons of money and some people went bankrupt?

B: No idea, this is all happening inside the box. None of these people are telling you their actual real-life money. This is all brokerage financials, net assets, paper valuations. It's like me telling you the discogs values for my record collection.

E: Whaaaa!?

B: What's anybody's time frame for taking money out of the box? Next week? 25 years from now? The only way you get to take that money into the real world is by actually selling your assets and closing out your account. It might affect somebody's dividends next quarter, they might lose everything tomorrow on some other trade. Just because your holdings are valued at millions or billions, doesn't mean anyone will actually buy them from you.

E: I'm so confused.

B: Of course you are. You're reading garbage information. Securities are no different from cars, or jewelry, or record collections, or baseball cards, or real estate, or any other investment. We're getting dangerously close to the capitalist/communist argument again, but you have to understand that the stock market is pure abstract capitalism, spending money for the sole purpose of getting back more money. It's raw capitalism superimposed on top of the real world. It's buying and selling claims to the profit/loss of buying/selling commodities.

GameStop isn't making tangible profits in the real world. They might with new leadership and a change of strategy, but right now they look like they are going to go bankrupt and fold in a year or two. Not a good investment to own any percentage of zero dollars. Likewise, not a good idea to blindly insert your life savings into the little black box.

What bothers me the most is the way the whole situation is being reported. This is a mechanics of trading episode with absolutely no connection to the real world other than keeping money out of general circulation.

Then, when the company tanks, the execs and majority holders get their money through liquidation. Real people lose their jobs and no one above the level of store manager cares because they haven't actually lost anything.

p(nmi)t – You Can Walk There From Here

B: Remarking on the freshness of garbage with each and every person that he meets.

X: 'Scuse me?

B: Oh, sorry, just thinking out loud. It's a lyric from a Spirit song. You ever feel like life seems to be one big round and round?

X: Sometimes. Who are you?

B: I dunno, but you can call me Bottle.

X: What do you mean you don't know?

B: I mean I don't know. No idea who I am. Well, no idea who I am to me, I am whomever you think I am.

X: That's cryptic, mister.

B: No, mister waters the plants mid-morning, I just hold things in my brain until it's time to pour them out.

X: Strange. Where are you headed?

B: Above my shoulders. Well, that's certainly a face on your face, uh, oh yeah, nowhere. I just wanted to sit for a while. Stew in my own juices sort of thing.

X: Oh, I thought you were waiting for a bus like me.

B: I assure you, the thought of comparing you to a bus never crossed my mind. Oh, oh, gotcha, no I find that wherever it is you can walk there from here. Sorry, I have a habit of thinking funny. Words mean too many things, so I often pick the wrong ones, the meanings that is. It takes me a while to figure out how to combine all the numbers, so it's best to just wait until it's obvious what to say, in my experience.

X: You live here?

B: No, I live way out in the fields. It's quite lovely.

X: Well, this is my bus. Nice talking to you Bottle. Uh oh, it's starting to rain, sure you don't want a ride? I'll pay if you need it.

B: No, no, I'm good. A little rain never hurt, and it always eventually stops in my experience. Plus, somebody has to hold down the sidewalk or it will float away. Enjoy your day.

Now, which direction was I headed? Oh well, when in doubt, walk forward and turn left at some point.

Bottle Gets Meta

Here's a little story about how my subconscious works:

B: Alright, which one of you hooligans did it?

C: Did what?

B: Put Donna Summer on top of the stack.

S: No one. We haven't touched 'em since Skip's little Kenny Rogers fiasco. Honest.

B: But, it's too much. It can't be coincidence.

E: What are you talking about, Bottle? You reviewed that album back before any of us got involved. Pinkie swears all around, we aren't playing a game here.

B: See! You're doing it right now. The whole album is pink.

S: No, we aren't doing anything!

B: Look, I ran out of ideas for what to do next, so I did what I always do, and went back to p(nmi)t's brain farts and Spirit to recalibrate. Had a nice conversation with some lady while she waited for a bus, then wandered the streets for a while with no particular destination in mind. Now here I am finally picking up what I thought would be a random album, and it turns out to be the very first Geffen album from the year of Mrs. Bottle's birth on her actual birthday, The Wanderer, full of songs about running off in search of adventure, but equally pointing out that your view of reality is all in your head and running back home. Wannabes getting a taste of ego steroids, big shots overreaching and losing. Even her story about Jesus and the plebes storming the gates of Heaven is relevant. You can't tell me it's random. It can't be random. One of you did it, I just don't know which one. But, judging from the faces on your faces (damnit! Even that's in here, too), I guess we'll never know. Fine. Whatever. It's hard to stay mad with this album playing in the background. Dance pop meets New Wave. Delicious. Oh well, we're all just spinning around and around anyway. Onward, space cadets. Grrr, even that's on this album! I can't find an original thought in my head for anything!

Cage the Elephant

Wanna know a secret? Mrs. Bottle doesn't like the album reviews where I talk to my imaginary friends. She thinks they make me sound like a crazy person. Joke's on her, I am a crazy person.

Not quite a year ago I said that the obnoxiousness of Cage The Elephant's Thank You Happy Birthday was the best part. Great news, it still is. I still don't like their first, or any of their subsequent albums, but this one is wonderful. Matt just trails off into mindless screaming on half the songs, and that's exactly what it's like walking around my head all night.

In between all the ads for used pinball machines, hypocritical hate mongering masquerading as humor, and whatever it is National Geographic thinks it's doing recently, lies my obnoxious nightly brick wall of text, and I like to think that ignoring it brings a little comfort to each and every one of you.

I'm am of course being facetious. Bottle isn't necessarily supposed to be a likable character. He's just supposed to signal the fictional nature of my writing, let you know that if the words I say hit a little too close to home, it's not personal. I have a grudge against bad ideas, so I call them out as vociferously as possible.

But honestly, I'm kind of mentally zapped, and we've plowed through all the good stuff in my record collection. I think I will take a break for a while. It's been fun and I'm sure he'll think of something clever in the near future, but for now it's sleepy time for Bottle and the Beefettes. Cheers.

My Favorite Soundtrack

I don't often listen to movie soundtracks, but when I do I prefer them to sound like the lead actor was homicided by negligence halfway through filming it.

That was way too dark and morbid. I apologize. But, holy crap the soundtrack to The Crow is amazing.

Starcastle – Citadel

Bottle's taxonomy of music criticism is filled with deep, probing questions like "what the hell am I listening to?," "who?," and "whaaaa?!" Today we get to use all three.

Now, I think we can all safely judge this particular book by its cover. Space fantasy, of the wackadoodle variety. And those guys can't exist outside the vacuum chamber of absurdity that is the 1970s. I'm not familiar with the band Starcastle, but this is clearly some variety of Prog, and there will be Moog. Oh yes, there will be Moog.

What's their story? The inner web of the networldtube tells me everyone thinks they're just Yes clones. Kay, that's not helpful, guess we'll just have to make up our own minds. Alright, first thing, it's going to take you a bit to get used to Terry Luttrell's voice. It's not weird or funny, but it is testicle-clenchingly high. It doesn't sound like falsetto, I think he's just a legitimate Alto. That's totally normal for Prog Rock and the 70s in general, it's his dead inside, lack of any color tone that I have to get used to.

Sure, fine, if Yes is your benchmark for 70s rock, then they sound like Yes. Synths and jammin' bass lines, hardcore chorus vocals, but that's like saying all Industrial rock sounds like NIN; your perception is a bit skewed toward celebrity as opposed to genre. This is definitely prog, and the Moog is strong on this one. It's also so sunshiny I'm worried about carcinoma. I wouldn't call it cheesy, though. Definitely eccentric, but so polished and happy you desperately want to punch them in the face.

As is often the case, this album is musically fantastic. But, and it's another one of those big buts that Becky's friend simply can't refrain from commenting upon, I can't tell you what any of the songs are about because I can't remember a single word he sang for the entire album. Some stuff about love, possibly the word "leper," and maybe a little bit of outer space. Lyrically, this is an example of how to guarantee you will be obscure in the future. That doesn't bother me, I like this quite a lot, there just isn't anything to really latch onto as far as statements go.

Rainbow – Right Between the Eyes

I bought a big bunch of records yesterday, but I don't have any story in mind for them. A lot of them are lead guitarist albums, though. I also left the charger cable for my phone at work, so I can't take pictures for today's album. Oh well, rainbows in the dark.

Yep, I now have a copy of Rainbow's 6th album, Right Between The Eyes. Wait a minute, where's Waldo, I mean Dio? Oh, this is after he quit to join Black Sabbath. Don't worry, we'll find him in a totally bizarre place later this week. Hey, I know track 2, Stone Cold. A Classic Rock staple, that one.

Rainbow was originally Ritchie Blackmore's hiring Ronnie's band Elf for a solo project after Deep Purple's lineup change and subsequent falling apart, but they became a hard rock and metal behemoth in their own right. Funny story about this album, Blackmore and David Coverdale quickly became not such good friends because Coverdale kept trying to claim copyright infringement any time Blackmore used the word "mistreated."

This isn't so much a coherent album in terms of concept, but it is a bunch of hard hitting early 80s rock songs with screaming guitar solos. And, these are great songs. Listening to this album is fun.

Traffic – On the Road

First let's take a moment to appreciate the sheer giddy joy I feel when looking at the cover of Traffic's live album On The Road. It's beautiful. Next, let's appreciate that it has 4 tracks. Yep, that's it, four extended live jams that critics weren't thrilled about the first time around in shorter studio form.

Some history on Traffic is probably in order. Steve Winwood formed Traffic as a psych Rock band, jammed with Hendrix a lot, then randomly quit to form Blind Faith with Eric Clapton. When that was over, he went back to his friends and they had a second go at Traffic, now expanding into Jazz Rock territory. That's why critics don't like this album. Critics hate it when you do whatever you feel like without their permission. Oh, sure, the playing is great, but who has an attention span longer than 3 minutes? Not us, Traffic sucks now.

Bugger that, this is fantastic. I simply can't understand the mentality that listening to people actually *make* music is a bad thing. This is great. It reminds me of Santana, just not quite so flashy. Oh, yeah, critics hated Santana too. That was a big theme in the 60s and early 70s, you're not allowed to like great bands succeeding on their own merits, stealing that hard earned revenue from our benevolent corporate pop overlords. Remember, this is Island Records (originally from Jamaica, but relocated to the UK) merely paying Capitol to manufacture it in the US so they didn't have to export it. Now it's all a nasty bowl of porridge under UMG, but back then they were legitimately competing.

Oh yeah, great stuff. Not gonna lie, I'd rather listen to Winwood than Clapton most any day of the week.

[Yeah, sure, leave another page blank, why not?]

IX. The Great Unbottling

The Empire Wakes Back Up

B: Skip! Wake up!

E: Whozamfuggh.

B: Wake up!

E: You can't put candles there it's a fire hazzamfff.

B: Skip!

E: I'm awake, I'm awake. What?

B: We're gonna do it.

E: Do what? [Yawn] I was having such a nice dream.

B: The book, man! The both books.

E: What book?

B: A year in the life. We're gonna make it real. But, that means you've got some real work to do. You left a lot of things uncapitalized, and there's factual errors, and stuff.

E: That sounds like work.

B: Of course it is. You gotta edit it. Comply's gotta compile the cibliography. Sandra's gotta colorform it a cover with basic geometric shapes, and maybe a clip art bus and a portrait of GREGORY or something.

E: Why don't you just do it? I liked sleeping, I could do that for eternity.

B: 'Cause I gotta go wake them up, and send a carrier pigeon to find Bridbrad, and write tonight's album review.

E: Hhhhh. Fine. Is there another computer lying around here? The one I was using melted after I listened to Music That Sucks a second time.

B: Yeah, sure, there's loads of 'em everywhere. Lucky it didn't 'splode if you ask me. Was it any better the second time around?

E: No. It's still absolutely atrocious, but I wanted to give that looking at it from all directions thing you do a try, and I think I at least get why it makes you giggle so much.

B: Birth comes to us all, my friend. Now get to work making me suck less and/or more. Chop, chop.

E: What would Sandra do if she heard you say that?

B: Kick me in the balls. You're not Sandra, you're The Editor. Edit.

E: Jeez, you sound serious, like you stole plutonium from some Libyans or something.

B: Ha! Sure, if the money the government gave me to spend is plutonium. Waaaaaaiiiiit. That counts as a joke down here. Did I miss something? What's your actual name, Skip?

E: Marvin Gardens.

B: Double Ha! No wonder I started this second book that way.

B: What are you talking about?

B: Who died and made Skip the editor? The Clown Died in Marvin Gardens. We Missy Elliot everything down here. You're growing a sense of humor. I just hope Bridbrad can convince enough people to buy the first one to pay for the second one. Nevermind, fraggle rock that.

E: Huh?

B: It's a worry for another day.

E: Oh, I get it. Okay, I'll get started, but it might take a while to spaceballs the whole thing.

B: Mwa! Combing the desert. That was beautiful and insulting at the same time. Now, if you'll excuse me, I have an empire to exploit.

Kerry Livgren – Seeds of Change

Told you I'd find Waldo, on a freshly reborn Kerry Livgren solo album, of all places.

I told you the story about Kerry's fascination with the Urantia Book, and how it infiltrated Monolith, but during the tour for that album he had nightly debates with their opening band, and Jeff Pollard finally convinced him that The Bible was a more authentic chronicle of Jesus than that other book of space alien dream sermons, so Livgren's an Evangelical Christian now. Spoiler alert, there's two more Kansas albums in this run, and one of them is the last "with Livgren" album before he tornadoed himself to Oz. No, I don't need to explain that joke, Skip. They get it. Get back to your actual work.

Where was I? Oh yeah, Seeds of Change. Ahem, excuse me waiter, but what's this baby doing in my diamond?

W: The backstroke, sir. Shall I fetch you another?

B: No, no, we're cool. Wait. What's Diablo Dio doing here?

W: Ah, a common misconception, sir. Though Mr. Ronnie James built a substantial second career singing *about* Satan, he himself was not "a Satanist." It was in fact his vocal versatility with which tonight's guitslinger was enamored.

B: Oh, ok. Sure, we'll give it a try. Well. It's an unexpected flavor. There're some interesting things going on. This album needs some serious contextualization, for sure.

Musically speaking, this is fun. The Dio tracks are spectacular. The part that's hard to deal with is the "evangelical" part. You have to make a choice. Is this Kerry Livgren telling you about his honest experience of life and how accepting Christ solved so many of his own psychological crises and existential angst, or is this annoying, self-righteous, hard right proselytizing?

KL: How can you live when nothing's there?

B: Just fine, Kerry, 41 years and counting. Like I've told everyone a thousand times, there's no empty space in my soul. I'm Stuart m'f'in Smalley. I'm super happy if this is working for you, but I'm telling you man to man, face to face, it doesn't work for me. No negotiation. I can meet you halfway at Whiskey Seed, alcoholically treating the pain isn't good at all. I'd be happy to compare and contrast my theory of complex causality, discuss the underlying metaphors, fully appreciate what it does for you, but Space Dad and Metatron aren't allowed at the Bottle of Beef Omni-Holiday Office Party. My brain, my rules.

I couldn't listen to this thing all the time, it takes a lot of work to filter out the condescension inherent in this ideology, but as part of the story of Kerry Livgren, or even a playlist of the weird stuff Dio did, it's a completely enjoyable listen.

Surf Zombies – Return of the Skeleton
We interrupt our regularly scheduled brain thoughts for this important joke I haven't yet tired of using:

Dear Bottle,

Merry Christmas from yours truly,

Last Week Bottle.

Oooh, what'd I get me? Sweet! My very own copy of Return of the Skeleton by Surf Zombies. Thanks, me. Double oooh, a guitar pick and sticker. Thanks, Brook Hoover!

I really can't recommend buying your future self presents from cool people enough, assuming of course you know yourself and your taste well enough to do a good job. Oh yeah, sounds fantastic guys. Keep up the great work, and cheers from the Basement. I'll be sure to be surprised when that Blendours split I also bought arrives in another day or so.

Old Wives/Blendours Split
Oh yeah, this is fantastic. If I could pump it straight into your earballs I would. Thanks, The Blendours! All the thumbs up.

Kansas – Masque

I've been trying to write about all the messed-up and downright confusing ways people think about money, but it's too big and too messy. I can't find a good entry point. Screw it, let's talk about a fascinatingly bizarre way some people experienced the band Kansas. There are people walking around the earth right now whose experience of Kansas is "Leftoverture and Point of Know Return are famous albums and I didn't hate them, let's see if their previous album Masque is any good."

Obviously, if you read my reviews, I've corkscrewed that particular view a little by inserting Monolith and Livgren's Seeds of Change, but it's a fascinating context to think about.

Hey look, it's a concept album about "reality" being a facade, and that's a face made up of sea creatures. Alright, I'm hooked, what fake way will this album portray the human experience?

Men and women need each other to be complete human beings. That is certainly a very narrowly defined context for meaningful existence, but there's no signifier for irony or sarcasm.

I wish I wasn't so scared of the world that I'm imbibing alcohol and hiding in my basement. Hey! I resemble those remarks, but not in the way you're assuming.

Icarus. More specifically, Icarus' actual perspective (spoiler alert, he never made it to manhood because the sun melted the wax that held his wings together).

The world's pretty awesome when people care about each other. Hmmmm.

I know what I did wrong. I was expecting sarcasm, but it's blatant sincerity. Masque, this silly little album is a clever disguise for our real-life philosophies. Kansas, we think you don't have to be a competitively aggressive jerk to live a happy and fulfilling life, and gosh darn it, try liking people for a change.

Guys, I don't mean to be a party pooper, but we're all going to die, and it kinda really sucks to feel like no one loves you. How do I know? Well, I met death in a nightmare, and realized that whatever bad thing you do to me will be Avenged Sevenfold for all eternity. I don't care if you're a jerk, I just don't like watching you suffer because I'm the Highlander, or whatever. Look kiddos, can you all please just play nice in the sandbox with each other so I can finally rest in peace?

Yep, that's quite a story. Not the Bible like everybody misinterprets it, though. Kerry Livgren and the book about the guy who was sleeping while the space aliens used him for their talk-radio program, remember?

It's good, though. Really good. I've said it before and I don't plan to stop, I freakin' love Kansas, and I can't wait to hear their trainwreckord. Sorry for using your word, Todd in the Shadows, but it's an unremovable part of my basic vocabulary now.

Jean Luc Ponty – Civilized Evil

Let's try to wash the nasty taste of politics out of our brains with some jazz fusion. And, nope. Clearly, we can't, even Jean Luc Ponty has something to say about demagoguery, and staying focused on removing its power over us.

Unfortunately, you put all your effort into it, but the critics get bored and accuse you of being formulaic, and boring. The trouble with that is that it's you, not the artist. You're the one who can't accept the larger picture. You're the stain that can't be removed without damaging the actual painting.

The trouble with Trump is that a lot of people mistakenly consider themselves part of the demographic he speaks to, the demographic he represents. So, let me try to describe the large-scale problem as I see it.

First of all, there is no "Government," only groups of people doing things, and other groups of people reacting to them. That's not a silly pedantic philosophical statement, it's a framework for understanding the world. When people say "the government," they are referring to an imaginary anthropomorphic skeleton, a GREGORY, if you will. In the real world, however, there are actual people performing governmental functions, holding office as representatives of "the will" of the people. Let's really drive that home, think of it like the will of a now deceased relative. That relative, in this case, is all of the people who lived and died for the ideals of personal (not corporate) liberty and the pursuit of happiness, without curtailing those rights of others.

There's one big problem at the moment, and that is the fact that the federal government recognizes the owning of branded commercialization as being more important than individual liberty. When Trump, or someone sharing his mindset, speaks of draining the swamp or removing regulations, he is talking about destroying the protections and compensation needed to protect "the people." The country in his mind is a hierarchical corporate structure, he sits at the top of the pyramid speaking to his closest few executive officers, who in turn instruct their departments according to strategic plans, pass them down to their management teams who break these strategies down into menial tasks and yell "keep firing, assholes" at the labor force. You, the person who drives to work in the morning and home again at night, are a menial laborer. You might also perform higher level functions in your specific context, but unless you're the governor, or the CEO of a fortune 500 company, or the manager of his resort, in the mind of Trump you are a nameless ant in the colony. Why do corporations love their layers of middle management? Because it is mentally damaging to watch yourself subjugate your fellow humans, reward or destroy their lives for arbitrary and often unrelatedly selfish reasons. The structure acts as a buffer, and removes that acute sense of personal responsibility.

Me? Yeah, I think that's Civilized Evil.

Now, are Biden and Trump diametrically opposed arch-nemeses? No. Politically speaking, Biden was the available compromise, the person we elected to steer the ship without actually throwing the people who don't want to head toward the scary, pirate-infested part of the ocean overboard.

I don't like using the metaphor of Warlords or Kings, but something similar is happening at the highest corporate level. Berkshire-Hathaway, Universal Music Group, British Petroleum, Wal-Mart, Amazon, etc. have all grown so massive in economic and political power that they are beginning to rival the actual States in these United States in their effect on our daily lives. Read the news some time, Warren Buffet is not an individual person anymore, he is the controlling interest of a vast commercial/retail/insurance empire. He's not particularly malevolent, but he easily could be.

Elon Musk has reached the point where he is literally directing his own space exploration program. Again, he's not being particularly villainous that I can see, but imagine if he changed his mind on Monday morning.

Imagine if we took away all the actual checks and balances of these international powers. Don't think of it in terms of good/bad or right/wrong, think in terms of capability, and recognize that removing governmental oversight from their organizations is akin to handing a fluffy kitten a hand grenade to bat around the living room floor.

Imagine waking up to find out that you have no choice but to work for one of these cross-border empires. Everything you wish to do is now owned by a major corporation; every idea or design is the legal property of some enterprising mogul. Every piece of software, every vehicle, every tree in the forest belongs not to you the individual, but to our supposedly benevolent corporate overlords.

Yes, we should encourage cooperation and big ideas, but we should also be prepared to let them go when they have run their course, accomplished their goal, or even just outright failed for most any reason. Success has become the acquired benevolence of the elite, but the common man bears all the weight of the consequences. We shouldn't punish each other just for the next guy's turn on the tire swing.

I haven't reminded you in quite a while, but these are just my thoughts. I could be wrong. However, at the end of the day, a civilized evil is still an evil. I don't want to play that game. I want to play this record.

Kansas – Drastic Measures
... and here it is, the punch line we've all been waiting for, I don't think we're in Kansas anymore, David Paich. Ha! The old Bottle switcheroo there. David Paich, Toto, you get it. Drastic Measures often require a sense of humor, and whoo! that bazooka as a chamber music instrument makes me chortle.

The bad news is that it's not a Kansas album. This is an Elefante Brothers 80s pop rock album, with 2 Kerry Livgren songs at the end (the 3rd Kerry Livgren song on Side A is literally "sorry we're making this garbage album, everybody").

But, here's the thing, it's good. Really good. If you're completely averse to Kansas making a Foreigner album, then you're gonna throw breakable things at the wall, but if you just accept that this is a different band in a different genre playing songs about how frustrating this runaway train crash really is, then it's thoroughly enjoyable. They know they're crashing, we know they're crashing, that's how this story plays out. They eventually work out their differences and get back together.

Believe it or not, that's the story of Capitalism. For the umpteenth time, capitalism isn't "business" or "freedom" or "the free market." Capitalism is a structural system superimposed on top of normal human relationships, a siphoning of money out of the system of trade. I'm tired of ranting about it. The war inside Kansas is between the members who don't want their music being used as a mouthpiece for Christian proselytizing and Kerry Livgren who is perfectly happy letting that happen. Kansas, according to Kansas, isn't "a Christian band." The irony is that they ended up making a great record about how much it sucks to compromise your ideals for the sake of chasing popularity, but nobody liked it and they broke up.

It's tricky because I can't hand Kansas any money; I can hand Steve a few bucks in exchange for a Kansas album. I want Kansas albums, but I can't make them magically appear.

Here's how the monetary system actually works. The Fed picks a number, let's say that number is 5,000, and it sells that 5k to three banks at some additional charge, say 1,000. It gives 2,000 to that bank, 2,000 to that bank, and 1,000 to that bank. Those 3 banks loan that money out to people for an additional charge, then slowly pay back the total 6,000. The original 5,000 is cancelled out, the additional 1,000 gets pushed back into the system wherever it needs to go, and the juggling show continues until it all crashes into a pile of rubble. Yes, that's a simplified description, we actually live in the in-between part, but it's structurally accurate. The system as a whole can't function if the money never gets back to the Fed. I can't repay my loan with interest if the people who have money refuse to pay me for something, I can't spend the same dollar twice. If everybody saves but nobody spends, the whole shebang falls apart. The tricky thing is that anyone can forget or misunderstand which function they serve at any given moment. People with money can mess up the larger system by refusing to exchange it with people who don't have money, or refusing to pay taxes, or wasting it by gambling on the side, or injecting it into the economy of another country. The more you save, the higher the cost of creating new money for everyone. Now, obviously, if you put a crazy moron in charge of determining interest rates and selling securities to the open market, then we're gonna have a problem. Conversely, if everyone starts following terrible advice from half-brained money manipulators, then we're gonna have a problem, too. The moral of the story, and my standard kind of joke that only I find funny because it's the title of the album plus a reference to another work of creativity, is this:

Stop creating situations where we all have to take Drastic Measures just to eat, pray, love on a daily basis!

Sea Level

I liked Sea Level's 2nd album so much I couldn't not bring home their self-titled debut found combing the deepest depths of a mile long record row. Biographically speaking, this is 4 years after the Allman Brothers Band recorded Ramblin Man and Jessica, and barely a few months after Gregg and Dicky stormed off for whatever reason in 1976.

Critics have nothing to say. I don't have much to say. It's fantastic. Funky jazz and southern rock getting along like biscuits and whatever you really like on your biscuits. There's a reason Chuck Leavell became a highly sought-after session player and a permanent studio member of the Rolling Stones, and it's because he's great.

The concept of the band is very much "hey, we're a great band, screw Gregg and Dickie, let's just follow Chuck's lead. Seriously, go check them out, you won't regret it.

Elvis Costello and the Attractions – Imperial Bedroom

B: Gentiles and ladymen, a toast.
E: A toast to what?
S: What are you talking about?

I LIKE TOAST, WITH APPLE BUTTER, IF AVAILABLE.

B: We made a book. We made it real. Well, we set it in motion, it should corporealize in a week or so, then hitch a ride with the ghost of John Candy to our humble abode. Planes, Trains, and Automobiles, possibly even Home Alone if you a) don't fail to recognize WHY the cameo makes sense like everyone else, and b) don't realize that John Candy received a whopping $414 (no millions attached, just that sad little 3-digit number) for traveling to the set, ad-libbing the entire day, and then traveling home while losing money. Cab fare in Chicago is 3.25/2.25/.25, and his agent probably took $150.

S: Seriously?

B: Which part? Doesn't matter, yes.

E: ...but, but ... nobody exploded ... no flames shot out of things that shouldn't normally catch fire ... Carl isn't screaming from the other end of the hallway...

B: So? Why did you think they would?

E: Because that's normal here. Every other day something goes completely haywire. This place is one catastrophe after another, nothing goes as planned, it's...it's...a...

B: a madhouse? Oh, yeah, totally. You get what you pay for.

E: What?

B: I paid some nice people in Ingram, California to make a few copies of our book and send them to us. We might convince a few of our not-so-imaginary friends to buy one or two, but I'm the one who wanted them.

E: You can do that?

B: Of course you can do that. Well, I mean it's a bad idea if you don't have any money, but if you do have enough money to pay for it, then pay for it. All the bad stuff happens because you're trying to not actually pay for it. Have you learned nothing, Skip? Compy, what's my damage?

C: $142 and change for 14 copies after shipping. That's 10 something a book. It's a $16.95 book in 1990s money, getting a single copy here in under 2 weeks would cost like $35, so it is what it is. Choosers can't be beggars.

B: Oh, Compy, magnifique on the word play. I (of course) want to postpone the real number analysis until I can take a picture of the actual book in my actual hand, we're playing Entrepreneur The Bored Game after all, but I think we can all agree that these are not at all price-gouging numbers. Real life is expensive.

S: Sorry for ignoring the template and making it take an extra day.

B: I'm not mad, I don't care. So, back to my toast. To all the things we can do if we tongue-in-cheekedly infringe on Nike's trademark and just do them. Like tonight's album. I just so happen to own a copy of Imperial Bedroom by Elvis Costello and the Attractions on vinyl, and we published a book. I certainly don't need to prove how awesome either of those things are. Cheers.

Compact Jazz's Miles Davis

Rush Limbaugh has died. Surely some of you assume that I am jumping for joy on the inside, but that's simply not true. I adamantly disagree with many of the ideas he expressed, his manipulation of words to render intellectual discussion impossible, and his penchant for celebrity above substance, but he was no less a person. His loved ones no doubt feel the same grief at his passing that I did when my father died. All things must end.

On this subject I can say only that his stance on issues clashed with mine not because our ideas were diametrically opposed, but because he made a great spectacle of obscuring the larger ideals of Liberalism that his ideology was founded upon. America, whether you choose to believe it or not, was founded on the principles of liberty and equality, two fundamentally Liberal ideas. The trick is to always remember that those ideals apply to more than just "people like me."

And so, may time work its magic for those who knew him, the same as it has for me.

B: Alright, you guys want to hear the real story of why the Allman Brothers Band broke up?

E: No.

S: Not really.

C: Probably drugs.

B: Of course it was drugs, but it's more complicated than just growing to hate each other. Like The Band, they were snorting, injecting, swallowing whatever they could find. They all agreed to stop abusing heroin, but they just doubled down on the cocaine in its place. Gregg stole Duane's cocaine stash, they had a fight, triangle wins. Duane crashed his motorcycle and died. Which reminds me. Compy, put on that bizarre Miles Davis compilation that travels backward through the 1950s.

Fast forward to the DEA trying to take down a Georgia mob boss. Turns out ABB's manager was by far their biggest client, so they arrest him and want Gregg to testify. Gregg didn't want to, but after the mob guy's death threats and his manager saying take the protection and testify against me, he did. Dickey, the now leader of the pack, was all "Gregg's a narc, and I just don't see how we can continue the high level of professionalism our organization is known for with such dissention and disloyalty in our midst. If there weren't so many passed out members of our entourage in the way, I would resort to fisticuffs." They made up and became friends again, by the way.

S: That's it? That's a dumb story.

B: Sandra, of course that's the story. Sure, I left out the many changes of pants in the middle, but those are the facts, Ma'am. Dave Mustaine wasn't wrong when he said he just assumed every manager was a drug dealer. Tracks 5-14 were actually created in Paris while watching the film they accompanied. We're still decades away from Miles Buck Cherrying on that Scratchy Polatchy abomination, this is his own heroin addiction bebop period.

    S: Why do you keep focusing on the drugs?

    B: Because they cared more about the drugs than their music. What's the punch line of that Bill Hicks joke about all the musicians who made the music that enhanced our lives? Rrrrrrrrrrrrrrreeeeeeaal fucking high on drugs. Crap, I guess we have to do the Tool discography at some point. What were we talking about? Oh, yeah, Miles Davis in retrograde. This is great stuff. Herbie Mann flutes all over a couple tracks at the beginning, you remember Herbie the Love Bug, right? Then we get the soundtrack, and last we get to hear him play with Charlie Parker. Miles dropped out of Julliard to play in Charlie's band.

    E: Was there supposed to be a moral to this story, Bottle?

    B: Nope. Never was, never will be. I can't stop you from learning things along the way, but not because I taught 'em to you. I'm just a couple ear holes and a mouth with an attitude.

The Tool Discography – 1. Opiate

    How in the world do you talk about Tool without mentioning bodily fluids, felonious inhumanity, sexual depravity, the more wackadoodle parts of Melchizadek's extension of Jungian Philosophy? You don't. You just accept that Tool is a giant wrench shaped like a dick, and fix the part of the plumbing of your house you broke last night. In my particular case it's the drain line for the kitchen sink/dishwasher.

I was going to replace the two 45s with a proper long sweep 90, but we didn't have any at work, so 45 + street 45 it is. You'll also need primer and glue, and a hacksaw.

Luckily, there's only 1 piece I need to actually measure, so I can cut and dry fit everything before I climb up on the washer and drier to dry fit everything in place.

Tool's first album is the Opiate EP. It's not really offensive at all, unless you're a hypocritical abuser. They all met through the standard mutual friends who would also become famous route. These are the heaviest songs they had at the time, but they were already playing a bunch of songs they saved for their first proper album, Undertow.

So, the secret to not messing up is to dry fit everything in place, and mark the fittings and pipe so that you don't glue something backward on accident. Just build what you are replacing and save the new parts for when you get it up there.

Like I said, mark all your fittings. You don't wanna climb up your appliances only to find out you squirreled the gluing and have to buy an entire second round of fittings tomorrow. Sure, they're cheap, but you might not be allowed to live another day without a functional kitchen sink/dishwasher.

Don't be a doof, prime and glue both parts. Twist fittings into place to ensure there's no air gaps in the glue. Plenty of time with medium set glue, but you only get one chance at it; do it right, or throw it in the dumpster and start over. Give each joint a minute or so to set before the next one... and violas (possibly an imaginary trumpet fanfare if you're needy) you're mostly done. Let it sit for 15 minutes.

Eventually, you'll get it all put back together. Sure, there will be some swear words involved, and the fumes from the primer will Mortal Kombat any little nicks or abrasions in your fingers from working in Sub-Zero temperatures over the last week, and even though you're wearing your mask, you will get fiberglass threads in your throat when you take it off and cough like a TB fit, but eventually you'll get your lightly alcoholed fizzy cola syrup and sit down to a rousing 27 minutes of Maynard singing about nightmares, censorship, self-loathing, hypocrisy, and the sheer horribleness we put each other through because we're terrible.

2. Undertow

So, when people talk about Tool they say "alternative metal." However, when they do, they invariably include Alice In Chains and Stone Temple Pilots, so it's jibber jabber. Sometimes they say "thinking man's metal," but fail to compare them to Helmet (Tool is nothing like Helmet, that's a lie they both used dropped-D tuning, but critics use the same description for both bands). Genres are dumb.

Now, these essays aren't really in-depth musical analyses, and they certainly aren't newspaper scuttlebutt, they are more like contextual frameworks, getting into the mindset of listening to them 30 or 40 more times for their real substance; trying to understand where they came from, or what they might mean for us now. Cultural artifacts. Yeah, my essays hold up the object and contextualize it from my personal point of view.

Undertow. What's this thing about? Well, it's definitely not happy-time, beers with the bros music. If ever an album deserved the explicit lyrics sticker, this would probably be one. That doesn't mean it's bad, or evil, or depraved, it just means you wouldn't really want a generation of children haphazardly reciting some of the more visceral lyrics in public. I'm totally against censorship, but I didn't need a counseling session after hearing this when I was 13 either, so proper definition of moot, I guess. Yes, a lot of this stuff is not suitable for polite conversation out of context, but which of the 1,000+ albums in my collection actually is? Still, we can't really walk through the world blissfully unaware of all the horribleness that lurks in the shadows, and we need to hear it expressed to fully come to terms with it. This album in particular requires an understanding that it comes from the perspective of being caught in the undertow of the polluted ocean of society. If you aren't ready for it, it can be quite a shock.

More so than most bands, Tool's discography is completely chrono-locked; you need the context of the albums as they unfold, because the albums themselves form a coherent narrative perspective. They are, in fact, the actual process of evolving into a better, more spiritually connected and psychologically complete consciousness. Partly that's the result of long-term legal and interpersonal struggles, but the final result is that they strip away more and more of the facade of reality, and ultimately replace it with a kind of mental equilibrium, an adventure in real time, from 1992 to 2020. I could certainly flesh that out, but I think you should flesh that out for yourself. I'm probably hundreds of listens ahead of you, and I'm still not done yet. If Opiate is the expression of rage about the bad stuff, Undertow is an expression of what it's like to be stuck inside it. It is disturbing, grotesque, offensive, frightening. Opiate calls out the abuser in rage, Undertow gives a voice to the horrors of the cycle of abuse. A kind of method acting approach to making music.

Now's a great time to delve into it, actually, what with the Joss Whedons and Marilyn Mansons and Boyd Tinsleys of the world being held accountable for their abuses of power. Sure, in the pantheon of depravity some might be more or less vile than others, but in reality they are very wealthy individuals demanding sexual gratification as the price of professional success (Sandra has a very convincing PowerPoint presentation about why that won't be tolerated), and Jean-Luc Ponty reminded us that a "civilized evil" is still an evil. Terrible people defend their piles of garbage, so all we're ever really doing is searching for some psychological equilibrium from which to move on with our lives. However uncomfortable it might be for us to hear it, our first step is simply to hear the story being told. How could you ever hope to begin the healing if you can't even bear to hear the pain being expressed?

Henry Rollins makes a guest appearance, that's a rib cage on the cover, and Adam's pet pig poses above a field of forks on the back. It's almost like they planned that alliterative description, isn't it? I won't describe the rest of the artwork so you can be disgustipated on your own (that's the title of track 10/69, in case you didn't know. They actually recorded the sound of shooting pianos with shotguns in the parking garage of Grand Master Studio for it). Fantastic album, by the way, and fully deserving of its 69-minute length.

3. Aenima

There are lots of interesting stories about Tool's career, too many for me to cover all in one go actually, but we get a 3-year gap before Aenima. Partly it's because their bassist left the band, but also because these guys do other stuff. Maynard has a foot in the stand-up comedy world, and his side project Puscifer was born as a way to improv on stage. He liked Bill Hicks a lot. He also eventually moved to Arizona and started his own vineyard. Adam is a full on sci-fi/horror effects artist. Danny was a session drummer and played with Carole King of all people before Tool.

This is also the pre-high-speed internet world. 56k modems are brand new and psychotically expensive. It's hard to generate national buzz when MTV refuses to broadcast your videos, even after midnight. They aren't driving a van all over the country to advertise themselves like everyone before them. They also have the old school kind of multi-album record deals to deal with, but Wal-Mart is demanding censored reprints and the few upper execs who bothered to listen to any of it are taking that calling out hypocrisy thing a little personal. Fans don't really know any of that stuff, they just want another Tool album.

So, all that stuff gets mixed into a delightful shade of brown for their next album. Tool is a music first, Maynard figures out what to sing over it, kind of band. He has 4 or 5 large-scale streams of thought going on, and each album gets bits and pieces of it.

I'll also point out that this album has an intermission that segues into the second half, a surprisingly common trope for the time (see Offspring's Ixnay...). And sadly, my copies of Aenima and Lateralus suffered their own deaths a long time ago, so I can't take photos. Oh well.

So, what is this thing? Without getting too technical, this is Maynard "assimilating his shadow" as a path to enlightenment. With getting technical, you need a professional arsenal of relevant personal and psychological details delivered by a Snap-On truck (tool joke, yay!):

Psychedelic drugs, new age gobbledygook, Jungian shadow theory, high level math (yes, involving infinity), a Bill Hicks archive marathon, his mom's stroke and 10,000 days of suffering, an intense hatred of LA and consumer culture in general, an equally intense aversion to supposed authority, a love of puns, and a 77-minute attention span.

It will take a long time to wrap your head around all of it, but it's not nearly as unsavory as Undertow probably was. Opiate was the rage, Undertow was giving the subconscious a voice and letting it take over, now we get the assimilation and a "becoming whole." He is literally prying open his third eye by any means necessary.

Aenima is probably my favorite album of the bunch, but the next two are pretty awesome as well. Their last album, Fear Inoculum isn't in my head like the others, but the few listens I've given it were quite enjoyable. We'll try to grasp it when the time comes.

Oh, yeah, Drunvalo Melchizedek's chromosome theory is total garbage (there are no 42+2 humans, aboriginal or otherwise), but Maynard is merely using it as an obscure metaphor for enlightenment, not suggesting he's about to spontaneously grow another pair of chromosomes.

I suppose it's worth noting that they all love the occult/sci-fi/horror/metaphysical/Alastair Crowley kind of stuff. Holy cow, look at the time. I mentioned these things are loooooong, and it's way past my bedtime. See you tomorrow night for the parabolic acid trip through the universe that is their next album.

4. Lateralus

My first round of books has a tracking number, so they really should be here next week! Yay, but back to Tool.

Christgau called Lateralus "meaning mongering," and the 78:51 run time was universally seen as egregiously pretentious. Yes, it's long, but it's worthy of the length.

Tool is about challenging your perceptions. It took so long to make this album because it took 4 years to settle the lawsuits with their label. Copyright technicalities, contract options, if we hand the next album to you will you actually manufacture and distribute it or throw it in the dumpster and tank our career? We want a label that will actually answer that question. In the end, Tool won.

But, now a new problem. It's the year 2,000 and file-sharing is a thing now. We all remember Metallica doing really nasty things to their fans, but Tool felt quite conflicted as well. This is a trickle-down problem. At the end of the ledger, the major label doesn't lose anything, period. Like every other corporation, the money goes straight to the top, and gets distributed down as negotiated, in a beautiful world with Mandelbrot-winged butterflies. If nobody actually goes out and buys the album, bands won't make any of that money when the tornados subside. The execs will make their money, but the band will take the hit. You have to look at it on a case-by-case basis to figure out who's stealing from whom; that's expensive lawyer work right there. The numbers are gigantic, but so too is the corporate machine. Thousands of people have a small role in making it all happen, and there's a pecking order when the money dispenser opens. Ignore sleazy managers and accountants gambling it away on the side while leaving the band with the tax burden, it's entirely possible for a band to generate millions of dollars in profit (not total revenue, pure profit), but still owe the label more and more money for all eternity.

How is that possible, Bottle? It makes absolutely no sense. I agree, it makes no sense to you, and that's because you have a one-directional view of reality. Take my statement to heart: the inverse of a binary opposition is equivalent. You think you work for a corporation and they pay you for that work. The Missy Elliot version (flip it and reverse it) is also true: the corporation works for you, and they will take every penny they can steal. When you sign here and initial here and here, the label has promised to make and distribute your album, and you have promised to pay for it, in the future with money you might not make. That's a tough one when you live in a van eating the cheapest peanut butter you can find and hoping you don't have a flat tire on the way to the next gig where you might get stiffed and/or robbed.

Anywho, Alex Gray and the death and transcendence thing LSD does for a lot of people. This album is about the schism between mind and body, and the search for a way to reunite them. The physical and psychological worlds bump up against each other, and each side misunderstands and misrepresents the other.

Damnit, need to buy more tools. The Fibonacci sequence and the spirals it creates, abstract geometry, occult philosophy and Enochian, the 16th-century constructed language of John Dee and Edward Kelley, oh and Area 51.

It's easy to get overwhelmed and frustrated and give up, like Christgau and everyone else who just want perky 3-minute synopses of small portions of the modern human condition. But, as Maynard says, be patient. If there were no reward for following this tedious path of actually living life, I wouldn't bother doing it. No one ever said it had to be fun. Think about it, if you can watch all the pieces fall apart, then logically they do fit back together like a trillion-piece jigsaw puzzle. How about we start by learning to talk honestly to each other again, huh?

One of the things that really connect with me is the choice to live in the experience. We tend to think that the mind is a fluke accident, sentience just magically popped out of our atoms vibrating together, but aren't we all desperately trying to look at it the other way around? What if consciousness is the eternal force, and this life is simply one stage in that process? I prefer to think of it as an interesting snapshot of complex causality, existence being the infinitely evolving vibrations of a singular pulse, an unpredictable binary on/off. If you need God to be the light switch operator, go right ahead, but we can't see what the "off" side looks like, and we never will. We will only ever experience half of reality.

This album sounds like being close enough to that singularity to see the chaotic ripples in the fabric of existence. That's my jibber-jabber, and I'm sticking to it.

5. 10,000 Days

The fun thing about guestimating numbers is that you can find all sorts of coincidences. Is 10,000 days the length of time Maynard's mom lived after her stroke, or is it the orbital length of Saturn, or is there just some magical universal force that makes approaching 30 pretty awful? Great news, coincidence says all three are roughly the same amount of inaccurate, so they all get to be true!

I'm skipping over the increasingly lavish packaging, but there's more lovely Alex Grey, DMT inspired artwork. The album is sort of meant to be the moment of breakthrough. The DMT breakthrough is generally when you meet the elves and feel like you're living in the higher plane of the eternal, then they say you've still got work to do so see you next time. Individual experiences vary on the details.

We start out being unwilling to accept death, now we have to come to terms with it in often excruciatingly painful ways, and finally we can step through. You get serious and intentionally juvenile silliness like any Tool album, because that's the way life works. The bass line of Jambi reminded Adam of Peewee's Playhouse, so Maynard wrote it about granting wishes.

Some critics bring up the length and pretense, and hate the interludes, but that's an intentional part of Tool, so it's hard to defend being surprised by them doing what they intended to do all along. As for living in your own world where every tiny little detail matters, that's what it's about. The album is literally the opportunity to transcend it. If some part if your psyche requires you to dismiss it, so be it. Keep in mind, this is their penultimate album. The next one is the last one and this is one more step toward the edge.

Personally, this album gives me whole-body ASMR chills, an every once in a while, does actually make me cry. It's intense.

I haven't really said much about production, but these things are so incredibly complicated and meticulous, foreshadowed echoes at the edge of hearing, tone blending and stacking, large scale structural and timing relationships, and on and on. You can pull tracks out, but the albums are designed to be listened to in one continuous stream without breaks.

Why the mishmash of real experience and pseudo-scientific occultism? Because we are metaphor machines, and we're always looking for some explanation why. It's not about the real, it's about listening to the repressed side of our psyche and trying to become whole, meeting in the middle and transcending. Maynard described this album as a hopeful gift, an attempt to demonstrate his own breakthrough. We get all the threads of thought again, pieces of the larger puzzle, the personal memories, the ritualized mysticism, the aliens, and the psychedelic drugs, with the added understanding that this is itself a vicarious experience. A lot of people find these albums insulting, tedious, pretentious, but I hear them as face value expressions of honesty. I can't know them as individuals, but I can listen to what they have to say and incorporate that experience into my own as much as possible. They aren't trying to trick anybody, in fact they take the creation quite serious as art.

I've told you about my own borderline episodes, and that's what Right in Two is about for me. And we conclude with some Latin about The Rapture. You see kiddos, after the rapture there's a period of peace, then a period of horror, and as fans of infinity know, we get to do it all over again. The universe has an infinite supply of anti-christs. Lots of beautiful numerological coincidences with the number 23, by the way.

And lastly remember, we've been dealing with binary oppositions this whole time, title puns, black and white, the real and the metaphysical, and so on. 13 more years of personal and legal gobbledygook before the next one.

6. Fear Inoculum

Long-time listeners know my dislike of Amateur Internet Interpretation Hour, and Tool's last album is a tragic favorite. It's about Trump, it's about vaccines, it's about mainlining fear... it's about whatever the words "fear inoculum" mean when placed together consecutively. It is an abstraction from their collective experience. Structuralism, ya jackasses, protagonist/antagonist in a never-ending battle to see who can devolve the fastest. That's Tool, we pick up a wrench and idiotically bash someone's head in instead of using it to tighten the nuts and bolts that hold us together. And, we don't give pause until the blood is flowing.

We're back to calling out the abuser. Deceiver means anyone who's lying. Also remember, we're trying to bring the two sides back together into one consciousness. How do you get through an argument? Well, you can focus on all the ways we disagree with each other and never solve it, just turn on the dopamine machine and love being a lab rat addicted to cocaine (a real-life interview answer straight from Maynard's brain into Joe Rogan's microphone), or you can look for any tiny shred of agreement and build on that collective progressivity without compromising your personal ideals in the process. Plus, releasing your last old-school album and wondering how people will respond after 13 years is a frightening prospect. All of everything goes into it, because this is honest art from thinking individuals trying to connect with the larger society. Bowie did that, Devo, Green Day, Throbbing Gristle, every other band along this adventure did that. That is the goal. Finding a way to inoculate yourself to the fear, and moving forward. That's all I'm doing. I'm certainly not done yet, but I'm light years away from where I was as a teenager watching the facade of reality falling away to reveal what's in the shadows. I rage at the blinders that everyone tries to put over their third eye because I won't tolerate it anymore. There's no mental anguish you can put me through that I haven't already sought out and grappled with for myself. I'm not afraid of the fight, I think the fight is stupid, and I'm getting impatient waiting here at the meet me half way point. I'm ready to get on with the moving forward, everyone's invited, hurry up and get here already. And bring your big-boy attention span, this one's 86 and a half minutes long.

Conclusion

And so, we return to where we started: Someone told me once that there's a right and wrong...

... but, it must not be true. How did we get back to Opiate? Well, I somehow wound up, at the end of the Tool discography, being tired of waiting. That wasn't intentional. I didn't plan it. Is it coincidence? Is it my subconscious? Is it structural consequence? Did Maynard have anything to do with it? Is the entire 27-year process intentional, or serendipity?

My answer, of course, is that it is all those things. There are no morals to these stories, because there is no morality, or rather, because morality exists only at the moment of action, a choice that leads to other choices, some expected, some unforeseen, unpredictable yet connected.

We abstract rules from the game by watching, test their validity by applying them to our own choices, reevaluate and continue. If consciousness itself is the eternal entity, fragmented across the shattered mirror of individuality, the puzzle pieces that have fallen away, waiting to be patiently reassembled, then the way forward must surely be to search tirelessly for more connection, more honesty, more understanding, while throwing away the fear and anger and hate that drives us apart. Step into the shadow, rather than repress and punish it. To change, to evolve, to transcend, to swing on the spiral of our divinity and still be a human.

Perhaps I'm wrong and there is a moral, but not in the assignation of good/bad, right/wrong. Perhaps it is one of my favorite sentences, one that hints at a fundamental law of complex causality, a fundamental truth that we can only express indirectly:

If when I say I might fade like a sigh if I stay, you minimize my movement anyway, I must persuade you another way.

GREGORY – Allow Me To Introduce Myself

B: Can we do your EP, GREGORY?

I'D RATHER NOT, BUT I SUSPECT YOU WILL ANYWAY. WHY?

B: Well, we did the Tool discography, and you hide in the shadows and screech, why not? Plus, I like it. It doesn't have words for anyone to interpret wrong. Well, there's the titles, but you know, no lyrics and stuff. Are you a pirate?

NO, THAT WAS MY BROTHER, ROGER. WE ARE A SEA FARING FOLK.

B: So, what's it about?

11 MINUTES.

B: No, what are you trying to say with it?

HELLO?

B: C'mon, it's your chance to tell us about it. Hook us in, make us want more, really connect.

I AM AN ANTHROPOMORPHIC SKELETON, I THOUGHT THAT WAS UNDERSTOOD.

B: Hhhhhhh. You're killing me, Talls. Give us some insight.

I BARELY OBSCURE THE VIEW, I HAVE NO INSIDES, YOU CAN SEE THROUGH MY RIBCAGE.

B: Ok, how did you make the EP?

I WAS RUMMAGING AROUND IN THE CLOSET WHERE YOU KEEP ALL THE STUDIO GEAR. THINGS MADE NOISE WHEN I TOUCHED THEM. P(NMI)T ASKED IF HE COULD PLAY OVER SOME OF THEM.

B: Oh, well I mean, yeah, that is a literal description of it. Why Turtles?

I LIKE TURTLES.

B: Oh, ok. Well, that was less interesting than I thought it would be.

I AM NOT AS SURPRISING OR COMPLEX AS PEOPLE TEND TO THINK I AM. HELLO, I AM GREGORY, WHAT SOUNDS DOES THIS MACHINE MAKE? I LIKE

TURTLES. THAT IS MY EP. PLEASE DON'T EXPECT ANOTHER.

B: Why not?

THE TOP HAT, I'M AFRAID, HAS MUFFLED MY SENSE OF ADVENTURE.

B: Sorry. You were eating my minions, I had to do something.

NO OFFENSE TAKEN. IT WAS A CHOICE YOU HAD TO MAKE. I WOULD NOT HAVE TAKEN YOU TO BE MENDED WITHOUT IT.

B: Touché, I do like being me. Thanks. Well, you know, at least you had the chance to introduce yourself before being assimilated.

INDEED.

Failure – Fantastic Planet

I miss having Failure's 3rd album, Fantastic Planet, on my shelf. It's a wonderful album, no matter what Dean Carlson says. You could condense his entire review down to "Simpson's did it. Nirvana's better, and Failure doesn't write catchy songs." Sure, think that if you want, but it's dumb and you're an incomplete human being with a limited mental toolbox, Dean. I'm sure you're a mostly wonderful person like most people, but if we were having a conversation, I'd probably tell you to go away.

We're riding the chemtrails of Tool, and Tool was a big supporter of Failure, bringing them on tour. APC even covered The Nurse Who Loved Me. Wait, I did too, that's hiding somewhere in Mopey Time if you know where to look, wink. The point of the Tool discography was the fact that the discography itself was structured around the content (intentional or not). The cool thing about Fantastic Planet is that they structured an unstructured album. The songs are all over the place thematically, but they are arranged as 2-segue-

3-seque-4-segue-5. Plus, it's cyclic (or possibly orbital), the same music-box sample begins and ends the album.

Technically, this is space rock, exploring "other worldly musical textures," and it totally connects with my mental image of old hack, pulp sci-fi. Losers in space. This is as much like Nirvana as Bush, which is to say, not. That's a false comparison from an extremely naive type of listening, the old familiar Industrial equals NIN problem: we'll just gloss over that annoying 20+ year history and compare the sound of the singers' voices, 'cause I'm lazy.

But, man I love this album.

The Pretty Reckless – Death By Rock and Roll

As you might suspect, my brain plays music virtually non-stop. It's quite jarring when it does stop, actually. It would be natural to assume that my nightly albums have some effect on what actually plays on the mental jukebox, but not as far as I can tell. I am at the mercy of an imaginary subconscious DJ so unpredictable a random number generator would say "damn, this guy is good." Every once in a while, though, an ear worm from the real world gets in there and replicates. I've been hearing Cindy Loo Hoo sing the chorus of And So It Went for 4 days now, and I guess we'll just have to exorcise the demons by listening to Death By Rock and Roll, this year's 5th album from The Pretty Reckless. I love the title track, I love the follow up single (though 4 days is testing my patience), but I don't expect to like it. Albums have been pretty dismal these last couple years (at least the few I've been interested enough to listen to), but there's only one way to find out...

... hello, naked Taylor Momsen. I wasn't joking earlier, she quit acting after confusing Jim Carey for Santa Clause, and joined a hard rock band. They are in general great, by the way. I only bring it up, because what's the point of her taking a nude nap on a concrete slab? This isn't exploitation, or scandalous. This is image marketing, but is the bisexual community an actual demographic? That's not a leading question, I really don't know.

What I do know, and I'd put money on it if you were here and in the mood to gamble, is that this is going to be a split personality album. Half the songs will be ball-crusher, biker-chick, the other half will be her internal emotional monologue (positive or negative). At first glance, she'll metaphorically live fast and die messy, but it could turn around at the end. The point is that it's Death By Rock and Roll by The Pretty Reckless. That's the inescapable concept. We're really just going to find out if they did a good job or not, and honestly, I'd be really impressed if they could find a way to screw it up.

1 - killer lead-off title track. Just a phenomenal hard rock banger, with the aforementioned motorcycle crash.

2 - pass. This is nonsensical filler. Technically all the lyrics make grammatical sense, but not in relation to each other. And that's the Chef Boyardee-iest solo I've ever heard. Maybe he was going for the sound of a bucket full of worms, but if not, eww.

3 - yes please, more of this. Well, not literally, 4 days, remember. Great, great song, and a completely acceptable use of chorus of children, and the ridiculous solo is totally great here.

4 - blech. Gag me. First of all, counting songs suck. Second of all, if you can't hit that note full out, don't back away from the climax, just cut this crap song from the album. Third, were you a child bride, or something? These numbers don't work no matter what they refer to. Fourth, what the hell does the bass drum and giblets bookends mean?

5 - I like it a lot, but I'm so confused. Are you running away from your horror show of a hick family to bury yourself in a field by the hanging tree? Like I said, I like the horror vibe, but I think you've mixed your metaphors a little too strong with incompatible ingredients.

6 - acoustic Lilith Fair ballad, nope. Not that it's bad, it just doesn't belong on this album.

7 - yep, fantastic. Horror, witches, pizzicato strings, best 39 seconds on the whole album.

8 - nothing has prepared this track. This track is a bit of a shock. It's like if Type O Negative were a southern rock band. It's great, but what the hell, lady?

9 - another acoustic ballad? Must we? Yes, walls are by definition taller than you. If it were shorter than you, we would call it a fence. Humpty Dumpty, everyone.

10 - sitar? Really? The seventh hour? Like, the Tracy Ward book? It is. It must be. I don't know why, but it must be.

11 - John Belushi the acoustics. I don't like this song. You can like it if you want, but it's cheap. Is she 27? Yes. I was gonna gloss over the spurious Harry Connick Jr. 25 connection, but why bother at this point?

12 - no, shove that harmonica somewhere uncomfortable. Spoiler alert, she didn't die, her boyfriend did. So, she sings a sad song to her motorcycle.

Yep, I'm impressed. They managed to screw up a completely airtight concept. This is two shuffled up EPs that aren't related to each other at all. It's a bad album. I could listen to all but one or two of the songs out of context, but altogether it's bad. The horror themed songs are fantastic, this could have been an amazing southern rock Misfits album. The acoustic tracks would be fine as a standalone EP.

Final verdict, this sounds like a mix-tape from a label with only 3 bands. I recommend tracks 1, 3, 5, 7, & 8. The rest just isn't up to par.

The Pogues – Pogue Mahone

Darned if we didn't just keep on rotating, I turned like 7,000 years old today. Kidding, I'm 41 now. Did you know that 41 is an incredibly boring number. Yes, it's on a bunch of lists of types of numbers, but those types of numbers are moderately useless. So, because Sum 41 feels way too easy, let's listen to the only album I know for sure I received as a birthday present. Here's the actual last album by The Pogues, Pogue Mahone.

Critics didn't like it, but since it's the rock-bandification of the Irish phrase they got their name from, who cares? That phrase, by the way, is "kiss my ass."

Shane MacGowan is nowhere near this album, he got fired two albums ago. Doesn't matter, it's still completely enjoyable Irish folk rock, and they all called it quits afterward. Luckily, not before covering one of my favorite Bob Dylan songs, When the Ship Comes In.

So, there's a distinction we have to make. This isn't punk rock from Ireland, this is Irish music played by punks. For 9/10ths of the Pogues' career, they were lauded, but by 1995 when this came out everyone had flipped and thought they were beyond passé. I believe the phrase "new age" was bandied about in a derogatory manner. I disagree, just because the whistles would fit on a Yanni or Kitaro album doesn't mean it's bad. Actually, there's a lot more Zydeco than New Age to my ears. It's not bad, it's lovely and sweet. This is the other side of the farthing from Boomtown Rats. Just because they aren't falling down drunk or bleeding/vomiting all over the studio, and you can understand what they're singing, doesn't make it suck.

I think everyone hated it because it's a hopeful album. These are "love will get us through it" songs, as opposed to the more familiar punk nihilism. It's also all over the place production wise, but that doesn't bother most people. I'll admit I was "meh" on it for a long time, but it has really grown on me over the years. I can see how it was totally out of place in the mid-90s, but I think it holds up pretty well, and even at the end The Pogues were better than "the average pub band" everyone tried to downplay. At the very least, if you just absolutely detested Shane's incomprehensible toothless garble, this will sound positively articulate.

Judgment Night Soundtrack

You guys remember Judgment Night, don't you? Emilio Estevez, Cuba Gooding Jr., Stephen Dorf, and Jeremy Piven getting chased through the ghetto by Dennis Leary and his gang of drug dealing murderers? No? Well, I do, so we're gonna listen to the soundtrack.

Brilliant idea, pair an alternative rock or metal band with a rap group. Some amazing songs on here. There are a couple "meh" songs, though: I'm looking at you Cypress Hill and Sir Mix-a-Lot. The point is that this is real rap rock, not rock bands rapping for no reason, and it's fantastic. My two favorite tracks are Another Body Murdered by Faith No More and Boo-Yaa Tribe, and the title track by Biohazard and Onyx. You might remember B&O from their collaborative version of Slam. I love, love, love Onyx, by the way. I loved them when I was 11, and now I'm gonna go binge watch their videos. See you tomorrow, when I might have exciting news. Hopefully Dennis Leary doesn't blow up my RV and send Everlast to hunt me down and shoot me before then.

We made a book!

B: Guys, guys, girls, and skeletons, look what just arrived, our book. We did it. We have 14 copies of my first 365 album reviews. Check 'em out. Whaddya think?

E: Uh, I think we got confused and formatted the page numbers to the wrong side.

B: Sweet, now everyone can use both top and bottom corners for flip book animations.

S: I'm appalled! Who would do that to a book?

B: Relax, Sandra, it's my book compiled from facebook posts, remember. Not exactly Pulitzer material, am I right?

C: Bottle? Why's there no bottom margin?

B: I admit, I was afraid that might happen. I was trying to cut down on page length, but I squeezed a little too hard. I suppose I could have used a smaller font, but I didn't. We could fix those things if we wanted to. Maybe for the next one.

Now though, we gotta Kai Risdoll this litter of puppies (do the numbers, if you're not up on your NPR personalities and their catchphrases).

The $49 setup fee is my cost. In the great ledger in the sky, I'd claim is as cost of doing business, depreciate it over the whole run, itemize it on my taxes, etc. That's my problem not somebody else's. I have 14 copies because it's a full case, and that's the most cost effective. I can buy more if I need to.

$142.68/14 = $10.20. I rounded up, but if you're mad about me gouging you a penny, so be it. I don't like being fiddly, I think $5 is a reasonable profit, but I'd lower that if you own a store and think you could sell multiple copies to other unsuspecting victims, I mean people. Now I'll round down and say $15 is totally tolerable. I have books just like this of similar size and quality that cost $16.95 20 years ago.

I have no idea how much it will cost to ship one to you. I had Calculator set up shipping through PayPal and UPS ground is gonna cost me $10 or less. Why don't we just say $25 gets a copy of this thing on your bookshelf no matter where you live. Plus, you have the mental equilibrium of knowing that 100% of that money goes to me and my imaginary friends, not a bunch of thugs settling their sexual harassment lawsuits out of court.

13 × 25 (I get to keep a copy of my own book) = 325. I make a dollar or lose one, and I'll do it all again for book 2 (that's the one where said imaginary friends come out to play).

So there you have it, if we did it a time or two I might make a 2 or 3 digit profit and you'd be out the cost of a couple books. A cynic might say, sheesh 2 years of work for that? Meh, it was fun and it was my own spare time.

Long story longer, if you want a copy of it, I'll send you one. I think there's a way to do a facebook link from PayPal, but you can also just go to paypal.me/pnmit and give me an address to send it to. If more than 12 of you actually want one (my mom gets the 2nd copy), I'll gladly order more, but it will take a week or two.

And finally, apologies in advance for how many times I shamelessly plug my book in the near future. Cheers.

R.E.M. – Monster

Understanding Monster:

1) it's the R.E.M. album, not the Steppenwolf album.
2) I didn't like it then, but now I do.

Got it? Great. Good night everybody.

Ok, ok, there's more to it than that. It's actually a fascinating album, and it isn't simply another R.E.M. album like you might think. I've talked about quite a few albums that were interrupted by real world things: riots, medical emergencies, airplanes crashing into skyscrapers, etc., and this album had a couple of its own. We'll get there, we just have to set up the real context first.

Critics mistakenly labeled this album Grunge. You already know I don't think that's a genre, but it does have some common tropes of the time period: crunchy distortion, character pieces, and a cynical view of celebrity and fame. The monster is fame, and the deaths of River Phoenix and Kurt Cobain are an integral part of the album because they were Michael Stipe's actual friends. River ODed while they were demoing the 40 something songs that spawned this album, and Kurt killed himself just as they were finishing up and Michael was getting ready to help him work on the next Nirvana album. Best laid plans. Rain Phoenix does background vocals on Bang and Blame. The Phoenix family, by the way, were missionaries to Venezuela as part of The Children of God cult, and that did play a large part in River's mental instability. Joaquin seems well adjusted, though (could you hear my eyes roll on that one?).

So, what was the original goal? Well, they were tired of the soft, slow, acoustic experimentation of their last two albums, and all agreed to make some kind of loud, electric guitar forward opus. Stipe ended up surprising everyone by singing as a bunch of different but equally jaded protagonists, some male, some female. However, as we all know, he gives his themes an entire continent to graze, so you get an assorted array of approaches to the downside of being famous for something.

The most famous story of course is the opening track, a truly bizarre moment in Dan Rather's life immortalized in an R.E.M. single. For me, I vividly remember people describing this album as "half fun, half filler," and a mere placeholder in the band's discography. Nope, I wouldn't call any of it fun. What's the Frequency slows down because Mills's appendix burst while recording it, Berry had a brain hemorrhage on the ensuing tour, their friends died while they were making it and nearly breaking up, they didn't like being famous like every other band at the time, to me this album has always sounded like riding the struggle bus.

But Bottle, you say, Shiny Happy People.

And I reply, what the hell is wrong with you? That was a sarcastic mistranslation of an actual Chinese propaganda response to the Tiananmen Massacre. To paraphrase Stipe, it's a pop song for children to assure them that the world isn't a terrifying cess-pool, please don't include a recording of it in the time capsule you blast off into space for distant aliens to decode.

Esoteric ennui is the baseline for R.E.M., and these random excursions are quite jarring in their original context.

So no, this isn't R.E.M.'s "rock" album, it's what they produced in the face of their world crashing to rubble all around them. I knew something wasn't quite right way back then, but I didn't have all that accumulated biographical knowledge to really put my finger on it. I know I've said that music doesn't point to some subconscious psychological impulse, and it still doesn't: this is intentional. This is an album about how much no fun they were having, and that really does put the whole thing in a proper perspective. As just another R.E.M. album, I agree it's "meh," but as a document of R.E.M. in 1994, this IS their razorblade suitcase while Gavin is literally in the middle of making Sixteen Stone. Put all that together, and yeah this is pretty stellar.

Traci Lords – 1,000 Fires
So, yeah, if you can follow the unwritten train of thought that leads from R.E.M.'s Monster to tonight's album pick, then knowing nod from me to you. That's some unsavory subject matter, right there. We're listening to Traci Lords's album, 1,000 Fires. If you're certain you're curious I'll explain it somewhere that isn't a public facebook post. For now though, let's just say I was gonna write about the 1995 Mortal Kombat soundtrack, but learned that Traci Lords did actually make a full album, so now I can't not listen to it. You remember her from the Jonny Depp classic Cry Baby. No, not Rikki Lake, the blonde one. No, not the ugly blonde, forget it. The Mortal Kombat soundtrack has a Juno Reactor remix of the lead off track, Control. They did a lot of the music for The Matrix, so you are actually familiar with their kind of industrial tinged techno. The whole soundtrack is a who's who of 90s Industrial Metal and EDM. But, we're here to hear Traci's album. I expect EDM/Techno and I don't expect her to be a great singer, but I've been wrong thousands of times, so tube me up the yoo-hoo-haw (that's a word order joke, not

innuendo or a chocolate flavored milk-adjacent beverage sponsorship, just so we're clear).

Control is a great track, but fair warning she whisper talks over it on the album. Sadly, she's no Rod McKuen. Like I said, I don't expect the vocals to be good, so it is in fact slightly better than I expected. 9 more tracks to ruin it, though, and keep in mind there's no second Traci Lords album to redeem herself.

Ok, this is one of those agree to disagree albums. I freakin' love this thing, but you will absolutely hate it. It's bad. These are Juno Reactor's trash folder files with Traci Lords talking over them. You gotta understand, though, I'm listening on multiple levels at once. Top layer Bottle is laughing because it's hilarious. Mid-level Bottle realizes that even though these are legit Ben Watkins throw-away tracks, he still put effort into the project. If I were to phrase it bluntly, he made sure he wasn't the reason this album went nowhere. A different vocalist could probably sell it better, borrow one from Lords of Acid or KMFDM if you want, but this is Traci's show.

And now, Deep-level Bottle will remind you that talent has no bearing on my enjoyment. How can that be? Ok, you listen to something bad and laugh out loud and say "omg, that was terrible," but I laugh out loud and think "that was amazing! Play it again, it's awesome." Maybe another example will help. You hear someone mess up the National Anthem and immediately start criticizing them, but I think "that's great!" It's interesting. Who would set out to try to mess up singing it in front of thousands of people? No one, that's who, you just watched someone have the most terribly embarrassing moment imaginable on live television, no take backs. Hopefully, they can laugh it off and move on.

Traci Lords is singing "bang, bang, he's an outlaw lover..." right now. Go ahead, try to find any possible context where that lyric isn't embarrassingly terrible. I'll wait...

... who prays for rain at 4am? Glancing ahead, the last track is called Okey Dokey, you think that's gonna be a banger?

I legit love this album. She clearly wanted to make it, she isn't phoning it in, no one is making her look bad. At the end of the day this is fun and I'm thoroughly enjoying it. Except the penultimate track. I can handle it, but you aren't prepared for Father's Field. You just aren't. And the last track is even worse than I expected.

So to recap, terrible album, thoroughly enjoyable, love it. No mention of even one fire, let alone a thousand. I'm legit thinking about buying a used copy from some store in Maine. Probably won't, but it's the thought that counts.

Dave Gedosh – Architectronics

Architectronics. Building sound worlds. These are the voyages of the sound sculptor Dave Gedosh.

A lot of you might think, why would I want to listen to the incidental sounds of a woodshop classroom, or a train station? To which I reply "awesome! You understand the basic building blocks, the raw materials being arranged and sculpted. Now let's find out what he's building with them."

Right from the get go, I can assure you that this isn't unfamiliar territory. You will almost instinctively hear these pieces like the ambient soundtrack of a movie. Probably a horror movie. Why? Because this kind of heightened sense of environment is also what happens when the adrenaline of fear kicks in, and the machete wielding madman could be right around the next corner. There is, however, a much wider and more interesting world beyond that conditioned response, you just have to keep putting on clean pants and walking forward. Luckily, Dave's really good at easing that tension with more traditional harmonic/rhythmic structures.

Which brings us to listening strategies. It should be obvious that these aren't pop songs, so why would you force yourself to listen to them that way? These are sonic environments, not mel-harmonic episodes. It's a chance to explore your own psychological reaction to pure auditory phenomena. It might be frightening, or peaceful, playful or angry. The sounds of water might strike you as naturally soothing, or they might make you have to pee. I don't know, you're learning about you. I have a slight disadvantage in this regard, because whenever you tune into Bottle's Funky Funtime Fiesta, you're watching me intentionally play with these parts of my brain like Legos. It's super fun, but the downside is that I have to manually change how I feel whenever I don't like it. It's like reprogramming a whole neighborhood of garage door openers in a single afternoon. Sure, I can see Hit The Brett-man Hartler in the Amazon box (because rectangles), but I don't have to believe that's real, even if BBC News runs an idiotic story about it. I can read Dr. Seuss or Sartre, listen to Michael Jackson, or say "pretend I don't know what your shop-talk means and describe what it looks like," because I'm a freethinking anarchist. I don't recognize authority. I recognize it when you're trying to exert it, that's not what I meant, I meant I don't equate function with value. I recognize intelligence, experience, passion, I recognize that you might need artificial structure and imagined agency, but I have to act based on what is actually going to happen. When you lie to me, I just think oh, ok, you don't know what you're talking about, and plan for it to not work out properly. Structurally speaking, lying and simply guessing wrong look pretty similar after it all goes haywire.

  Business is buying and selling commodities, staff meetings and greeting scripts and color schemes and uniforms are not business. I have no clue when UPS will show up, because I don't work for UPS; stop promising things you can't control. Man, I'm so far afield it's like I wandered into a different stadium. Get back on track, Bottle.

By complete coincidence, track 4 reminded me that I have quite a few recurring dreams that feature unreal architecture. Houses connected by intangible secret passageways, invented structures overlaid on top of real directions and spatial relationships, amorphous locations with detailed mental mappings of the surrounding but unseen area. My brain naturally wonders what things look like from the other side, inside out, skewed at a 12-degree angle. Amazingly enough, I can't say I remember there ever being a thunderstorm in there. Oh, hey, there's Megadeth's Foreclosure of a Dream from the subconscious cellar, because word substitutions. Not about the farm mortgage crisis and the rise of corporate agribusiness. Focus.

And we end with the wonderful Point Flow. What makes that center section sound so wet, and the outer bookends so vibrantly electric? I don't know, but fountain inside a Faraday cage is what my mind says it looks like.

The real subject here is decoupling the sound from its source. Some signals are very strong and coherent, rain and thunder for example. Other less familiar sounds can become highly abstract and intangible. Somewhere in the world, someone might be able to differentiate types or even brands of power saws (I can tell the difference between circular saws and reciprocating saws), but for some people that signal might degrade to a mere "metallic" connotation, or even take on the qualities of some shrieking animal (real or mechanical). And now that we're juggling Piercian Interpretants like professional dinner theater entertainers, I will step back into the shadows and let you explore those secret synapses of your own think box.

Oooh, I just had a memory. One time Dave forbade me from singing in a bar, so I stopped. I don't blame him, my voice is irritating even by DIY gutter folk standards.

What was my point? Oh yeah, what are your thoughts? No, not about the lady who put glue in her hair, about the pieces on Architectronics. I'm anxiously awaiting the arrival of my copy of the physical CD. I'm an old-school tangible media kind of guy, as you might have guessed, but I certainly can't complain about the accessibility modern technology brings to the table. I tried taking the turntable along in the car one time, but it just wasn't practical. Cheers.

Carson Murphy – Bad Habits

X: Everyone, we have a new friend joining us today. Would you like to introduce yourself?

B: Peg leg? Stone belly? Oh, sorry, I'm with you now. Hi, everybody. You can call me Bottle, and I haven't reviewed an album in 7 days.

X: That's wonderful! We're all recovering critics here, so we know what you're going through. Would you like to try sharing what you're listening to without any context or ulterior motives?

B: Oh, geez, I dunno. Gene Simmons says rock is dead because bands aren't maxing out 12 credit cards and signing away their future royalties, and while that's half true if you squint into the sun, it's also not true at all, and...

X: Don't feel bad, Bottle. It's ok. You're not ready.

B: Bugger that! I'll just drop this DIY album I found on Bandcamp here, and b-line for that coffee table over there.

Bottle's Gift Card-stravaganza (with a side of politico-economics)

Mastodon – Emperor of Sand

C: How ya gonna review Emperor of Sand, B-man?

B: What do you mean, Compy?

C: What do you mean, what do I mean? Are you going to review it, and if so, how?

B: It's the inner monologue of a fictional character doomed to die in the Peruvian desert.

C: Well yeah, sure, that's what it *is*, but what about the background, the production, the fact that it's skipping even though you've been unusually careful with it, the fact that we're four years later and all we've had is an EP of b-sides.

B: Compy, Mastodon is just a band. I happen to like them a lot, but they are real people with real lives and we're trying to literally reboot the economy here. Not that it deserves to be rebooted, but still. It's an album about the curse of death. Yeah, friends and family dealing with cancer were the impetus, but it's just a Mastodon album.

C: So, you don't like it?

B: No, I love it, it's fantastic, it's gorgeous. None of the guys from Mastodon are T.S. Eliot or Ezra Pound, but why would you need them to be? It's lovely, I never have things to say about lovely albums. They're lovely.

I mean, this isn't a convince you to like Mastodon album by any means, and who knows what 2nd-world country actually aluminum-coated and shellacked the disc itself, but I'm certainly not booking a trip to early 20th-century Italy to pretend old fashioned fascism will wash away our economic woes, like Ezra did. True story, that one. I agree there's more than a fair bit of usury behind our direct-deposited paychecks, but I'm about as anti-fascist as it gets. The problem is that nobody understands that our modern economy is 100% debt propelled. Nobody has a passion for assembly-line animal slaughter or pressure-cooking corn syrup. Back when you could retire at 45, sure yeah bring on the temporary misery, but an entire life of drudgery for 2 good years before the osteoporosis kicks in isn't worth it.

I guess I could point out how I called Brendan O'Brien the "evil corporate doppelganger of Steve Albini," but I'm not gonna deny this album sounds amazing in spite of its 1 dynamic marking from start to finish.

There's an entire army of critics and fans who really do believe that "Mastodon is the savior of heavy metal" nonsense, and think this album is a bit of a lull, but they are just a band. I happen to love it, but it wouldn't be the one album I implore people to go listen to. I'm not known for lying.

    C: You suck.
    B: Thanks! I appreciate that.

Screaming Females – Chalk Tape
    S: Geez, Bottle. Where did that doom and gloom in last night's album review come from?
    B: Glad you asked, Sandra. We have money now, right? But, by and large, we're all stuck in various vicious cycles of buying Giffen goods.
    E: What the hell are Giffen goods?
    B: That's where the price of things you have to have to function inflate for normal reasons, Skip, but you and everyone else still needs to buy them so they keep inflating, and because they are inflating even more people start buying them as "investments," so everything actually gets worse. Think Irish potato famine, or the housing bubble, or the recent weather-related hyperinflation of natural gas in Texas. My problem is repaying my student loan debt, but I'm well past the moral crisis stage, and Congress isn't addressing the lack of lender responsibility that bankruptcy is supposed to ameliorate, they just aren't collecting on it at all. I've been bankrupt for my decade, but that 6-digit monolith is still not crumbling and I'll still be out at sea when it starts back up again. Plus, the situation as a whole is impossible to encapsulate in a few facebook posts, so I'm just back to treading water.
    Economics isn't about money. It's about trying to predict human behavior in relation to money. However, if there isn't anyone with the ability or willingness to solve a

specific problem, then none of it matters. I have to earn enough money to pay the debt, but that's still another decade away, and who knows what things will happen to mess it up. Nobody's making a plan to succeed as far as I can tell. I could hand a measly 4 digits back to the department of education today, but that doesn't do anything about tomorrow, and I still have to buy food and gasoline in the meantime.

    M: But, we can't just wipe out all that debt. It wouldn't be fair.

    B: Who invited you, Milton? Fair doesn't factor into it at all. Let that notion go, we aren't talking about everyone else, we're talking about me.

    M: Now you're just being selfish.

    B: Yes, it's my problem. I'm the person I'm talking about. Yes, this is a macro-economic problem, but there is no macro-economic solution. I have to hand money to a real person, and that person has to deduct it from my debt; I have to have money to do that. I have to earn money to have money. Anyone with a calculator can do the math and come up with a number that I CAN repay in a reasonable time frame, the rest is up in the air, but we're talking years not 3 or 4 months. I don't hear any ten keys clickety-clacking, do you?

    M: Umm.

    B: I work full time. Bankrupt. I can't pay for reeducation or relocation, I can't ask for a huge loan, I don't own enough stuff to sell or use for collateral. I can hand over a few hundred dollars a month. Who has 200k to hand me, anyone? No? Nobody? Problem still there, I'm sitting at an empty table. I could buy a lottery ticket every day if you're prepared to never get that money, but until some benevolent force of the universe actually solves the problem, I'm doing the best I can do in a system that doesn't have a solution. Some actual person has to pay it, or hand me the money to pay it, or we really do have to accept that it will never get paid back before I die. That's not morbid, it's a cold hard fact. I can do all sorts of stuff, but if nobody can or will "overpay" for it, then all I can do is shrug and say "sorry."

M: You sound so angry. It's not like I can magic it all away. It's better for society at large that The Firm pays back its investors and continues to provide abstract employment than meddle in philanthropy.

B: I'm not actually angry, I'm just frustrated and tired of watching everyone dance around in circles while complaining that we have to dance around in circles all day. Your ideas are one-sided garbage, Milton. Of course you can't magic it away, it's a doing problem. I'm doing exactly what everyone, including you, thinks is right and proper, but it actually makes the larger situation worse. Market economics has winners and losers. I am one of the losers, but I'm not the type of loser you want to see, because you can't blame me for making bad choices. I'm not the homeless drug addict you can write off, I'm not the thug or the con man, I'm the polite, friendly, hard-working, nice guy who takes care of himself and tries to help the people around him. I don't want a mansion, or a luxury car, or a yacht. I want a simple life with my chickens and vegetables and family, and my records. Unfortunately, the ghost of student loans past keeps tapping me on the shoulder and asking for huge tracts of money from the future that never seem to teleport into my checking account.

Oooh, speaking of. Two of the albums from my Christmas gift card-stravaganza arrived today. Navient doesn't accept gift cards or chickens as payment, by the way.

So, as I once again shrug and apologize for a system I think is dumb, but don't have the power to change, I'll put on Chalk Tape by Screaming Females, and thoroughly enjoy the demos they recorded in 2013 that only existed on 100 cassette tapes that sold out at the first show they played after an extended illness break.

It's great by the way. It's raw, it's unpolished, it's delicious. It's really just an EP, but pressed as a 12" 45. And thanks again to Plaid Room Records, hope all is as well as can be over in Ohioland.

Between the Buried and Me – Colors

M: Ok, I sort of get it. I can see how you're stuck in limbo. But, we can't rearrange the entire economy to pay off your debt, even if you represent a wider demographic.

B: That's where you go wrong. I'm not a demographic. I'm 1 person, being selfish. I can't pay it, but I'm also perfectly willing to not even try. I make enough money to live a comfortable life, and the promise of possible fortune has no power over me. All I have to do is make an annoying phone call every once in a while to explain reality to a 20-something collections agent. She types in my numbers, sees that they are exactly what the IRS report says they are, and slumps down in her chair because she isn't legally allowed to take away my grocery money. I'm paying more than the maximum federal wage garnishment. I'm exceedingly tired of playing that game, so instead I'll play some adult contemporary progressive death metal. I'm not thrilled that it's remixed/mastered, but I am thrilled that it's Between the Buried and Me's fourth album, Colors. I'll keep buying records one gift card at a time until it's a million-dollar collection, but I'll also keep listening to them for fun and tank that value at the same time. Floating toward the sun, the sun of nothing.

Oh man, this album is gorgeous. It's got everything: piano, screaming, circus music, jazz guitar solos, more screaming, an out of nowhere honky-tonk banjo interlude, trumpets and synths and dueling lead guitars, the whole album is one continuous work and only one or two tracks fit on a side. I like some of their later albums more, but Colors is a monumental epic of an audio masterpiece. We're gonna keep going tomorrow and really delve into stuff when the next batch of records gets here, but I beg you to carve out 65 minutes of your life to listen to Colors by Between the Buried and Me. I just made it to the accordion part at the end of Side C. Delicious.

A truly magnificent work of art.

Swaps

Runaway compound interest is stretching the definition of a Giffen good a bit, but it's certainly true that I have to devote more and more of my paycheck to it as the balance keeps rising. At some point, it will overtake 100% of my potential future earnings, and theoretically zoom off to infinity. Who gets the blame is somewhat immaterial, the point is that someone with authority has to physically put a stop to it.

So, how do we solve it? First, the compound interest has to permanently stop compounding. Congress and the next few Presidents can't keep changing their minds every time it rises to the top of the agenda. Set some criteria, set up a payoff plan, and make a legitimate end point. Stop speculating on my unpayable debt, and properly budget what I *can* pay. Yes, your precious shareholder profits will take a hit, and the billionaires will have to take responsibility for their own bad investments.

Second, realize that Universities are not an acceptable substitute for skills training, they are communities and repositories of knowledge and philosophy. Apprenticeships and professional training are important, but they need to be supported by industry and trade organizations, not the mandatory entry fee to being alive. Passing on practical, useful skills and ideas to future generations should be the ultimate goal for everyone, not just the economically privileged, and not just in our "school system." Likewise, bad ideas and corruption need to be held accountable for the havoc they cause. Regardless, all I care about is paying back the loans without starving or being more punished in the process.

You can look at things from various viewpoints, but the American corporate sector is simply too big for everyday consumers to support. It takes too much money, too many resources, and too much environmental damage to sustain at a reasonable level of consistency. Most major corporations and large businesses are just as insolvent as I am, but they're also "too big to fail." One factory closing is enough to bankrupt the surrounding towns and destroy thousands of lives with no real safety net to ease the burden. There is no reset button, just pointless starvation and urban decay until someone decides to pay people to rebuild.

Which brings us to taxes. Your taxes don't go to other people. Taxes are merely a way to force money circulation through the macro-economic formulas of the Fed and the Reserve banks. What do you think the deductions represent? They represent legitimate expenses that help keep everything moving, your positive economic impact on the world around you. Whether or not that's true or real isn't the issue, it's the assumption behind the system. At the heart of it all, we are individual people trying to navigate through the blanket generalizations of local, state, and federal government because most people aren't willing or prepared to live every moment as a complete surprise the way I do (totally true, by the way).

The Fed's job is to try to keep things functioning. Interest rates are only 1 little tool, and can't solve every problem. Sometimes you have to buy $1,000 toilet seats to get money flowing where you think it should go. If you think Congress is messing with the money supply at a dangerous level, then you have to realize that your precious private citizens aren't actually spending enough to keep the whole thing running smoothly without government intervention. If it were functioning properly, Congress wouldn't have anything to congregate about. Markets crash all the time, and big companies crash big. Little companies don't cause as much damage, so big companies get bailed out, little companies don't. Fair or nice doesn't factor into our system because every part of it is based on a mathematical guesstimate. Investors are literally thinking up new ways to trade money back and forth, just to see how it turns out. A whole bunch of people seem to think that's a more productive use of money than using it to buy and sell tangible commodities. I don't need this 3 million right now, let's see if I can turn it into 4 million with some creative accounting. Oops! Guess we'll need to adjust this variable over here and try again. Sell that land, those buildings, and lay off 900 workers to get us back in the black.

This is all getting a bit dry and abstract, let's play a record. I doubt it will be relevant, but I've got a whole new stack of weird stuff. A 10"? Didn't realize when I bought that. This whole batch of records is sub $20 stuff from Barnes & Noble, by the way. That means these bands didn't really make any money from them. Swaps? Whaddya know, it is relevant.

Interest rate swaps are just that. The most common is fixed for floating, meaning one guy sends money to another at an agreed fixed rate, but receives return payments according to a floating (variable) rate schedule in the future. Heads up guys, next year you gotta have 20% growth or go bankrupt. It's one of the many instruments hedge funds use to speculate with their hoardings. What you need to know is that behind the scenes, people are playing around with lending money back and forth just to see if their mathematical models are accurate.

The album Swaps is two 11+ minute tracks of glorious cacophony. If I really did own a record store, this would be in the Delightful Gibberish section. It's experimental noise music, like your children might play if you hand them 27 different instruments and a hammer. Actually, it's the perfect soundtrack to my nonsensical ramblings about the economy. Go torture your brain a little with Pair Bonds and Aether

Defects by Swaps. I have hand numbered copy 117/483, in case you wanted to know.

Spoon – Ga Ga Ga Ga Ga

If you feel like I'm just going Ga Ga Ga Ga Ga, don't make me a target. I love Spoon. Now I can add their 6th album to my collection.

Did you know Pete Loeffler is surprised and frustrated by the fact that Chavelle doesn't make any money from album sales? Why is he surprised by that? Pete isn't selling those records. They aren't Pete's records, they aren't Chavelle's records, they are Sony's records. The band signed away their profits for global distribution. It's one thing to understand what your contract says, it's another thing to understand what it means and decide what you really want. In the case of a major label, it invariably means you created a work for hire. Dear Pete, Epic bought your album with Sony's money, hope you negotiated enough of an advance to live until the next one.

I know what's happening in Pete's head. He thinks that fans are buying his albums and he'll get some portion of that money. That's not what his contract says will happen. It could say it MIGHT happen, but I doubt Epic has much left after payroll and pay-up to Sony. Epic's job is to pay Sony with revenue generated by its roster, not the other way around. Pete's job is to re-capitalize on the gargantuan marketing, publicity, and distribution to get fans to shows, but he doesn't own the venue, or tickets, or merch. There isn't anyone handing Pete money, so....

Spoon, on the other hand, is an indie band. They have a much better contract than Chavelle, in large part because Spoon is paying their fair share. Spoon has a stake in their own career, tours, distribution. I'm not ragging on Chavelle just to be mean, I'm merely pointing out the sloppy, naive thinking. Chavelle is at the mercy of Sony, using Sony subsidiaries for the profit of Sony. Spoon is on Merge, who uses AMPED for distribution. Merge cares about producing great new music. AMPED cares about getting Merge artists into stores and fans hands. Everyone is paying for a service and expecting tangible results, but Sony is just slapping through product the same way it has been for decades, hit or miss, drop them if they miss too many times. Merge doesn't want to miss.

Is that actually true? No idea, it's what the illusion looks like to me. Hold on Bottle, says my imaginary audience. This is all getting too abstract for me to follow. What are you trying to say?

I'm just rambling. We're looking at a problem. We all have this notion that people know what they are doing, that there are systems in place to take care of problems, that things *should* work out. Things don't just work out. Yes, it's entirely possible to make it worse by doing dumb things, but we have enough experience to prioritize, and we should have enough integrity to suck it up and do the work.

In the case of Spoon vs. Chavelle, all the little private companies are focusing on succeeding at their task, but Sony only cares about Sony. If you start to make a dent in one of their markets, they will try to buy and/or squash you. Sony has a massive economic footprint, and if they fold, the whole world will feel it. They are "too big to fail." There's no exit strategy if they do, the same way that there's no exit strategy for the education loan system failing. We need to take a look behind the scenes, and try to understand how we got where we are. That means the Fannie Mae/Sally Mae/Freddie Mac problem. I don't want to dive into the deep end, though. We'll take the following statement as our context: things got so bad that the Department of Education bought most of that debt, and people like me with graduate degrees are ultimately paying back the Federal government through various servicers.

There are strict rules about how much can be collected, but there is no actual plan for the really bad ones like mine. Average outstanding debt is 30k, mine's over 200k at this point because the interest kept compounding through two years of unemployment without any benefits (a different story).

Once I finally got a job, I resumed paying what I could, but the interest on my loans was more than my salary. Everyone with three firing brain cells understands that's an impossible situation, but nobody has an actual plan to resolve it, because everyone wants it to magically work out; I'll get 200k for buying that 80k principal balance (or whatever, I'm just using approximate numbers at the moment). So, they kept trading my debt around until the federal government said "no more." But, they don't have a plan either, and partisan bickering is the opposite of doing something. If it were a house, the bank would foreclose and kick me out, if it were a car they'd repossess it, but it's the stuff in my brain we're talking about. Most people don't think my thoughts and creativity are worth much money. They certainly aren't worth grocery money. Spoon's 6th album isn't worth grocery money, no matter how much I like it. Food is more important than music. But, Barnes & Noble doesn't sell groceries, so records it is.

One last thing before we move on to the weekend, I make more than enough to live a lovely life (and you've been watching me do it for years now). I shouldn't have to sit here watching the federal government argue with the federal government about how much of my salary from working a full-time job at a plumbing/hvac wholesaler they can take to pay back my unpayable student loans from my Master's and PhD studies. I wanted a career that required a doctorate, but it failed to materialize for reasons beyond my control. It's gone forever. I'm paying the cost of my failure (and I started back at ground level $9.50/hr), but no one is paying the cost of the bad investment that I turned out to be. Statler and Waldorff never come down from the balcony, Mortimer and Randolf don't become bums at the end. That doesn't seem fair; I'm small enough to fail, but the predatory lenders aren't? I have to payroll my own third-party debt collector?

I think tomorrow we should look at my book, how it illustrates the reality of business without the illusive fallacies of financial finagling. I can't guarantee it will make this whole train of thought come together, but it should at least be interesting to watch while it makes you late for work as it's passing through town. Plus, I still have 4 more records in this batch, so who knows where we'll end up?

Mirror Travel – Cruise Deal

Let's travel through the mirror and look at it from the inside, show you what happens when you step through reality into the Imaginarium. Don't worry, the escalator of doom knows the difference, and you can ride right back up it when we're done.

We need a soundtrack, though. Well, would you look at that, I have the Cruise Deal EP by Mirror Travel. Pouty post-punk on a pretty sea-foam platter. Poyfect.

Hi, I'm Bottle, welcome to my media empire. I am a publisher. I publish music, videos, and books. In terms of actual work, I get the material, make sure it looks and/or tastes the way I want it to, then shove it in the innertubenetweb and go do something else. I have some big advantages, like no employees to pay, buildings to rent, licenses or fees, we call that stuff overhead. I let all that stuff sail over my head; we're in the basement, after all. Sure, I have corporate functions like any other schmuck (you've met Sandra and Skip and Gladys and Compilerson and possibly caught a glimpse or two of GREGORY or Bridbrad or p(nmi)t), but they qualify as imaginary minions; all they cost is a little bit of brain power.

What does cost money is the book I recently published. Real things cost real money. On this occasion, I borrowed some money from this super nice guy named Paul. I eventually have to pay him back, but there's no time frame or trickery. He paid to make 14 real copies of my year of album reviews, but he set the exit strategy at $250 no time limit. I kept notes, so I know it cost him just shy of 200. He'll make $50 profit from lending it to me. Certainly can't complain about 25% when I've got eternity to accomplish it. Truth be told, it doesn't have to come from actually selling the book. If I made some money some other way, I could divert that to Paul and he wouldn't care, our deal was a pure money exchange and he isn't morally or legally responsible for what I do to pay it back.

      How to price this thing? Well, there's the physical cost of each book, the cost of shipping it, and some profit. If I charge less than the cost of making it, I'll lose money. If I charge too much, nobody will buy it. This book looks and feels like all the other 15 to 20-dollar books in my library, and it would cost about $32 to buy 1 copy from the printing company, so that's my target range, more than 15, less than 32. Ok, 200/14 = 14.29, so far so good. Should cost less than $10 to ship it 2-3 day ups, but I could use the post office for less if I needed to. I want it in your hand as quick as possible, so we'll say $10 for shipping and go with $25 total cost. The discerning amongst you will notice that my actual profit is only a couple dollars. That's ok, no time frame or restrictions on that loan; I have to hand Paul $250 at some point, but he agreed not to speculate on that $250 until I actually hand it to him. He's pretending that he got whatever he paid for, and that deal is done. Did I mention what a nice guy he is?

      Alrighty, sloppy thinking 101: some of your brains might say "sell 10 of the books at 25 and pay Paul back, easy peasy." No, you forgot all the internal expenses, books don't teleport. My transaction fee on 25 is 1.30, and the real cost of shipping so far is 8.58. So, 25 - 9.88 = 15.12. I get to keep 15.12 out of every book I sell. Grab your calculators, that means I have to actually sell 16 books to have the 250. I only have 14 books, so I'll either have to buy more books to do it, or find a way to keep more money from each sale. My sales model has some gremlins, but at least I'm not losing any money. Sell a bunch more books, find cheaper shipping, eventually it will get there as long as nothing actually changes. I can still fail, but I'm not doomed from the start. As long as someone finds $25 a fair price and I don't spend any extra money, that is.

Oh, I almost forgot, I kept a copy for myself and I sent a copy to my mom. I'm 38.82 behind on this first case. Let's try to use the real numbers to figure out how many books I have to sell.

15.12 x 12 = 181.44. The next 14 will cost 143. 181.44 - 143 = 38.44. That's how much I could pay Paul from the first 14 books. No silly stuff on the next round. 14 x 15.12 = 211.68 + 38.44 = 250.12.

There you have it, if I can sell 26 copies, I can pay Paul his money and make 12 cents for myself. I think I'm still under the radar of having to collect and document sales/income tax, but that would certainly throw a huge monkey wrench in my calculations, considering I actually made 12 cents on this whole kerfuffle.

That's enough for today. Time to shovel some chicken poop.

Narrative Interlude

When last we saw Bottle, he was showing us how his investor made $50, but he made 12 cents. He then walked away, because shoveling chicken shit was a more productive use of his time and energy than being a businesspeople.

We know that Bottle and Paul and all the rest are the same person, we know that this is a structural sandbox, but Bottle is a decently smart chap. He's showing us the underlying structure of American business, and how the rich get richer/poor struggle to break even without anyone taking any advantage of anyone else. The structure itself causes this problem, even when the people involved are the nicest, sweetest, good intentioned people imaginable.

He'll come back tomorrow with more records, but even a well-functioning narrator such as myself can't possibly know what words will come out of his mouth, or what record will be playing while he says them. It is an adventure, after all. So as Bottle might say, catch you on the flip side, and cheers.

Parts & Labor – Mapmaker

No, you know what, Mr. Narrator? I don't have to follow your rules. I can do another album if I feel like it. Call me Happy David Gilmour, 'cause I'm not feeling lazy anymore.

Have you ever wished that there were such a thing as catchy frantic pop-punk buoyed by electronic gobbledygook instead of power-chord chugging and strumming? Jangly guitar melodies with total drum and distortion cacophony behind them? A Devo/Merzbow collab? Well, I've got Parts & Labor's Mapmaker from 2007. I'd say their brand of noise rock is pretty close. It might be the only good album I've heard from the decade of the naughts. What does that have to do with the price of cheese, I mean higher education? I don't know. Nothing. I mean, we were talking about real people vs. corporate functions, trying to understand why it's so hard to keep track of the real cost of living in a technologically advanced society, how the little guys and gals get swept aside for the sake of not having to constantly dodge those 40-ton dinosaurs as they heart-attack and die above our heads, and earthquake us into oblivion when they collapse, 'cause we just assumed those crazy titans of industry knew what they were doing. We assumed the world would rearrange herself to do the same for us. Damn you, totally unrelated coincidence! How do you keep doing it to me? How do you make random crap I bought last week so relevant? Hold on...

... ok, I just reread my own book, and reminded myself of that subplot where we just avoided all these problems for the last 52 years. Yep, nothing new under the sun. Maybe Nixon 4.0 will do a better job in 4 or 8 years (I seriously doubt it). Also keep in mind, at no point in that book did I defend Kennedy or Johnson, I was simply pointing out that Nixon, Reagan, both Bushes, and Trump were absolutely, categorically, undeniably, and vomitously not the "answer to our prayers." They weren't even just a band like Mastodon. They were nastier than the nastiest Bradley Whitford characters. They set us back decades every single time, because their ideas and theories were outdated, completely lopsided, and in a lot of cases blatantly discriminatory.

Let me give you some examples. The mission statement of police and law enforcement is noble and justifiable, but quite a lot of the things police officers do on a daily basis are counterproductive at best, homicidal at worst. 90% of lawsuits are childish garbage, meaning the few actual important cases don't get proper judicial review and consideration. All 50 State governments are such absolute garbage that the federal government has to actively prevent them from bankrupting/imprisoning their minding-their-own-business citizens, and/or bulldozing their neighborhoods to build bigger highways for their downtown financial center/recreation expansions, while garbage businesses with money to throw around get rewarded for undercutting innovative startups and family shops. Trust me, a whole bunch of people would ecstatically farm, garden, and raise animals way out in the country if they were actually paid decent money to do so. Hand me a tractor and some in the meantime grocery money, I'll plant whatever kind of edible food you want to eat 4 months from now, and drive it straight to your house the day after harvest day. Build me a greenhouse and I'll grow tomatoes and bananas all year long. Pay me to stay home with the chickens and I'll give 'em away, they make more of themselves than I can butcher in a weekend. By all means make the reward for success bigger than failure, but don't look a farmer in the face and tell him it's his own fault that it rained too much or too little so he gets to be homeless now. Don't pretend that the map is more important than the land, that the nation is more important than half its people, that this whole reality is anything more than a false facade. There's more to life than right or wrong. Building bigger and bigger fortresses of solitude and fighting bigger and bigger wars over who gets to dig in the mines for shiny rocks is a pitiful and pointless form of existence. It might take a few listens, but this album is pretty straight to the point once your brain wraps around it. I highly recommend it.

The Mopes – Accident Waiting to Happen

Look, Bottle. As the narrator, I know that you're exasperated, but you can't fly off on a subtly humorous tangent related to the lyrical content of an album as it interacts with your secondary subject. The reader can't follow it.

Yes, I can. I've been doing it the whole time. My imaginary reader can follow it. This isn't light, diversionary, casual reading. This is heavy, intricate philosophical investigation type stuff, albeit framed in the silly context of hiding in the basement listening to my rapidly growing record collection while leaving out a lot of the big words and jargon. Illustrations of the subject, rather than dry boring op-ed rants in the Sunday paper. I prefaced the whole project that way. Two years ago I said I was showing everyone how to do it, how to interpret real life, you just have to understand that you're along for the ride on my bus, and I don't have a map or route to follow. I apologized for hating some albums, said I don't know why I like this but I do, even the worst of the worst has some redeeming quality, wrestled with ideas that were too large for anyone to fully comprehend, said if it doesn't connect that's totally fine. If I think I went too far, or that some people forgot the perspective, I bring it back up like now. I've made it very clear that it's a horror show inside my head, and that's why I consciously choose to be objective, fair, humble, honest, friendly, and patient. I do have a borderline personality. Everything is fantastic or everything is horrible, and I have to actively talk myself back to the middle and do the one thing that keeps us all floating. I have to regulate myself, I can't have too much happy or too much sad. I have to avoid actual anger like the plague, so if your idea has fleas, I'm not sticking around to get bit.

Sometimes I get the mopes, but I don't want to have a duel at high noon. Today, I literally have The Mopes, Accident Waiting To Happen. This is a project by a bunch of friends, recorded around holidays during breaks from their respective bands in 1999. They got together when they could and recorded a couple songs by everyone. It caught my eye because Dan Vapid is here. I bought two of his albums on the spot when I randomly encountered him last summer, remember? This is pure, glorious, good-natured pop-punk, and I'm a huge fan. No single member traveled less than 500 miles alone to make it. I have one of the first 500 orange-marbled repressings, the very first Sounds Rad release. It might be the only album that's legitimately worth more than I paid for it, even after opening and listening to it. It's amazing.

So, I'll try to meet you half way. I know I still have to address the ends and means justification debate, and I know I have to talk about my book example because I intentionally stopped at the breakeven point. I did my standard state a problem AND its conclusion right at the start, fleshed out the innards, and now we're headed for the serendipitous accident that's waiting to happen at the end. Remember that time Skip's office flipped sideways and the sprinklers came on? Spoiler alert, the end of this story involves a deep look at agency. Specifically, is there actually a villain being villainy? I don't know, I haven't written it yet. But, until then, please enjoy one of my favorite pop-punk practitioners and his friends making great 50s pop songs about modern feelings and experiences. Check out anything Dan Vapid's involved with, he's fantastic.

Villainy – Villainy II: Dim

I don't know anything about Villainy. That cover art screams foreign extreme metal, though. Opening it up, I see the very first lyrics are "when the structure is done...."

Total coincidence that this is the penultimate album before the out-of-nowhere random record that magically ties the whole thing together in my mind. Your mileage may vary, but I'm highly attuned to the shape and feel of an unfolding process. It's an illusion our brains create to navigate the constant bombardment of stimuli. It's one of many doorways into the wild west of Gestalt Psychology (see how The Mopes just travelled right along with us?). It's the opposite of Structuralism in some ways, arguing that we perceive larger patterns and cycles all at once, rather than assembling meaning from individual components. It's where the idiom "the whole is greater than its parts" comes from. I, of course, have been doing both at the same time, constantly flipping back and forth, double and triple rechecking my thoughts, pulling out the weeds and letting the new growth evolve. I think the oscillation itself is meaning, the thing that propels us forward, or overwhelms us until we jump off the bus at cruising speed, whether or not it kills us. Unexpected surprises, nonsensical gibberish, traveling through the mirror with or without a map. But, for me, there isn't a map yet that's been accurate enough to be useful. I have all the tools I need to go wherever I want, but there's always someone or something trying to take that freedom away. That's the real villainy.

First track called Res Cogitans, Decartes' binary opposition to res extensa, the mind and the material world respectively. See, told you this was deep stuff, even if it happened by total accident. I bought things that cost less than

$20 with gift cards, and ended up right back at the deep schism of Structuralism like I always do. I, Bottle, am a discorporate mind after all, totally separate and detached from the real person who is Paul.

And now we're magically back where I said we would be; I never renege. Paul made $50, Bottle made $0.12. Is that fair? Is Paul the villain, Bottle the victim? No idea, we have two tasks to accomplish. 1) we have to define the whole situation, and 2) we have to deconstruct it. We should probably reassemble it afterward, but I can't guarantee we actually will.

What are the parts? Well, first Paul loaned Bottle money and Bottle used it to accomplish something. Second, Bottle gave money back to Paul. That second part is currently a cat inside Schroedinger's paradox box, we don't know if it's alive or dead until we look inside, but once we do, we have to remember that the act of observing it creates the reality we observe. Looking at the exact moment Bottle succeeds at giving Paul $250 dollars tells us a different story than what happens before and after that moment.

$50 vs. $0.12 certainly looks vastly unequal, if that's the stopping point. The story could unfold two different ways from there: Bottle could keep investing in the book, but he'd have to borrow money again, and the whole thing would start over. We could calculate how much it would take to get Bottle to the point where he had enough money to invest in the book himself, but we can easily see that Paul's profit would expand exponentially compared to Bottle's. Bottle will always make a minuscule fraction of the profit that Paul makes, even when the lending deal is completely fair and agreeable to both parties. There's no actual person being a villain, but there is a coherent evil taking place. Granted, we don't have to interpret that result as evil, but I think most every mind WOULD. It's hard to accept that kind of unfair reality, so we attach it to the closest agent available. If Paul steadfastly defended the system because it works (for him), Bottle would call bullshit and show how it will always keep him down in the basement without any structural mobility at all. Success is still comparative failure in this situation.

But, that's actually not reality at all. We know it's all the same person and this is a thought experiment. I know the real Paul pretty well, and he would look at the 50/.12 disparity and hand me, Bottle, back half of it. Not because he's desperate for me to like him, and not because he was trying to teach me some pedantic lesson, and not because he sloppily thinks the desperation of paying back the loan somehow helped me succeed, but because he didn't need the money in the first place, he doesn't need the profit from investing it, he wouldn't care if I had failed, and it just seems fair to split the actual profit equally. Bottle couldn't do it without Paul's money, so they should both get the reward. If either party were desperate for the money, all sorts of terrible things might have happened.

All those corporations, businesses, executives, investors, traders, gamblers, liars are absolutely desperate for the money. The only success they understand is finding an unequal system to exploit, then claiming the self-deluded ego boost of being good at exploiting it. There is no Paul up there interested in other people's success, only various sizes and colors of Bottles, no idea what secret poisons are hiding inside, or what anybody will do after they take a couple swigs. Truth be told, there aren't many Bottles like me up there either, just a bunch of incomplete minds looking for any dopamine escape hatch they can squeeze through. Most people love being way too happy and way too miserable and don't care if it kills them, or anyone else.

This album is lovely, by the way. It's proggy deathy/black-ish type stuff like BTBAM or Opeth, but not quite as spastic or bewildering or harsh. Some people might call it middle of the road, but I think it's great. I'll definitely be listening to it more than a couple more times, and trying to find some info on them.

So, did we get somewhere? Did we accomplish anything? I dunno, I'm not invested in winning, I just enjoy actively living the process. I'm ready for that surprise album whether I did a good job or not. There's nobody up there ready to solve the student loan crisis, so I'll just keep opening the Bottle to see how it's fermenting inside. It won't be a 5th Dimension album (if you can remember that far back), but it will be a surprise. Until then, thanks for sticking with me through this longer than anticipated trek through the wilderness. Cheers.

Conclusion: David Bowie

So, in the spirit of Spirit revolving and weaving itself through the whole tapestry of the first book, hello David Bowie's first album. All those little lonely people trying to navigate a big scary complicated uncaring world of other people's realities.

It's a favorite saying that the poor can't become wealthy by taking away the wealth of the wealthy, but it's also a favorite saying that you can't make money by dividing money, and everyone should have to work for their wealth. I can't hold all that cognitive dissonance in my head for very long without screaming at people that they are thinking like morons. I showed you exactly why that's the mirror image of tangible reality with my own real-life money (4 Seasons style), and I went into great detail about the difficulty of actually keeping track of which function corresponds to which agent, and how sloppy thinking creeps in at every possible moment. Each one of those statements is perfectly logical thinking in isolation, but they do not combine the way you think they combine, and they collapse the actual structure by confusing which pronouns attach to which agent/function.

For example, $50 and $5 a month for 10 months appear equivalent if we are outside the system looking in, but they have vastly different potential meanings and consequences inside the system as it operates. Our available choices, feelings, and actions might be drastically different if we choose one or the other, and it is impossible to state that they are truly equivalent without actually participating in the consequences of that choice AND realizing that neither choice is inherently right or wrong, good or bad until we connect them to their actual consequences. We try to predict the consequences of each choice, but ultimately choose the one we think is more logically valuable. However, if the logic behind the options of a choice is faulty or arbitrary, then the situation itself is absurd. If I offered you the choice of A) cow, B) grapes, or C) vacuum cleaner without any context or indication of structural consequence, you would rightfully think that's insane. That's how those 3 statements above appear to me; each idiom exists in an unrelated context to the other two, and they contradict each other when conflated into the same structural level. Paul didn't do jack for his $50, but Bottle worked his ass off for 12 cents, then Paul divided his money equally and everyone profited.

The good news for my facebook friends reading this is that I've seen multiple people share similar statements recently, and I can honestly say I have no idea who did or didn't. A while ago I told you all that I intentionally don't look at the avatars, so I have no idea if any particular person did or not. I don't even try to guess. But, it is a thing I saw, it affects the way I think, and it ends up infiltrating my writing. My posts do the same to you, and I assume quite a lot of people have unfollowed me by now. I'm fine with that, but I do wish more people were willing to tough it out and search for some value in it, the way I search for some value in all these records whether I like them or not. I wish more people could openly separate their thoughts from their actions, and pick apart all the gremlins they find. Some days it's not fun for me at all, but I want you to see what it looks like while I do it. I tried things the other way around for 20 something years and it shattered me over and over again. I have no room in my head for sloppy thoughts, so I eat the available protein, throw in whatever fruit is in season, and vacuum all the garbage out of my brain as often as necessary, whether I want to or not. See, even those arbitrary things turned out useful. I feel better, and I hope you got something out of it too. I chose to listen to the stereo version of David Bowie this time, but this repressing gives me the option of mono or stereo each time. I like that. Mrs. Bottle doesn't like his first album, and gave me the stink face when I told her I bought it. Just to give you that perspective. Happy next week adventure, I'll see you tomorrow in some form of something. Toodles....

So, back to the starting point for the continuation. Paul has $250, Bottle has $0.12 and 2 books. Let's say he sells those books plus 9 more out of nowhere. Bottle needs to order another 14, but he only has $30.36. He needs 143 - 30.36 = 112.64 to get them.

This is only one of many possible continuations, by the way. Bottle really could call it quits, Paul could be done investing, Bottle could have kept going without actually paying Paul back yet, you get the idea. This chain of choices splinters off into an infinitely complex web of possibilities at every single point. For this thought experiment we're closing out every transaction, and I'm intentionally steering toward succeeding. Bottle might not sell any more books at all, or Paul might get tricky with his lending schemes, or a tornado might roll through. Anything could happen. We waved bye-bye to actual reality quite a while ago.

Paul, the nice guys that he is, says same deal, he'll pay the 143 but he wants back 200. That's just as fair as the first deal, right? 57/200 = 28.5%. Paul is making a little more than last time, but not really enough to quibble.

15.12 x 11 = 166.32 +.12 = 166.44 and 5 books. 5 x 15.12 = 75.60 + 166.44 = 242.04.

Paul gets his 200, Bottle has 42.04. We're making progress. Paul has made $107 profit, Bottle is at 42.04. We've speculated, of course. Still, though, another round is still 143, assuming that cost hasn't changed in the meantime. 42.04 isn't enough to hire an accounting major to keep track of this stuff, so we have to do it ourselves. How many hypothetical books have we sold now? Hold on, calculator time...

... 42 books, and we're about to do it again for the 4th case of 14. Remember, we're trying to get Bottle to that magic 143. That's the actual end of the cycle. We're also eternally grateful to Paul for not changing his terms based on how well this whole thing is going.

The next round is pretty magical, though. Paul has already made $100, so his actual risk at this point is a $1.96. Paul is basically just loaning the profits from Bottle's work back to Bottle. We started out with Paul making a profit, Bottle getting screwed, but we ended up with Paul making barely any money, and Bottle owning the full financial stake in the book. How did that happen?

First, I designed it to happen that way. Second, the short answer is that we were never talking about money, we were talking about the exchange of ownership of that money. Like I said, I'm not using big silly words that nobody understands, I'm trying to describe the shape and movement of the system so that you can picture it in your mind.

The only available action in this system is exchanging money in proportion to the financial stake. If Paul walked away after the first exchange then Bottle gets nothing, but if Paul lends the way I described it, the original sum will fully transfer to Bottle (from the wider world now, rather than Paul's pocket). In this well-functioning system, the investor doesn't make any money. If Paul mistakenly thought he would make money in this system, he might also mistakenly think Bottle is the villain.

Everybody looks glass eyed. Did I go too fast? Did I miss a step? The system I described is just a Rube Goldbergian transfer of $143 from the outside world to Bottle by way of Paul loaning money to a friend. Paul knew he wasn't going to make any money, and he was smart enough to know better than to speculate with the mirage of profit.

The end result of successfully completing the process is that Paul didn't actually spend or gain any money.

I did warn you this was complicated. Any part of it you want me to explain in more detail?

Times up, the answer is yes, I did skip a step. Bottle hasn't paid back that 101.96 yet. Paul pays it and wants $150. 48.04/150 = 32%. Ok, now Paul's percentage is looking suspicious. Where is Bottle?

9 x 15.12 = 136.08 + 42.04 = 178.12. Pay Paul his 150, Bottle has 28.12. Kris Kristofferson, this is confusing! Paul has $157 and Bottle has $28, I think. Aw crap! I don't know, I can't keep track of this gibberish. We'll have to start all over again. We need more detail. Loaning money to yourself is confusing!

N: Don't worry, Bottle. We'll get there. The one lesson we did definitely learn is that opening the alive/dead box is a sure-fire way to get completely confused. I know I'm the imaginary narrator, but will you trust me?

B: I guess.

N: Ok, then in the next post I'll help everyone keep better track of what's happening where and when.

B: Sure, fine, I mean I couldn't do it.

N: No, no, you were doing fine. You just went a little haywire toward the end. We just have to calm down and define WHEN we are allowed to look at the system and what that snapshot is supposed to tell us. You can't jump to conclusions just because it looks good.

So, from me, the Narrator who isn't Paul or Bottle, stick with us. I promise, we will eventually get some real answers. The trick is that no 1 way of thinking about it is an accurate snapshot. I need some time to make some proper notes and diagrams. Please enjoy the rest of your evening, and I promise we will all get there. I might even convince Bottle to stop talking in the 3rd person.

Paul and Bottle play games with numbers

Hello, you can call me Narry. Bottle was doing a really good job of following the exchanges of money in publishing his book, but wandered into the wild web of complexity that trying to predict the structural consequences of choice weaves.

As you astute readers might have guessed, he accidentally reverted to normal people thinking, and Carl is currently sweeping him back up into an old snow shovel for Chriscrosstopher Robin to reassemble.

After 26 books, Paul had $50, Bottle had 12 cents. What happened after that was that Bottle forgot what the rules of the game were, lost track of how many books he had or hadn't sold, and got bit by the cat because he looked into the box at too many random times for no reason. That's what people do all the time in the real world, and it's nonsensical gibberish.

We need to understand the rules if we want to see what happens. From that 50/.12 split, Paul agrees to buy each new crate for $143 if Bottle agrees to pay him $200 after he sells all of them. That's the game, let's see how it plays out.

Bottle's revenue from each crate is 211.68. That's just 14 books times 15.12 from each book. Bottle then gives 200 to Paul and we do it again. So, for every crate sold Paul makes $57, Bottle makes $11.68. How many crates to get Bottle past the 143 mark? 13 crates of books. $13 \times 11.68 = 151.84$.

Paul's side is equally simple, he makes $57 from every crate. After the 13th crate, Paul makes $741. Bottle's original point is that that system is inherently unfair.

Now, let's try to show you the other system Bottle tried to weave in there with catastrophic results. What if Paul only paid the difference between the cost of a crate and Bottle's balance? That's a little trickier because we have to keep a running total of both accounts. I don't know about you, but I'm tired. Let's tackle that tomorrow…

Welcome back! Let's try to untangle Bottle's thoughts from yesterday. For this first game, we'll remove the real variation of the first case, and look at an ideal simple exchange. Each case costs 143, and returns 211. We can watch Bottle's account go up and down like this.

0
211
68
279
136
347

… and so on. Seeing how Paul's account changes is a little more complicated. First, we need to watch how the negatives accumulate. Remember, Paul is paying the difference whenever Bottle falls below 143.

0
-143
143 - 68 = -75
143 - 136 = - 7

This is what Bottle thought Paul actually payed each time he bought a case of books, 225 altogether. Unfortunately, that's nonsensical gibberish. The numbers don't actually look like that when we combine them. We need to look at how Bottle might pay back this investment. We could play all sorts of games here, but let's say Paul wants a 25% return on each purchase.

143 x .25 = 35.75

Paul wants 178.75 for the first case of books. Can Bottle pay it? Yes, but notice that it will change Paul's subsequent investments. For the second case, Bottle only has 32.93, Paul will have to pay 110.07. Paul wants 25%, so he wants 137.59 from the second case, and so on.

Let's try to keep a running ledger for Bottle with all this information built into it. The steps are hidden because we only see the actual transactions in and out of Bottle's account. I hope I did it right, but you might want to double check my numbers:

0
211.68-178.75 = 32.93
211.68-137.59 = 74.09
211.68-86.14 = 125.54
211.68-21.83 = 189.85

We can now see that Bottle owns full financial control of the book; he will never drop below 143 now, so he doesn't need to borrow more money. We can also see his payments to Paul as debits, but we don't see Paul's actual profit. Paul's profit is simply 25% of whatever he paid for each case:

35.75 + 27.52 + 17.23 + 4.36 = 84.86

In this particular game, Paul only made 84.86, and Bottle now owns the book. Obviously, we aren't accounting for any gremlins or trickery, but this system is quite fair. Both parties make money, and ownership transfers completely. Paul earned his 84.86 by taking on the initial risk, but he compensated for it by giving Bottle ownership and unlimited earning potential as the reward for success. Whether or not there is a Paul or a Bottle who actually understands that is beyond the scope of this ideal system.

B: Uh, excuse me, Narry. Hi, it's me Bottle. So, I just got carried away and jumped to conclusions and fumbled numbers, so I apologize and we move on?

N: Sure, Bottle, you can do that, but I'm not done. I want to teach you that both Paul and Bottle are guessing about which choices are most valuable in relation to their actual intentions. We have to know those intentions, how the system they agree upon is supposed to work, whether or not Paul and Bottle actually understand what they agreed to do, and how any of that might be accomplished in the real world for other people. We've barely even started, I'm afraid. We already know real life doesn't match these numbers, but we do know the system should work out quite fairly if everything succeeds. Now, we could start slowly introducing real world glitches, hiccups, problems, etc., and begin to plan for them. Be warned, it keeps getting more and more complicated, and we can only look at 1 out of millions of possibilities at a time.

So, games 1 and 2 were basic money lending games. Game 1, though simple to understand in general, was actually a sloppy nightmare behind the scenes. Paul always made 57 and Bottle always made 11. Bottle could make a million dollars, but Paul would always make 5 times the money that Bottle makes.

Game 2, much more difficult to follow on paper, was actually a very simple interest plan. Paul wanted a fixed rate of return, which in turn capped Paul's profit and resulted in a gradual transfer of liability. Each round cost less for Paul, so he made less profit, until Bottle didn't need Paul's money anymore.

Now though, I have to try to show you a simple compound interest game. I don't mind saying that's much tougher. We have to know how compound interest works, and we have to place that formula in an actual real-world context. Let's give it a shot.

The formula for compound interest is $P(1 + r/n)^{(nt)}$, where P is the initial principal balance, r is the interest rate, n is the number of times interest is compounded per time period, and t is the number of time periods.

Let's define our scenario (the numbers are arbitrary, by the way. We simply want to watch it play out no matter where it ends up): Paul says to Bottle "I'll give you $2,000, I only want 3%, compounded monthly, but I want a lump sum payment in 5 years." Bottle has absolutely no idea if that's a good idea or a bad idea, so he has to figure it out.

Where do we start? We start by plugging in our numbers.

P = 2,000
R = .03
N = 12 (12 months in a year)
T = 5
$2{,}000\,(1 + .03/12)^{(12 \times 5)}$

Plug all that into your calculator and you get: 2,323

We assume Bottle is doing whatever he needs to do with that $2,000 (it's his working capital and he wants to make 2,323 from selling the book and keeping the change as his future working capital), let's see how many books Bottle has to sell. 2323/15=155 books, or 31 books a year (Bottle gets to keep a little over $400 after paying back the 2,323). That might seem insignificant, but remember it's only 1 book, and we don't know Bottle's actual situation. If he pushes 500 of these things out into the world in a few years, then he'll make real profits. If only Bottle's closest friends buy it, then he shouldn't do it at all. If he has thousands of potential buyers a month from other activities, then it may or may not be worth it, but he's probably better off just borrowing a couple hundred from an actual friend (provided that friend offers Bottle a fair deal like in game 2). All things perfect, Bottle actually makes slightly more profit than Paul.

As you can see, we had to inject some real-world criteria into this 3rd game, because it happens over time, and involves 20 times the money of our earlier scenarios. The longer the time or the more money involved, the more difficult it will be to determine if the goal is achievable, because that interest will keep compounding every month. 5 years is relatively short, 25 years is a different story. In this actual scenario, with this actual book, it's not a good idea for Bottle to court small investors, but only Bottle can actually make that decision.

Now, as the narrator, I've shown you a few lending scenarios and how they function. If I were to make a pedantic point of the whole thing, it would be this: if the vast majority of people can't do this for small numbers in a hypothetical sandbox like I have, then it is completely unethical to force them to make those choices about things that will affect them for decades, like cars, houses, career paths, insurance policies, higher education. People need to understand the systems their governments and banks use to make these kinds of financial decisions at large, and they need access to that ability to learn at all stages of life without the constant shock that greed is the primary motivation behind every major decision that affects the things they can't control. Education is not optional. It's not acceptable for any nation to deprive any of its citizens access to that education, the same way that's it's not acceptable to deny basic health and emergency services to people who cannot afford them, the same way it's not acceptable to discriminate based on gender or ethnicity or any other stereotype. I realize that I am merely the narrator acting like the world's dad, but Paul doesn't think he is particularly smart, Bottle doesn't think he is particularly good at anything, yet I think they have more integrity, determination, and inventiveness in their toenail clippings than many of the so-called most financially successful people in the world. Does that make us the Id, Ego, and Superego, respectively? I don't know, but I am probably more surprised than you that that's where we ended up.

B: Thanks, Narry, I think Bottle, I mean I, can take it from here. That was quite the adventure, but I suppose we did learn something after all. I'm bizarro Stuart freakin' Smalley on the inside. Cheers.

[A lesser man would cheat and format the subsections to hide these inconvenient blank pages.]

X. Final Sequence: The end is somewhere in the beginning
of the middle

Between the Buried and Me – Automata I

Album review, meandering post-structural inquiry, both, or neither? Choices, choices...

... both it is!

Problem solving is a narrative structure that involves 3 components. 1) the application of a good/bad dichotomy and a classification as "bad"; 2) the application of learned strategies and consequences to flip that classification to "good"; and 3) the observation or affirmation that the dichotomy has been resolved. We need an example.

I want to place things on a table, and I want them to stay on the table. Every time I place something on the table it moves to the other side, falls off the edge, and shatters. That entire gestalt is an identifiable problem, I need to apply some action to prevent it, and observe to my satisfaction that it has been prevented for future repetitions.

In order to do that, we have to step inside the system and analyze its component parts. Thus, we have to define what is or is not a component. We could make a list of all the component actions like this:

1 - placing on table
2 - object moving
3 - object falling off table
4 - object shattering on floor

Next, we need to evaluate each component in terms of its effect on the gestalt, whether or not it contributes to the failure of the system. Most people would intuitively understand that the table is the real source of the problem, but that tells us nothing about the actual process used to reach that conclusion. We need to understand how to think through it without that invisible intuition.

Logically, choosing to stop placing things on the table would prevent the problem from occurring at all, but that does not solve the problem as we have defined it. Placing things on the table is our intention, therefore it lies outside the system.

At this point, reversing our thinking is a common strategy. I can prevent the things from shattering, then I can prevent them from falling, then I can prevent them from moving. This is a typical structural strategy of alleviating the symptoms until the system behaves accordingly. However, I think we can all see that it is the least efficient way to solve the problem. It would be better to prevent the objects from moving, as that eliminates the chain of events and accomplishes our evaluation criteria at the same time.

This is all logical thinking. I could keep going, but you probably think it is silly. It is silly, but only because we already understand the gestalt. What if we take a step back from the system? What if we have no observation of that internal system? We set an object on the table reach down for the next one, but when we turn around the first one is gone and we hear a crash. What sorts of possible explanations might we invent?

> Someone stole it and jumped through the window.
> It magically vanished.
> I hallucinated putting the first object on the table.
> There must be a hole in the table.
> I guess we'll never know.
> I'll set the next one down and watch it.

These are the kinds of reactions that point to the real structure of our approach to problem solving, and we can train ourselves to reject or prefer certain reactions. You might notice that some of the reactions might better be described as 'Blame,' 'Avoidance,' or 'Testing,' or other such descriptive outlooks. These descriptions ultimately boil down to

Avoidance or Investigation in relation to gaining knowledge. Keep in mind these are structural terms: do we avoid analyzing a system, or do we investigate how the system operates.

That precognitive moment is an example of what I call binary flipping. Binary flipping is a moment when two separate instances of the same dichotomy clash, and the resulting cognitive process proceeds along the "wrong" path. In my example, there is a good/bad dichotomy attached to avoidance/investigation and a separate good/bad dichotomy for the system under observation. The moment when these two oppositions meet is a point of instability that allows the participant to proceed under an ironic fallacy; the investigation becomes contaminated by an underlying avoidance of knowledge, or being shocked by completely logical occurrences, and other well-known analytical biases.

Back to my descriptions of false agency (blaming the disappearance on an imaginary thief, for example). In this context we might reject that as silly, but it is not as trivial as it might appear. We falsely ascribe agency all the time. Santa and Elf on the Shelf spring to mind, but the left-eating sock monster, my favorite Gremlins, Murphy's Law, stereotyping, all these things are a constant part of our actions and communication a million times a day. We tend to frame this false-agency as humor, moral lessons, etc., but it can also be seen as a constant reinforcement of lying as an escape from challenging intellectual activity; the invention of Blame to excuse our preference for the pleasure of learned predictability, and protect ourselves from the embarrassment or pain of failure or ignorance. It might sound like I am dancing around the topic of "ego-death" that comes up in relation to psychedelic drugs, and that's because it is very similar (possibly the same phenomenon described from a different direction).

I joke about reprogramming my brain all the time, but it is a useful metaphor. I've found that slipping into the underlying mode of Blame is a major psychological trigger for me, and by consciously choosing to adopt an Investigative mindset I can avoid the worst of my anger and depressive tendencies. Some might call that a high degree of "objectivity." I tend to think of it as playing with binary oppositions like Legos: good/bad, up/down, forward/backward, motion/stasis, alive/dead, etc. combined in various ways to form an observational perspective. A stupefying web of contextualizations. I have to constantly "untrain" my reactions and keep a mental catalogue of plausible sequences.

What does any of that have to do with Between the Buried and Me's 8th album, Automata I? Probably something, I'm still trying to comprehend how the lyrics fit into the concept of a corporation called Voice of Trespass broadcasting someone's dreams for entertainment. Maybe part 2 will clear that up, but it won't get here for another week. Automata I is a pretty great listen, though. Harder to follow than Coheed & Cambria or Mastodon, but who doesn't love the intellectual challenge of progressive death metal?

I haven't listened to Procol Harum in a while

You know, if at times my nonsense rhymes, then I'll stand trial. It's certainly true that I sat me down to tell a simple story, but my goodness the places we've explored. I thought it might be interesting to go way back near the beginning. No, not Vanilla Fudge, I was thinking of A Salty Dog by Procol Harum. As I recall, I didn't have much to say because it's lovely. I was also just clumsily starting to write the story I sat me down to write, so where the devil did that suggestion come from? Where's Narry, the Metatron, the Mouth of my subconscious Sauron? Nowhere? Ok, guess I'll wing it. I don't have any proof, but I suspect it's that the actual dream in BTBAM's Automata is supposedly about finding his family and returning home. This album is clearly the first half of that process, sailing off and finding yourself in the middle of the journey.

There's a fair bit of garbage amateur musicology about this album, critical blather as I call it. Supposedly, you can hear that Robin Trower has begun to head off in a different direction and will quit soon. No, he's just panned hard right (not counting that one track where they just randomly twist the knob back and forth so he sounds like a fly buzzing around your head), in a completely different room, and playing sloppy. Sure, David Gilmour did exactly the same thing on tracks he thought were dumb, but these songs aren't dumb. This is a great album. For starters, all the protagonists are muddling through the middle of their adventures, and they can't stop adventuring them even if they wanted to.

Hey guys, you're not gonna believe this, but I think the album might have a nautical theme.

Are you sure?

Well, I mean there's a lighthouse on the cover, and that's how I'd paint water if I knew how to paint. His hat says he's a hero, but he kind of reminds me of the Player's Navy Cut Cigarette logo.

Do you think it's the same lighthouse as the Lighthouse lighthouse?

Enough of that, you two! I didn't invite you here to talk over my talky talk like dumb dumbs. I invited you here to point out that the wider array of styles and changing vocalists signifies that we are all on our own adventure through life, we're all out at sea, we don't know what we'll find when we get to where we're getting, but hopefully we'll have the chance to party on the beach somewhere in the middle.

Even better, the album is a proper cycle: he starts telling the story, lives through it, sits down to start telling the story, and you guessed it, proceeds to start telling the story. If that doesn't make you feel warm and fuzzy on the inside, then you just aren't even trying, are you?

The Presidents of the United States of America

How have we not listened to The Presidents of the United States of America? The band, I mean. They made 6 albums, but I only care about their self-titled debut. They were originally a punk rock busker duo whose shtick came from Sandman, a series of graphic novels by Neil Gaiman. No, I'm being told it was Mark Sandman, the front man of Morphine. Morphine was one of those super famous and influential bands no one ever heard on commercial radio. Regardless, the gist is that you take one guitar and fit it with two bass strings, and another guitar and fit it with the 3 thickest-gauge guitar strings you can find. Tune it all down to C# so you have essentially one 5-string bass, write songs about the most mundane topics possible, and eventually hire a drummer. It's the 90s so you got Smurfs, obscure regional supermarkets, getting scratched by your cat, finding your pet lizard dead under the furniture, a dune buggy, and canned peaches. Oh, and an MC5 cover. Realistically, nobody wants to be naked and famous at the same time, and in spite of trying our damnedest to not make it, we seem to keep stumbling down the seemingly never ending, dramatically ironic Republican rabbit hole.

To all my Republican friends, we already live and work in your ideological paradise. The things you are mad about are the parts that suck about that socio-political structure for everyone, but you're so busy fighting the people who want to make those parts suck less that you don't realize it will still suck for you too. You'll still have to sit at the little kids table and eat the same sun-baked, salmonella-flavored potato salad as the rest of us, while Uncle Harvey talks about space hookers and car parts. Apologies if you have an Uncle Harvey, I didn't mean him specifically.

As you might expect, this band tended to side with Democrat candidates; the dune buggy is little and blue, after all. Why? Because the Republican party is garbage. I hope you understand me well enough by now to not be personally insulted by that statement, but the party is feather-plucking insane. Whether you like it or not, America is a decidedly right-wing country compared to the rest of the whole world. Please keep in mind, I'm way down in the lower left-hand corner of the political compass with Noam Chomsky and the actual Marxists-Anarchists. Politically speaking, even Biden and Obama were too right-wing/authoritarian for my liking. Sanders (even though I dislike him for many other reasons) is barely left of center, with believe it or not Teddy Roosevelt. These are actual political compass rankings determined by analyzing actual speeches and policies, by the way.

My point is that all that stuff about "the extreme left" and "cancel culture" and "oppressive political correctness" is an ideological war between the authoritarian right and the radical centrists. If that's confusing to you, then we'll just go back to Lord of the Rings and I'm back in the second age saying "hey guys, you just gonna let all of us over here on Numenor drown? Oh, ok, rings of power and whatnot? Well, have fun with that gurgle, gurgle."

Automata II – The second part of the first part of the analysis of Automata

"It's here, it's here! Now we can get to the bottom of this Automata thing."

Three heads simultaneously jerked up from their computers, with matching left eye squints and nose crinkles. After several eternities of awkward silence, Sandra remarked with the delicate meekness of a 19th-century English orphan in some dismal London rookery. "Oh, Bottle. Please, no. We would gladly listen to the wood chipper again, if it pleases you."

"Whaaa, with an emphatic interrobang," replied Bottle. "What have you got against Between the Buried and Me? They're great. I suppose this particular concept might turn out to be nonsense, but the music is awesome. You just hate the death growls that much?"

"Yes. It is a stench upon the nose of our ears most foul."

"It's supposed to be horrible. I talked about that way back with Black Dahlia Murder. Ok, what if I put it this way? The parts where Tommy actually sings, what do those do for you?"

"Oh, those are a choir of angels, sir. If he sang all their songs like that we'd be totally on board." The head bobbing corroboration for this response was quite unanimously emphatic, complete with widened eyes and an exuberance not seen in the bunker for quite some time.

"What's that tell you?" To call Bottle's peculiar form of nonchalant snark a blow to the collective psyche would be glossing over how much they clearly did not wish to participate in the evening's festivities. Nevertheless, it was at this point that Bottle ascended his soapbox of doom, and began his by now familiar orational madness. Thus, I take my own leave, good reader. May we meet again after the distance between the buried and ourselves has been shortened by some tangible, yet mayhap not irredeemable distance...

[The voice of Bottle]

The singy parts are the deranged insanity ideas that represent the real world, the screaming represents what it actually feels like on the inside. When it comes to this band, you won't even consider what they have to say. Well, we're doing it whether you want to or not. First, we're just gonna listen to Automata II, then we're gonna try to figure the whole thing out. It might be good, it might be bad, but gosh darn it, I'm gonna understand it if it's the last thing I do. Callback in 3, 2, 1, roll that beautiful bean footage....

Lovely, just lovely. Do yourself a favor and listen to it. Pretend it's in a foreign language, let yourself be lost, taste the rainbow, or something. I'm a rum and coke guy, but bring your chocolate milk, or apple juice, or Windex. Heck, even youtube ad interruptions would be hilariously apropos. You don't have to like it, but there's really very little to not like, in my opinion. Meet me back in the place where I put that thing that time (Hackers reference), and we'll do that thing I do *all* the time....

Part 2 of part 2 of part 1 of the analysis of Automata
Some preliminary points:

1) I was hoping this would be the case, and it is: the whole thing is out of order. Thank goodness I've built my entire writing style around that theme. You're welcome.

2) we have some proper nouns, and the band's minimalist user manual to work from. There is a protagonist. There is a corporation. Dreams are involved. Various songs share various words. I'm not saying it can't be bad, but I am saying there's every possible chance it will be good.

3) these two albums are an actual puzzle for us to figure out. We get to use spreadsheets, draw arrow diagrams, type random things into the googlemafetchbox, it's like a structuralist scavenger hunt made of cardboard and plumbing pipes.

4) you can cheat and buy Tommy's actual book about these albums for $25 on sheet happens dot com. You can also buy my book of album reviews for the same price without the extra cost of shipping. Who's more interesting? Tommy, obviously, but that's not the point.

Is North Carolina a Mecca for death metal? Houston, sure. Scandinavia, obviously. Brazil, why not? All I know about NC is Petey Pablo, shirt helicopters, and raising up. Yes, of course, it's north of South Carolina, but this is a Deltron 3030 type anti-corporation type album. I promised you pie charts and infographics, but Sandra's not fully cooperating, so while I go find a box of crayons to draw them myself, why don't you guys and gals work on getting some tangible mental grasp on what the corporation called Voice of Trespass is doing, what the hell "the grid" actually is, and whether having yellow eyes is a good or bad thing. Photos wouldn't do it justice, the record is the most delectable shade of raspberry syrup.

Automata – where do we even try to begin?
First thing's first (it's like step 9 by now, but who's counting?), we need a list of chronological (for us) vs. in order (for the story).

1. Condemned to the gallows [night 1]
2. House organ [day 2]
3. Yellow eyes [night 4/morning 5]
4. Millions [before]
5. Gold distance
6. Blot [rehearsal]
7. The proverbial bellow [night 6]
8. Glide [night 4]
9. Voice of trespass
10. The grid [the premier]

Now, there's definitely some wiggle room here, but if I were going to rearrange those tracks in order of the story timeline, it would be this:

4, 6, 10, 1, 2, 3.1, 8, 3.2, 7

Sure, the dreams actually took place before they were broadcast, but the story is about the actual broadcasting of these dreams. Tracks 5 and 9 aren't given a sequential reference, and that's because they are musical nouns. Whatever the "gold distance" is, it's the purely musical track 5, and track 9 is a character study of "voice of trespass." Tommy already told us it's a corporation, so track 9 is the musical personification of that corporation, regardless of what it actually does throughout the story. Skip, you're looking a little too splodey for my liking. I had Gladys roll a roll of Tums down the escalator before we started, so here, chew 4 of 'em before things get really confusing.

From our chronological experience, the later songs actually point backward to earlier songs, so track 9 for example sends us back to track 1. The yellow eye thing is in tracks 3 and 7, there's a sun and moon battle going on not merely in terms of night and day, something about a wooden frame, the gold distance (track 5) is first mentioned back in track 3, and the corporation itself always has some type of reptile associated with it. Musically speaking, the technical death metal is reality for the protagonist and all the other styles are some form of sarcasm/irony/unreality. It's a giant mess is what I'm saying.

Believe it or not, I'm tired and we've barely even started. Hows 'bout we all take a nap and try again tomorrow? Oh, that motion was seconded, thirded, and fourthed, I see you're still not won over. Well, tough titties, or whatever less provocative thing you think is a good metaphor for difficult, we'll be listening to all 4 sides again tomorrow, and every night after until the analytical epiphany smacks me on the forehead like a can of tomato juice. Hope you brought your raincoats to SeaWorld, 'cause you're all in the splash zone. I'm gonna try to avoid buying Tommy's Kinko's copied Cliff's Notes (spiral bound for your pleasure), but I've got a feeling this is gonna be like that time my dad took me down to the bottom of the 9' deep end at the YMCA and I wasn't entirely sure I would maintain consciousness on the way back to the surface.

Automata – Scene 4

[Day 2]

Bottle awoke with a stuffy nose, and a general desire to not do anything. Though he longed for nothing so much as to go back to blissful sleep, he nevertheless conquered the invisible force that pinned him to the bed, and as they say, put on pants. Onward, he goes.

[Voice of Bottle]
Millions, according to the conceptual timeline, is the first song. We have to try to understand it, but you're not gonna like how much grammatical analysis it's gonna take. Oh well.

Millions of something flying overhead. Birds, UFOs, cans of peaches, Professor Xavier's room with all the psychic web links to people's brains, people watching The Truman Show, owls, spy satellites, I don't know. Way too many to count, is the point. He wants to be back up there with them, but they are flying away without him. Whatever they are, he feels like they have abandoned him and he's scared, possibly cold. That might seem like barely a fragment of an idea, but it is a coherent framework for the project as a whole. Is that "the frame"? No idea, but now that possibility is in our brains. "Wooden frame" could also just simply be a house, but I'm getting ahead of myself.

Whenever you're confronting something this obtuse, a good strategy is to find all the places a word or idea pops up, and compare them. We'll start doing that in a bit. At the moment, I want to try to parse the truly bizarre fragment that is "fog dancing slavery." What the hell does that mean? Noun-participle-noun, think of some others: airplane flying poodle, muck raking journalist, shit eating grin. In those examples the noun-participle pair acts as an adjective for the object. If you turn it back around that would mean there's fog and slavery is dancing in it. Weird, but not completely incomprehensible.

Maybe it's a simile, the fog is like dancing slavery. There's some corroboration for that in the alternate ending "like snakes circling." Possibly the whole structure is that the concept of slavery is dancing through the fog like snakes circling their prey. I'm good with that, it gives us a mental image of what the situation feels like for the narrator/protagonist. Now I think we can zoom back out and try to grapple with the large-scale themes.

[Aside]
As Bottle reemerged from his orational stupor, it slowly dawned on him that not all of his minions had fully crossed over into similar wakeful exuberance. Skip, for example, was still snoring and twitching his arms in a manner much like a rabbit scampering through a field. Sandra, though ostensibly awake, appeared to be staring off into space, lost in some intangibly slow thought process. The Compiler was nowhere to be seen.

Having fully digested the lack of happenings around him, Bottle simply shrugged and wandered off, mumbling "meh, I'll just come back later, I guess."

Automata – Final Sequence

Everybody here now? Ok, analysis is a tricky thing. For one, you have to have a goal. That goal could be tiny, like when we tried to figure out what order makes the tracks actually mean something. The brackets helped a lot, because they outlined the context of a performance: there's a rehearsal, a premier, and an ordered sequence of scenes. Whatever it is we're hearing, it's being performed for an audience. Now we can proceed to the actual stuff being performed.

As far as I can tell, there are only two participants. There's an entity that says "me," and an entity that says "we." I'm skipping over the fact that it morphs from "me" to "we," the important part is that it says "we are the Voice of Trespass." Voice of Trespass is a corporate (plural) entity. I don't think we have to delve too deep into it, they explicitly call themselves evil, and equally explicitly take advantage of the protagonist. Actually, they are the clarification that the person at the beginning is in fact a protagonist. Voice of Trespass defines itself as the antagonist, and that forces us into a specific interpretation of the situation. Everything the first character says or does happens inside the context of struggling against an enemy.

While we're on the subject of pronouns, Glide uses "it," but "it" has the capacity to exhibit nervousness, and the capability of dancing. So, "it" is at the very least human shaped.

What else have we got? Yellow eyes, blood on snow, a death sentence, a house, a thing that a wanderer can wander too far from called "gold distance," and something called "the grid." Start at the start, I guess.

Yellow eyes. What has yellow eyes? Cats, owls, lemurs, raccoons, people in liver failure, turtles maybe. Creatures. He's scared, so scary creatures. Yellow eyed creatures tend to be nocturnal, so we got that going for us.

Pretty sure on day two he lights his house on fire. It's called House Organ, and he says ignite a couple times.

The hard one is dreams. Sure, we can point to some serious time dislocation, frequently changing landscape, some technological vs. biological interaction, electricity is involved, but it's only in track 9 that we finally get the statement "wake up," and we end with the protagonist locking the metaphorical door and moving on.

BN, by the way is how Tommy's son said "the end" at the end of a story. That's everyone's favorite tidbit from the book about the writing of the lyrics.

S: Uh, excuse me, Bottle. Are we done now?
B: You don't want to keep going? Analyze more scenes? Talk about how the music emphasizes mood and stuff?

E: No.
S: No.
C: No.

B: Fine. Nice ergodic responses there. Ok, we can leave it at that, I guess. Did it at least make the whole experience less agonizing?

[Epilogue]
Bottle never did get an answer to that question. Some say they sat there glaring at each other for the rest of eternity. Empires rose and fell, the sun fused all its hydrogen into helium and long ago ceased laughing at its resulting high-pitched voice, galaxies swirled away, the fabric of space-time grew thinner and ripped so that things kept falling out of its pockets. But even after all that, the echoes of Sandra's final words still vibrated between the last two extant atoms of existence with a remarkable vibrancy: shut up, Bottle.

Fin.

I lied, there is a moral to my story
The political compass is a Klein Bottle.

Spin Doctors – Turn It Upside Down

I cannot tell you how great it feels to get the end of the story out of the way. It's on the blog, but I didn't actually publish it on facebook. Now we can just keep filling in random middle parts. Like mid 90s funk rock. You probably know 1 or 2 songs by Spin Doctors, but they aren't on their second album Turn It Upside Down. You probably didn't know John Popper was an early member (prior to their name change).

Spin Doctors is a jam band. I don't mean that in a bad way, I just mean you have to take them completely on their own terms because there isn't any larger statement they try to make than "hi, we're a band, hope you came here to hear some random funky rock songs about drug euphemisms." Dirt means heroin, by the way. Especially if it's in a bag.

Ok, normally I don't like this album, but today it's totally fine. It could just be that finishing the story is a big mental relief, but probably anything sounds a little more chipper and light after all the screaming. Funnily enough, the band had to sit out a year because Chris Barron woke up with vocal-chord paralysis one morning in 1999. We ended up taking the timeline fork tine where it came back and they kept playing and made 2 more albums in the 21st century, but it was a legitimate coin toss back then.

Critically speaking, this is a "meh, it's fine, I don't completely hate it" album. I'd call it an album for people who specifically want to hear more Spin Doctors songs. They're fine. They're a weeknight bar/festival, good time band, not a theatrical headliner. They're also as excessively 90s as Dave Matthews Band, in the same way Uriah Heep or Citadel are decidedly 70s. I'm surprised this album didn't come with weed and patchouli scented scratch-and-sniff stickers. If you don't mind my asking, what's it like for you to go from Between the Buried and Me to Spin Doctors? Do you feel anything? I personally don't feel anything, I'm tired and hungry all the time anyway.

The End, or Knot

Bottle wandered the hallways, lost in thought.

Is it really over? Did I miss a thing? Watch out for that pothole. Did we already do it, or did I just imagine not having done it yet? I need a spin doctor, or something.

The rest of his thoughts were somewhat less coherent, more flashing lights and pretty colors than actual grammatical sentences.

There was a lot of snapping, though. Lost in his mind, he didn't seem to notice that every snap blinked another architectural anomaly into the wake of his existence. An escalator appeared, then a frighteningly ornate wood-framed mirror. A hallway that stretched as far as visible sight would allow, but almost certainly farther than that. From a distance, his path traced a giant spiral through space, as though his left leg were ever so imperceptibly shorter than his right leg. Suddenly he stopped and turned back to retrace his steps, when a voice stopped him again. "Hey, mister. Where are you headed?"

Without so much as a blink of a pause, Bottle replied "mister waters the plants, you can call me Bottle."

"I know that, silly" replied the voice.

"You sound like a Sandra."

"How could you possibly remember that?! It was lifetimes ago." The voice, still invisible as far as any spectators could tell, seemed somehow bewildered and giddy at the same time. After an awkward pause, probably due to Bottle's misinterpretation of the question as rhetorical, she said "up here."

"Oh, ok, good. I wasn't sure if you were real or imaginary. Not that that makes a difference. You remind me of someone I used to know."

"Named Sandra?"

"That depends, Sandra was her name, but people called her lots of other things that weren't. Even useless superheroes have alter egos. It's all well and good to ask why are you here, but you aren't, you're up there and my neck's not as stretchy as it used to be."

"I'll come down then."

Again, the proverbial spectator might remark on the absence of actual happenings, but somehow the two now stood facing each other.

    B: Hi, Sandra. What brings you here?"
    S: My legs.
    B: There's the bite. Lovely
    S: I'm hiding.
    B: Ok.
    S: You're not even going to ask why?
    B: Why ask why? Bullfrogs and wasabi [snap] football puppies [snap, snap] not my beverage. It is what it is.
    S: That's refreshing. Still, what is it?"
    B: The epic question. The answer, of course, is it's it no matter what it is. Everything's connected in some way or another. You just have to figure out which path you're supposed to be taking at the moment.

S: I don't know, I kind of like it back up there watching you bumble around.

B: Ok, suit yourself. You're welcome to tag along whenever you want. It's nice to face a familiar face.

S: What are you planning?

Bottle looked around, and finally seemed to notice the haphazard structures assembling around him. "No plans. But, I'm apparently world building. I ran out of labels, so I have to open 'em up one at a time to remember what's inside. All in all, though, this feels like the right place to be. So, how'd you like an office up there?"

S: Can I have a bean bag chair?

B: Don't see why not [snap] don't be a stranger, though.

S: Thanks, Bottle. You can come back here anytime, too.

B: What if I get lost?

S: If you're lost and you look.... Just make a permanent path. How'd you get here the first time?

B: 3 lefts and a right. Yeah, that'll work. Just do me a favor.

S: What?

B: Keep track of it all for me, like draw a map or something. Oh, and tell me to shut up whenever I look about to wander off. Helps me focus on the now and its actual later.

S: That's two favors.

B: Yeah, I count wrong sometimes, and I tend to round up or down too often. I like the process, but I don't have much interest in the actual answer. Do it or don't's my motto. Now, if you'll excuse me for a while, there're some strange sounds over thataway, and I'd quite like to find out who or what is making them.

As she watched Bottle amble off, a trail of assorted doodads and curiosities falling out of the holes in his overstuffed pockets with every step, Sandra smiled.

It does feel like the right place to be, she thought. It feels like home.

And now, a word from our sponsor:

Welcome to the metaphysical end of the meta-fictional book. As I was editing it in these waning days of April, 2021, it smacked me in the forehead like a deftly hurled can of tomato juice. Whether you've enjoyed it or not, this book and its predecessor A Year in the Life… are my contribution to the universe. These were actual daily chronicles of a real person living in Iowa in 2019-2021. I thought those thoughts, I listened to those records every night, I wrote stories about the whole experience, and I'm working on making them real tangible objects. It feels self-aggrandizing, to be honest, but how many other similar accounts of real life in real time do you get to experience like this? At the very least, I think we can all agree that mine was, for good or bad, unique.

Welp, pants, work, on and back to, respectively. Apologies to future historians if my books are all you've got to work from.

Paul Tompkins III (Miss Bottle, if you're nasty).

P.S. This second book wouldn't exist at all without the inspiration of Steven Stark's 2018 album Wandering Woven World (which I surreptitiously reviewed on MLK Day for all the obvious and secret reasons back on page 328). You really should go search it out, it's lovely.

P.P.S. Onward, space cadets!

P.P.P.S. No index for this one. The last one was such a pain, I said buggerit. Sorry.

P.P.P.P.S. I'm kidding, on with the index.

Artists being reviewed

A Perfect Circle, 168
AC/DC, 59
Accept, 133
Achilles & The Tortoise, 142
After The Fire, 192
Air Supply, 183
Alice Cooper, 273
Alice In Chains, 115
Argent, 112
Arlo Guthrie, 231
Armageddon, 317
AWOLNATION, 52
Bad Religion, 157, 212, 262
Beastie Boys, 184
Between the Buried and Me, 410, 441, 447
Biohazard, 155
Black Pumas, 343
Black Sabbath, 268
Born Of Osiris, 140
Breaking Benjamin, 151
Brian Setzer, 255
Brian Wilson, 167
Cage the Elephant, 356
Cake, 155
Camel, 110
Carson Murphy, 405
Charles Gershwin, 123
Charles Ives, 306
Chavelle, 150, 167
Classics IV, 182
Coheed & Cambria, 229, 328
Cypress Hill, 215
Dan Vapid and the Cheats, 55
Dave Gedosh, 402
Dave Matthews Band, 307
David Bowie, 427
Delaney & Bonnie, 178
Die Krupps, 57
Dizzy Gillespie, 337
Dominique Guiot, 46
Donna Summer, 355
Elton John, 154
Elvis Costello/Brodsky Quartet, 56
Eric Burdon and The Animals, 245
Evans Blue, 119
Failure, 391
Fall Out Boy, 235
Flyleaf, 340
Genesis, 122
Good Rats, 326
Green Day, 167
GREGORY, 390
Gustav Mahler, 303
Harry Connick Jr., 240, 242, 244
Incubus, 163
Insane Clown Posse, 212
Iron Maiden, 236
It's Immaterial, 189

J.J. Hrubovcak, 260
Jean Luc Ponty, 368
Jean-Luc Ponty, 134, 145
Jethro Tull, 219, 252
Joe Cocker, 228
John Coltrane, 159
John Denver, 334
John Lee Hooker, 332
Judgment Night, 396
Judy Collins, 342
Justice, 239
Kansas, 270, 320, 367, 371
Katie Perry, 97
Kenny Rogers, 336, 338
Kerry Livgren, 364
Kettel, 238
KMFDM, 238
Leonard Bernstein, 231
Lighthouse, 346
Linda Ronstadt, 47
Loggins and Messina, 183
Marty Friedman, 265
Marx (Karl, not Richard), 193
Massive Attack, 173
Mastodon, 64, 167, 279, 405
Meat Puppets, 214
Meatloaf, 299
Men At Work, 190
Michael McDonald, 63
Miles Davis, 375
Ministry, 158
Mirror Travel, 417
MLWTKK, 309
Modern English, 109

Modest Mouse, 132
Moon Hooch, 142
Moron Manor, 121
Mr. 76ix, 237
Mr. Bungle, 332
Mumford's Music, 50
My Chemical Romance, 166
Nancy Sinatra, 129
Neutral Milk Hotel, 275
New Found Glory, 164
Nine Inch Nails, 174
Nirvana, 280
NOFX, 170
Offspring, 150, 234
Old Wives/Blendours, 366
p(nmi)t, 69, 354
Parts & Labor, 420
Pete Seeger, 125
Peter, Paul, & Mary, 126
Petula Clark, 127
Phoebe Snow, 144
Pirates of Darkwater, 261
Premiata Forneria Marconi, 124
Pricewise, 159
Prism, 109, 217, 322
Procol Harum, 444
Queens of the Stone Age, 230
R.E.M., 398
Radiohead, 130
Rainbow, 358
Rammstein, 169

Red Hot Chili Peppers, 177
Red Rider, 146, 216
Rev. Horton Heat, 255
Ric Ocasek, 117
Roger Miller, 214
Rolling Stones, 68
Rotary Connection, 258
Roulette Records, 46
Roy Orbison, 125
Rudy Ray Moore, 255
Sandal-core, 136
Screaming Females, 407
Sea Level, 251, 373
Sevendust, 116
Skid Row, 160
Skinny Puppy, 165
Smash Mouth, 48
Snail, 248
Soundgarden, 225
Spin Doctors, 456
Spoon, 118, 135, 414
Squirrel Nut Zippers, 51
Starcastle, 357
Steely Dan, 191, 325
Steven Stark, 331
Stone Temple Pilots, 303
Stonks, 348
Surf Zombies, 366
Swaps, 411
Sylvan Esso, 143
The B52's, 142
The Band, 176
The Boomtown Rats, 271
The Bottle Rockets, 132
The Crow, 357
The Eurythmics, 319
The Grasshoppers, 49
The Hollies, 145
The Killers, 261
The Lazy Cowgirls, 62
The Misfits, 54
The Mopes, 422
The Motels, 249, 316
The Pogues, 394
The Presidents of the United States of America, 446
The Pretty Reckless, 392
The Specials, 276
The Tubes, 147, 250
The Vandals, 264
Thelonious Monk, 159
Tiger Lillies/Kronos Quartet, 56
Tool, 377
Traci Lords, 400
Traffic, 359
Type O Negative, 134
Uriah Heep, 171
Villainy, 424
Violent Femmes, 220
X-Files, 61
Yanni, 157

v

v

CPSIA information can be obtained
at www.ICGtesting.com
Printed in the USA
BVHW072034070621
608943BV00001B/5